1400

Reading, Writing, & Race

Reading, Writing, & Race

The Desegregation of the Charlotte Schools

Davison M. Douglas

THE UNIVERSITY OF NORTH CAROLINA PRESS

Chapel Hill & London

Library of Congress Cataloging-in-Publication Data
Douglas, Davison M.
Reading, writing, and race: the desegregation of the
Charlotte schools / Davison McDowell Douglas.
    p.   cm.
Includes bibliographical references (p.) and index.
ISBN 0-8078-2216-7 (alk. paper). —
ISBN 0-8078-4529-9 (pbk.: alk. paper)
1. School integration — North Carolina — Charlotte —
Case studies. I. Title.
LC214.23.C43D68   1995
370.19'342 — dc20   94-39347
                            CIP

99 98 97 96 95   5 4 3 2 1

Publication of this volume was aided by a generous grant
from the Z. Smith Reynolds Foundation.

To my parents

JOHN MUNROE DOUGLAS

&

MARJORIE LUTZ DOUGLAS

who taught me the value of education

Contents

Illustrations

Acknowledgments

I received a tremendous amount of support along the way in writing this book. The staff of the following libraries were most helpful in allowing me to use their manuscript collections: the Special Collections at the University of North Carolina at Charlotte, the Public Library of Charlotte and Mecklenburg County, the Southern Historical Collection and the North Carolina Collection at the University of North Carolina at Chapel Hill, the North Carolina State Archives in Raleigh, and the Manuscripts Division of the Library of Congress in Washington, D.C. In addition, the *Charlotte Observer* graciously opened its files to me, as did the Charlotte-Mecklenburg Community Relations Committee. The Charlotte-Mecklenburg Public Schools, the Charlotte Chamber of Commerce, and the United States Courthouse in Charlotte also provided valuable assistance. Carlton Watkins and Paul Ervin, Jr., allowed me to examine their personal papers. The library staff and administration at the William and Mary Law School were particularly supportive of my research efforts. I am also very grateful to the National Endowment for the Humanities and the William and Mary Law School, both of which provided me with generous financial support.

Many people assisted me in this project. My two dissertation advisers at Yale University, John Blum and John Butler, each gave me a great deal of critical encouragement and support at various stages of my work. Drew Days, Neal Devins, Steven Gillon, David Goldfield, Paul LeBel, William Link, Michael Okun, Rodney Smolla, Mark Tushnet, and Stephen Wasby each read earlier drafts of the book and offered valuable criticism. Ellen Ferris, Erin Hawkins, Jonathan Koenig, John McGowan, Joan Pearlstein, Manesh Rath, and Stephen Schofield tirelessly and cheerfully helped me track down endless newspaper articles and cases.

I would also like to thank the staffs of the *Northwestern University Law Review* and the *Chicago-Kent Law Review*. Chapter 2 first appeared in revised form in the fall 1994 issue of the *Northwestern University Law Review*. Parts of chapters 3 and 4 first appeared in the spring 1995 issue of the *Chicago-Kent Law Review*.

At the University of North Carolina Press, executive editor Lewis Bateman, editor Pamela Upton, and copyeditor Teddy Diggs each provided valuable encouragement and assistance and greatly strengthened the book.

Mike and Melva Okun, Peggy Link, and Steve Evans graciously opened their homes to me during my many research trips. Dozens of participants in the events described in this book shared their recollections and insights with me, greatly enriching my understanding of desegregation in Charlotte.

Finally, I must note that I attended the Charlotte-Mecklenburg Schools from 1962 until 1974 and hence experienced firsthand many of the events described in this book. To my friends—both black and white—in the Class of 1974, I give thanks for your courage and faithfulness through a trying time. I hope this book in some small way will enhance our understanding of what those years were all about.

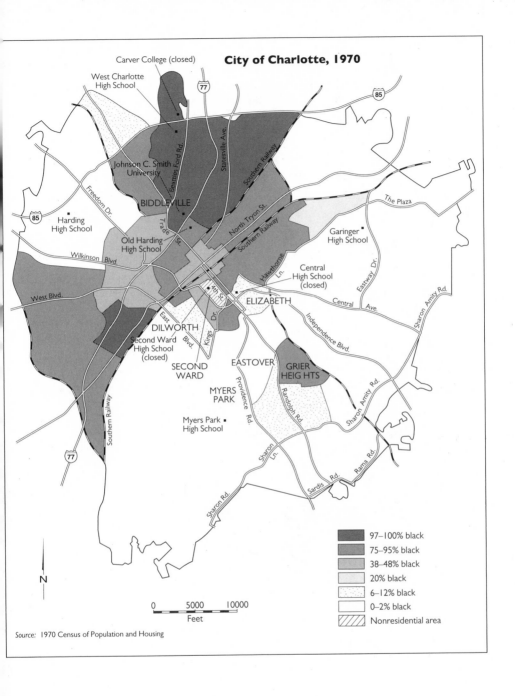

City of Charlotte, 1970

Carver College (closed)
West Charlotte High School
Johnson C. Smith University
BIDDLEVILLE
Harding High School
Old Harding High School
Freedom Dr.
Trade St.
Wilkinson Blvd.
West Blvd.
Southern Railway
Beatties Ford Rd.
Statesville Ave.
North Tryon St.
Southern Railway
The Plaza
Garinger High School
Central High School (closed)
Hawthorne Ln.
ELIZABETH
Eastway Dr.
Central Ave.
Independence Blvd.
Sharon Amity Rd.
DILWORTH
Second Ward High School (closed)
SECOND WARD
East Blvd.
Kings Dr.
4th St.
EASTOVER
GRIER HEIGHTS
MYERS PARK
Myers Park High School
Providence Rd.
Randolph Rd.
Sharon Amity Rd.
Sharon Ln.
Sardis Rd.
Rama Rd.
Sharon Rd.

N

0   5000   10000
Feet

97–100% black
75–95% black
38–48% black
20% black
6–12% black
0–2% black
Nonresidential area

Source: 1970 Census of Population and Housing

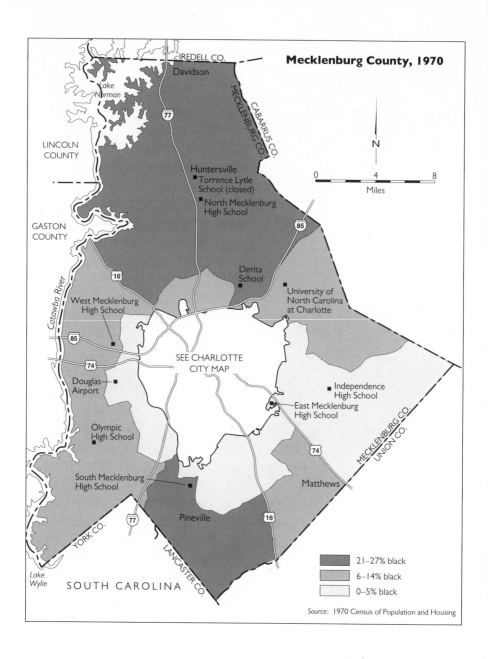

Mecklenburg County, 1970

IREDELL CO.

Davidson

Lake Norman

MECKLENBURG CO.

CABARRUS CO.

77

N

0   4   8
Miles

LINCOLN COUNTY

Huntersville
■ Torrence Lytle School (closed)
■ North Mecklenburg High School

85

GASTON COUNTY

Catawba River

16

Derita School

■ University of North Carolina at Charlotte

West Mecklenburg High School

85

74

SEE CHARLOTTE CITY MAP

Douglas Airport

■ Independence High School

East Mecklenburg High School

Olympic High School

74

South Mecklenburg High School

Matthews

MECKLENBURG CO.
UNION CO.

16

Pineville

77

YORK CO.

LANCASTER CO.

Lake Wylie

SOUTH CAROLINA

21–27% black

6–14% black

0–5% black

Source: 1970 Census of Population and Housing

Reading, Writing, & Race

Introduction

Race, today as much as ever, is the American dilemma. For over three centuries, since a Dutch ship brought twenty Africans to Jamestown in 1619, America has struggled with the question of how to square the oppressive treatment of African Americans with the American credo of equality under law. For most of this nation's history, white society has maintained legal superiority over African Americans. Until the Civil War, the ownership of black slaves enjoyed legal protection throughout the American South. Although the war's conclusion carried with it the promise of freedom, that promise proved hollow. A system of enforced racial separation in various aspects of public and private life emerged during the last quarter of the nineteenth century and persisted until the 1950s and 1960s. Although by the early 1960s, most of the explicit government-mandated segregation had been eliminated, the legacy of centuries of discrimination left the nation divided — economically, culturally, and even geographically — along racial lines.

Since the end of the Civil War, the African American community in this country has struggled to secure for itself the promise of equality seemingly guaranteed by the Fourteenth Amendment to the U.S. Constitution. Those efforts enjoyed little success, however, until the middle decades of the twentieth century. White state legislatures and school boards consistently viewed demands for equal treatment as unwanted intrusions into the southern way of life. At the same time, the African American community lacked sufficient resources and power to challenge the racial status quo. The courts, the one institution specifically committed to the vindication of constitutional rights, offered little relief to black litigants until the middle of the twentieth century.

Since the 1940s and 1950s, however, there has been a profound reordering of the legal and social order in this country around issues of race. Indeed, the civil rights movement of the 1950s and 1960s constituted one of the most significant social and political readjustments in this nation's history. Scholars have differed over the primary impetus for these changes. Many have focused on the role of national civil rights leaders, such as Martin Luther King, or the actions of national civil rights organizations, such as the National Association for the Advancement of Colored People (NAACP), the Congress of Racial Equality (CORE), the Southern Christian Leadership Conference (SCLC), and the Student

Nonviolent Coordinating Committee (SNCC).[1] Others have emphasized the importance of political institutions, particularly the federal courts, Congress, and the president, in fostering racial change.[2]

Many scholars have considered the importance of these various factors by examining, in considerable detail, the experience of one community.[3] This book contributes to this genre of scholarship by examining the struggle to desegregate the schools of Charlotte, North Carolina, from the *Brown v. Board of Education* decision in 1954 until the mid-1970s.[4] The choice of both education and Charlotte as focal points is deliberate.

Over the course of the last half century, education has functioned as perhaps the most critical arena in which the struggle for racial equality has taken place. Beginning in the early 1930s, the African American community identified the public school system as the best place to attack Jim Crow segregation. As a result, the NAACP initiated a litigation campaign that was directed against school segregation and that ultimately culminated in the momentous *Brown* decision.[5] By the same token, to attack segregated schools was to attack Jim Crow at its most sensitive point. White fears and anxieties about racial mixing were never greater than when children were involved. Hence, the battle for integrated schools engaged southern racial hostilities at their deepest level.

Moreover, as the pursuit of racial justice in this country evolved from eliminating legal separation in the mid-1950s to taking affirmative steps to overcome the effects of past discrimination in the early 1970s, the public schools once again emerged as the central arena in which the battle over appropriate racial policies would be waged. By the late 1960s, the nation had reached a consensus that legally mandated school segregation was inconsistent with American notions of equality, yet most urban schoolchildren still attended single-race schools because of extensive residential segregation. As a result, by 1970, the concern in urban America had shifted from the elimination of de jure segregation to overcoming widespread residential segregation through race-conscious pupil assignments aimed at increasing integration. In the process, the urban school system emerged as America's new racial battleground. "Busing" became the issue on which the conflict centered.

Charlotte was chosen as the subject of this study for three reasons. First, Charlotte responded more quickly to the racial demands of the post-*Brown* era than did most other southern cities and hence affords a particularly suitable venue for exploring the dynamics of racial change in the "moderate" American South. Charlotte became one of the first cities in the South to admit African American students to white schools in the

1950s, engaged in more extensive pupil mixing than did most other metropolitan areas in the 1960s, and ultimately adopted one of the nation's most ambitious school busing plans in the early 1970s.

Second, Charlotte emerged as the focal point in the national debate over the use of school busing by virtue of the fact that the U.S. Supreme Court used Charlotte's pupil assignment plan in 1971 to define, in the landmark case *Swann v. Charlotte-Mecklenburg Board of Education*, the constitutional obligations of urban school boards to overcome residential segregation.[6] An examination of the legal efforts to integrate the Charlotte schools thus affords an opportunity to examine both the way in which the courts emerged in the early 1970s as the primary institution responsible for giving meaning to the concept of equality in urban America and the social and political tensions that resulted from the primacy of the judicial role.

Finally, the desegregation of the Charlotte schools has been widely regarded as more successful—measured by the extent of white flight, improvements in educational achievement, and community acceptance—than similar efforts in most other American cities. Thus, an examination of Charlotte's desegregation experience may shed light on the various factors that contributed to the relative success or failure of the efforts to integrate America's urban schools during the 1970s.

The desegregation of the Charlotte schools was but one small piece of a national struggle to eliminate racial inequality during the two decades following the *Brown* decision. This book, by examining in considerable detail the desegregation experiences of one city, seeks to illuminate some of the broader themes surrounding the dynamics of racial change in post-*Brown* America.

Historians have placed differing degrees of emphasis on the relative importance of various institutions and individuals in securing the racial gains of the two decades after *Brown*. To many, the courts—the one political institution not directly responsible to the whims of the white majority—played the central role in moving this country away from its deeply embedded system of racial segregation and oppression. Hence, for many, federal judges loom large in the hagiography of the civil rights movement, with the Supreme Court's *Brown* decision serving as the signal event that unleashed the second Reconstruction.[7]

For others, the role of the courts has been overstated. For these historians, meaningful racial change did not occur in the American South until the elective branches of government—the president and the Congress—

entered the fray in a substantial way in the mid-1960s with the Civil Rights Act of 1964 and the Voting Rights Act of 1965, coupled with executive enforcement of those statutes. Consequently, these historians emphasize the importance of the pressure applied by the African American community on the elective branches of government through direct action protest that helped reshape public and political opinion around issues of racial justice.[8]

The twenty-year effort to desegregate the Charlotte schools following the *Brown* decision offers an excellent opportunity to assess the relative importance of litigation and direct action in achieving greater school integration. During the first fifteen years after *Brown*, significant pupil mixing took place in large measure as a result of executive and legislative action, particularly the Civil Rights Act of 1964 and its enforcement by the U.S. Office of Education. During these years, litigation proved far less effective than did political action at both the local and the national levels. Urban desegregation during the early 1970s, however, took place almost exclusively as a result of court orders and in spite of various executive and legislative initiatives to restrict integration efforts in America's cities. Whereas those who have questioned the traditional emphasis on the courts as facilitators of school desegregation have some support in the first decade after *Brown*, the integration of urban schools through busing was driven almost exclusively by judicial decrees. This focus on Charlotte and its school desegregation litigation thus provides insight into the relative importance of the federal courts throughout the post-*Brown* era in defining the meaning of racial equality in urban education.

Efforts to eliminate racial segregation and oppression were greeted in dramatically different ways across the South. Some cities, such as Charlotte, responded relatively quickly to demands for greater integration, whereas other cities, such as Birmingham, staunchly resisted. These variations depended in significant measure on the value that white leaders placed on the retention of racial segregation in comparison with other civic concerns, particularly economic growth. Charlotte's business and civic leaders in the 1950s and early 1960s realized, as did their counterparts in other "moderate" southern cities such as Atlanta and Dallas, that token and controlled integration, conducted in an environment of "civility," could avoid damaging racial demonstrations that might undermine efforts to attract new business and industry to their city.[9] The desegregation process in Charlotte thus supports the conclusions of those who have noted that white business leaders, motivated by economic considerations, positively influenced the breakdown of racial segregation in southern communities.[10] Yet the second phase of desegregation in Charlotte — the elimination of majority-black schools through widespread school busing — tested the commitment of white leaders to racial integration in new ways. Busing, particularly when it involved sending white children to schools in black neighborhoods, affected white interests in an unparalleled manner compared with that experienced in the earlier desegregation efforts. As a result, Charlotte's business and civic leaders stood largely silent during the first two years of the city's busing "crisis," as did such leaders in communities across the nation. In time, however, these leaders understood that Charlotte's long-term interests required the maintenance of a stable public school system. Eventually, therefore, Charlotte's business and civic leaders embraced the city's busing program. Once again, the perceived importance of preserving a vital local economy overrode fears of extensive racial mixing.

Some observers have argued that the *Brown* decision resulted from a convergence of interests in the black and white communities — the black community's obvious interest in overthrowing racial segregation and the white community's interest in gaining the moral and political capital, particularly in foreign affairs, that ensued from the decision striking down enforced racial separation.[11] In Charlotte, the interests of the black community in integration and of the white community in avoiding public strife converged in favor of limited desegregation in the late 1950s and early 1960s. In the early 1970s, those interests would converge again as the white community ultimately came to value a stable educational system over continued efforts to avoid school busing. In this way, racial desegregation in Charlotte is squarely within the tradition of much of the civil rights activism of the 1940s, 1950s, and 1960s: white economic, political, and moral interests and black dignity interests converged in a manner that resulted in greater racial integration.

The desegregation of the Charlotte schools thus brings together several themes in the social and legal history of the struggle for racial equality in the post-*Brown* South. By focusing on one community's desegregation experiences over a twenty-year period, this book aids in a better understanding of the complex dynamics of racial change in contemporary America.

It is hopeless for the Negro to expect complete emancipation from the menial social and economic position into which the white man has forced him, merely by trusting in the moral sense of the white race. . . . However large the number of individual white men who do and who will identify themselves completely with the Negro cause, the white race in America will not admit the Negro to equal rights if it is not forced to do so. Upon that point one may speak with a dogmatism which all history justifies.

—Reinhold Niebuhr, *Moral Man and Immoral Society* (1932)

CHAPTER I

Challenging Separate and Unequal Education in North Carolina before *Brown*

When the U.S. Supreme Court announced in 1954 in *Brown v. Board of Education* that racially segregated schools unconstitutionally denied African American students the equal protection of the law, it challenged almost a century of separate and unequal education throughout much of the nation, particularly the South.[1] Since Reconstruction, North Carolina, like other southern states, had required that black and white children be taught in separate schools, which invariably were unequal.

Although African American parents occasionally invoked the authority of the courts to secure the educational equality mandated by both the federal and the state constitutions, the courts — until the middle of the twentieth century — offered little protection for the constitutional rights of black schoolchildren. The difficulties facing African American parents in bringing sophisticated constitutional challenges to unequal education and a generally unreceptive judiciary to claims of educational inequality rendered the courts an ineffectual forum for most of the pre-*Brown* era. During the fifteen years preceding the *Brown* decision, however, the NAACP orchestrated an effective litigation campaign attacking racial inequality in public education. At the same time, the federal courts became increasingly receptive to claims of racial discrimination. As a result of this litigation, by 1954, the dramatic differences between black and white schools had been substantially reduced. As the nation awaited the Supreme Court's decision on the constitutionality of segregated education in the *Brown* case, the African American community had already learned a valuable lesson: litigation and the threat of litigation were the most effective means of challenging educational inequality.

The North Carolina General Assembly first established a system of public education in 1839 but provided only for the education of white children.[2] In the aftermath of the Civil War, North Carolina's Constitutional Convention of 1868 drafted a constitution that provided for the creation of a free public school system for all children, black and white.[3] Yet from the beginning, consistent with the practice in other states, North Carolina segregated its students by race. Although the Constitutional Convention of 1868, after much debate, declined to require racially segregated schools, few members of the convention favored educating black and white schoolchildren together. Indeed, at the behest of an African American delegate, the convention adopted a nonbinding resolution that stated, "The interests and happiness of the two races would be best promoted by the establishment of separate schools."[4] African American leaders in North Carolina, like those throughout the South, well understood that promoting integrated education could undermine support for any system of public education.[5] North Carolina State Superintendent of Public Instruction Alexander McIver urged Congress in 1874 to reject legislation requiring integrated public schools, noting, "Opposition to mixed schools is so strong that if the people are free to choose between mixed schools and no schools, they will prefer the latter."[6]

In 1869, the North Carolina General Assembly, with the support of its African American members, codified the segregationist sentiment of the Constitutional Convention of 1868 by enacting a statute mandating separate schools for white and black schoolchildren.[7] Finally, in 1875, another constitutional convention amended the constitution to state, "The children of the white race and the children of the colored race shall be taught in separate public schools."[8] In so doing, North Carolina became one of the first southern states to require by constitutional provision segregated public schools.[9] Yet the amendment was superfluous: those black and white schoolchildren who attended school in North Carolina already did so on a segregated basis.[10]

Throughout the nineteenth century, North Carolina schools were woefully underfinanced, since tax revenues were insufficient to support the four-month school term mandated by the state constitution.[11] The state legislature would not adequately finance the schools to support a four-month school year until the first decade of the twentieth century. The state's public school system struggled during these early years, with only about 40 percent of eligible children receiving any public education.[12] Wealthy white parents sent their children to private schools or employed private tutors; those children not so fortunate either attended no school or went to school for only a few weeks a year.[13] As a result, illiteracy actually increased during the 1870s.[14]

To be sure, a few school systems, primarily in the larger towns such as Charlotte, improved their lot by gaining legislative permission to levy supplemental local taxes for school support. Even at this early date, some North Carolinians understood the relationship between strong public schools and economic prosperity. The *Charlotte Observer*, for example, claimed, "Of all the questions before the southern people at this day, that of education transcends all others in importance, for upon it depends the future progress, greatness and glory of our section."[15] The city responded; as a result of increased local taxes, schools in Charlotte and Mecklenburg County were among the best financed in the state in the nineteenth century.[16]

Throughout North Carolina—including Charlotte and Mecklenburg County—white schools were consistently better financed than black schools during the nineteenth century.[17] Although the state constitution mandated that there should be "no discrimination in favor of or to the prejudice of either race," that constitutional provision was widely ignored.[18] The state's schools would not be adequately financed until the twentieth century; in the competition for scarce resources, schools for African American children suffered. There was little white support for black schools, as well as overt hostility to black education in many quarters, in part due to feelings that educated African Americans would be more likely to challenge whites socially and economically.[19]

The differences between black and white schools, modest in the 1870s, became more substantial over time. In the early 1880s, the North Carolina General Assembly took several actions that permitted increased expenditures on white schools without comparable expenditures on black schools. Confronted with an underfinanced public education system and realizing that few whites would vote additional taxes for public education if some of that tax money supported African American schools, the general assembly in 1880 enacted legislation allowing the town of Goldsboro the option of establishing separate black and white graded schools financed by local supplemental taxes imposed on the respective racial groups. The plan allowed whites to tax themselves solely for the support of white schools.[20] Although separate taxation schemes had previously been used in other southern states immediately after the Civil War, this marked the first time that the North Carolina legislature had permitted such a system.[21] The general assembly subsequently gave similar authorization to several other North Carolina towns and in 1883 enacted legislation that authorized every local district in the state to adopt a separate taxation scheme.[22] As a result of these statutes, a number of jurisdictions voted additional assessments on white property to improve white schools.[23]

In 1885, the general assembly enacted additional legislation providing that local school board members would henceforth be appointed by local justices of the peace and county commissioners. Since these two groups were appointed by the legislature, few if any African Americans could expect to win school board appointment.[24] Of equal significance, the 1885 law gave local school boards broad discretion in the disbursement of funds for education, an act that permitted further discrimination against black schools.[25]

As a result of these legislative actions, by the end of the century white schools were significantly better financed than black schools, particularly in the eastern part of the state, which had a substantial African American population.[26] In many school districts there were no schools for black children; no school district provided any schooling for black children beyond the elementary school level.[27] By 1890, only about half of the black school-age children in North Carolina attended school.[28] The results were apparent. By 1900, almost half of the African American population in North Carolina was illiterate, whereas for whites the figure was less than one-fifth.[29]

This growing disparity between black and white schools appeared to violate the state constitutional provision that prohibited racial discrimination in the provision of public education. Nevertheless, the general assembly, controlled by white interests, simply ignored the pleas of African American representatives who claimed that the separate taxation bills would decimate black education.[30] Moreover, the courts, charged with interpreting and enforcing the state constitution, were not readily accessible to black schoolchildren. Securing legal representation for a major constitutional challenge to school funding was a daunting task. By 1890, there were only fourteen African American lawyers in the entire state, in part because no formal legal training was available to African Americans until Shaw University in Raleigh established a fledgling law school in 1890.[31] Moreover, black lawyers typically represented black clients in small civil and criminal matters. Although black clients sometimes sought representation by white lawyers, a state supreme court challenge to educational inequalities was both an expensive and an unpopular venture. The absence of an organization financially prepared for and institutionally committed to challenging educational inequalities (an institution such as the NAACP) hampered efforts to seek judicial consideration of the educational disparities between black and white schools.

The interests of African American schoolchildren received an unexpected boost when a group of white taxpayers in Gaston County who objected to paying additional taxes filed suit challenging the separate taxation scheme; the case ultimately made its way to the North Carolina Supreme Court.[32] In 1886 the court declared, in *Puitt v. Commissioners of Gaston County*, that the division of school revenues on a racial basis violated the state constitutional provision that mandated no discrimination between black and white schools.[33] In an opinion remarkable for its concern for the rights of African Americans, the court noted, "Nor can we shut our eyes to the fact, that the vast bulk of property, yielding the fruits of taxation, belongs to the white people of the State, and very little is held by the emancipated race; and yet the needs of the latter for free tuition, in proportion to its numbers are as great, or greater than the needs of the former."[34] The *Puitt* decision put to rest, at least in theory, the ability of local school systems to finance black and white schools through separate taxation.[35]

Although the North Carolina Supreme Court had struck down separate taxation, a device that was gaining favor in other southern states to the detriment of African American schools, the court in the *Puitt* decision did legitimate North Carolina's strict segregation of black and white schoolchildren. Although not directly raised by the litigants, the court considered whether the state constitutional provision that required segregated schools could be squared with the equal protection clause of the Fourteenth Amendment to the U.S. Constitution. The court concluded that as long as North Carolina provided children of both races with "substantially equal school advantages," segregated education did not deny African American children the equal protection of the law.[36] Yet the North Carolina Supreme Court's insistence on "substantially equal school advantages" was meaningless if it could not be enforced. And because of the difficulties in bringing this type of litigation, few African American litigants would challenge educational inequality in North Carolina until the middle of the twentieth century.

The North Carolina Supreme Court's interpretation of the Fourteenth

Amendment was consistent with that of other state courts that had considered the issue.[37] Moreover, for the next half century, with the exception of one Pennsylvania trial court, no state or federal court would conclude that the equal protection clause of the Fourteenth Amendment barred segregated schools.[38] Indeed, in 1896, the U.S. Supreme Court appeared to put the issue to rest in *Plessy v. Ferguson,* a case involving segregated rail transportation, by holding that legally enforced racial separation did not violate the Fourteenth Amendment.[39]

Interestingly, the *Puitt* decision was one of only a handful of nineteenth-century southern state supreme court decisions that did find some form of racial discrimination in the operation of the public schools.[40] It is not entirely clear why the North Carolina court held the separate taxation scheme unconstitutional; the three justices were conservative Democrats, and hence their support of black rights could not have been predicted. Moreover, other state supreme courts split on the issue.[41]

Yet the *Puitt* decision cannot be understood as a victory for African American education. Although the court did strike down the separate taxation scheme, to the relief of many financially pressed white North Carolinians who feared new tax increases, the decision expressly upheld segregated schools and left untouched the discretion of local school boards to distribute school monies as they saw fit. Thus, although the *Puitt* decision did eliminate one means of discriminating against black schools, it left intact the legal basis of segregated and indeed unequal education.

Still, parts of the state greeted the *Puitt* decision with defiance. Some towns, such as Wilson, simply ignored the supreme court ruling and continued with a separate taxation scheme for a number of years. Other towns, such as Kinston and Goldsboro, responded to the *Puitt* decision by abandoning their public schools, a tactic that certain southern school districts would follow in the 1950s to avoid desegregation.[42] Within a short period of time, however, public schools in these towns were reestablished when it became apparent that school closures were counterproductive to white interests.[43] At the same time, some eastern North Carolina newspapers suggested that the decision should deprive the three supreme court justices of reelection. Yet all three justices won reelection just months after the *Puitt* decision was announced, reflecting in some measure the intense distaste of large portions of the populace for increased taxation.[44]

In the wake of the *Puitt* decision, very few jurisdictions voted additional tax assessments to support local education. As a result, North Carolina schools, already hurt by the state's poor economy, were some of the most poorly financed in the nation by the end of the nineteenth century.[45] At the same time, due in significant measure to the unavailability of separate taxation, the discrepancies between black and white schools in North Carolina at the end of the century were smaller than those in nearly every other southern state. In 1899, for example, black schools in North Carolina received a higher portion of the total school fund — 27 percent — than did black schools in any other southern state, even those states with a much higher black population.[46]

African Americans in North Carolina had been politically active throughout the post–Civil War era, with substantial electoral success. At the end of the century, however, the political voice of black North Carolinians fell silent, with unfortunate consequences for black education.

The 1890s marked the rise of white supremacy movements throughout the South, eliminating for more than half a century the participation of African Americans in southern public affairs. The race issue exploded with particular fury in North Carolina during the election of 1898. The Democratic Party, unsuccessful in the previous two elections due to a political alliance, or "fusion," between the state's Republican and Populist parties with significant black support, began a virulent white supremacy campaign. Paramilitary units, called Red Shirts and Rough Riders, terrorized Republicans, Populists, and especially African Americans. Race riots following the 1898 election in Wilmington left many African Americans dead and the legitimately elected local government forcefully driven from office.[47] In Charlotte, as in many North Carolina towns, thousands of onlookers thronged to watch a preelection "white supremacy" parade through the center of town.[48] On the day following the election, the *Charlotte Observer*'s banner headline announced: "WHITES TO RULE."[49]

In the wake of the 1898 election, the Democratic general assembly passed a number of segregation laws and a suffrage amendment to the state constitution that established a poll tax and literacy test for voters, the effect of which was to disfranchise most African Americans.[50] The populace ratified the suffrage amendment in the 1900 election, completing, in the words of Democratic leader Charles Aycock, "the final settlement of the negro problem."[51] Moreover, after 1898, several North Carolina towns enacted segregation ordinances mandating residential segregation.[52]

Aycock, elected governor in 1900 on a platform that emphasized white supremacy and educational reform, orchestrated an extraordinary campaign to increase expenditures for education during the first few years of the twentieth century.[53] Aycock promoted his education program in part to gain the illiterate whites' support for the disfranchisement amendment and to take the issue of educational reform away from the Populists.[54] The campaign succeeded beyond all expectations; total funding for public education in North Carolina increased from $1 million in 1900 to $4.7 million in 1915, one of the largest increases of all the southern states.[55] Because local school boards exercised considerable discretion in the allocation of educational monies, however, African American schools continued to receive an unequal share of the available revenues, typically no more than the black contribution to the property tax base would warrant. Even in counties with a majority-black population, white schools received a majority of the available funds.[56] Moreover, throughout the first decade of the century, the North Carolina General Assembly passed a number of statutes that permitted the creation of separate white school districts within the confines of existing school districts, thus allowing greater differentiation between black and white schools.[57]

Governor Aycock, in his public addresses, insisted that the increase in educational expenditures benefit both races and helped defeat a proposed constitutional amendment that would have reversed the *Puitt* decision and allowed the division of school monies based on the respective tax contributions of the two races.[58] Aycock and his colleagues who helped defeat the amendment believed in the supremacy of the white race but did not favor completely decimating black education. The motives were mixed. To some extent, the legislators possessed a paternalistic concern for the newly disfranchised race. Moreover, many understood that black education could yield economic benefits for the state. James Y. Joyner, later superintendent of public instruction, argued that underfinancing the black schools might encourage black emigration from the state, thereby eliminating a necessary part of the work force.[59] Concerns about black emigration were legitimate; in the wake of the 1900 ratification of the disfranchisement amendment, a large number of African Americans, including Congressman George White, left the state, seeking better opportunities in the North, creating labor shortages in some areas.[60]

Yet the defeat of the constitutional amendment did not mean that black schools would be adequately financed. By the end of the first decade of the twentieth century, the gap between black and white schools in North Carolina was the greatest it had ever been. In 1910, black schools received about 17 percent of total school monies, even though African Americans accounted for about one-third of the school population.[61] Just ten years earlier, black schools had received 28 percent of available school funds.[62] Those numbers would continue to decline. By 1915, African American schools received only 13 percent of total school monies; at that time, the state spent on average $7.40 for each white child and $2.30 for each black child.[63] Nathan Newbold, a white man who would later serve as North Carolina's first state agent for black schools, issued a stern indictment of the status of black education in 1914: "The average negro school house is really a disgrace to an independent civilized society, . . . [and reflects] injustice, inhumanity, and neglect on the part of white people."[64] But for the efforts of northern philanthropists, black education in North Carolina and indeed in the entire South would have lagged even further behind white education. A number of northern foundations, including the Southern Education Board, the Rosenwald Fund, and the John F. Slater Fund, provided tremendous assistance to black education, particularly in rural areas, throughout the South. In some years, in fact, the money supplied by the Rosenwald Fund for African American schools in North Carolina exceeded the amount spent by the state.[65]

This dramatic discrepancy between black and white schools was due in significant measure to the broad discretion that local school boards exercised in the distribution of tax monies for education and to the absence of black representation on any school board in the state. Although the constitutional amendment mandating separate taxation schemes had failed, individual school boards consistently left African American schools underfinanced. A 1909 study suggested that African American schools received even less money than they would have under a separate taxation plan.[66]

Once again, the disparity between the financing of black and white schools appeared to violate the state constitution's prohibition on racial discrimination in the provision of public education. Yet the difficulties confronting African American parents seeking to initiate constitutional challenges and the unreceptiveness of courts to claims of racial discrimination in education curtailed efforts to rectify these inequities through litigation.

Initially, it appeared that the North Carolina Supreme Court would enforce the state constitutional provision mandating no discrimination between black and white schools. In 1902, in *Hooker v. Town of Greenville*, another suit brought by a white taxpayer objecting to the issuance of school bonds, the court enjoined the issuance of the bonds in question on the grounds that the revenues would disproportionately benefit white schools.[67] The court unanimously concluded that the state constitution required school districts to provide African American children the same per capita share of school revenues as was given to white students: "One white child of the school age shall have the same amount of money *per capita* as a colored child, and no more; and the colored child shall have the same amount *per capita* as any white child, and no more; . . . both races shall have equal opportunities for an education, so far as the public money is concerned."[68] It was an extraordinary statement—probably the most liberal construction of the rights of black schoolchildren to date by a southern state supreme court. The *Hooker* opinion theoretically provided a legal blueprint for a challenge to every North Carolina school system's education financing: monies would have to be spent equally for blacks and whites. No southern court had ever so held.

The remarkable *Hooker* decision was clearly an aberration in the context of contemporary southern jurisprudence and reflected the explosive politics of the day. Four of the five justices who rendered the decision were Republicans who had joined the court during the tumultuous "fusion" years of the mid-1890s.[69] The Democrat-controlled House had impeached two of the justices the previous year in part because of their suspected liberal views on racial matters.[70] Although the Senate failed to convict, the *Hooker* decision constituted the last gasp of an embattled court from another political era; within three years, the four Republican justices had been replaced by Aycock Democrats.[71]

The new Democratic supreme court eviscerated the *Hooker* principle in a series of decisions that legitimated grossly disparate financing of black and white schools. In 1905, the court explicitly overruled the *Hooker* requirement of equal spending in *Lowery v. School Trustees of Kernersville*, substituting in its stead a requirement of "equal facilities."[72] The court defined "equal facilities" in a curious manner. Such equality meant only a school term "of the same length" and the employment of "a sufficient number" of teachers in both black and white schools.[73] In articulating such an amorphous standard of equality, the court in *Lowery* indicated a reluctance to scrutinize closely the actions of local school boards, to whom the court granted essentially unreviewable discretion: "Much must be left to the good faith, integrity and judgment of local [school] boards in working out the difficult problem of providing equal facilities for each race in the education of all the children of the State."[74] The court well understood that every school board member in North Carolina was white and that the "good faith" of local school boards held little promise for African American schoolchildren.[75] In his 1910 biennial report, State Superintendent of Public Instruction Joyner conceded the effect of the *Lowery* decision: "The apportionment of the school fund in each county is practically placed absolutely under the control of the county board of education, the only restriction laid upon the board therein being that the funds shall be apportioned among the schools of each township in such a way as to give *equal length of term* as nearly as possible."[76] Three years later, the court held that creating a new school district in an all-white section of a town and then improving the schools in the new white district through local tax supplements was not discriminatory.[77] The nondiscrimination clause of the state constitution had been rendered meaningless.

The court's decisions on equality were not surprising. These new Democratic justices had been chosen by an electorate devoid of African Americans and that cared little for racial equality. Moreover, virtually all of the legal challenges had been brought by white taxpayers who objected to a new tax increase or bond issue. In several of the opinions in which the court found the tax increase or bond issue to be lawful, it expressly noted that the question of whether school monies were subsequently spent in a discriminatory manner was not before the court—white plaintiffs had no interest in raising those issues. Indeed both the white plaintiff and the defendant school board in the *Lowery* case agreed that the insistence on "per capita" equality in the earlier *Hooker* decision exceeded the requirements of the state constitution, a proposition that the newly constituted supreme court readily accepted.[78] Once again, the barriers confronting African American schoolchildren in bringing sophisticated lawsuits—particularly the absence of an organization committed to this type of litigation—prevented legal challenges that squarely presented the unequal expenditure issue. Disfranchisement was a contributing factor. Between 1900, the year the disfranchisement amendment was ratified, and 1910, the number of African American lawyers in North Carolina declined by almost 25 percent.[79] In part, the decline was due to the emigration of African American lawyers from the state in search of more favorable environments in which to practice law.[80] Moreover, in 1914, Shaw University in Raleigh closed its law school because of low enrollment. Shaw had educated over fifty African American lawyers during the previous quarter century and had been the primary source of black legal education in North Carolina.[81]

To be sure, had the state supreme court been confronted directly with the issue of unequal expenditures—which it was not—it most likely would have declined to find unlawful discrimination. Nevertheless, the inability of African American parents to mount legal challenges contributed to the foreclosure of the courts as a forum for legal redress.

The blatant discrimination by the North Carolina General Assembly and local school boards against African American schoolchildren in the provision of school monies was not unique to North Carolina; nor were the unfavorable decisions of the North Carolina Supreme Court. During the first decade of the twentieth century, the gap between black and white education widened throughout the South, aided by disfranchisement efforts. Moreover, legal challenges to racial discrimination in education were sparse throughout the region, and no southern court — state or federal — offered relief to litigants challenging racial discrimination in education.[82] It would take an organized and sustained challenge to rectify this educational inequality, and as of the early twentieth century, black southerners had never been capable of mounting such a challenge.

Yet ultimately an organization emerged that was both committed to and capable of challenging the educational inequalities that persisted throughout the South: the NAACP. Founded in 1909 by a group of black and white leaders committed to ending black disfranchisement, lynchings, and racial segregation, the NAACP spent its early years engaged in lobbying efforts and occasional court appearances attempting to improve the political status of African Americans. In the early 1930s, the NAACP determined that the courts offered the best hope for challenging educational inequality. Armed with financing from a foundation grant, the organization initiated a modest litigation campaign challenging both the exclusion of black students from southern graduate and professional schools and the salary inequities between black and white teachers.[83] The NAACP offered what had previously been lacking in the southern black community: legal expertise and financial backing. Before 1930, southern courts considered few legal challenges to educational inequality, and most of those had been brought by white plaintiffs concerned not with the inferior status of black education but with the threat of increased taxation. The NAACP was poised to rectify that situation.

The NAACP's litigation efforts, however, particularly in North Carolina, were seriously hampered by the lack of support among the state's African American educational leadership, which had a vested interest in the maintenance of segregated education. In March 1933, Thomas Hocutt, of Durham, represented by two local African American lawyers, Conrad Pearson and Cecil McCoy, initiated the first lawsuit ever filed seeking the admission of a black student to a white professional school. Hocutt had been denied admission to the pharmacy school at the all-white University of North Carolina, notwithstanding the fact that the state offered no pharmacy education to African American students.[84] Although the national office of the NAACP did not initiate the litigation, it did offer its support and sent William Hastie, a black lawyer from Washington, D.C., to handle the case.[85] Within two weeks of filing suit, the court conducted a trial, after which it dismissed Hocutt's claim for failure to prove that he was sufficiently qualified to enter the university.[86]

The opposition of Dr. James E. Shepard, president of both the North Carolina College for Negroes in Durham and the black North Carolina Teachers Association, undermined Hocutt's efforts. Shepard, who had long discouraged political and legal activism as a means of improving the status of black North Carolinians, worried that Hocutt's attempt to integrate the white University of North Carolina would subvert his efforts to secure segregated graduate programs for African American students at his college.[87] Under pressure from North Carolina Director of Negro Education Nathan Newbold to oppose the litigation, Shepard refused to release Hocutt's undergraduate transcript from the North Carolina College for Negroes or to supply recommendations in support of his application, making Hocutt's claim fatally defective.[88] Accordingly, the trial court ruled that the university had appropriately exercised its discretion in declining to admit Hocutt. Significantly, the court noted that it left open the question of whether the university had an obligation to admit qualified African American applicants to its graduate programs if no such programs were otherwise available for black students.[89]

The NAACP declined to appeal the *Hocutt* decision, and it would be more than fifteen years before the NAACP initiated additional litigation in North Carolina.[90] The lack of support among the state's African American leadership proved decisive in the organization's decision to carry on its litigation campaign elsewhere. Indeed, in the early 1950s, Thurgood Marshall, legal director of the NAACP, claimed that lack of support in the black community—particularly among educational leaders such as Shepard—was one of the primary barriers to more extensive litigation challenging educational inequalities in the South.[91]

Conrad Pearson, the Durham lawyer who initiated the *Hocutt* challenge, had recently graduated from Howard Law School in Washington, D.C. North Carolina at that time afforded no legal education for African American students. Pearson was clearly influenced by Howard's dean, Charles Houston, who strongly encouraged his graduates to use their legal skills to fight racial discrimination.[92] Over the course of the next few decades, Pearson, who would serve as the state NAACP legal director, initiated a number of desegregation suits, including successful challenges to segregation at the University of North Carolina's law school and undergraduate program. Houston's vision, however, was not shared by most of the leading African American educators in North Carolina.

Shepard, in particular, would continue to oppose both integration in general and litigation in particular as a means of improving the status of black education in North Carolina. When challenged about the need to increase black teachers' salaries in 1938, Shepard wrote that such a movement "should be directed not by an outside agency" such as the NAACP, "which in the beginning resorts to the courts," but through negotiation conducted by the state's traditional black leadership.[93] Later, in 1947, Shepard told a statewide radio audience that he still opposed "any recourse to litigation to hasten the ending of discrimination," notwithstanding the substantial success enjoyed by the NAACP in its litigation campaign during the 1940s.[94] Shepard's accommodationist attitudes — shared by many of the state's leading black educators — in conjunction with his statewide prominence made litigation in North Carolina difficult.[95] Shepard was ultimately rewarded for his opposition to integrationist efforts; when the North Carolina General Assembly finally established graduate education for African American students in the late 1930s, Shepard's North Carolina College received the bulk of the new programs that he had long sought.[96]

Despite the dearth of lawsuits in North Carolina challenging racial discrimination in education, the threat of litigation spurred the general assembly into action in three areas: graduate education for African American students, the equalization of teachers' salaries, and the equalization of support for elementary and secondary schools. In each of these areas, favorable court decisions in other jurisdictions signaled that continued discrimination against black students and teachers in North Carolina would invite judicial intervention.

In the area of graduate education, the first critical decision came in 1938, when the U.S. Supreme Court found Missouri's failure to provide legal education for African American students constitutionally defective in *Missouri ex rel. Gaines v. Canada*.[97] The Court ordered the state of Missouri either to admit an African American student to the state's white law school or to make some other provision for his education. Since no southern state provided any such educational opportunities for African

Americans, all were vulnerable to similar legal challenges. North Carolina was one of the first southern states to respond to the *Gaines* decision. In 1939, the general assembly established some of the first state-supported graduate and professional programs for African Americans in the South at the North Carolina College for Negroes and the North Carolina Agricultural and Technical College in Greensboro.[98] The quick action of the general assembly in response to *Gaines* reflected a calculated desire to prevent judicially compelled integration of North Carolina's white colleges and universities. Indeed, shortly after the *Gaines* decision, Pauli Murray, an African American woman and later distinguished lawyer and poet, had unsuccessfully sought admission to the University of North Carolina graduate school.[99] Although Murray decided not to challenge her exclusion in the courts, the lack of graduate education for blacks had left the state vulnerable in light of the *Gaines* decision.

Successful litigation in other jurisdictions also prompted the North Carolina General Assembly to take action regarding unequal salaries for teachers. In 1940, the U.S. Court of Appeals for the Fourth Circuit, with Judge John Parker of Charlotte writing, held in a Norfolk, Virginia, case that disparities in teachers' salaries violated the equal protection clause of the Fourteenth Amendment.[100] The decision enjoyed wide publicity. The NAACP subsequently won similar victories in other states throughout the South.[101] Cognizant of the potential for similar litigation in North Carolina, the state superintendent of public instruction persuaded the general assembly to increase the pay of African American teachers. As a result, throughout the early 1940s, the North Carolina General Assembly appropriated increasingly larger sums of money to provide for the ultimate equalization of black and white teachers' salaries.[102] Whereas in 1938 white teachers' salaries exceeded black salaries by about 25 to 30 percent, by 1945 salaries of black teachers actually exceeded those of white teachers due to the higher qualifications of black teachers.[103] Every other southern state legislature took similar action during the 1940s to avoid litigation.[104]

Before this successful litigation, there had been serious but unsuccessful efforts in North Carolina to equalize teachers' salaries. In 1934 and 1935, the biracial Commission for the Study of Problems in Negro Education, appointed by Governor John C. B. Ehringhaus, had revealed significant disparities between the salaries of black and white teachers and had recommended that those disparities be completely eliminated within three to five years.[105] The North Carolina General Assembly, however, ignored the commission's recommendations. Without any judicial precedent compelling such salary equalization, the commission's recommendations carried little weight.

The African American community in North Carolina had divided over the question of whether to pursue litigation to force the general assembly's hand on the salary issue. The North Carolina Teachers Association, under the leadership of Shepard, eschewed litigation as a method for achieving such equalization, as did J. N. Seabrook, president of a state-supported black teachers college in Fayetteville.[106] On the other hand, Pearson and McCoy, the Durham lawyers who had handled the *Hocutt* case, urged Walter White at the NAACP national office to provide assistance in bringing a legal challenge to unequal teachers' salaries. Pearson and McCoy enjoyed the support of Louis Austin, the editor of a black newspaper in Durham, *Carolina Times*; Austin favored litigation and castigated the state's black leaders for their accommodationist views.[107] Ultimately the national organization declined to pursue litigation in North Carolina due to the opposition of substantial portions of the state's black leadership. In White's view, it was better to pursue litigation in those states where there was less opposition in the black community. Hence no litigation was brought in North Carolina challenging unequal salaries, and the general assembly took no action to equalize salaries until the successful litigation in other jurisdictions compelled the legislature to change its posture.

In the late 1940s, the national NAACP's litigation strategy expanded to include challenges to unequal elementary and secondary school facilities. In several North Carolina cities, local NAACP branches threatened litigation if conditions in black schools did not improve.[108] Although most local branches of the organization ultimately declined to initiate litigation, a few lawsuits were filed.[109] In May 1949, for example, a group of African Americans in Durham, with NAACP support, filed suit in federal court challenging unequal support for black schools in that city; two years later, a federal court found that black schools in Durham were indeed unconstitutionally underfunded.[110] Within a few years, additional lawsuits were filed challenging unequal support for black schools in Wilson, High Point, Old Fort, Lumberton, New Hanover County, Pamlico County, Washington County, and Gaston County.[111]

Even though many of these suits were unsuccessful, the North Carolina General Assembly once again acted in response to the threat of litigation.[112] Many of the legislators well understood that the failure to provide equal facilities could result in court-ordered pupil mixing, since the status of segregated schools was technically dependent on equality. Hence, the general assembly in the late 1940s and early 1950s appropriated increasingly larger amounts of money for African American schools. The steady increase in appropriations had tangible results. Whereas in 1940 the state spent 71 percent more per white pupil than per black pupil, by 1952 the difference was 17 percent, the lowest in the South.[113] Other state legislatures throughout the South took similar action. Between 1940 and 1954, every southern state significantly reduced the wide discrepancy in per capita expenditures for black and white students.[114]

The significant actions by the North Carolina General Assembly — as well as other southern state legislatures — in the areas of graduate education, teachers' salaries, and educational expenditures during the fifteen years before the *Brown* decision were in large measure due to the legislature's desire to avoid judicial intervention in the administration of the public schools and the possibility of court-ordered racial mixing. Beginning in the late 1930s the federal courts, particularly the U.S. Supreme Court, had issued a series of favorable decisions that signaled a shifting judicial mood on the question of racial inequality in education.[115] For the first time, the federal courts were a significant threat to the continuation of separate and unequal education in the South. Moreover, the NAACP offered the African American community its first substantial opportunity to utilize the courts effectively as an instrument for racial change. Recognizing the shift in judicial attitudes and the enhanced potential for litigation, the North Carolina General Assembly moved to avert judicial intervention in the state's educational system.

Yet the general assembly's relatively quick response to changing legal expectations was influenced by other concerns as well. Throughout most of the twentieth century, North Carolina's political leaders, although strong proponents of racial segregation, supported black education for reasons of paternalism and potential economic benefits to the state. North Carolina's Democratic leaders had embraced disfranchisement in 1900 to eliminate the perceived "disruption" of black participation in electoral politics but, having done so, refused for the next half century to engage in racial demagoguery and espoused on occasion a paternalistic concern for the economic welfare of black citizens. The general assembly, particularly after the end of World War I, made serious efforts to improve the quality of black education; as a result, the differences between black and white schools — although quite dramatic — were generally less in North Carolina than in any other southern state throughout the pre-*Brown* period.[116] Governor Clyde Hoey, explaining his support for black graduate education in 1939, commented, "North Carolina does not believe in social equality between the races, and will not tolerate mixed schools for the races, but we do believe in equality of opportunity in their respective fields of service."[117]

By midcentury, the NAACP had learned a valuable lesson in North Carolina as well as in other parts of the South: litigation or the threat of litigation could serve as a highly effective tool in the quest for educational equality. The next issue the organization addressed was whether to use the courts to challenge segregation itself. During the 1940s, a number of NAACP leaders favored an outright attack on segregated schools. North Carolina State NAACP President Kelly Alexander, for example, in his 1949 address to the state NAACP convention, called for "a county by county campaign" to fight segregated education in North Carolina: "This fight should include court action on the elementary, secondary and university level. The goal is an integrated school system."[118] For the next several years, Alexander would repeat that call in his annual presidential address.[119] Alexander's demand for integration stood in stark contrast to the accommodationist views of men like Shepard and Seabrook.

In June 1950, the NAACP won two critical Supreme Court cases requiring racial integration in graduate and professional schools.[120] Relying on these precedents, the organization prevailed in several challenges to segregation in southern graduate schools. For example, in 1951, a federal court required the integration of the University of North Carolina Law School, notwithstanding the opposition to that litigation by one of the state's most prominent black educators, Alfonso Elder, Shepard's successor as president of the North Carolina College for Negroes.[121] The next question was whether the courts would require pupil mixing in elementary and secondary schools. In 1952, the U.S. Supreme Court announced that it would decide that issue in the case of *Brown v. Board of Education.*[122]

But putting small children of different races together in a classroom ran afoul of southern mores in a way that equalizing school expenditures or mixing graduate students did not. To challenge public school segregation was to challenge a foundation stone of southern culture that divided even those of liberal sensibilities. In 1949, for example, the progressive North Carolina Commission on Interracial Cooperation dissolved, after nearly three decades, due to internal disagreements over the wisdom of racial integration. Throughout its tenure, this biracial organization of distinguished North Carolina educators and church leaders had confronted an array of racial issues; integration proved to be its death knell.[123] Even

Frank Porter Graham, perhaps the South's leading white liberal, had held the line against racial integration during his tenure as president of the University of North Carolina during the 1930s and 1940s.[124] Nevertheless, Graham's suspected liberal racial views led to his defeat by Willis Smith in a runoff primary for the Democratic nomination to the U.S. Senate in June 1950. During the runoff primary campaign, Smith's allies charged that if Graham was elected, pupil mixing would follow. One pro-Smith handbill asked voters if they wanted "Negroes going to white schools and white children going to Negro schools"; another was more direct and demanded, "WHITE PEOPLE WAKE UP." Smith's racial charges undoubtedly influenced the election.[125]

The North Carolina that awaited the Supreme Court's decision in *Brown* in the spring of 1954 had taken significant strides in equalizing black and white schools, but the issue of integration was a wholly different matter. North Carolinians might be a bit more willing than their southern neighbors to put a new set of books in a black school or pay a black teacher a fair wage, but they shared their neighbors' profound aversion to seating black and white schoolchildren together in the same room. In the aftermath of the *Brown* decision, North Carolina passions on the issue of school integration would not be stirred quite as deeply by demagogic sputterings as in other parts of the South, but the state would nevertheless be severely tested by the new social order.

The choice is not between segregation and integration; it is between some integration and total integration. . . . [If we resist all integration], it is a foregone conclusion that the winner will be total integration, or that the schools will be closed. . . . Token integration . . . will save the state and save the schools.

This is moderation.

—North Carolina State Judge Braxton Craven, *Chapel Hill Weekly*, April 28, 1960

CHAPTER 2

The Pursuit of Moderation
North Carolina Struggles with the
Demands of *Brown*

On May 17, 1954, the U.S. Supreme Court forever altered the fabric of American life. In one of the most momentous political events of the twentieth century, the U.S. Supreme Court, in *Brown v. Board of Education*, declared segregated education unconstitutional.[1] In so doing, the Court directly challenged three centuries of well-entrenched social patterns and initiated a cultural upheaval of immense proportions. The legitimacy of one of the cornerstones of southern society—racial segregation—had been profoundly undercut.

For the next several years, the white South struggled to make sense of the new order. In the early years after *Brown*, those who sought to maintain the old traditions in defiance of the Court held sway. In some parts of the South, defiance came easy, accompanied by inflammatory rhetoric. North Carolina, a state that prided itself on a more progressive racial heritage, responded to *Brown* with appeals to "moderation." In so doing, the state avoided much of the inflammatory rhetoric that dominated the response to *Brown* in other southern states and won itself a reputation as a state willing to adapt to the new order. Although North Carolina's political leaders were no more eager to allow black children into white schools than were their counterparts in other southern states, they well understood that defiance could harm the state's reputation for racial moderation, forestall new economic development, and invite judicial intervention in the operation of the schools. North Carolina in the post-

25

Brown period therefore resisted the more extreme legislative responses adopted in other states.

North Carolina's "moderate" response to *Brown* did not open the doors of the state's white schools to black children. By engaging in well-publicized, but decidedly token, integration, North Carolina managed to maintain an almost completely segregated school system for the first decade after *Brown*. Indeed, North Carolina's schools remained more segregated than those in most southern states, including some of the more defiant states such as Virginia, whose leaders opposed any desegregation in what became a badge of honor.[2] On the tenth anniversary of *Brown*, only one in a hundred southern black children attended a desegregated school; in "moderate" North Carolina, that figure was one in two hundred.[3]

The *Brown* case was actually a collection of cases from four states challenging racial segregation in public education.[4] Having successfully challenged segregation in graduate education as unconstitutional in 1950, the NAACP had refocused its attentions on elementary and secondary education.[5] The Supreme Court was well aware of the significance of the cases when it first considered them in December 1952; because of divisions on the Court as to the proper result and because of serious qualms about a split decision, the Court held the case for an additional year. Over the course of that year, Earl Warren replaced Fred Vinson as chief justice. Warren was staunchly committed to a decision declaring segregated schools unconstitutional and possessed the requisite skills of persuasion to fashion unanimous agreement around such a decision. In a short opinion, the Court, citing recent social science research, concluded that segregation denied African American children the full benefits of education. "To separate [black schoolchildren] from others of similar age and qualifications solely because of their race," the Court announced, "generates a feeling of inferiority . . . that may affect their hearts and minds in a way unlikely ever to be undone."[6]

The initial reaction to the *Brown* decision varied throughout the South. Some southern leaders were defiant. Senator James Eastland of Mississippi announced, "The Supreme Court of the United States in the false name of law and justice has perpetrated a monstrous crime."[7] Mississippi Governor Hugh L. White announced: "We're not going to pay any attention to the Supreme Court's decision. We don't think it will have any effect on us down here at all."[8] And in fact, no black child would attend school with a white child in Mississippi for over a decade. Other states, such as

Georgia and South Carolina, had already taken action in anticipation of the Supreme Court's decision by abolishing the constitutional requirement of public education.[9]

Political leaders in North Carolina initially responded to the *Brown* decision in subdued tones. Most of the state's politicians, reflecting the sentiment of the state's white population, opposed school integration. But most were also unprepared to engage in hopeless defiance of the Supreme Court, a move that could hurt the state's broader interests. Hence, for the next several years, the state's political leaders sought to avoid as much integration as possible while taking no action that would undermine the state's education system or its reputation for moderation on matters of race, since they believed such action would harm the state's economic environment. Effectively utilizing limited token integration, North Carolina's leaders pursued a course of well-publicized "moderation," in contrast to its more obstreperous southern neighbors.

On learning of the *Brown* decision, North Carolina Governor William Umstead, although noting that he was "terribly disappointed" by the decision, refused to counsel defiance of the Supreme Court and instead stated, "The Supreme Court of the United States has spoken."[10] He added, "This is no time for rash statements or the proposal of impossible schemes."[11] The day after the decision was announced, the Greensboro, N.C., School Board became the first in the United States to decide to study ways of complying with the decision; the board chair announced, "We must not fight or attempt to circumvent this decision."[12] Two days later, Irving Carlyle, a prominent North Carolina attorney and Democratic leader, addressed the North Carolina Democratic Convention and urged the state to obey the decision: "As good citizens we have no other course except to obey the law laid down by the United States Supreme Court."[13] The convention adopted a resolution affirming "the supremacy of the law for all citizens."[14] The resolution was not an endorsement of *Brown*, but it did reflect the fact that much of the political leadership of North Carolina did not care to flout the Supreme Court's authority.

Within weeks of the *Brown* decision, Governor Umstead directed the North Carolina Institute of Government, a branch of the University of North Carolina, to prepare a report analyzing *Brown* and outlining possible responses to the decision. The selection of the institute to prepare the state's initial analysis of *Brown* was significant. The institute, under the leadership of Director Albert Coates, had since the 1930s offered the state an impressive array of critical analyses of public policy issues.

Governor Umstead met with Coates and his assistant, James Paul, to discuss their work. The governor articulated his fear that a demagogue might exploit the school desegregation issue for political advantage, which could do serious damage to the state and its reputation. Umstead reminded Coates and Paul that just four years earlier the Democratic primary for the U.S. Senate between Frank Porter Graham and Willis Smith had unleashed a great deal of racial bitterness throughout the state. Umstead feared that the *Brown* decision, if mishandled, could cause similar problems.[15]

Within three months, the institute submitted a lengthy and detailed analysis of both the Court's decision and the various legal alternatives open to the state in response. The report, written in large measure by Paul, a Philadelphia Quaker who had recently finished a Supreme Court clerkship with Chief Justice Fred Vinson, was one of the most balanced and dispassionate analyses of the *Brown* decision prepared during the 1950s. This achievement was all the more remarkable in light of the rancor of much of the contemporaneous discussion of the *Brown* decision throughout the South.[16]

The institute report analyzed several of the proposed responses that were gaining favor in other southern states, such as the creation of a state-supported private school system and the utilization of private school tuition grants. The report concluded that the constitutionality of such proposals was doubtful and that, for the state to avert judicial challenge to its pupil assignment scheme, some black students must receive assignments to white schools.[17] That conclusion was a reasonable reading of *Brown* but overestimated the willingness of the federal courts in the near term to scrutinize closely the actions of southern school boards.

Although the institute report did not make explicit recommendations, it suggested that the state not openly defy the Supreme Court, the result of which would be "litigious harassment, damage suits, and possibly considerable court supervision." The authors instead encouraged a program of gradual desegregation, which would allow "a minimum of court interference and a minimum of sudden change."[18] The institute report clearly contemplated some desegregation, in marked contrast to the declarations of several other southern states, although it recognized that such desegregation efforts would take time, given the political realities of the mid-1950s.

In August 1954, having received the institute report, Governor Umstead appointed a nineteen-person committee—including three African Americans—under the leadership of former Speaker of the House Thomas J. Pearsall to study the desegregation issue.[19] The governor presented the committee with copies of the institute's report and emphasized its gradual approach.[20] Like Umstead, Pearsall opposed pupil mixing, but he also wanted to preserve the state's public schools and strong economic climate.[21] Pearsall announced at the outset that his primary goal was to preserve the public schools, an obvious reference to the discussion in many southern states about abandoning the public school system.[22]

Throughout the fall, as the committee did its work, Umstead continued to resist pressure from segregationists to publicly defy the Supreme Court. In September 1954, for example, Umstead refused to endorse a petition from a large number of his constituents favoring the continuation of school segregation.[23] When other southern politicians joined the call for defiance, Umstead resisted such action and sought to avoid any racial demagoguery that could harm the state.

Although North Carolina's leaders publicly eschewed defiance, they did seek to persuade the U.S. Supreme Court to reject school desegregation in the rehearing on the *Brown* case. In the fall of 1954, the state's attorney general submitted a brief to the Court on the remedy question in the *Brown* case; the brief argued that desegregation was simply not feasible in North Carolina. Drafted in large measure by Beverly Lake, an assistant attorney general, the brief concluded, based on a survey of opinion of law enforcement officers and school superintendents, that desegregation would cause substantial disruption and even violence in North Carolina's schools. Any attempt to desegregate the schools, Lake argued, could lead to the abandonment of public education.[24] That the state would take such a strong position in its *Brown* brief was not surprising. The governor and the attorney general had studiously avoided counseling defiance of the Supreme Court, but they were quite anxious about pupil mixing, which they hoped to avoid by any lawful means available. In a statement that betrayed a profound misunderstanding of the direction that school desegregation law would take, Lake concluded that in the state's cities, such as Charlotte, with significant residential segregation, the *Brown* decision would have little impact; he worried instead about rural North Carolina, where blacks and whites lived in desegregated residential patterns and where a race-neutral pupil assignment plan would likely result in extensive desegregation.[25]

The Pearsall Committee completed its report four months later, on December 30, 1954. Governor Umstead had died on November 7, so the committee submitted its report to his successor, Governor Luther Hodges, a former textile executive who had entered politics in 1952 with his election as lieutenant governor. Hodges perceived of himself as a businessman first and foremost; he entitled his autobiography, published a few years after his tenure as governor, *Businessman in the Statehouse.* Throughout his six years as governor, Hodges was an aggressive proponent of economic development; one of his lasting legacies was the creation of Research Triangle Park, west of Raleigh, for the purpose of promoting corporate and government research.[26] Hodges's concern for the way in which his policy decisions affected business animated his administration, including his treatment of the desegregation issue.

At first blush, the Pearsall Committee's report seemed to dash any hope that the state might move toward substantial desegregation, gradual or otherwise. The committee, including its three black members, unanimously concluded that "the mixing of the races forthwith in the public schools throughout the state" could not be accomplished and "should not be attempted" because it "would alienate public support of the schools to such an extent that they could not be operated successfully."[27] Although the use of the word "forthwith" introduced a degree of ambiguity into the committee's conclusions, leaving open the question of whether the committee contemplated the eventual desegregation of the schools, the report nevertheless expressed strong opposition to school desegregation.

On the other hand, the report avoided recommending legislative actions, such as school closings or the use of private school tuition grants, which were gaining popularity in other southern states and which might undermine the public schools. Indeed, the only legislative action that the committee recommended was the transfer of authority over pupil assignments to local school boards.[28] The report set the state on a course that it would follow for the next several years: avoid the strident responses to *Brown*, which might damage the state's moderate reputation, but minimize as much as possible the amount of school desegregation.

The support of the committee's three African Americans, although troubling to many in the black community, particularly the NAACP, was not surprising. Each of the three was employed by the state and hence disinclined to dissent from the majority view. Moreover, two of the three members were heads of all-black state colleges that had benefited from the legacy of segregated education in the state. The NAACP issued a statement claiming that the three "were not free to express their personal opinion" and did not reflect "the majority opinion of fellow Negroes of North Carolina."[29] Yet that latter claim was open to question. An American Institute of Public Opinion survey found, in February 1956, that 47 percent of African Americans in the South did not support the *Brown* decision — in large measure because of fear of mistreatment of black children in white schools.[30] Although the support of southern blacks for school desegregation would dramatically increase over the course of the next few years, during the first years after *Brown* the NAACP's integrationist agenda was not shared by all members of the black community.

When the North Carolina General Assembly convened its regular legislative session in January 1955, one of the legislature's primary items of business was consideration of the Pearsall Committee's report. Governor Hodges endorsed the report as an appropriate and moderate response to the crisis brought about by the *Brown* decision. Hodges, echoing the concern of his predecessor Umstead, announced of the suggestions outlined in the report, "[They] protect what we think are our rights without any demagoguery."[31] On March 30, 1955, the North Carolina General Assembly enacted legislation that vested local school boards with exclusive authority over pupil assignments.[32] The statute expressly directed local school boards not to consider race as an assignment criteria. Assistant Attorney General Lake informed the Supreme Court, during oral argument in April 1955 in the *Brown* case, that the statute would permit a local school board to operate mixed-race schools.[33]

Although the new legislation appeared to be racially neutral and hence to contemplate some pupil mixing, in fact it contained certain features that inhibited desegregation. First, the legislation decentralized assignment authority, making it impossible to challenge pupil assignments without bringing suit against each individual school board. Second, the legislation established a complicated system of administrative appeals through which challenges to school board assignments had to be made and transfer requests filed. No black student could challenge an assignment to a segregated school unless that student had faithfully adhered to all specified administrative procedures. Many black children lost their opportunity to challenge a school assignment because they failed to comply with some detail of the administrative appeal process. Thus, although on its face the legislation appeared to constitute an abandonment of previous race-based pupil assignments, in practice every school board in the state would continue to assign students to schools on the basis of race until the early 1960s. At the same time, most school boards denied every request filed by a black student to transfer from an assigned black school to a white school.

The actions of the North Carolina General Assembly, however, were perceived as moderate and enlightened when compared with those of most other southern states. Unlike some other southern state legislatures, the general assembly had resisted efforts to pass a constitutional amendment abolishing the requirement of public schools and providing tuition grants to parents who wanted to place their children in private schools. In addition, the assembly had rejected legislation providing that any school district that permitted desegregation be denied state funds.[34] Governor Hodges, concerned about the negative impact these proposals would have on the state's relatively strong public school system and economic climate, labeled them "extreme and untimely."[35] Hodges ultimately persuaded the legislators who sponsored these bills to withdraw them pending the Supreme Court's upcoming remedial decision in the *Brown* case.[36] Hodges understood that the delegation of assignment authority to local school boards would likely achieve the same results as the proposed constitutional amendment but that, unlike outright defiance, it would avoid rancor and damage to the public schools. Recognizing the broader economic interests of the state, the governor sought to avoid the harm that would ensue should the general assembly abolish the constitutional requirement of a public education system.

Yet one year later, in 1956, the North Carolina General Assembly enacted a more ambitious legislative program that aimed at reducing the threat of school desegregation and that appeared at first blush to embrace certain of the more extreme positions taken in other states. In the spring of 1955, the North Carolina General Assembly had created a second education commission, also known as the Pearsall Committee, to conduct further study of the desegregation question. Hodges appointed seven white men to the new committee, later explaining that African Americans would have been under too much pressure from groups such as the NAACP to push for immediate desegregation.[37] In April 1956, this second Pearsall Committee, having worked in close consultation with Hodges, issued its report, which explicitly expressed a desire to maintain segregated schools: "The educational system of North Carolina has been built on the foundation stone of segregation of the races in the schools. . . . The Supreme Court of the United States destroyed the school system which we had developed—a segregated-by-law system. . . . [The committee is] proposing the building of a new school system on a new foundation—a foundation of no racial segregation by law, but assignment according to natural racial preference and the administrative determination of what is best for the child."[38] In a reversal from the prior year, the committee's "Pearsall Plan" provided for constitutional amendments allowing both private school tuition grants for parents whose children were assigned to a desegregated school and local referenda whereby a community could decide whether to close certain schools instead of desegregating them.[39] Both the governor and the general assembly had rejected legislation closing schools a year earlier, but now the Pearsall Plan gave local communities the option of taking that course of action.

Governor Hodges publicly embraced the Pearsall Plan with its more extreme provisions.[40] It was a clear reversal for the governor. One year earlier, Hodges had successfully led an effort to defeat legislation allowing school closings; the prior summer, in a statewide broadcast, Hodges had argued that closing the public schools was "a last-ditch and double-edged weapon." He added, "If that weapon is ever used in North Carolina, its result will be appalling in ignorance, poverty, and bitterness."[41] Now, Hodges supported a constitutional amendment permitting the closure of the public schools. When Hodges went before the legislature during the summer of 1956 to defend the Pearsall Plan, he offered a much more aggressive defense of racial segregation than he had in 1955: "It is my firm belief that . . . the people of North Carolina expect their General Assembly and their Governor to do everything legally possible to prevent their children from being forced to attend mixed schools against their wishes."[42]

The general assembly ultimately ratified the Pearsall Plan, following a special four-day session in July 1956, and submitted the proposed constitutional amendments to the electorate for a statewide vote. Two months later, in September 1956, the voters of North Carolina approved, by a four-to-one margin, the constitutional amendments allowing tuition grants and local referenda on school closings.[43]

Although the Pearsall Plan seemed to mark a significant shift in the public policy of North Carolina on the segregation issue, in fact the plan did far less than did legislative schemes adopted in other southern states. Four states abolished constitutional requirements of public education.[44] Four states passed legislation to withhold aid from schools that desegregated.[45] Eight states enacted interposition resolutions urging either outright defiance of the Supreme Court's *Brown* decision or at least every possible action to avoid its reach.[46] Ten states passed legislation that severely inhibited the activities of the NAACP.[47] North Carolina was the only southern state to take none of those actions. Indeed, the North Carolina General Assembly enacted fewer statutes and promulgated fewer resolutions in response to *Brown* during the 1950s than did any other southern state legislature.

Moreover, on close inspection, the Pearsall Plan promised more than it actually delivered. The plan did not mandate school closings in the face of desegregation; it merely permitted a local referendum on the question at the school board's discretion. The distinction was an important one. On at least one occasion, when a citizens' group sought a school closing referendum over token integration, the local school board simply denied the request.[48] Indeed, no school was ever closed in North Carolina under the closing provision. By comparison, legislation enacted in other states, such as Virginia, *required* that schools close in the face of desegregation orders.[49] Dozens of schools were eventually closed throughout the South to avoid desegregation.[50]

Likewise, no student ever received a private school tuition grant in North Carolina, even though thousands of these grants were provided in other southern states.[51] When a student finally requested a private school tuition grant for the first time in North Carolina, the grant provision was deemed unconstitutional in a court challenge.[52] Significantly, the attorney arguing that the tuition grant provision was unconstitutional had been a member of the Pearsall Committee responsible for its adoption.

Accordingly, the Pearsall Plan did not reflect a major shift in the attitudes of the state's political leadership on the issue of school integration. Rather it reflected the increasing militancy of southern segregationists and the need to defuse the pressure to take more extreme action. In effect, the tuition grant and school closing components of the Pearsall Plan served a symbolic function: they placated segregationists but left the state's public schools essentially untouched. Hodges referred to them as "safety valves."[53] Pearsall himself later explained his perceptions of the committee's motivations: "What we were doing was buying time. The people had to have a psychological safety valve. They had to know that if things really got terrible, they could close the schools. . . . The plan gave desperate people something to hang onto while we proceeded, little by little, with integration."[54] Although Pearsall's comments were clearly self-serving, he was probably on target. Desegregation would inevitably come to North Carolina, but the Pearsall Plan gave the state's political leaders an opportunity to appease segregationist sentiment without undermining public education. This was moderation, North Carolina style.

To be sure, the southern mood on desegregation had noticeably stiffened by 1956.[55] Although there had been some resistance to *Brown* during the first year following the decision, many southern politicians, understanding that political capital could be gained from resistance, began to take more aggressive postures of defiance in early 1956. Beginning in February of that year, one southern state legislature after another promulgated nullification or interposition resolutions defying or at least challenging the Supreme Court's authority and enacted legislation aimed at thwarting efforts to integrate schools within their borders.[56] During the first three months of 1956, the legislatures of Alabama, Georgia, Mississippi, South Carolina, and Virginia—five of the most defiant states—enacted a total of forty-two prosegregation statutes.[57]

Moreover, in March 1956, 92 of the 106 southern members of Congress, including most of the North Carolina delegation, signed a "Southern Manifesto," drafted in part by North Carolina Senator Sam Ervin, which claimed that *Brown* was illegitimate and that they would do everything they could to reverse it.[58] The manifesto legitimated defiance. As one contemporary observer noted, "The true meaning of the Manifesto was to make defiance of the Supreme Court and the Constitution socially acceptable in the South—to give resistance to the law the approval of the Southern Establishment."[59]

At the same time, the White House remained aloof from school desegregation efforts, giving further encouragement to those urging resistance. President Dwight Eisenhower steadfastly and repeatedly refused to endorse the *Brown* decision.[60] Public opinion polls taken in the summer of 1955 indicated that the public perceived the president as encouraging the retention of racial segregation.[61] In February 1956, when questioned about the various interposition resolutions enacted in southern states challenging the Supreme Court's authority, Eisenhower weakly responded that the issue was "filled with argument on both sides." One month later, he declined comment on the "Southern Manifesto."[62]

As a result of the more aggressive activities of segregationists, pressure increased on southern politicians to take additional action against the threat of pupil mixing. In large measure, the Pearsall Committee's 1956 proposals were intended to mute the demands of North Carolina segregationists, such as assistant Attorney General Lake, who were ready to abandon the public school system altogether over the issue of segregation and who were building a political base around that issue. In July 1955, Lake delivered a widely publicized speech in which he called for an amendment to the state constitution that would abolish the requirement of public schools.[63] In August 1955, within weeks of Lake's speech promoting legislation to close schools, Hodges hinted, in a statewide address, that school closings might ultimately be required if his program of voluntary segregation failed: "If we are not able to succeed in a program of voluntary separate school attendance, the state within the next year or so will be face to face with deciding the issue of whether it shall have some form of integrated public schools or shall abandon its public schools."[64]

Hodges changed his posture on the school closing and tuition grant issues to deflect the attacks of segregationists such as Lake. At a conference of editorial writers in May 1956 he justified his shift: "If I hadn't come out for [the Pearsall Plan], a racist would have run against me [for governor] and torn our state apart with hatred."[65] Hodges thwarted that threat by simply embracing certain aspects of the segregationist agenda while positioning both himself and the Pearsall Plan as the "moderate" alternative. As Lake became more vocal during the summer of 1955 on the segregation question by attacking the NAACP, Hodges increased his own attacks on the NAACP as an "extremist" organization composed of outsiders who did not represent the views of most black North Carolinians. Moreover, Hodges supported Lake in the face of calls by the NAACP for Lake's removal.[66] In so doing, Hodges recognized that Lake was a potent political force who gave expression to the resentments of many white citizens. Pearsall later explained: "We didn't want Lake fired because he would become a martyr and a symbol. He could probably have gotten elected governor, and a segregationist would have destroyed everything."[67]

Hodges' fears concerning Lake's political popularity were not unfounded. Lake was well known throughout the state and by 1955 had emerged as the leading spokesman for the prosegregation position in the state. Although several of the state's newspapers attacked Lake as an extremist, particularly when he called for legislation permitting school closings, Lake enjoyed considerable popular support.[68] Ultimately, Lake decided not to enter the 1956 gubernatorial race, but Hodges did have to fend off a primary challenge during which he was attacked for his "very lukewarm stand" on the desegregation issue.[69] In those same 1956 primaries, in campaigns dominated by the "Manifesto issue," only one of the three North Carolina congressmen who had refused to sign the "Southern Manifesto" won renomination; the one survivor assured voters that, notwithstanding his failure to sign the manifesto, he favored the continuation of segregated schools.[70] Segregation was a potent political issue in North Carolina in 1956, as Hodges and the general assembly well understood.

As North Carolina's leaders debated the wisdom of the Pearsall Plan during the summer of 1956, participants on both sides of the debate sought to characterize their views as the "moderate" position. State Senator Terry Sanford, one of the more progressive politicians in the state and Hodges's successor as governor in 1960, championed the plan as advancing the cause of "moderation, unity, understanding, and good-will."[71] William Joyner, vice-chair of the Pearsall Committee and a prominent North Carolina lawyer, promoted the plan as "the moderate course."[72] The state's leading newspapers urged passage of the Pearsall Plan as a moderate response to the desegregation problem. The *Greensboro Daily News*, for example, editorialized: "North Carolina wants no violence and North Carolina wants no abandonment of its public school system. The path is tortuous and narrow. But with moderation, goodwill, understanding, and wise, sound and far-seeing statesmanship, we can and shall tread it safely."[73]

Politicians who opposed the Pearsall Plan on the grounds that it could undermine public education also claimed to represent the "moderate" position. Irving Carlyle, for example, one of the chief opponents of the plan, urged North Carolinians to follow the route of "moderation and not one of extremism" and defeat the plan.[74]

That the politicians of the day would claim to represent the "moderate" position speaks much about North Carolina and its self-perceptions during the 1950s. Throughout much of the South, those politicians who called unapologetically for defiant segregation were winning elections. Yet the rhythmic chants of segregationists such as Georgia Governor Ernest Vandiver—"not one, no, not one"[75]—were not spoken by most North Carolinians who captured high political office. North Carolina politicians made competing claims of taking a "moderate" position on racial issues.

Historian William Chafe has aptly described the "civility" of much of the North Carolina debate over school segregation, a debate in which appearances of moderation often proved more important than realities.[76] To be sure, most white North Carolinians were no different from their southern neighbors in their opposition to pupil mixing. Governor Hodges adamantly opposed pupil mixing, pleading with the state's African American population to accept voluntary segregation and castigating the NAACP for suggesting otherwise. Hodges's administrative assistant, Paul Johnston, assured constituents, "Governor Hodges will continue to do everything in his power to keep the races separated in all walks of life."[77] What distinguished Hodges and the majority of white politicians in North Carolina from their counterparts in many other southern states was a recognition that more was at stake than merely preserving racial segregation.

At an early date, much of the state's business and political leadership recognized that defiant resistance to school desegregation, including school closings, could potentially damage the state's economic future. As early as 1956, several prominent newspaper editors urged the state to adapt itself, for economic reasons, to school desegregation demands. Reed Sarratt, executive editor of the *Winston-Salem Journal and Sentinel*, noted that the state's failure to adapt to *Brown* would cause "untold damage . . . to our economy."[78] C. A. McKnight, editor of the *Charlotte Observer*, made a similar claim.[79] Likewise, North Carolina Attorney General Malcolm Seawell told a group of bankers that although he objected to the *Brown* decision, defiance was inappropriate because of the social and economic havoc it could cause the state.[80] The Charlotte-Mecklenburg Council on Human Relations circulated a speech delivered by the executive vice-president of the Baton Rouge Chamber of Commerce in 1956 in which he predicted the economic costs of resistance to *Brown*: "Boycotts, economic reprisals, the possibility of abandoning our public schools, incidents of violence, irresponsible statements—these are new factors which will now be given consideration by industry and business when they consider a Southern location."[81] The Southern Regional Council sounded a similar theme in 1956, calling on chambers of commerce throughout the South to urge "sensible" solutions to the desegregation problem as a matter of "long-range economic benefit to the region."[82]

By the late 1950s, business leaders throughout the South were well aware of the economic impact of defiant opposition to the *Brown* decision. The severe downturn in new business after the resistance to school desegregation in Little Rock, Arkansas, was widely publicized. Likewise, Virginia, which adopted a statewide policy of massive resistance, experienced a sharp decline in new business growth. During the first three years of the 1950s, Virginia added approximately thirty-one thousand manufacturing jobs per year; during the last three years of the 1950s, after implementation of the state's widely publicized program of massive resistance, Virginia added approximately five thousand new manufacturing jobs per year.[83] Martin Gainsburgh, chief economist for the National Industrial Conference Board, explained the economic impact of defiance: "[Businesses] eliminate from further consideration areas which have this school problem, because of the friction involved in them and the difficulty of getting top personnel to move to such places with their children."[84]

Governor Hodges, one of the region's most active gubernatorial business recruiters, was particularly sensitive to the impact of the region's racial problems on the recruitment of new business; at least one company in the mid-1950s declined to locate in North Carolina expressly because of the state's racial problems.[85] Both Hodges and his successor in the governor's mansion, Terry Sanford, aggressively used the state's reputation for racial moderation to recruit new industry.[86] Both men recognized that overt resistance to the *Brown* decision could cause economic damage to the state. North Carolina's moderation ultimately produced tangible economic benefits. Preston Holmes, a Richmond banker, contrasted North Carolina's "moderation" with Arkansas's defiance in a 1959 article: "North Carolina, with legal compliance with the Supreme Court decision and little social unrest, had new plant investment in 1958 totaling $253 million, while Arkansas, with its massive resistance and unsettled conditions, had only $25.4 million in 1958 compared with $44.9 million in 1957 and $131 million in 1956."[87]

Yet North Carolina's more moderate response to the *Brown* decision was motivated by more than a desire to avoid economic damage to the state. The state's political leaders also understood that legislative pronouncements and resolutions expressing defiance of *Brown* could lead to judicial intervention in the state's school system, resulting in even more widespread pupil mixing. Indeed, North Carolina's political leadership, while consenting to the school closing and tuition grant features of the Pearsall Plan, well understood that the plan must not operate as a device to maintain rigid segregation. Just as the state in the pre-*Brown* period had opened graduate programs for black students, improved the salaries of black teachers, and increased expenditures for black schools in order to avoid judicial intervention, many North Carolinians now understood the need to engage in token desegregation to avoid judicial meddling in pupil assignments.

In a widely publicized speech to the North Carolina State Bar in November 1956, two months after the enactment of the Pearsall Plan, William Joyner, the vice-chair of the Pearsall Committee and a distinguished Raleigh attorney, noted that several other southern states had vowed never to admit a black child to a white school. According to Joyner, those states would eventually face either the abandonment of public education or court-mandated integration; neither option was acceptable. According to Joyner, who described himself as a "man in the middle" on the desegregation issue:

> Some mixing in some of our schools is inevitable and must occur. I do not hesitate to advance my personal opinion and it is that the admission of less than 1 percent, for example, one-tenth of 1 percent, of Negro children to schools heretofore attended only by white children, . . .

is a small price to pay for the ability to keep the mixing within the bounds of reasonable control.

One of the nightmares which besets me on a restless night is that I am in a federal court attempting to defend a school board in its rejection of a transfer [to a white school] requested by a Negro student, when a showing is made in that court that nowhere in all of the state of North Carolina has a single Negro ever been admitted to any one of more than 2,000 schools attended by white students.[88]

Subsequently, Joyner told Kenneth Whitsett, the Mecklenburg County head of a segregationist organization called the Patriots of North Carolina, "[The] sacrifice of some children to mixed schools must be made so that many other children will not similarly be subjected to the evils of mixed schools."[89] Joyner's comments reflected the pragmatism of white political leadership in North Carolina in the 1950s.

Likewise, North Carolina was the only southern state to resist passing legislation inhibiting the activities of the NAACP. In May 1957, the North Carolina General Assembly, prompted by assistant Attorney General Lake, considered legislation to require the organization to disclose its membership lists and to prohibit the organization from paying litigation costs. Eventually every other southern state enacted legislation inhibiting the activities of the NAACP.[90] Governor Hodges, having been accused by his conservative critics of being unduly sympathetic to the NAACP, threw his weight behind the proposal, arguing that the organization was an outsider interfering with North Carolina's efforts to work out its school problems.[91]

The North Carolina chapter of the NAACP attempted to fend off the legislative efforts. State President Kelly Alexander, seeking to appeal to the anti-Communist feelings of most North Carolinians, told the North Carolina General Assembly that his organization had fought against the Communists' aim "to capitalize on the justifiable resentment Negroes feel against segregation and discrimination" and that the legislation threatened the state's "reputation for friendly race relations."[92] Ultimately, the North Carolina General Assembly defeated the proposed legislation. Although the legislation passed the state House, J. Spencer Bell, the newly elected Charlotte legislator and later a federal judge, successfully led the opposition to the legislation in the Senate.[93]

In significant measure, the general assembly rejected the proposed legislation because of fear of judicial intervention in the state's school desegregation efforts. Representative Frank Snepp of Charlotte, one of the primary opponents of the anti-NAACP legislation in the state House, argued that the legislation not only would cause "bitterness and disunity" and "would open the way for economic reprisals" against NAACP members but also might lead a federal court to scrutinize more closely the state's recently enacted pupil assignment plan.[94] Snepp claimed that the bill was "unconstitutional on its face"; he added: "All we are doing is putting the State to a court test. . . . We've been fortunate in this matter, but if the federal court knocks this down it will set a pattern, our school laws on the subject would be in danger."[95] Snepp had a keen sense of the broader picture. Taking retributive action against the NAACP could undermine the more important goal of fending off judicial interference with the pupil assignment process.

At the same time, others feared that the legislation could damage the state's reputation for racial moderation, causing untoward economic consequences. In Charlotte, from which came many of the bill's most avid opponents, the *Charlotte Observer* claimed that the legislation would harm "North Carolina's good name as a progressive, enlightened, fair state."[96] North Carolina's refusal to take retributive action against the NAACP can be attributed in part to a less harsh racial environment within the state. Nevertheless, the desire of the state's political leaders to avoid both judicially mandated pupil integration and damage to the state's economically beneficial moderate reputation on racial matters was a critical factor as well.

But why did Hodges and the North Carolina "moderates" ultimately prevail over Lake and those North Carolinians calling for a more defiant response to the *Brown* decision? Why did North Carolina not adopt the more extreme segregationist measures adopted in other states? The answers lie in large measure in two factors: the domination of North Carolina politics for much of the twentieth century by a business and financial elite committed to economic advancement and the avoidance of racial strife; and the relative lack of political influence of the majority-black, rural counties of eastern North Carolina.

Unlike many southern states, North Carolina, with a relatively small slave population, had no rural planter elite that dominated the state's politics during the antebellum or Reconstruction eras.[97] Instead, a financial and business elite emerged in the late nineteenth and early twentieth centuries; described by one observer as a "progressive plutocracy," it would dominate the state's politics for much of the twentieth century.[98] This business elite committed itself to the aggressive promotion of industrial growth; indeed, during the first half of the century, North Carolina enjoyed a substantially greater increase in its manufacturing activity than did any other southern state.[99] Moreover, North Carolina's business and political elite had long understood the relationship between economic prosperity and positive race relations.

For example, throughout the first half of the twentieth century, North Carolina's political leaders, although unwavering proponents of racial separation, supported black education for reasons of paternalism and the potential economic benefits to the state. In 1902, when Governor Charles Aycock and his allies helped defeat a proposed state constitutional amendment that would have allowed the division of school monies based on the respective contributions of the two races, they argued in part that underfinancing the black schools might have negative economic consequences by encouraging black emigration from the state.[100] Similarly, for most of the first half of the century, North Carolina maintained a smaller gap in per pupil expenditures for black and white children than did any other southern state and was the first southern state to provide graduate education programs for black students. Moreover, repression of the African American vote was less severe in North Carolina than in other southern states; for much of the civil rights era, a higher percentage of blacks were registered to vote in North Carolina than in nearly every other southern state.[101]

This racial paternalism may have been influenced by the fact that lawyers have traditionally played a dominant role in North Carolina's politics. For the first half of the twentieth century, every governor of North Carolina was a lawyer, as were large numbers of the state's leading legislators.[102] In such a context, arguments that antiblack measures could lead to judicial intervention carried considerable weight. As a result, North Carolina responded more quickly than did most other southern states to changing legal expectations pertaining to the financing of black education during the late 1930s and early 1940s and pupil mixing in the 1950s.

Yet North Carolina's racial "moderation" was also influenced by the fact that the majority-black counties in eastern North Carolina did not exert the same degree of political influence as did similar "black-belt" areas in other southern states. Political scientists have recognized a positive correlation in southern voting patterns between areas of high black population and support for segregationist measures.[103] But in North Carolina, political power for most of the twentieth century has been linked to the business and financial interests of the state's central Piedmont section, as opposed to the rural farming areas of the state's eastern counties.[104] This distribution of political power in North Carolina sharply contrasts with that in the more defiant southern states of the Deep South or Virginia, where political power was far more likely to be linked to counties with high black populations. Indeed, North Carolina had a smaller black population than did most of the defiant states of the South and substantially fewer majority-black counties. In 1950, for example, less than 10 percent of the state's counties were majority black; each of the six most defiant southern states had a significantly higher percentage of majority-black counties than did North Carolina.[105]

Significantly, the only election in the post-*Brown* South in which a moderate segregationist defeated a militant segregationist in a head-to-head primary election occurred when Terry Sanford defeated Beverly Lake in the 1960 Democratic runoff primary for governor of North Carolina. Lake enjoyed strong support in the state's black-belt counties, but Sanford's strong support in the Piedmont and the western section of the state allowed him to capture his party's nomination. Sanford made it clear that he opposed "mixing the races in the schools" but that he also understood the necessity of token integration in the service of larger interests: "Nobody likes the Supreme Court decision and nobody intends to let the NAACP dominate North Carolina, but it is not going to serve any constructive purpose to keep saying this over and over. The more we stir it up, the harder it is going to be to keep the Supreme Court out of North Carolina's affairs. [Lake's] approach is leading us to closed schools or mixed schools, and we have got to stop his approach."[106] In a state where the preservation of racial separation at all costs was no longer the highest goal, Sanford captured well over half of the votes cast.[107]

Yet North Carolina's "moderate" response to *Brown* did not mean that African American children were welcome in the state's white schools. Indeed, ten years after the *Brown* decision, less than 1 percent of the schoolchildren in the state attended school with a child of another race. Other southern states that engaged in more strident resistance actually had more integrated schools in 1964 than did North Carolina. How did North Carolina's course of "moderation" result in the retention of segregated schools?

In effect, North Carolina "succeeded" in retaining segregated schools because it understood that voluntary token desegregation and avoidance of statements of defiance would allow the state to continue with segregated schools without judicial interference. Following the enactment of the 1955 pupil assignment statute that vested local school boards with the discretion to make pupil assignments on a nonracial basis, every North Carolina school board ostensibly abandoned the long-standing practice of race-based school assignments. Yet in reality, most of the state's school boards would continue to assign children to schools on the basis of their race until the mid-1960s. African American children who lived within walking distance of a white school—including many in Mecklenburg County—were frequently assigned to a distant and inferior black school.[108] In a few instances, when a school system provided schools only for white children, African American children were required to travel by bus to schools in neighboring counties.[109] From the perspective of the black community, "busing" was not an invention of the late 1960s; throughout North Carolina, busing was used extensively until the mid-1960s to maintain racially defined public schools.

The pupil assignment statute did give African American children the right to request a transfer to a white school, and many students initially assigned to a black school sought such transfers. Not one of the fifty black students who requested a transfer to a white school during the first two school years under the new placement statute, however, was successful.[110] Even counties that offered no black education denied transfer requests.[111] By the summer of 1957, no school board in North Carolina had ever assigned a black child to a white school and no school board had ever granted a black child's transfer request to attend a white school.

In time, however, many North Carolinians argued that continued refusal to admit African American students to white schools could leave the state's school systems exposed to judicial challenge. Accordingly, some of the state's political leaders, including Joyner, the Pearsall Committee vice-chair, urged several of the state's local school boards to admit a few African American students into white schools to demonstrate to the courts that North Carolina's pupil assignment system was not designed to preserve segregated schools. Ultimately, three North Carolina school boards—Charlotte, Greensboro, and Winston-Salem—became among the first in the South to desegregate their schools when they simultaneously announced in July 1957 that they had granted the transfer requests of twelve black students to white schools.[112] That this early desegregation would come in these three cities was not surprising. Each was a Piedmont city, removed from the large African American population of eastern North Carolina; each constituted one of the state's largest urban areas; and each had a thriving local economy. All of these conditions contributed to an environment in which modest racial change was most likely.[113]

In agreeing to voluntary desegregation in the summer of 1957, these three school boards operated with the understanding that their action would fend off broader, court-imposed desegregation orders.[114] The Charlotte School Board announced that in granting the transfers, it had acted to "preserve the public schools of Charlotte."[115] Several of the state's newspapers argued that the token integration would forestall widespread pupil mixing. The *Raleigh Times*, for example, suggested that the three school boards' action would allow other school systems to keep their schools segregated: "[This action] will make it possible for schools in areas where integration is surely not possible or even feasible to continue completely separate schools. This action has been taken for the benefit of the whole school system of the State, not just for the benefit of the 12 Negro children involved."[116]

Many of the state's political leaders also claimed that the decision of the three boards would fend off broader, court-imposed desegregation. State Representative Edward Yarborough of Franklin County, chair of the state House Education Committee and a member of the Pearsall Committee, commended the three school boards for their decision: "I think it certainly strengthens our hands in the courts because it shows we have non-discriminatory laws, administered by local boards."[117]

When schools opened in the fall of 1957, North Carolina was one of only four southern states, along with Arkansas, Texas, and Tennessee, to operate integrated schools.[118] Yet the voluntary desegregation of these three school systems did not bring broader desegregation to North Carolina. During the same summer that the three urban school boards granted the twelve transfer requests, the requests of almost two hundred other African American students throughout the state, even those living in counties with no black schools, were denied.[119] Moreover, even in the three desegregated school systems, the number of African American students attending integrated schools did not increase during the next few years. By the spring of 1959, in fact, fewer African Americans were attending integrated schools in North Carolina than in September 1957.[120]

Finally, during the 1959–60 school year, four school systems outside of the original three cities permitted black students to transfer to white schools for the first time. Two of these school systems — Wayne County and Craven County — were the sites of major military installations, and the desegregation in those counties took place at schools attended primarily by the children of military personnel, many of whom were non-southerners. More black students in those two school systems attended integrated schools during the 1959–60 school year than in all of the other school systems in the state combined.[121]

By 1960, no school board in North Carolina had ever initially assigned a black student to a white school, and most of the hundreds of transfer requests filed by black students had been denied.[122] At the same time, no court had ever found a North Carolina school system to be unconstitutionally segregated, even though the NAACP initiated more school desegregation litigation in North Carolina during the 1950s than in any other state and even though a few courts had found unlawful school segregation in other southern states.[123] The obvious fact that every North Carolina school board was continuing to maintain a dual assignment system by initially assigning children only to schools of their own race went uncorrected by the courts until the early 1960s.[124] Token integration, unaccompanied by defiant rhetoric, enabled the state to escape judicial intervention in a manner that other, more defiant southern states could not. North Carolina's policy of moderation stood vindicated.

But if the *Brown* decision declared segregated education unconstitutional, why did the lower courts in North Carolina, charged with carrying out the *Brown* mandate, refuse to require school boards to cease race-based pupil assignments and grant the transfer requests of black students? The reasons are several: the failure of the Supreme Court to insist on meaningful desegregation, the dearth of plaintiffs ready to challenge segregation practices, and the willingness of the lower courts to conclude that token integration and the absence of statements of defiance indicated that the state was operating its schools in a nondiscriminatory manner.

First, the Supreme Court failed to give lower-court judges detailed guidance in enforcing the *Brown* mandate. Although the second *Brown* decision in 1955 concerned itself in large measure with the issue of enforcement, the decision offered little in terms of specific direction. In a statement that offered great comfort to southerners intent on resisting compliance, the Court noted: "Full implementation of these constitutional principles may require solution of varied local school problems. School authorities have the primary responsibility for elucidating, assessing, and solving these problems."[125] Significantly, the Court did not impose any timetable on desegregation efforts, rejecting the Justice Department's proposed ninety-day timetable for the submission of desegregation plans.[126] The Court instead merely indicated that school boards should make a "good faith" start toward desegregation and should proceed "with all deliberate speed." Not surprisingly, the second *Brown* decision was greeted with relief throughout the South.[127]

Furthermore, following the second *Brown* decision, the Supreme Court largely abandoned the school desegregation field for the next several years, seriously undermining compliance efforts. Between 1955 and 1960, although the Court was active in striking down state-supported segregation in a broad range of public facilities, it issued only one full opinion in a public school desegregation case—in the crisis situation of Little Rock—and a few other per curiam decisions and affirmances.[128] For the most part, the Court's decisions came in extraordinary cases where the very authority of the federal courts was challenged and Supreme Court intervention demanded. Otherwise, the Court remained silent on a large number of issues concerning school desegregation, such as the need for plaintiffs to exhaust administrative remedies before seeking judicial relief and the validity of one-grade-per-year desegregation plans, notwithstanding widely divergent decisions in the lower courts on these and other issues.[129] In cases in which the Court did speak, it reaffirmed the general principles of *Brown* but declined to offer specific guidance to lower courts on how to enforce its mandate. Calls for the Supreme Court to offer more guidance to lower courts went unheeded.[130]

The Supreme Court had initiated a "second reconstruction" with the *Brown* decision but had left it to southern federal judges to supervise the accompanying social revolution, with little guidance or support. The failure of the Court to at least reconcile conflicting lower-court opinions, if not offer further guidance as to what *Brown* required, made the job of the federal district court judge charged with the responsibility of overseeing desegregation decrees all the more difficult.[131] As a consequence, in the face of considerable local pressure from segregationists, many state and federal judges simply refused to order school boards to desegregate their schools.

The second reason for the dearth of successful school desegregation lawsuits in North Carolina during the first decade after *Brown* was the difficulty in bringing such litigation. Many African Americans did not want to send their children to white schools because of fears of mistreatment and hence had no interest in litigation seeking to force the admission of their children. Moreover, several of the African Americans who did sign petitions asking for desegregation or who did file lawsuits in the early years after *Brown* were subjected to harassment or retaliation, which further dampened enthusiasm for litigation.[132] The difficult transfer procedures that black students challenging their pupil assignments were required to follow, coupled with the substantial expense and expertise required to support litigation, made it virtually impossible to mount a successful legal challenge to a pupil assignment without some type of organizational support. Moreover, until the 1964 Civil Rights Act authorized the Justice Department to file school desegregation suits, the NAACP was the only organization committed to challenging school segregation through litigation. Even though the North Carolina General Assembly ultimately declined to enact anti-NAACP legislation, the attacks on the organization and its members in North Carolina restricted its effectiveness and undermined the willingness of black plaintiffs to step forward and pursue legal remedies.

The final reason North Carolina's "moderate" response to the *Brown* decision survived judicial challenge until the 1960s was the ability of local school boards to utilize both the complicated transfer process and the few instances of token integration to deflect claims that the state maintained a dual school system. The North Carolina courts early established that black plaintiffs seeking assignments to white schools would be entitled to no judicial relief unless they went through the detailed transfer and administrative appeal process established by the state pupil assignment statute.[133] This exhaustion requirement proved to be a major hurdle; nearly every judicial challenge to school segregation considered by a North Carolina state or federal court during the 1950s was ultimately dismissed on the grounds that the plaintiff had failed in some manner to exhaust administrative remedies. At the same time, the fact that such transfers were possible and that a few African Americans did actually receive transfers enabled the courts to conclude that the North Carolina assignment plan passed constitutional muster, despite the fact that every schoolchild in North Carolina was still assigned to school on the basis of race. Significantly, shortly after the three North Carolina school systems opened in the fall of 1957 with limited desegregation, a three-judge court in Alabama upheld the Alabama pupil placement statute, noting that North Carolina's placement statute, on which Alabama's had been modeled, had resulted in the admission of black students to white schools.[134] The U.S. Supreme Court affirmed the three-judge court's decision.[135]

By 1960, no North Carolina federal or state court had ever ruled in favor of a black plaintiff in a school desegregation case.[136] By the same token, courts during the 1950s struck down pupil assignment practices in other southern states that had excluded *all* black children from white schools as part of a well-orchestrated strategy of massive resistance and ordered black students admitted into white schools.[137] On the tenth anniversary of *Brown*, less than 1 percent of the African American students in North Carolina attended school with white children. Eleven of the sixteen southern and border states had a higher percentage of black students in white schools than did North Carolina, including Virginia and Louisiana with their policies of massive resistance.[138] Token integration and the avoidance of extremist rhetoric enabled North Carolina to mask its own, more subtle, form of resistance and to escape judicial intervention in a manner that its more defiant southern neighbors could not. In a region historically beset with profound ironies when it came to matters of race, this result could not have been surprising.

[In admitting a few black students to white schools,] the Charlotte City School Board has acted to preserve the schools. It has acted to prevent massive, court-decreed integration.

—*Charlotte News*, July 1957

CHAPTER 3

A Moderate Southern City Responds to *Brown*

The Token Integration of the Charlotte Schools

As North Carolina nurtured an image of racial moderation, so did Charlotte. Although by the time of the *Brown* decision in 1954, Charlotte was one of the most racially segregated cities in the United States, during the late 1950s the city captured national acclaim for the token integration of a few of its schools. This early desegregation resulted from a mixture of motives: a moral disquiet with some of the harsher aspects of segregation and an understanding that voluntary, controlled integration could help the city retain a healthy business climate while avoiding unwanted judicial intrusion. Charlotte's business and political leaders understood, as leaders in many other southern cities did not, that token integration would well serve a range of civic interests.

Since the nineteenth century, Charlotte has thrived as one of the major economic centers of North Carolina and, more recently, the South. Charlotte's growth in the early nineteenth century was due in large measure to its close proximity to the leading gold-mining area in the United States.[1] Although the importance of gold mining to the region's economy declined with the discovery of gold in California in the mid-nineteenth century, the linkage of Charlotte with the region's growing network of railroads during the 1850s and 1860s facilitated Charlotte's eventual development as an important distribution center.[2] By 1880, Charlotte was the third-largest town in North Carolina, behind Wilmington and Raleigh; by the early twentieth century, Charlotte had become the largest town in the state, although with a population of only 20,000 people.[3]

In the latter years of the nineteenth century, the opening of a large number of cotton mills transformed Charlotte into one of the region's leading textile centers. By 1903, half of the looms and spindles in the South were located within a hundred miles of the city.[4] The growth of banking and the distribution of manufactured goods in the early twentieth century helped solidify Charlotte's status as the leading commercial center in the state.[5] The favorable placement of roads and highways in the 1920s and 1930s facilitated the rapid growth of Charlotte's trucking industry; in time the city would become one of the leading trucking centers in the United States.[6] In the 1980s and 1990s, Charlotte emerged as one of the country's leading banking centers; due in significant measure to the rapidly expanding NationsBank, Charlotte became the third-largest banking center in the United States. At the end of the twentieth century, the city rivaled Atlanta as both the retail and the trade center of the southeastern United States and as the nation's leader in new job growth.[7] This consistent economic prosperity was accompanied by extraordinary population growth. Since 1900 the population of the city has more than doubled every twenty years, with a current population of over 400,000.[8]

Much of Charlotte's prosperity during the twentieth century flowed from the city's unflagging commitment to the recruitment of new business and industry. Charlotte's leaders have long understood the value of new business development and hence, under the leadership of the chamber of commerce, consistently engaged in vigorous promotion and protection of the city's image as a good place to do business. This spirit of boosterism continues to the present. When college basketball brought its "Final Four" tournament to the city in April 1994, *Creative Loafing*, a weekly newspaper, greeted the city's guests with the headline: "Welcome to Charlotte! Final Four Fans, We'll Do Anything to Please You." The *Charlotte Observer* was more direct, pleading with the throng of visitors: "Please Try to Like Us a Lot. Please."[9]

When the Supreme Court decided the *Brown* case in 1954, Charlotte was a city of two very different worlds: one black and one white. The city's rapid growth and development during the half century before *Brown* had proceeded along well-defined racial lines, producing one of the most residentially segregated cities in the United States.[10] During the nineteenth century, Charlotte, along with many other southern towns, had displayed a high degree of residential integration. As families clustered around the intersection of Trade and Tryon streets, wealthy white homeowners were likely to live on the same block with modest African American laborers. To be sure, by the turn of the century, certain blocks within the city were occupied exclusively by people of one race, but very few neighborhoods had attained a racial identity.[11] At the same time, racial separation emerged during the nineteenth century as a fact of social life in Charlotte. Certain bars and restaurants served only white patrons, and other establishments, such as the Opera House, established separate seating by race.[12]

Residential patterns in Charlotte began to change during the early twentieth century with the beginnings of suburban development. In the early 1890s, developers of Charlotte's first suburb, Dilworth, sought to attract both white and black residents.[13] The racial furor of the late 1890s, however, which resulted in disfranchisement of black voters and more aggressive efforts to segregate various aspects of public life, precipitated a steady trend toward residential segregation. In the wake of disfranchisement, many African Americans left Charlotte to seek a more hospitable environment in the North.[14] Those who remained behind soon learned that racial separation would underlie the city's future development.

New residential development in Charlotte during the first few decades of the twentieth century generally followed racial lines. To be sure, unlike several other North Carolina cities, Charlotte never adopted municipal ordinances that mandated residential segregation.[15] Nevertheless, in the early years of this century, residential developers ensured the racial homogeneity of new white neighborhoods through the use of restrictive covenants that prohibited the sale of property to African Americans. Between 1900 and 1930, for example, developers created three new neighborhoods east and southeast of the downtown area — Elizabeth, Myers Park, and Eastover — that specifically excluded black as well as lower-income white families through racial and house-cost restrictive covenants, creating a haven for upper-class whites.[16] North Carolina courts enforced these racially restrictive covenants, as did courts throughout the country until the Supreme Court's 1948 decision in *Shelley v. Kraemer* declared them unconstitutional.[17]

Other suburban neighborhoods that developed in the early years of the twentieth century also assumed identities based on race and class even in the absence of racially restrictive covenants. For example, Wesley Heights, located west of the center of town, attracted middle-class whites; Villa Heights, Belmont, and Optimist Park, north and northeast of the center of town, attracted white mill workers; and Biddleville and Washington Heights, also west of the center of town near Biddle Institute, attracted black middle-class homeowners. Biddle, a black college founded in the aftermath of the Civil War by the northern Presbyterian Church and renamed Johnson C. Smith University in 1923, would prove to be a strong draw for new black development in the area west of the center of town. Yet the most substantial African American neighborhood in the early twentieth century was Second Ward, or Brooklyn, located immediately southeast of the town square. By 1920, Second Ward had developed its own commercial center complete with a large number of black-owned businesses.[18]

Even though Charlotte's new neighborhoods developed along race and class lines during the first three decades of the twentieth century, no section of the city attained a rigid racial or class identity; indeed, both black and white neighborhoods of all social classes were located throughout the city in a checkerboard fashion. But by the beginning of the second decade of the 1900s, some white Charlotteans foresaw the eventual distribution of the city's residents in a much more rigid fashion, with African Americans in the northwest section of the city near Biddle Institute and whites scattered throughout the rest of the city. The *Charlotte Observer* provided an ominous prediction along these lines in 1912: "The opinion is quite generally held among white citizens of Charlotte that the solution of the question of housing the colored population for the best interests of all concerned is afforded by sites west of the city, where their educational center [Biddle] is already established. The Second Ward is already populated by [African Americans], many owning comfortable homes, but farsighted men believe that eventually this section, because of its proximity to the center of the city, must sooner or later be utilized by the white population."[19] The predictions of those "farsighted men" would ultimately come to pass: urban renewal efforts of the 1960s included the razing of Second Ward and the relocation of its black residents.

This movement toward residential segregation received significant encouragement from various government and private influences during the 1930s and 1940s. In the wake of the collapse of the private housing market during the Great Depression, the federal government established several housing programs to encourage homeownership. The National Housing Act of 1934 created the Federal Housing Administration (FHA), which in turn insured private mortgages on residential property that met the agency's standards. The FHA, by lowering the cost of home mortgages, made homeownership possible for millions of middle-income Americans. Yet the FHA, to reduce its risks, imposed strict requirements on the types of home mortgages that it would insure. The *FHA Under-writing Manual* stipulated that the FHA would insure loans only on property in neighborhoods protected by racially restrictive covenants and deed restrictions that prevented the construction of new homes of widely differing value.[20] The FHA justified these requirements on the grounds that racially and economically homogeneous neighborhoods were more stable and more likely to hold their value than were mixed neighborhoods. As a result, the FHA would generally insure only homes for black families in black neighborhoods and homes for white families in white neighborhoods covered by covenants not to sell or rent to African Americans. The Veterans Administration (VA) followed suit when it began extending VA loans in 1944.[21] Although these racial requirements were eliminated in 1947, real estate developers endeavored thereafter to preserve the racial and economic homogeneity of new neighborhoods.[22]

A significant portion of the new housing built in Charlotte beginning in the 1930s enjoyed FHA support. Local developers, responding to a booming population and the availability of FHA insurance, built large numbers of new homes that they explicitly advertised for sale on a racial basis, describing, for example, new housing in the northwest sector for "the colored citizens of Charlotte."[23] Newspaper real estate advertisements in Charlotte would continue to advertise housing by race until the 1960s.[24] The FHA mortgage insurance program helped initiate a migration of black families to the northwest section of the city; during the 1940s, over four thousand black residents, armed with FHA insurance, left center-city neighborhoods to live in new homes in the northwest.[25]

At the same time, the FHA policy manual explicitly encouraged the retention of racially segregated schools as a means of preserving stable neighborhoods.[26] The Charlotte School Board responded, locating West Charlotte High School in 1938 at the edge of a black neighborhood on Beatties Ford Road in northwest Charlotte. With the only other black high school located in Second Ward in the center city, the placement of West Charlotte High School encouraged further development of new black neighborhoods in the northwest.[27] The Charlotte-Mecklenburg School Board would continue to build new schools in racially homogeneous neighborhoods until at least the mid-1960s.[28]

The placement of federally assisted public housing in Charlotte further enhanced segregated residential patterns. The Wagner-Steagall Act of 1937 made federal money available to localities for the construction of municipally owned, low-income housing. City leaders were sharply divided over the wisdom of accepting federal dollars to build public housing that would compete with privately owned housing. Ultimately, aided in part by a series of articles published by the *Charlotte News* on the appalling condition of slum housing in Charlotte, the city decided to seek federal dollars to build low-cost public housing.[29] In 1940 and 1941, the city built its first two federally aided low-income housing projects.[30] Fairview Homes, located in a black neighborhood near Beatties Ford Road, would house only African Americans until the 1970s; Piedmont Courts, placed in a white residential area northeast of the downtown area, would house only white tenants until the late 1960s.[31] Likewise, in the early 1950s, the city built two more public housing projects, one for black tenants in a black neighborhood—Southside Homes—and one in a white neighborhood for white tenants—Belvedere Homes.[32]

Finally, in 1947, the Charlotte Planning Commission developed the city's first comprehensive zoning plan. Whereas white neighborhoods were zoned for residential use only, black center-city neighborhoods, such as Second Ward, were zoned "industrial," which harmed residential resale and further encouraged black migration to the northwest section of the city.[33]

As a result of these various actions, by the time of the *Brown* decision Charlotte was one of the most residentially segregated cities in the United States. Indeed, only thirteen of the one hundred largest cities in the country had more residential segregation than did Charlotte.[34] Moreover, by 1954, the various quadrants of the city had attained a certain racial and class identity: African Americans lived primarily in the northwest section of the city, lower-middle-class whites primarily in the northeast and southwest sections of the city, and upper-middle-class whites primarily in the southeast section of the city. At the same time, the white residents of southeast Charlotte had emerged as the dominant force in the city's economic and political life.

Yet the city's black and white communities were separated by more than mere geography. Blacks and whites lived in disparate worlds in terms of income, employment, education, and quality of housing. In 1950, over 90 percent of the employed black men in the city engaged in manual labor; only about 7 percent held some type of white-collar job. On the other hand, about half of the city's white men held a white-collar job. Likewise over half of the city's working black women held low-paying jobs as domestics in white homes; only about 10 percent of the working white women were so engaged. These differences were reflected in the incomes that black and white workers earned; in 1950, the median income of white workers in Charlotte was more than twice that of African Americans, a disparity greater than in every other North Carolina city except Raleigh and greater than in most other upper South cities.[35]

This dramatic disparity in employment and income was due to a range of factors, one of which was the remarkably different educational backgrounds of the two groups. Whereas the average white adult in Charlotte in 1950 had completed 12.2 grades of school, the average African American adult had completed only 6.6 grades of school.[36] In significant measure, that difference resulted from the fact that a high school education was not widely available for black students in North Carolina until the 1940s. Indeed, in 1933, only 7 percent of the eligible African American children in the state attended high school.[37] Moreover, the quality of education available to black and white children varied dramatically, since expenditures for white education far exceeded those for black education until the early 1950s; the average value of white schools far outpaced that of black schools until well into the 1960s.[38]

Those educational inequalities persisted in Charlotte as well as in other parts of the state. When a Howard University professor in 1948 conducted a detailed study of the Charlotte schools, he concluded that there were substantial inequalities between black and white schools, particularly at the junior and senior school level.[39] Inequalities were even greater in the rural Mecklenburg County school system. One schoolteacher later recalled that many of the black county schools in the 1940s had "no running water, . . . no teacher's manual, no construction paper, . . . no library."[40]

In addition, African American houses were generally inferior to white houses. White families were much more likely than black families to own their own home. In a city in which about 28 percent of the residents were black, about 90 percent of the owner-occupied houses were inhabited by white families. Moreover, white-owned houses were worth about 50 percent more than black-owned houses and were far more likely to be newly constructed.[41] Many black homes lacked proper toilet facilities.[42]

In addition to this extensive residential and economic separation, the city also enforced state laws and local ordinances that mandated racially separate schools, playgrounds, parks, swimming pools, and cemeteries.[43] Furthermore, no African American played any role in the governance of the city. From the 1890s until the mid-1960s, no African American held any type of important governmental position in Charlotte, whether by election or appointment, notwithstanding the fact that black candidates

Billingsville School, Grier Heights neighborhood, Charlotte, 1951.
(Courtesy of the *Charlotte Observer*)

had begun to win local elections in other North Carolina towns and cities by the late 1940s.[44]

To be sure, since the late nineteenth century, Charlotte had been home to a small middle-class black community.[45] The political influence of this community declined substantially, however, following disfranchisement in the early twentieth century.[46] Nevertheless, many members of Charlotte's black middle class, particularly those affiliated with Johnson C. Smith University, would provide critical support for desegregation initiatives during the 1950s and 1960s. Black teachers and administrators, although opposed to desegregation initiatives in many parts of North Carolina because of legitimate fears of job loss, generally supported school integration efforts in Charlotte.[47]

By the time the Supreme Court issued its *Brown* decision in 1954, racial segregation in Charlotte was significantly more pronounced than it had been in 1900.[48] In this divided city of the 1950s, the most common point of contact between the two races was the domestic service that black women provided in white homes. Julius Chambers, the city's most prominent African American attorney during the 1960s and 1970s, would later comment that Charlotte could teach Rhodesia "something about apartheid."[49]

Token Integration of the Charlotte Schools

The *Brown* decision constituted a challenge of unknown proportions to these patterns of racial separation. Although much of the South reacted to *Brown* with cries of defiance, white Charlotte reacted to the decision in a muted fashion. None of the city's political, civic, and religious leaders counseled defiance of the Court, and a few even endorsed the decision.[50] Moreover, during the first few years following the decision, many of Charlotte's civic leaders helped facilitate the desegregation of certain aspects of the city's life.

In September 1955, a few months after the Supreme Court issued its second *Brown* decision, forty-five prominent white and black citizens under the leadership of a white physician, Raymond Wheeler, organized the Charlotte-Mecklenburg Council on Human Relations to improve racial relations in the city.[51] To some extent, the council was the successor to the pre-*Brown* Commission on Interracial Cooperation, which had been active in Charlotte for three decades before the 1954 decision.[52] The new council, consisting of business and professional leaders, helped move the city toward early desegregation in a number of areas. Exercising quiet persuasion, the council convinced managers of the largest department stores in the city that they should open their restrooms to black customers and persuaded the board of directors of the Charlotte library to operate on a fully desegregated basis.[53] The actions of the Council on Human Relations were illustrative of much of the desegregation activity that the city would undertake over the next decade: behind-the-scenes persuasion that quietly moved the city toward increased desegregation.

In 1954, the Mecklenburg County Medical Society became the first such society in the state and one of the first in the South to desegregate its professional membership, a decision that ultimately forced the state chapter to do likewise.[54] Shortly thereafter, the city became one of the first southern cities to desegregate its bus service, in sharp contrast to the stormy bus boycott in Montgomery.[55] A few years later, in 1960, Charlotte received national attention by becoming the first city in the state and one of the first in the South to integrate a public swimming pool; other North Carolina cities had closed public swimming pools rather than allow them to operate on a desegregated basis.[56]

Several factors influenced the city's early desegregation efforts. First of all, the widely read *Charlotte Observer* played an important role in creating a climate favorable to desegregation initiatives. Following the Supreme Court's 1954 *Brown* ruling, the *Observer*, unlike many other southern newspapers, did not attack the decision but instead commented that it required "a reappraisal of educational policies at the public school level."[57] The *Observer*'s moderate stance on *Brown* ultimately cost it several thousand subscribers, particularly in South Carolina as subscription agents from the *Charleston News and Courier* contrasted the *Observer*'s stand on *Brown* with that of the more defiant *News and Courier*.[58] Likewise, following the second *Brown* ruling in 1955, the *Observer* urged local schools "to make a 'prompt and reasonable start' toward opening their classroom doors to all eligible pupils, regardless of race," noting, "We see no reasonable alternative to compliance."[59]

To be sure, the *Observer* had had a mixed record of editorial support for racially progressive issues throughout its history, having been a forceful proponent of white supremacy during the late nineteenth and early twentieth centuries.[60] The *Observer* had championed the constitutional amendment of 1900 that disfranchised black voters, heralding its passage as "one of the greatest days that ever dawned upon North Carolina."[61] Moreover, at the same time that the paper's editorial pages promoted integration efforts, many of the paper's employees privately opposed such efforts. When the *Observer* hired its first black reporter in 1966, the paper's composing room employees placed a packet of Ku Klux Klan pamphlets on his chair with a note reading "For Your Nigger-Loving Friends."[62] Nevertheless, during the post-*Brown* era, the paper would publish some of the most racially liberal editorials in the South, particularly after C. A. "Pete" McKnight became editor in early 1955.[63]

McKnight had long been concerned with the injustice of racial segregation and its negative effect on the economic development of the South. In 1950, while editor of the city's afternoon paper, the *Charlotte News*, McKnight wrote, "Segregation, as an abstract moral principle, cannot be defended by any intellectually or spiritually honest person."[64] It was a bold claim. The *News*, one of the South's most liberal newspapers during the 1930s and 1940s on race issues, had frequently complained about racial violence, inadequate public facilities for African Americans, and the absence of black representation on juries or city commissions; segregation, however, had been off-limits as a target of editorial criticism.[65] Yet by 1950, McKnight was questioning the central fact of southern social life.

Thereafter, McKnight helped organize and became the first editor of the *Southern School News*, a publication established to provide coverage of southern school desegregation efforts in the wake of *Brown*. Under McKnight's leadership, throughout the various race-related crises that confronted the city over the course of the next two decades, the *Observer* usually favored desegregation efforts, serving as an important voice in a city confronted with the demands of racial change.[66]

Moreover, on several occasions McKnight crossed the line between journalist and civic leader by becoming an active participant in the desegregation process. The local school board frequently consulted with McKnight about the wisdom of certain contemplated board actions. In 1963, McKnight drafted a chamber of commerce resolution that resulted in the desegregation of the city's public accommodations. As a member of the Mayor's Community Relations Committee in the 1960s charged with improving the city's race relations, McKnight declined to report on the committee's activities except to publish its press releases.[67]

Indeed, one of the striking aspects of desegregation in Charlotte during the 1950s and 1960s was the active role played by the city's journalists. Rather than simply report on desegregation initiatives, many of the city's leading journalists helped shape those initiatives through their personal involvement. Representatives of both the *Charlotte Observer* and the *Charlotte News* encouraged desegregation as members of the Mayor's Community Relations Committee until the 1970s. Moreover, on several occasions members of the city's print and broadcast media met informally with civic and political leaders to decide how to cover a particularly delicate racial issue and to discuss what course of action the city should take.[68]

The city's early desegregation efforts were also aided by the growing awareness that defiance of the *Brown* decision could have a negative impact on the city's economic climate. McKnight was one of the first southerners to understand the negative economic effect of resistance to *Brown*. At a March 1956 symposium on North Carolina public affairs, McKnight argued that deteriorating race relations in the wake of resistance to school desegregation could potentially damage the state's economic future.[69] The Charlotte-Mecklenburg Council on Human Relations repeatedly emphasized that smooth adjustment to the *Brown* decision would benefit the city's economic prospects.[70] The Southern Regional Council supported the Council on Human Relations by calling on local chambers of commerce to find "'sensible' solutions to [school] integration petitions as a matter of long-range economic benefit to the region."[71] In time, many of the city's business leaders would come to agree, a factor that had a profound impact on the city's evolving race relations.

Litigation helped push the city in some of these desegregation efforts. On December 16, 1951, a group of black men arrived to play golf at the city's municipal golf course in Revolution Park in southwest Charlotte. The city had always restricted use of the park to whites, since the original gift of the land to the city provided that if African Americans were granted access, the land must revert back to the donor's estate. On being denied the opportunity to play, the men petitioned the Parks and Recreation Commission to operate the park on a nondiscriminatory basis. The commission denied their request but filed suit to gain a judicial opinion as to whether the park could be used on an integrated basis consistent with the terms of the deed granting the land to the city.[72] The North Carolina Supreme Court upheld a ruling of the state trial court finding the reverter clause in the deed to be valid: if the city allowed African Americans to use the park, then the land would revert back to the donor's estate.[73] In the meantime, the NAACP filed its own lawsuit challenging the exclusion of African American golfers from the city-owned facility, arguing that such exclusion violated the Fourteenth Amendment. Superior court judge Susie Sharp, North Carolina's only female state court judge, agreed and ordered the city to either purchase the reverter clause from the donor's estate or close the park. A few weeks later, the city purchased the reverter clause and operated the park on an integrated basis.[74]

Notwithstanding these modest desegregation efforts during the first few years following the *Brown* decision, school integration posed a far more difficult problem. Pupil mixing aroused passions of an order entirely different from that involved in the desegregation of golf courses and city buses.

For the first three years after the *Brown* decision, the Charlotte and Mecklenburg County school boards did little more than study the issue of school desegregation; during that time period, both boards continued the long-standing practice of assigning children to schools on the basis of their race.[75] At the same time, the NAACP, under the leadership of State President Kelly Alexander of Charlotte, sought to pressure the Charlotte and Mecklenburg County school boards to desegregate their schools.

Alexander would serve as one of North Carolina's leading civil rights figures for over forty years. Alexander's father, Zechariah Alexander, worked for several years as a district manager for North Carolina Mutual Life Insurance Company, one of the largest black-owned businesses in the United States. Subsequently, during the 1930s, Zechariah Alexander founded Alexander Funeral Home in Charlotte, which became one of the city's leading funeral homes servicing the African American community. Kelly Alexander's own sensitivity to racial issues had been shaped by his experiences as a salesman in the Deep South in the 1930s, when he gained a firsthand appreciation for the second-class status of African Americans. In the late 1930s he returned to Charlotte to work in the family funeral home and in 1940 founded the Charlotte branch of the NAACP. In 1948, Alexander became statewide president of the NAACP, a position he held until 1984. In 1983, Alexander would be elected national chair of the NAACP.[76]

The Alexanders, who were also personal friends with W. E. B. Du Bois, were one of the city's most prominent black families for much of the twentieth century.[77] Kelly Alexander's older brother Fred put his energies into politics, becoming, in 1965, the first black member of the Charlotte City Council and, in 1974, one of the first two black members of the North Carolina Senate since Reconstruction.[78]

Kelly Alexander had for years challenged the accommodationist attitudes of much of the state's traditional black leadership, criticizing their "complacency as to civil rights."[79] Beginning in the late 1940s, Alexander argued that significant racial progress would not occur in North Carolina until the black community used the courtroom to confront the white political leadership with its claims for racial justice.[80] Under Alexander's leadership, the North Carolina chapter of the NAACP would be one of the most aggressive state chapters in the South. Indeed, it petitioned more school boards and brought more school desegregation lawsuits during the 1950s than any other state chapter.[81]

The NAACP initially sought to achieve its desegregation goals by appeals to school boards without resort to litigation. One week after the *Brown* decision was announced, NAACP representatives from seventeen southern and border states met in Atlanta to discuss the organization's response to the decision. The representatives agreed to ask NAACP branches throughout the South to petition local school boards to abolish school segregation without delay.[82] During the summer of 1954, Alexander prepared petitions seeking immediate desegregation and distributed them to local NAACP branches for presentation to school boards.[83] Although several NAACP branches, including Charlotte's, filed these petitions with local school boards, these efforts met no success.[84]

During the summers of 1955 and 1956, the NAACP presented petitions for immediate school desegregation to the school boards of Charlotte and Mecklenburg County and threatened litigation if the boards failed to act on the petitions.[85] Both boards rejected the petitions. In March 1957, the NAACP presented another desegregation petition to the

Charlotte School Board; this time, the board told the NAACP leaders that those African American students who wanted to attend a white school should file individual transfer requests in accord with the new pupil assignment statute.[86] In the meantime, the U.S. Court of Appeals for the Fourth Circuit underscored the importance of the administrative transfer process by upholding the exclusion of a group of black students from a white school in Old Fort, North Carolina, on the grounds that these students had not properly requested a transfer to a white school before filing their lawsuit.[87]

As a result, Alexander sought to stimulate interest among African Americans to seek transfers for their children to white schools. During the spring of 1957, Alexander held a number of public meetings in Charlotte during which he advised parents on the necessity of filing transfer applications; Alexander also approached certain parents whose children were thought to be particularly good candidates for transfers and specifically encouraged them to seek assignment at a white school. Ultimately, African Americans filed forty transfer requests with the Charlotte School Board during the summer of 1957.[88]

Not everyone in the African American community favored school desegregation. Many black parents did not want to subject their children to the harassment they feared would accompany attendance at a white school.[89] Others did not perceive the benefits of a desegregated education and did not care to risk the retaliation that could accompany a transfer request. The Charlotte branch of the NAACP ultimately concluded: "Parents find it difficult to understand the harmful, detrimental psychological and educational effects of segregation. It is essential that we continue to educate them as to the meaning of [the *Brown* decision]."[90] African Americans who had sought entry for their children into white schools throughout North Carolina had suffered economic consequences for their actions; more than once, the national office of the NAACP had been called on to help a black family suffering a foreclosure or some other adverse action occasioned by a transfer request.[91] Some blacks claimed that they had lost their jobs after filing transfer requests.[92]

Throughout the 1950s and 1960s, one of the most prominent black Charlotteans, Nathaniel Tross, criticized school desegregation efforts. Tross, who had been born in the Caribbean and educated at various American and English universities, including Harvard and Oxford, was one of the most influential black ministers in the city from the 1930s until his death in 1971. In 1939, the city's leading radio station, WBT, began broadcasting Tross's sermons, a practice it continued for over a quarter of a century. In 1949, Tross became editor and publisher of the city's only black newspaper, the *Charlotte Post*.[93]

Tross was a firm opponent of pupil mixing.[94] When Governor Hodges proposed voluntary segregation in August 1955 as a means of dealing with the demands of *Brown*, Tross endorsed the governor's plan: "We can avoid racial friction on the whole question of integration only on a voluntary basis. . . . I think the governor was right in castigating the false prophets of the NAACP."[95] Throughout the 1950s and early 1960s, Tross opposed desegregation efforts, bringing him into public conflict with other African American leaders. The Western North Carolina Conference of the A.M.E. Zion Church, Tross's denomination, ultimately passed a resolution criticizing him for the part he had "played in behalf of those who would stave off integration."[96]

Tross not only opposed racial integration but also criticized the use of pressure tactics, such as demonstrations, to achieve racial gains of any type. In 1945, he told a radio audience, "It is nonsensical . . . to think that we can improve a race, or better race relations . . . by threatened demonstrations."[97] Later, Tross would attack Martin Luther King's confrontational actions, claiming that King's voice had become "false" and was "a distinct discord in the chorus of interracial goodwill and understanding."[98] Tross's newspaper, unlike many other black newspapers such as the *Carolina Times* in Durham, reported almost exclusively on social events in the Charlotte black community, ignoring larger political issues.

The white community of Charlotte held Tross in high regard, which Tross reinforced by his emphasis on the responsibility of the black community to improve itself through hard work and by his public criticism of those black leaders who were pushing too forcefully for racial change.[99] Tross would later recount asking a Charlotte bank to fire its first African American bank teller because she was rude and inefficient and would not help advance black interests by her conduct.[100]

It is unclear whether the public Tross accurately represented the true feelings of the distinguished minister. Reginald Hawkins, one of Charlotte's most outspoken black activists of the 1950s and 1960s, later commented that in private Tross fully supported more aggressive action by civil rights activists but wanted to preserve his inroads into the white community by publicly attacking those black leaders engaging in more confrontational actions.[101] Another of the city's black leaders, James Polk, agreed with Hawkins's assessment: "The real Dr. Tross never stood up, except to a very few people."[102] Nevertheless, Tross's prominence, coupled with his accommodationist views, made the work of the NAACP far more difficult.

The NAACP had a few white allies in its request for school desegregation. The biracial Charlotte-Mecklenburg Council on Human Relations supported the NAACP's integration efforts. The council argued that school desegregation would bring "great prestige [to] Charlotte throughout the nation and the world" and would be "good for business."[103] The council insisted that only a fraction of the black population would actually attend white schools in Charlotte because of the city's extensive residential segregation. At the same time, Harry Golden, the outspoken and sardonic editor of the *Carolina Israelite* and one of the city's leading social critics, urged desegregation coupled with the removal of all chairs from the public schools, noting that whites seemed to object only to sitting, not standing, with blacks. Golden's "Vertical Negro Plan" received national attention.[104]

Just as Charlotte's political and civic leaders were confronted with the thorny issues presented by the *Brown* decision, so were the city's religious leaders. Imbued with considerable moral and cultural authority in a deeply religious city, Charlotte's ministers took various positions on the issue of school desegregation. The fact that the city's churches were uniformly segregated at the time of the Supreme Court's decision made the issue particularly complex.

Charlotte in the 1950s was a center of Presbyterianism. Many of the city's leading white citizens were Presbyterians of Scotch-Irish ancestry and belonged to churches affiliated with the Presbyterian Church in the United States (PCUS), which had split from its northern counterpart, the United Presbyterian Church, a century earlier over the slavery issue. The PCUS was the first denomination to meet following the *Brown* decision; two weeks later, the general assembly of the denomination adopted a statement commending the principles set forth by the Supreme Court and urging its members to aid those charged with its implementation. The denomination also resolved to end segregation in its own churches and assemblies. To be sure, there was dissent throughout the denomination, and a denominational publication, the *Presbyterian Journal*, claimed, "Voluntary segregation . . . is for the highest interest of the races and is not un-Christian." Another denominational publication, however, the *Presbyterian Outlook*, favored integration, as did a majority of the denomination's clergy.[105]

A few of Charlotte's white Presbyterian clergy, in particular John Cunningham of the Presbyterian Foundation and Warner Hall of Covenant Presbyterian Church, took on influential roles in civic efforts to improve race relations through their leadership of the Mayor's Community Relations Committee, established in 1960. Moreover, several white Presbyterian laypersons, such as Judge James McMillan and Joseph Grier, both elders at Charlotte's First Presbyterian Church, and Margaret Ray, of Myers Park Presbyterian Church, took significant action in pushing the city toward greater integration.

The Episcopal Church, though much smaller in membership than the Presbyterian Church, was even stronger in its support of the *Brown* decision. The diocese of western North Carolina, including Charlotte, endorsed integration, as did seven of the city's eight Episcopal rectors. Thomas Blair, the rector of the city's largest and most prominent Episcopal church—Christ Episcopal—would later take a leadership role in community efforts to facilitate integration.[106] Another rector of Christ Episcopal, Harcourt Waller, would eventually be forced to resign, in part because of his outspoken support of an array of liberal social issues, including school integration.[107] As with most denominations, however, there was dissent. Shortly after the initial integration of the Charlotte schools in 1957, the rector of St. Peter's Episcopal Church, the city's oldest Episcopal church, delivered a widely publicized sermon in which he told his parishioners, "It is not God's will to mix the races."[108]

The Methodist Church took a much weaker position; in the fall of 1954, the Western North Carolina Conference of the Methodist Church, including Charlotte, rejected a resolution that would have recognized "the obligation of all citizens to obey the law of the land"; instead the conference resolved to "study" the issue.[109] Few of the city's Methodist clergy would be outspoken in their support of school integration efforts. The Baptist clergy, consistent with their church's nonhierarchical structure, took various positions in response to integration initiatives. Some Baptist pastors bitterly opposed integration efforts.[110] Others, such as Claude Broach, of St. John's Baptist Church, and Carlyle Marney and, later, Eugene Owens, of Myers Park Baptist Church in southeast Charlotte, endorsed desegregation initiatives. Both Marney, in the 1960s, and Owens, in the 1970s, were particularly outspoken on racial issues. Marney published a book in 1961, *Structures of Prejudice*, in which he wrote that segregation and racism threatened to destroy "our lives as a potential people of God."[111] In the Lutheran Church, Herbert Mirly, of Resurrection Lutheran Church, was an outspoken supporter of desegregation initiatives throughout the 1960s.[112]

The Catholic Church, which had a limited presence in Charlotte, quickly embraced school integration. Following the *Brown* decision, the Catholic bishop of North Carolina ordered the immediate desegregation of all Catholic high schools in the state; from 1954 until 1957, Catholic schools — including Charlotte Catholic — were the only integrated schools in North Carolina.[113] Probably the most outspoken white minister in Charlotte, however, was Sidney Freeman, of the Unitarian Church of Charlotte. Freeman frequently walked the picket lines with black protesters in the early 1960s, at a time when few white people would offer such visible support.[114] The North Carolina Association of Rabbis also endorsed school desegregation; moreover, Charlotte Rabbi Israel Gerber would later support Judge James McMillan's busing orders, explaining to his congregation that the white community's lethargy following the *Brown* decision had made such orders necessary.[115]

Black clergy were generally far more supportive of desegregation efforts than were their white counterparts. Several of the city's most prominent black leaders, including many Smith professors, were United Presbyterian Church ministers. Confronted with widespread racial discrimination in the southern Presbyterian Church, most black Presbyterians had chosen to affiliate with the more liberal United Presbyterian Church. Many of these ministers, in particular Reginald Hawkins, were among the leading supporters of various desegregation efforts during the 1950s and 1960s. Other black clergy played active roles in desegregation initiatives as well. Coleman Kerry, for example, pastor of Friendship Baptist Church, helped organize the Clergymen's Christian and Civic Association in 1965 to promote black interests in civic affairs and would subsequently be the first African American to serve on the Charlotte-Mecklenburg School Board.[116]

Ministers in Charlotte, particularly in the white community, were generally more likely to favor desegregation efforts than were their parishioners. In an important study of integration efforts in the 1950s, two prominent social scientists concluded, "The Christian ministry in the South is the only significant group throughout the area willing to stand up for integration."[117] In Charlotte, many clergy, both white and black, supported integration efforts; the Mecklenburg Christian Ministers Association, for example, would be one of the first groups to respond favorably to the student sit-ins of 1960.[118] Yet the city's white clergy, with significant exceptions, did not urge their parishioners to accept integration initiatives, particularly when token integration of the late 1950s and early 1960s turned to massive busing in the late 1960s and early 1970s.

Few white ministers endorsed school busing, particularly in the early years. To some extent, this silence may have reflected the limits of the clergy's moral authority; moreover, some reports indicated that those white ministers who urged support for busing suffered a decline in collection-plate contributions.[119]

In the meantime, the Charlotte School Board decided that accepting the transfers of a few black students to white schools served the city's interest in controlling the pace of desegregation without judicial interference. Beginning in 1955, the Charlotte School Board met secretly with the school boards of Greensboro and Winston-Salem to discuss the eventual desegregation of their respective school systems.[120] The school boards brought media representatives into the discussions to solicit advice and cooperation; the media cooperated by declining to report on the negotiations.[121]

During the spring and summer of 1957, the local boards of these three school systems agreed to accept the transfer requests of a few African Americans to white schools for the 1957–58 school year. The three boards decided that each would announce on July 23 that the transfer requests of twelve black students in the three cities had been granted.[122] All of the students whose transfer applications were granted lived closer to a white school than to the black school to which they were initially assigned and were among the top students in their black schools.[123] In Charlotte, five of the forty students who requested a transfer were successful; one of the five moved from Charlotte shortly thereafter, leaving four students to integrate the schools. Among those students whose transfer requests were rejected were NAACP President Alexander's children.[124]

In agreeing to voluntary desegregation in the summer of 1957, the Charlotte School Board operated with the understanding that this action would fend off more extensive court-ordered desegregation. The board announced that in granting the transfers, it had acted to "preserve the public schools of Charlotte."[125] Both of the city's newspapers and a number of respected business and professional leaders articulated this perspective. The *Charlotte Observer* described the voluntary desegregation as a "legal and effective instrument for keeping desegregation a limited and selective process," thereby avoiding "an inevitable court order for mandatory desegregation" and enhancing "the progressive tradition of the three communities and of this state."[126] In a widely covered speech Fred Helms, a prominent Charlotte attorney and a member of the original Pearsall Committee, told a civic club audience that business and professional people should lead the community in acceptance of desegregation. North Carolina's "course of moderation" would succeed, urged Helms, whereas courts would strike down the more extreme school statutes in other states.[127] The Charlotte Chamber of Commerce supported the school board's actions; one year earlier, the chamber's president, Stowe Moody, had asked the board to form a biracial committee to forge a "moderate approach" to the resolution of the city's racial problems.[128]

This token school desegregation, however, sparked opposition from parts of the white community. Representatives of a white segregationist organization, the Patriots of North Carolina, challenged the Charlotte School Board's decision to admit black children into white schools. A group of prominent North Carolinians had organized the Patriots in August 1955 in the wake of Assistant Attorney General Beverly Lake's widely publicized attack on the NAACP. Established for the purpose of maintaining "the purity and culture of the white race and Anglo-Saxon institutions," the Patriots included among its members some of the most prominent North Carolinians: three former speakers of the state house, a trustee of the University of North Carolina, three members of the state legislature, and a number of prominent business leaders.[129]

Yet the organization enjoyed little lasting support, particularly in Charlotte. In 1957, the Patriots mailed letters to the parents of over one thousand students at Charlotte's Central High School—one of the schools slated to receive a black student—encouraging them to pull their children out of Central. The organization received only one favorable response, which was later withdrawn.[130] By the following summer, the Patriots had disappeared from the scene in North Carolina, the most short-lived of all southern segregationist organizations.[131] Unlike resistance groups formed in other southern states, the Patriots did not originate in the heavily agricultural black-belt section of the state, but rather in the urban Piedmont. In time, the organization disbanded as the Piedmont cities came to understand the advantages of token desegregation.[132]

The Patriots failed because of the unwillingness of the state's urban areas to engage in a "resistance at all costs" response to desegregation. Significantly, in Charlotte, unlike in other parts of the state and other parts of the South, few business or professional people of prominence ever associated with segregationist groups. White segregationist organizations ran counter to the dominant sensibilities in the city. For much of the 1900s, Charlotte's business and political leaders studiously avoided racial demagoguery, sensitive to the civic and economic importance of the city's reputation for racial moderation. Charlotte resolved its problems quietly, without resort to extreme rhetoric; that style would serve the city well during the tumultuous 1960s. The Patriots' leader in Charlotte, Kenneth Whitsett, later noted that the prominent business leaders in Charlotte refused to support his organization, fearing that such support would hurt business. Whitsett claimed that his organization never had more than thirty-five members in Mecklenburg County and that it ultimately wielded little influence.[133]

Charlotte largely avoided the violent resistance to desegregation efforts that took place in other southern cities, such as Little Rock, in the fall of 1957 because those who favored segregation took their grievances to the courts rather than to the schoolyards. Shortly before the opening of the schools in September, over two hundred white parents in Charlotte sought an injunction from a state superior court judge barring the admission of the black students to the white schools. Earlier, the Patriot leader Whitsett had unsuccessfully attempted to persuade the Charlotte School Board to rescind its decision on the transfers by presenting it with a petition allegedly bearing sixteen thousand signatures.[134] The petition, however, failed; the school board stood by its decision on the transfers. Lawyers for the white parents argued that desegregated schools were inconsistent with the "customs, ideas and beliefs" of the community and would jeopardize the health and welfare of the students.[135] Will Pless, a longtime state superior court judge, declined to issue the requested injunction, explaining his decision as the lesser of two evils: if he enjoined the board's token desegregation, the city would "be put under the orders of a federal court," which in Pless's view would lead to wholesale race mixing in the schools. Pless reminded the white parents, "We can't secede from the Union."[136] Pless did not necessarily favor desegregation, but like many of his fellow Charlotteans, he desired to avoid federal intervention in the operation of the schools. Pless had previously shown himself cognizant of changing legal expectations regarding race. Over twenty years earlier, Pless had been one of the first judges in North Carolina to hold that a jury pool was illegally constituted because blacks were excluded from the jury list.[137]

The white parents eventually sought a school closing vote in accordance with the Pearsall Plan, but the Charlotte School Board refused to grant the request.[138] Thus, in its first major test, the Pearsall Plan's provisions for closing schools had been ignored, underscoring the significance of North Carolina's decision not to *require* school closings in the face of desegregation, as required by other states such as Virginia. Charlotte's leadership was not prepared to allow the abandonment of the public schools over token desegregation.

The most strident reaction to the Charlotte School Board's decision to integrate came from outside the city. Shortly before the Charlotte schools opened, John Kasper, an itinerant New Jersey segregationist who traveled throughout the South during the 1950s inciting opposition to school desegregation, came to Charlotte from Clinton, Tennessee, where he had just served a six-month jail sentence for interference with that city's school desegregation efforts.[139] Kasper addressed a crowd of about three hundred on the courthouse steps on Sunday, September 1, 1957, three days before the Charlotte schools were scheduled to open. Using inflammatory language, Kasper urged community pressure on the school board to force a reversal of its decision to desegregate: "We want a heart attack, . . . we want suicides, we want flight from persecution."[140] He distributed leaflets featuring a photograph of a black man kissing a white woman and urged his white followers to "load your shotguns."[141] Kasper's effect on Charlotte, however, was minimal. He announced the formation of a Mecklenburg White Citizens' Council but could recruit only fifteen members; the organization disbanded within weeks. He encouraged a student strike and picketing of schools, but to no avail.[142] Kasper left Charlotte a few days later, never to return. Within a week, Kasper would be jailed in Nashville, Tennessee, for inciting a riot in another school desegregation conflict.[143]

In large measure, Kasper's failure to foster resistance to the token desegregation in Charlotte was due to his conflict with local sensibilities. The majority of Charlotteans did not favor desegregation, but most were repelled by Kasper's extremist language and tactics. His speech and manner violated the parameters of acceptable political discourse. When Kasper first announced that he might come to Charlotte to stir up opposition to school integration, Whitsett, the leader of the segregationist Patriots, announced that any Patriot who had anything to do with Kasper would be "drummed out of the group."[144] The *Charlotte Observer* dismissed Kasper as a "hate-monger."[145]

Similarly, the Ku Klux Klan, though active in Charlotte, had little impact on school desegregation, due in part to vigorous law-enforcement efforts to control its nefarious activities. In 1956, the county police raided a Klan meeting, resulting in several arrests and convictions.[146] Aided by documents seized in that raid, both county and city police began to keep local Klan members under surveillance.[147] Charlotte Police Chief Frank

Littlejohn assigned an undercover agent the task of infiltrating the Klan with the purpose of destroying it. The informer advised county police of a scheme by the local Klan in February 1958—five months after the initial desegregation of the Charlotte schools—to dynamite a black school.[148] Police arrested three Klansmen on their way to the school; all three were subsequently convicted and received prison terms.[149]

The initial desegregation of the three North Carolina school systems was relatively peaceful, with one exception: Harding High School in Charlotte. Early in the summer of 1957, the state NAACP president, Alexander, had approached Herman Counts, a professor at Charlotte's Johnson C. Smith University, about seeking a transfer for Counts's daughter Dorothy to the all-white Harding High School. Counts agreed, and Dorothy was one of the Charlotte students whose transfer request was granted. On Wednesday, September 4, the same day that nine black students made their first attempt to enroll at Central High School in Little Rock, Arkansas, Dorothy Counts enrolled at Harding. Two persons who were leaders in Kasper's fledgling White Citizens' Council in Charlotte, truck driver John Warlick and his wife, appeared at Harding and encouraged students to prevent Counts from enrolling. Mrs. Warlick told a group of boys, "It's up to you to keep her out." She urged another group of students to "spit on her, girls, spit on her."[150] Several students did spit on Counts; some threw sticks while others taunted, "Nigger, go back to Africa."[151] A *New York Times* reporter described Counts as "a comely lady of unmistakable gentleness and breeding," who confronted the jeering crowd "with a quiet dignity that made theories of Negro inferiority seem grotesque."[152] Police ultimately arrested two students for disorderly conduct. Counts declined to return to school on Thursday and Friday on account of illness but returned the following Monday.[153]

The harassment continued the next week, with little intervention from the white Harding principal, J. R. Hawkins. Hawkins downplayed the harassment of Counts, noting she had reported no misconduct to him while ignoring the fact that her plight was widely covered in the local press.[154] At the end of the second week, after Counts was pelted again with debris and after her father's car window was shattered, Counts withdrew from Harding and enrolled in an integrated school in Philadelphia. Herman Counts explained that the threat to his daughter's safety made the move necessary, but he added, "Our cause is just and ultimately must win."[155]

Counts's experience received nationwide and even worldwide attention as photographs of her walking through the hostile crowd were transmitted throughout the world. Counts received hundreds of letters of sup-

Dorothy Counts arrives for her first day of classes at Harding High School, September 4, 1957. (Courtesy of the *Charlotte Observer*)

port from across America and from more than a dozen foreign countries.[156] Although the simultaneous and far more tumultuous integration of Central High School in Little Rock eventually overshadowed Counts's experience, the extensive publicity of Counts's ordeal had a profound impact on Charlotte and particularly on its leadership. A city jealous of its public image as a moderate southern city had been embarrassed before the world. Henceforth, having learned their lesson, the city's leaders would strive to avoid any negative publicity on racial matters. As one community leader later explained, "There was a resolve it would never happen again."[157]

The three other black students in Charlotte who ultimately attended a white school in the fall of 1957 — Gus Roberts, Girvaud Roberts, and Delores Huntley — had a less traumatic experience than did Counts, in large measure due to the support of school officials. Ed Sanders, the principal at Central High, the other white high school to receive a black student, sought to prevent any interference with integration at Central.[158] When Sanders first learned that Gus Roberts would be transferring to Central, he feared problems: "I grew up in the South and I was aware of how strongly people felt about mixing the races."[159] On one of the first days of the new school year, a group of white boys blocked the entrance to the

Protesting students await Dorothy Counts at Harding High School, September 4, 1957. (Courtesy of the *Charlotte Observer*)

school to prevent Roberts from entering the school. Sanders responded by personally escorting Roberts through the line of students. Roberts remained at Central until graduation, two years later. Likewise, Piedmont Junior High School Principal Don Newman met Girvaud Roberts at the door to the school and personally escorted her to her classroom.[160]

The relative success of this initial school desegregation in Charlotte, particularly in comparison with the far more tumultuous school desegregation in Little Rock, was due in large measure to the fact that no statewide or local leader—such as Governor Hodges—chose to exploit the issue for political advantage. On the contrary, a significant number of state and local leaders made the case for token desegregation as a means of avoiding judicial intervention and preserving the state's reputation for positive race relations.

Notwithstanding the harassment of Dorothy Counts, the stark contrast between Charlotte and Little Rock gained wide notice. In the fall of 1957, the Voice of America radio broadcast compared the Charlotte and Little Rock desegregation experiences, citing Charlotte as illustrative of the nation's peaceful transition to an integrated society.[161] Two years later, an Atlanta television station made arrangements to film a documentary

Gus Roberts during the first day of classes at Central High School, September 4, 1957. (Courtesy of the *Charlotte Observer*)

on school desegregation in Charlotte.[162] Over the next several years, at a time when many southern cities reported downturns in business growth as a result of racial problems, the Charlotte Chamber of Commerce reported generous increases in new business in the city.[163]

But the initial desegregation of the Charlotte schools was truly token. The following year, the Charlotte School Board assigned no additional African Americans to a white school and approved only two out of twenty-three transfer requests; only four African Americans attended a white school in Charlotte that year. In 1959, the Charlotte School Board denied every transfer request, continuing its policy of denying all transfer requests of black students who lived closer to their assigned black school than to the desired white school. Only one African American attended a white school in Charlotte during the 1959–60 school year, three fewer than two years earlier.[164] In the meantime, the Mecklenburg County Board of Education continued to deny every request by a black student to attend a white school. Charlotte had shrewdly captured national publicity as a pioneering southern city on race issues without any real commitment to school desegregation.

The Charlotte-Mecklenburg Council on Human Relations chastised the board in 1959 for its actions: "It seems increasingly clear that initial token desegregation, rather than paving the way for future compliance, is becoming a means of evasion of the law." The council argued that such tokenism was actually damaging: "Token desegregation, as we have it in Charlotte today, with one Negro child assigned to each of two formerly all-white schools, grossly violates the principle of equal protection of the law. . . . Such a policy, conceivably, may be more harmful to the values of our society than no compliance at all, for it sets up an apparently re-spectable front behind which the law is ignored."[165]

For years to come, Charlotte's political and civic leaders would cele-brate the school board's decision to integrate its schools in 1957. This early desegregation played a central role in efforts to promote the city's progressive racial image during the 1960s and 1970s. What was often lost in such efforts, however, was the truly token nature of this early integra-tion. For example, when the Charlotte-Mecklenburg School Board ap-peared before the U.S. Supreme Court in 1970 to defend its assignment policies, the school board's attorneys boasted, "In 1957 Charlotte led the South in opening its schools to students of both races." The school board's attorneys further claimed, somewhat disingenuously, that few students in 1957 "took advantage of this option" to attend an integrated school. Left unsaid was the fact that few students "took advantage of this option" precisely because the school board denied them the opportunity to do so.[166]

As the decade ended, the Charlotte and Mecklenburg County school boards took a seemingly innocuous action that would have a profound impact on the future of desegregated education in the city. In January 1960, the Charlotte City Public Schools and the Mecklenburg County Public Schools, the two largest school systems in North Carolina, con-solidated, thereby creating one of the largest school systems in the na-tion.[167] Since the late 1940s, many North Carolinians had promoted the consolidation of city and county school districts as a means of improving the educational quality of rural schools. The issue of school consolidation came to a head in Charlotte when the city sought in 1957 to expand its limits. This proposed expansion threatened to take a sizable portion of the county's tax base, further eroding the financial support for the county schools at a time when many county residents already sent their children to schools in the city because of the superior education offered. Recog-nizing that the continued operation of two school districts would inhibit the city's expansion while at the same time disadvantaging students in the county schools, the Charlotte Chamber of Commerce proposed a consolidation of the two school systems. After an extensive chamber-led public relations effort, the voters approved the consolidation in a June 1959 referendum, to take effect the following January.[168] Although civic leaders promoted the consolidation for reasons of administrative convenience and educational efficiency, the creation of such a large school district would have the unintended effect of making it extremely difficult for the city's white residents to flee the school system to avoid desegregation. But it would be years before that consequence of school consolidation became apparent.

In the meantime, on February 10, 1959, eight African American students whose transfer requests to a white elementary school had been denied in both 1957 and 1958 filed suit in federal district court against the Mecklenburg County School Board with the assistance of NAACP lawyers, including Thurgood Marshall from the national office.[169] The school board had assigned the children to Torrence Lytle School, a black "union" school in the northern section of the county that educated children from grades one through twelve and that would be forced to close within a few years due to inadequate facilities. Most of the children lived about ten miles from Torrence Lytle but within walking distance of Derita Elementary, the white school to which the transfers were sought. Many of the white students assigned to Derita lived much farther from the school than did the black plaintiffs.[170]

In August 1957, within a few weeks of the Charlotte School Board's decision to allow black students to transfer to white schools for the first time, the Mecklenburg County School Board denied the transfer requests of these students. The students properly exhausted their administrative remedies, seeking a hearing before the board, at which their requests for reconsideration were rejected. In the summer of 1958, the black students again sought a transfer to the white Derita school; met with another rebuff, they initiated litigation challenging their exclusion from the white school.

Federal judge Wilson Warlick of Statesville ultimately considered the case at a hearing in Charlotte. Judge Warlick had earlier commented: "I'm a states' rights individualist and I always have been. If I had anything to do with schools in North Carolina, I wouldn't let the federal government have any part of it."[171] Of course, as a federal judge, Warlick was obliged to have a "part" of the local schools by reviewing the constitutionality of the school board's pupil assignments.

The fundamental question for Judge Warlick was whether the board's decision to deny these black students' request to attend the all-white school within walking distance of their homes was made on account of their race. If so, then the school board's actions violated the equal protection clause of the U.S. Constitution. Warlick answered that question in his June 1961 decision by stating that he did not think the school board had violated the Constitution:

> After a careful study of the evidence, the court is of the opinion that the defendant Board has conscientiously complied with the requirements placed upon it, and that the plaintiffs have failed to show wherein they were discriminated against because of their race. In their requests for reassignment the plaintiffs all state as their reasons therefor that they lived closer to the Derita School than to the Torrence Lytle School, and that they desired a desegregated education. It has been defendant's position throughout that *distance from a school has never been a determinative factor in the assignment of pupils* because of the extensive use of busses throughout the State and the county.[172]

Eight years later, the same school board would argue that distance from a school was indeed *the* determinative factor in the assignment of pupils and that busing children to distant schools subverted the educational process. But those arguments were for another day. Now, in 1961, confronted with the delicate question of how it could justify requiring these black children to ride a bus twenty miles a day instead of walking to school, the board argued that school busing had a long and distinguished history in North Carolina and that a child's physical proximity to a school was hardly decisive in terms of pupil assignment. Judge Warlick agreed, elaborating at great length on the extensive use of school busing throughout the state, noting that some North Carolina children rode buses as far as one hundred miles a day.[173]

Warlick's decision was difficult to justify. The board's initial assignment decisions were obviously race-based and hence unconstitutional. Nevertheless, the decision was indicative of the fact that the courts were not yet a receptive forum for black parents seeking to realize the promise of the *Brown* decision. The plaintiffs appealed but failed to do so on a timely basis, and the appeal was dismissed.[174] But the problem of black children seeking admission to nearby white schools would remain. Although Charlotte had a high degree of residential segregation, there were several black neighborhoods located near white schools, presenting the school board with the problem of how to keep white schools in those areas segregated.[175]

In the meantime, in January 1961, two African Americans filed suit to force the city to consolidate its two community colleges into one school serving both races. The Charlotte City School Board had created Charlotte College in 1946 to educate white veterans returning from the war, utilizing Central High School for evening classes. In 1949, the board established Carver College for black students at Second Ward High School, notwithstanding NAACP State President Alexander's demands that the board integrate Charlotte College instead of providing a separate school for black students.[176]

In time, the two schools outgrew their modest facilities, and in the late 1950s, local officials scheduled a bond referendum to raise funds to establish a separate campus for each of the two community colleges.[177] The NAACP opposed the establishment of two separate colleges and urged that the bond referendum be restructured to raise money for one facility. Despite the NAACP's opposition, the bond referendum was successful.[178]

Construction began on the two campuses, with the black Carver College located near black neighborhoods in northwest Charlotte and the white Charlotte College located northeast of the city and far removed from black neighborhoods. Even though each school was technically open to students of both races, almost no students chose to attend the college for students of the opposite race. The Charlotte-Mecklenburg Council on Human Relations joined the NAACP in opposing the establishment of two campuses and in January 1961 threatened litigation if college trustees began construction of the new Carver College campus.[179]

When the trustees failed to respond, the council helped organize a lawsuit to enjoin the construction, winning the financial backing of a liberal white woman, Marion Cannon, and securing the cooperation of two African American doctors to serve as plaintiffs.[180] Cannon, the widow of a wealthy textile executive, supported a number of desegregation efforts in Charlotte in the early 1960s.[181] The suit alleged that the bond money was being unlawfully utilized to establish two segregated community colleges. Within a week of the filing of the suit, however, state superior court judge Susie Sharp dismissed it. Sharp accepted the college trustees' arguments that the plaintiffs, who had not been denied entry to either college on account of their race, could show no injury.[182] The plaintiffs appealed to the North Carolina Supreme Court, but several months later the supreme court agreed with Judge Sharp. The court emphasized, "Plaintiffs do not allege that any qualified prospective student has been or will be excluded from attending either Charlotte College or Carver College solely on the basis of race."[183] Hence there was no basis for relief. It might be bad policy for the trustees to establish two colleges offering substantially similar programs in one community, but wastefulness did not establish a constitutional violation. And yet wasteful it was. Within four years, the new Carver College closed its doors due to a lack of students, and the buildings were sold at a loss.[184]

The North Carolina Supreme Court's decision was not surprising. The courts at this time looked with disfavor on "taxpayer" suits whereby a citizen attempted to block the expenditure of tax money. A better suit might have been one brought by an African American denied admission to Charlotte College, of which there were several.[185] But even that suit would likely have failed. In the wake of the threat of litigation, the trustees formally announced that both colleges would henceforth accept students without regard to race. Shortly thereafter, a few black nursing students were admitted to Charlotte College. As a result, even though the establishment of the two colleges was clearly intended to perpetuate segregation, the formal open policy would probably have been sufficient to defeat any litigation efforts.

Over the course of the next three years, the level of school desegregation in Charlotte slowly increased. Whereas in 1960, the newly merged Charlotte-Mecklenburg School Board approved only one transfer request by a black student, during the summer of 1961 the board granted twenty-six transfer requests. During the summer of 1962, the Charlotte-Mecklenburg School Board considered for the first time abandoning race-based pupil assignments in favor of a geographic assignment scheme pursuant to which pupils of both races would be assigned to the same school. The issue for the board was whether the white community would accept such action. Following a pattern it had established with the initial desegregation in 1957, the board consulted with the editors of the *Charlotte Observer* and the *Charlotte News* as well as representatives of local television stations in order to get a sense of the community's willingness to accept further desegregation.[186] Again following the 1957 pattern, the media representatives agreed not to report the board's deliberations on the desegregation issue. Ultimately, the board voted to try geographic pupil assignments on a limited basis for the 1962–63 school year.[187] Thus, eight years after the *Brown v. Board of Education* decision, the Charlotte-

Mecklenburg School Board became one of the first school boards in the South to assign children to schools on some basis other than their race.

The board chose two previously all-white elementary schools — Sedgefield and Bethune — to receive students on a geographic basis. Four black students and 636 white students were assigned to Sedgefield Elementary in southwest Charlotte. For these black children, the new assignment meant the opportunity to attend a neighborhood school for the first time; these students had previously been bused about twenty miles a day to attend a twelve-grade "union" school in the southern part of the county. On the other hand, 371 black students and 61 white students were assigned to the previously all-white Bethune Elementary in northwest Charlotte, reflecting the fact that there had been a recent influx of African Americans into nearby neighborhoods.[188] In accordance with the state's pupil placement statute, all students assigned to a desegregated school were given the option of transferring to another school.[189] As a result, all but fifteen of the white students assigned to Bethune, now a majority-black school, elected to transfer, whereas almost all of the white students assigned to Sedgefield, which was still predominantly white, accepted their initial assignment.[190]

In addition to this limited geographic assignment system, the board experimented with a limited freedom-of-choice assignment scheme whereby a few other students were granted the opportunity to choose between a black or a white school. Of the forty African American students offered such a choice at the elementary school level, twenty-four chose a white school. As a result of these changes, during the 1962–63 school year forty-two of the more than eighteen thousand black students in Charlotte-Mecklenburg attended a majority-white school.[191] Although still a fraction of the total black student population, that number was roughly equal to the total number of African Americans who had ever attended a white school in Charlotte. In adopting this plan, Charlotte-Mecklenburg became only the second school system in the state — along with Chapel Hill — and one of the first systems in the South to convert at least in part to a geographic assignment plan.[192]

During the summer of 1963, the Charlotte-Mecklenburg School Board offered seventy-eight additional black students the choice of attending either a black or a white elementary school; only fifteen chose to attend a white school.[193] During the 1963–64 school year, twelve of the system's approximately one hundred schools were desegregated as a result of this combination of geographic school assignments and freedom of choice.[194]

Another twenty-six schools also received students on the basis of non-racial geographic assignments, but all of these were single-race schools due to the high degree of residential segregation in Charlotte.[195] During the 1964–65 school year, the geographic attendance zones were extended to fifty schools.[196] It would be a few more years before the Charlotte-Mecklenburg school system would abandon the old dual system completely in favor of geographic assignments, but the school board was inching its way in that direction, in advance of most other southern school systems.

The Charlotte-Mecklenburg School Board converted to a limited geographic attendance plan in the 1960s because of its concern that the courts would order more extensive desegregation if the board failed to act voluntarily. Although Judge Warlick had upheld the school board's assignment practices in his 1961 decision, the board recognized that the courts would eventually demand greater desegregation. Paul Ervin, one of the school board's attorneys and a cousin of U.S. Senator Sam Ervin, advised board members that they could not continue to expect court decisions such as the one from Judge Warlick and that the board would ultimately have to move away from race-based pupil assignments to satisfy judicial requirements.[197]

Ervin's advice was a correct read of the law.[198] In September 1960, Judge Warlick himself had ordered the Yancey County School Board to allow African Americans to attend a white high school, since the board did not operate a black high school.[199] In August 1961, two months after Warlick's decision in the Charlotte case, another federal judge ordered the admission of an African American student to a white school in Chapel Hill, finding that the student had been excluded from that school in favor of a black school solely because of his race.[200] It was the first such decision in the state's history. One year later, the U.S. Court of Appeals for the Fourth Circuit found that the Durham School Board had unconstitutionally assigned African American students to black schools because of their race and ordered the board to cease its discriminatory practices.[201]

With these decisions, the school desegregation jurisprudence in North Carolina had shifted. The courts were no longer dismissing desegregation challenges on the grounds that administrative remedies had not been exhausted or that school boards had acted within their discretion. Now, the courts were paying closer attention to the realities of school board actions and were prepared to strike down race-based assignment plans. The

Charlotte-Mecklenburg School Board could no longer rest confident that its pupil assignment system would survive judicial scrutiny.

At the same time, the African American community stepped up its demand for integrated schools. In May 1961, one month before Judge Warlick's decision in the Charlotte case, Thurgood Marshall, the NAACP national legal counsel, visited North Carolina and told a statewide NAACP rally that it was time for a massive assault on segregated education in North Carolina. At the time of Marshall's address, fewer than one hundred black students attended white schools in North Carolina.[202] That summer, the Charlotte branch of the organization initiated an intensive campaign to persuade black parents to seek transfers for their children to white schools; in response, the Charlotte-Mecklenburg School Board granted more transfer requests during the summer of 1961 than ever before. The initial legal effort to further desegregate the Charlotte schools had failed, but it was clear that the demand for greater school integration would not abate. Over the course of the next few years, the demands of black Charlotteans for integrated schools would dramatically increase.

Charlotte did not engage in meaningful desegregation for several years after the *Brown* decision. Nevertheless, because of the school board's comparatively early decision to grant the transfer requests of a few black students, the city captured national acclaim as a model of racial moderation. The Charlotte School Board understood, in ways that most of its southern counterparts did not, that well-managed token integration could fend off unwanted judicial intervention. The city would draw on that understanding again and again over the course of the tumultuous 1960s.

When will racial segregation in the South finally be eliminated? The answer is fairly simple; — when the Chambers of Commerce, bankers, and manufacturers decide that the time has come for them to step in and settle the matter.

—Harry Golden, *Carolina Israelite*, 1956

CHAPTER 4

The Convergence of Morality and Money

Charlotte Confronts the Civil Rights Movement

In the early 1960s, the dynamics of racial protest in America altered as African Americans increasingly turned to public demonstrations as a means of challenging racial discrimination. Civil rights leaders in Charlotte embraced this confrontational strategy. Although during the 1950s the city's African American community had utilized petitions and an occasional lawsuit to secure desegregation, during the early 1960s the city's black leadership supplemented this litigation strategy with public demonstrations as a means of pressuring the white community to yield to additional integration demands. Charlotte's white leaders would respond to this new pressure by drawing on their experience with school desegregation in the 1950s. Voluntary and controlled integration could fend off unwanted public demonstrations, control the pace of desegregation, and preserve the city's progressive national image as a good place to live and do business. By 1963, Charlotte had once again received national acclaim for its integration efforts, this time of its restaurants and hotels.

During the pre-*Brown* era, African Americans had conducted a handful of racial demonstrations in Charlotte. A group of black ministers orchestrated an unsuccessful boycott of Charlotte's segregated streetcar system in 1907; such streetcar boycotts failed throughout the South during the first decade of the twentieth century.[1] In the 1940s, several African Americans, led by a reporter from the *Pittsburgh Courier*, picketed the Charlotte post office to challenge the postal service's discriminatory employment practices. In 1953, a group of African Americans sat down and demanded service at the Dogwood Room at the Charlotte airport; as a result, the restaurant began operating on a nondiscriminatory basis.[2] None of these incidents, however, led to a sustained use of public demonstrations to challenge patterns of racial segregation in Charlotte.

The first sustained demonstration challenging racial segregation in Charlotte began on February 9, 1960, when Charles Jones, a theological student at Johnson C. Smith University, led several hundred other students in a sit-in protest at several downtown Charlotte lunch counters that refused service to black customers.[3] The Charlotte sit-ins came on the heels of similar protests that had begun in Greensboro one week earlier and that spread throughout the state and the South during February 1960.[4] Johnson C. Smith students would play an important role in much of the city's public demonstration activity over the course of the next several years. Although Smith did not have a tradition of social activism similar to, for example, that of Howard University in Washington, D.C., an increasing number of both students and faculty had become committed to pressing for racial change. Few racial demonstrations would take place in Charlotte during the early 1960s without a substantial contingent of Smith students.

Jones would prove himself to be a savvy leader of the nascent protest movement. Though only twenty-two years old, Jones, whose father was a Presbyterian minister and whose mother was a Smith English professor, had considerable worldly experience. During the summer of 1959, as a regional officer in the National Student Association, Jones had traveled to the Vienna Youth Festival, where he had extolled the benefits of American democracy to students from around the world. Jones's comments in Vienna received broad coverage in Charlotte, and on his return, Charlotte Mayor James Smith called Jones "a credit to [his] race." In early February, Jones had testified before the House Committee on Un-American Activities to counter an appearance of Paul Robeson, Jr. While driving home from Washington after his congressional appearance, Jones heard a radio report describing the Greensboro sit-ins that had begun a few days earlier; he realized that "this was the handle that [was] needed" to challenge racial segregation in Charlotte. On his return, Jones, who was vice-president of the Smith student council, announced at a council meeting his plan to conduct a sit-in the following day. The next morning, over two hundred Smith students joined him, sitting down and demanding service at the lunch counters in eight Charlotte stores, including Woolworth's, Belk's, and Ivey's. Each of these stores permitted black customers to take food away from the lunch counters to eat elsewhere but denied them the opportunity to sit down and eat in the store. In the following days and weeks, the students continued their efforts, and their numbers steadily increased.[5]

The students enjoyed considerable support within the community. The *Charlotte Observer* backed the students in its editorial pages and helped apply pressure on the recalcitrant storeowners by publicizing the results of a survey that indicated that most Charlotteans would patronize a store that operated an integrated lunch counter.[6] Many people, in fact, canceled their credit cards at the stores targeted by the protesters.[7] In March, the Mecklenburg Christian Ministers Association unanimously moved for an end to racial discrimination in the city and county.[8] One white minister, Sidney Freeman, of the Unitarian Church of Charlotte, joined the student demonstrators. Freeman taught English and speech classes at Johnson C. Smith; several of the student protesters were his students and solicited his involvement in the sit-ins. Freeman, an affable Wisconsin native who had come to Charlotte in 1957, would become a familiar white face in racial demonstrations throughout the early 1960s.[9]

The students also enjoyed considerable support in the African American community. Black professionals and business leaders organized a caravan of Cadillacs to transport the students from the Smith campus to the downtown stores. Black women who worked as domestics in the homes of prominent white families reported to Jones those conversations they had overheard concerning the sit-ins. Many African Americans wore old clothes at Easter church services in April 1960 as a show of support. Not everyone in the black community, however, endorsed the sit-in protests. Black minister Nathaniel Tross sharply criticized the students for their actions. The students responded by hanging Tross in effigy on the Smith campus.[10]

Jones carefully distanced his group of demonstrators from national civil rights organizations such as the Congress of Racial Equality, which had identified with the sit-in movement in other cities. Concerned to deflect local antagonism to "outside agitators," Jones emphasized that all his group wanted was to "sit down and eat" when they were tired. Jones would later identify with national civil rights efforts, however, becoming a leader in the Student Nonviolent Coordinating Committee.[11]

Mayor Smith and Chamber of Commerce President Stanford Brookshire met in February 1960 to discuss the impact the protests could have on Charlotte's image and business climate. Smith was entering his last year as mayor; Brookshire would take his place in the mayor's office in 1961, a position he would hold until 1969. During those eight years, Brookshire emerged as one of the central figures in Charlotte's desegregation efforts. Brookshire, a native of the town of Troutman, north of Charlotte, had moved to the city in the late 1920s after graduating from Duke University. Brookshire established his own business, Engineering Sales Company, and eventually became one of the city's most important business, civic, and political leaders. In addition to serving as president of the chamber of commerce and as mayor, Brookshire headed the city's United Appeal and chaired the board of one of the city's most prominent churches, Myers Park Methodist.[12]

Before entering public life, Brookshire had said very little about issues of racial discrimination and did not enjoy significant black support in his first election bid. During the course of his tenure as mayor, however, Brookshire would become increasingly outspoken about the evils of racial discrimination, describing such discrimination as both immoral and bad for business. On several occasions, Brookshire urged both the city and local businesses to hire more African Americans.[13] To Brookshire, expanding job opportunities made good economic sense; in his view, many of Charlotte's black citizens were an "economic liability" to the city, and increased employment would enable them to make a stronger contribution to the economic health of the community.[14]

Brookshire and Mayor Smith agreed on the need for the mayor's office to take a prominent role in the resolution of the lunch counter controversy. In mid-March, Smith announced the establishment of a biracial community committee devoted to improving race relations, known as the Mayor's Committee on Friendly Relations.[15] Both Smith and Brookshire perceived significant advantages flowing from the resolution of racial differences in the context of committee meetings rather than street demonstrations. Brookshire in particular would rely quite heavily on this biracial committee during his tenure as mayor to resolve racial disputes out of the public eye. Public demonstrations, Brookshire believed, "set up tensions" and created ill will that would "retard progress."[16]

Smith's choice for committee chair, John Cunningham, gave the group immediate legitimacy. Cunningham, the former president of nearby Davidson College and executive director of the Presbyterian Foundation in Charlotte, was highly respected throughout the city. Cunningham immediately undertook negotiations with the local merchants who were resisting the desegregation of their lunch counters, and he appealed to the students to suspend their demonstrations in the interest of "community welfare." Cunningham managed to secure a hiatus in the sit-ins from mid-May until mid-June while negotiations continued.[17]

In June 1960, when the negotiations between the Mayor's Committee and the merchants had born no fruit, the students resumed their protests, this time calling for a boycott of the entire downtown business area. A threatened July 4 demonstration proved decisive. The owners of the targeted businesses requested a meeting with the Mayor's Committee, which resulted in a settlement providing for integrated lunch counters. On July 9, black students were served at seven Charlotte lunch counters for the first time; by agreement, the local newspapers did not report the desegregation until after the fact, to avoid conflict.[18]

The success of the sit-ins flowed in large measure from their perceived and actual economic disruption. Chamber of Commerce President Brookshire later conceded that the city's business leadership evaluated the desegregation issue in economic terms: "It seems odd now that Mayor Smith and I and, I think, the rest of the white community throughout the South, were overlooking both the legal and moral aspects of the problem." Brookshire later noted: "The Chamber was aware of and concerned about the boycotts and disruption of business in [other cities], apprehensive that Charlotte might suffer in a like manner unless the protest movement could be contained here."[19] The *Charlotte Observer* saw it the same way: "Charlotte merchants have now made their decision after full consideration of both their economic and moral position."[20] The ability of the students to apply economic pressure on the merchants had proven decisive. Charlotte was not the only southern city to integrate its lunch counters in response to the sit-ins of 1960. By midsummer, stores in over twenty-five upper South cities had opened lunch counters on a nonracial basis.[21]

The sit-ins during the spring of 1960 unleashed several years of direct-action protest throughout the South, a supplement to the litigation orientation of earlier civil rights activity. In some measure, the courts' weak enforcement of *Brown* had signaled that direct action would be required to force racial change. The NAACP would continue its desegregation litigation with increasing success, but with the sit-ins of the spring of 1960, the dynamics of racial protest in the American South had shifted. In cities, like Charlotte, that were acutely aware of their national image on racial issues, demonstrations would be highly successful at forcing city leaders to take action.

During August 1961, public demonstrations erupted over a separate issue: school segregation. In April of that year, the school board had decided to convert an old white high school in northwest Charlotte—Harding, where Dorothy Counts had sought entry in 1957—into an all-black junior high school, renaming it Irwin Avenue Junior High School. As part of the conversion, the board transferred over eight hundred African American students and teachers from Northwest Junior High School to Irwin Avenue. All of the white students and faculty at old Harding High were moved to a newly constructed school building in the western section of the city. The new school was slated to operate as an all-white high school, whereas Irwin Avenue would educate only black junior high students.[22]

Although traditionally a white school, the old Harding High School, located near the downtown area of the city, was the closest school to a number of black residential areas. Over the years, a number of nearby black students had sought transfers to the white school. Although the school board had denied most of these requests, pressure to desegregate Harding High School was increasing in light of its proximity to African American neighborhoods.

The school board's actions engendered protest in both the black and the white communities. About 150 white parents, who lived in neighborhoods close to Harding, petitioned the school board to make Harding available to both white and black children at the junior high level, although with black children required to pass an entrance examination before being admitted. The unexpected white push for a neighborhood desegregated school was motivated largely by economic considerations. The decision to change Harding from a white to a black school had caused a drop in property values in white neighborhoods near the school; white residents believed that it was better to have a neighborhood desegregated school than a neighborhood black school.[23]

At the same time, a group of African Americans, calling themselves the Westside Parents Council, under the leadership of Reginald Hawkins, complained that the white students from old Harding were being provided a new school, leaving the black students with an old school.[24] They asked the school board to retain old Harding High School as an integrated facility.

During the course of the early 1960s, Hawkins emerged as the leading black activist in Charlotte. Born in Beaufort, North Carolina, Hawkins had been educated at Johnson C. Smith, where he quarterbacked the football team, and at the dental school at Howard University in Washington, D.C. Hawkins's years at Howard were particularly significant, since he was exposed to a community that took seriously the need to challenge directly the discriminatory treatment of African Americans. Hawkins spent the early 1950s in the army, during which time he developed an awareness of the potential of religion to influence the political development of African Americans. One of Hawkins's army colleagues, a Jewish psychologist, explained to Hawkins the significance of religion in the political and social development of the Jewish people. After leaving the army in 1953, Hawkins returned to Charlotte to open a dental practice and to enroll in the theological seminary at Johnson C. Smith. On completing his theological degree, Hawkins did not enter the full-time pastorate — choosing instead to maintain his dental practice — but did begin a long history of close work with the United Presbyterian Church on issues of racial discrimination.[25]

In 1959, Hawkins organized his own political group — the Mecklenburg Organization on Political Affairs (MOPA). Although MOPA initially focused its attention on increasing black voter registration, in the early 1960s the organization began to challenge various aspects of racial segregation — particularly in the schools and hospitals — through public demonstrations. In the early 1960s, Hawkins established close contacts with both the Sanford administration in Raleigh and the Kennedy administration in Washington, ties that enabled him to supplement his public demonstrations with governmental pressure. Ultimately Hawkins would run for governor of North Carolina in both 1968 and 1972; Martin Luther King was assassinated in April 1968 when he postponed a campaign appearance with Hawkins to remain in Memphis in support of a sanitation strike.[26]

In time, Hawkins would alienate much of the city's white power structure.[27] Moreover, many blacks kept their distance from Hawkins because of his outspoken nature, though at the same time they respected his courage to take on the white establishment.[28] Unquestionably, Hawkins's confrontational actions quickened the pace of racial desegregation in Charlotte.

Reginald Hawkins campaigning for governor of North Carolina, May 1968.
(Courtesy of the *Charlotte Observer*)

During the summer of 1961, Hawkins argued that the school board, in converting Harding High School from a white to a black school and providing a new school for the white Harding students, was simply continuing its practice of closing certain white schools that were under increasing pressure to admit neighboring black students and replacing those closed schools with newly constructed ones in distant white neighborhoods. The group had a legitimate point. Earlier, the board had closed Central High School, a white school that had been desegregated in 1957 and that was located in downtown Charlotte near a significant black population. In its place, the board had built Garinger High School, located in a predominantly white section of east Charlotte, to educate white students. Likewise, Alexander Graham, a white junior high school that had also been desegregated in 1957 and that was also relatively close to some black residential areas, had been torn down in 1958; to take its place, the board had built a new school in a white residential neighborhood in southeast Charlotte. At the elementary school level, the school board had converted Zeb Vance, Hutchison, and First Ward from white schools to black schools in response to changing neighborhoods.[29] As Hawkins complained at the time, "When a neighborhood begins to desegregate and its Negro residents become eligible under the Pupil Assignment Act to apply for admission to an all-white school, the school is abandoned, moved somewhere else, to suburbia."[30]

To publicize his complaints, Hawkins organized a student boycott of the newly named Irwin Avenue school. When schools opened on the morning of August 30, 1961, picketers greeted the arriving African American students, urging them to return to Northwest Junior High, their previous school. Hawkins marched at the head of the picket line, carrying a sign that read, "Desegregate on a Geographical Basis." The boycott won broad support; approximately five hundred of the eight hundred students assigned to Irwin returned to their old school—Northwest—and attempted to enroll. When they were denied admission to Northwest, a number of the students simply stayed home.[31]

Hawkins attempted to apply further pressure on the school board by threatening to embarrass the city during the upcoming North Carolina World Trade Fair. Charlotte was scheduled to host the trade fair in October 1961, and Hawkins announced plans to use the fair to publicize the city's discriminatory practices. Hawkins told a reporter that he planned to write letters to President John Kennedy and the presidents of Mexico and Finland, each of whom might attend the trade fair, explaining his protest and telling them that all was "not fair in Charlotte." He noted that business leaders had warned him against causing the city "embarrassment" during the trade fair. "But what do they know of embarrassment? We have been embarrassed all our lives."[32]

Confronted with the ugly specter of an ongoing school boycott, the school board chair, David Harris, agreed to meet with Hawkins; at the same time, Brookshire's newly named Mayor's Committee on Community Relations passed a resolution urging an end to the boycott and authorizing the appointment of a permanent subcommittee on education to assist with racial problems in the public schools. In the meantime, the school board announced plans to build a new junior high school that would operate on an integrated basis. Following these actions, Hawkins called off the boycott.[33]

Although the boycott was ostensibly a failure — the transformation of Harding from a white high school to a black junior high was not rescinded — it did have the effect of increasing pressure on the school board to eliminate race-based assignment practices in the Charlotte-Mecklenburg school system and to convert to a system of assignments based on geography. Whereas in 1960, the school board had approved only one request by a black student to transfer to a white school, during the summer of 1961, amid threats by Hawkins to boycott Irwin Avenue, the board granted twenty-six such requests. Moreover, the school board initiated its limited nonracial geographic assignment plan the following summer. Unquestionably, the pressure tactics of Hawkins and his group influenced the school board in reaching that decision.

Yet at the same time, the Irwin Avenue boycott brought to light certain conflicts between the litigation-oriented NAACP and the direct-action stance of Hawkins. When Hawkins first threatened the school boycott in the summer of 1961, NAACP leader Kelly Alexander criticized him, commenting that the black students in question should request transfers and exhaust their administrative remedies as a prelude to litigation.[34] According to Alexander, Hawkins was "steering his own course," which was "not one charted by the NAACP."[35] Hawkins, however, perceived the need to do more than file lawsuits, given the lack of success of previous litigation efforts. "We feel that this matter has gone beyond the courts," Hawkins explained. "The city and state can keep cases like this in the courts for ten years, [and] we haven't got ten years."[36] To be sure, Hawkins would also use litigation and threats of litigation to pursue desegregation goals, as in his successful lawsuit to desegregate the North Carolina Dental Society, but he was far more willing than the local NAACP leadership to use public demonstrations as a supplement to litigation.[37]

These disagreements between Hawkins and Alexander would continue. In 1963, Hawkins's political organization, MOPA, threatened to withhold support for a school bond issue unless the school board adopted a far more ambitious desegregation plan. The NAACP disagreed with Hawkins. Alexander explained, "The need for expanding educational programs and facilities for the total community is so great that the matter of desegregation should not be used to hobble an educational bond issue at this time."[38] Once again, Alexander announced that the NAACP preferred to pursue its desegregation goals through a legal challenge to the school board's assignment system.[39] Hawkins remained a member of the NAACP and performed an active role in much of the organization's litigation efforts of the 1960s, including the challenge to segregated schools, but he retained certain differences with Alexander over appropriate strategy.

As the decade wore on, the NAACP in Charlotte—as happened nationally—came into increasing conflict with other, more aggressive civil rights organizations and leaders. Much of this conflict centered on the NAACP's integrationist agenda and its reliance on a litigation strategy as a means of seeking racial change. Alexander, for example, sharply criticized the separatist goals of the emerging Black Power movement as racist in origin and contrary to the policies of the NAACP.[40]

In the meantime, Hawkins expanded his focus to challenge the city's segregated hospitals. During the 1950s, the only hospital in the city that would serve black patients was Good Samaritan, an inadequate facility that the Episcopal Church had established in the early 1890s.[41] A study in the 1950s by United Community Services concluded that efforts to modernize Good Samaritan would be futile. At the same time, the *Charlotte Observer* ran a series of stories detailing the inadequacies of Good Samaritan. Yet neither Memorial Hospital, the publicly owned facility, nor the privately owned Presbyterian Hospital and Mercy Hospital admitted African American patients.[42]

In response to the complaints about the poor condition of Good Samaritan, the Charlotte Hospital Authority proposed in early 1960 the issuance of $800,000 in bonds to renovate the hospital. The Charlotte Medical Society, an organization of black health care professionals under the leadership of Hawkins, opposed the bond issuance, requesting instead that African Americans be admitted to Memorial Hospital, and threatened litigation if Memorial failed to act.[43] Memorial Hospital appeared divided over the desegregation issue. The director of the city's Hospital Authority, Rush Dickson, claimed that Memorial did not have adequate facilities to handle both white and black patients.[44] The hospital's medical staff, however, opposed efforts to renovate Good Samaritan and urged that Memorial operate on a desegregated basis.[45] Dickson rebuked the staff, noting that it was the hospital board and administrators—not the medical staff—that were charged with responsibility for operating the hospital.[46] Ultimately, however, Memorial agreed to set aside a small percentage of its beds, all located on one floor of the hospital, for black patients.

Subsequently, in 1962, Hawkins increased pressure on Memorial to admit additional black patients by announcing that he would begin public demonstrations outside the hospital unless it fully desegregated its facilities. Memorial agreed to open twenty more beds to African Americans in response to the threatened demonstrations. Hawkins rejected the hospital's effort to prevent demonstrations: "This appeasement by allocation of Negro beds isn't the answer. They don't show good faith by continuing segregation."[47] In March 1962, Hawkins initiated picketing outside of Memorial.[48]

Brookshire, who had moved to the mayor's office in 1961, attacked Hawkins. Brookshire issued a statement in March 1962 that accused Hawkins of destroying the city's good race relations: "These belligerent acts of pressure will result in building resentments and antagonisms. Such acts tend to destroy the good will, so necessary to any progress which this community has been working to establish. For these reasons I regret that the students and their leaders have resorted to coercion, instead of lending their support and cooperation to the community leadership, both white and Negro, which seeks peaceful solutions to these problems through constructive efforts." Brookshire attempted to isolate Hawkins as a radical, claiming that his actions did "not meet with the general approval of the masses or leaders of either race in Charlotte." Hoping to contain the demonstrations, Brookshire attacked Hawkins for taking his grievances to the streets rather than to the Mayor's Community Relations Committee: "Furthermore, these actions are in violation of agreements expressed by the leaders involved, who had previously agreed before witnesses to work through the Mayor's . . . Committee. I am convinced that this strong biracial committee, composed of leaders of both races, can do more in a quiet way that any biased group can do by exploitation and/or public exhibition."[49] Hawkins understood, however, that public demonstrations had a greater chance of compelling change than did negotiation with the Mayor's Committee. Consequently, he refused to back down.

When the demonstrations had little immediate impact, Hawkins undertook additional action to force the full integration of the city's hospitals. First, he filed a lawsuit, with legal assistance from the NAACP, to prevent the expenditure of any additional funds to renovate Good Samaritan.[50] Second, he contacted both Attorney General Robert Kennedy and the Department of Health, Education, and Welfare to complain about discrimination at Memorial in the admission of black patients.[51] Hawkins's complaint triggered a federal investigation of the hospital; the investigators eventually concluded that Memorial did discriminate on the basis of race in its maternity and dental clinics. One year later, in 1963, Memorial agreed to operate on a fully desegregated basis.[52] Hawkins's use of demonstrations, threatened litigation, and federal pressure had again forced racial change in Charlotte.

Hawkins enjoyed his greatest success in forcing the desegregation of Charlotte's public accommodations. These desegregation efforts placed Charlotte in the national spotlight and helped define the city's race relations for the rest of the decade.

Following the sit-ins of 1960, the Johnson C. Smith students engaged in a few sporadic demonstrations in 1961 and 1962 challenging the exclusion of African Americans from local restaurants.[53] Student demonstrations during 1961, for example, succeeded in opening restaurants at two department stores—Belk's and Ivey's.[54] Brookshire had again intervened, helping to persuade the department stores to desegregate in exchange for a promise from the students to bring future racial complaints to the Mayor's Community Relations Committee before resorting to public demonstrations.[55]

During the spring of 1963, civil rights marches protesting discrimination in public accommodations spread throughout the South, including a number of North Carolina cities. No marches were held in Charlotte during the first several months of 1963, but Hawkins announced that he would lead such protests if the city's restaurants and hotels failed to serve African Americans.[56] Charlotte planned to host once again the North Carolina World Trade Fair during April 1963. Recognizing the importance of the trade fair to the city's local economy, Charlotte's civic leaders sought—as they had in 1961—to avoid any controversy that might sully the city's reputation.[57] Moreover, Martin Luther King was scheduled to speak in May at the graduation exercises of the city's black high schools, bringing a national spotlight to the city on issues of race.[58]

Shortly before the opening of the trade fair and in the face of threatened demonstrations by Hawkins, Brookshire's Mayor's Committee announced that several of the city's hotels had agreed to operate on a desegregated basis: "The latest step which we believe the community will accept as both morally and economically sound has been taken by a number of our hotels and motels in the opening of registration for the trade fair on a non-restricted basis."⁵⁹ That announcement thwarted planned demonstrations. Within a few weeks, however, it became clear that the hotels, after the conclusion of the fair, had reneged on their agreement to serve African Americans; Hawkins himself was denied service at the downtown Manger restaurant and hotel.⁶⁰ Shortly thereafter, Hawkins ascertained that only two Charlotte hotels—the Queen Charlotte and the Barringer—would accept black patrons.⁶¹ Accordingly, Hawkins announced that he would lead a new round of public demonstrations. On May 20, a day traditionally celebrated in Charlotte as the anniversary of the signing of the Mecklenburg County Declaration of Independence in 1775, Hawkins made good on his threat, leading a march of about sixty-five persons, most of whom were Smith students, through the downtown area and complaining of the exclusion of black customers from the city's hotels, restaurants, and theaters.⁶² Hawkins promised additional demonstrations.

Mayor Brookshire worried about the effect the threatened demonstrations could have on the city's business climate. Brookshire knew that other southern cities such as Greensboro, Raleigh, and Birmingham were suffering adverse publicity from public demonstrations and that Charlotte must act quickly to avoid a similar fate.⁶³ Consequently, on May 19, Brookshire approached the president of the Charlotte Chamber of Commerce, Ed Burnside, to discuss ways of avoiding a lengthy round of racial demonstrations.

Brookshire's choice of the chamber president as a fellow strategist was no accident. Throughout the 1950s and early 1960s, the Charlotte Chamber of Commerce had functioned as the most powerful institution in the city. During that time period, the chamber led a number of important city reform efforts, including the expansion of the city's limits and the consolidation of the city and county school systems. As part of its activities, the chamber frequently sponsored trips for business leaders to visit other American cities to study ways of resolving community problems such as urban renewal and park development.⁶⁴ Community initiatives that gained chamber support generally succeeded. The chamber also functioned as a keeper of the city's image, facilitating favorable coverage of the city in the national press.⁶⁵

The *Charlotte Observer* repeatedly cited the chamber for its important role in civic affairs. In 1958, the paper noted, "Scratch beneath the surface of any local government program in Charlotte or Mecklenburg these days and you're likely to find a Chamber of Commerce committee lending aid, comfort, and more than a little push."⁶⁶ In a 1960 editorial entitled

"Guess Who's Boss of Our Town," the paper wrote: "Charlotte is run, primarily and well, by its Chamber of Commerce. . . . We are pleased to acknowledge its bossism and to wish it continued health."[67] Columnist Ed Yoder, then of Greensboro, described the chamber's importance in a 1961 column: "The Chamber of Commerce . . . is the mainspring of Charlotte, the clearing house for what is done politically and even culturally."[68] The chamber had performed this role for several decades; in 1933, *Charlotte News* reporter W. J. Cash claimed of Charlotte, "Nowhere else in Dixie . . . is the Chamber of Commerce more an oracle."[69]

The chamber's leaders and the city's political leadership had always been closely linked. From 1935 through 1975, every Charlotte mayor except one had been a chamber member and the president or owner of his own business.[70] The chamber presidency frequently led directly to the mayor's office. From the early 1960s until the late 1970s, every mayor of Charlotte was a former president of the chamber of commerce; every chair of the Mecklenburg County Board of Commissioners during the late 1960s and early 1970s was also a former chamber president.[71] The chamber frequently approached local business leaders and encouraged them to run for office with a promise of financial support; Brookshire, for example, had entered the mayoral race in 1961 at the chamber's behest.[72]

When Mayor Brookshire met with Chamber President Burnside in May 1963, each man understood the damage that racial unrest could inflict on the city's business climate. Investment in new facilities in Arkansas had dramatically dropped following Little Rock's 1957 school desegregation crisis, a fact that was well publicized and widely perceived as due to the negative publicity that flowed from the racial unrest.[73] Both Brookshire and Burnside understood that recent racial conflict in other southern cities—especially in Birmingham—had been costly. Indeed, the *Wall Street Journal* estimated that Birmingham's violent resistance to the freedom riders in 1961 had cost the city more than $40 million in potential new capital.[74] Confronted with racial conflict that threatened the city's strong business climate, the chamber threw its considerable weight into the struggle to forestall demonstrations over segregated public accommodations. The chamber itself had opened its membership the year before to African Americans to avoid public embarrassment on the eve of a visit from Secretary of State Dean Rusk to address the group's annual meeting.[75]

Brookshire proposed to Burnside that the chamber orchestrate an effort to secure an agreement from Charlotte's restaurant, hotel, and theater operators to stop discriminating against African Americans. If the entire business community acted in solidarity, no individual business would suffer from disturbing long-standing racial mores. Burnside agreed and arranged for *Observer* editor C. A. McKnight to draft a resolution recommending that all Charlotte businesses "be opened immediately to all customers without regard to race, creed, or color."[76] In the meantime, McKnight published an editorial encouraging the chamber to adopt a strong nondiscrimination policy and citing the chamber's unique ability to forge "community acceptance of change."[77] Two days after Hawkins's May 20 demonstration, the executive committee of the chamber unanimously approved McKnight's proposed resolution, and the next day, the full chamber board of directors did likewise. In the wake of the announcement of the chamber's actions, Hawkins canceled additional scheduled demonstrations.[78]

The next issue for the chamber was that of compliance with the resolution. One restaurateur, J. W. "Slug" Claiborne, suggested that white business leaders invite black leaders to lunch at certain cooperative restaurants and hotel dining rooms to "break" the color line. The chamber leaders agreed and invited several restaurant and hotel operators to a meeting to solicit their cooperation. Stressing both the economic and the moral reasons for integration—and citing the negative impact of racial unrest in Little Rock and Birmingham—the chamber persuaded several hotel owners to desegregate their restaurants.[79] From May 29 to May 31, several white business leaders went to lunch with black guests at a number of prominent hotel restaurants.[80] By agreement, the local papers did not specify the restaurants involved until after the fact to avoid any possibility of unseemly reactions.[81] To avoid publicity, one restaurant date was changed to a new location to avoid a cameraman from a national television network. By the time the story broke in the local papers, many of the leading restaurants in the city had already desegregated a few days earlier. Shortly thereafter, several hotels and theaters and about one-third of the city's restaurants were desegregated in a similar fashion.[82]

Brookshire sought compliance with the desegregation resolution for the next few months, meeting individually with restaurant owners to win their support.[83] Of particular importance, Brookshire persuaded Frank Sherrill, owner of the popular S & W Cafeteria, to operate his restaurant on a desegregated basis. Many other restaurant operators had waited to see what Sherrill would do before taking action themselves. Finally, in mid-July, Sherrill relented, leading the way for several other restaurants to open their doors on a desegregated basis.[84]

The steps taken by the chamber to ensure that the city's businesses complied with its resolution proved to be important. In Greensboro, for example, the chamber ultimately adopted a similar resolution, but it was not widely followed and the demonstrations continued.[85] In that city, police arrested over fourteen hundred demonstrators between May 11 and June 7, 1963.[86] Charlotte had no arrests. John Parramore of the Greensboro Chamber of Commerce later complained that the demonstrations of May 1963 had crippled efforts to attract new industry to his city.[87]

The efforts of Brookshire and the chamber to move the city forward on the public accommodations issue were facilitated by the fact the city was not plagued by a large contingent of aggressive segregationists eager to preserve the traditional racial order at all costs. Throughout the early 1960s, white resistance groups were largely quiet, although Brookshire did receive threats on his life and had a cross burned in his yard.[88] A Charlotte White Citizens' Council had formed in 1962 in response to earlier demands for public accommodations desegregation but had little effect. Like earlier segregationist groups in Charlotte in the 1950s, no prominent business leaders, professionals, or politicians associated themselves with the Citizens' Council, and the organization was ineffectual during the 1963 desegregation efforts.[89] The *Charlotte Observer*, which criticized the council's efforts to establish in Charlotte, claimed that the organization's views did not square with those of most Charlotteans: "Our people, though opposed to radical, overnight changes, have been recognized throughout the nation for their accommodation to moderate, sensible change."[90]

By contrast, in other southern cities, business leaders helped lead the resistance to integration efforts. In St. Augustine, Florida, for example, a number of leading business leaders joined the John Birch Society and were more committed to maintaining the racial status quo than economic development.[91] St. Augustine successfully resisted the desegregation of its public accommodations until such action was required after the passage of the Civil Rights Act in July 1964. In other southern cities, the business community remained silent on racial issues, allowing segregationists to control the public dialogue.[92]

Those southern cities that desegregated their public accommodations voluntarily before the Civil Rights Act, such as Charlotte and Atlanta, are distinguishable from those that did not in large measure by the posture of the business community and the mayor's office. In both Charlotte and Atlanta, for example, the business community, under the leadership of a moderate probusiness mayor, understood that desegregation would translate into increased economic growth and took the lead in promoting desegregation.[93] In cities of the deeper South that resisted public accommodations desegregation, the felt need to hold the line on segregation outweighed all other concerns. Historian James Cobb, in his 1982 study of the efforts of southerners during the twentieth century to promote their region to outside investors, concluded that southern business leaders, "concern[ed] about a location's image in the eyes of new industrial investors," gave important support to desegregation initiatives in a number of southern cities.[94]

Charlotte thus became one of the first major southern cities to drop discrimination in public accommodations a full year before the passage of the Civil Rights Act of 1964 mandated such action by law. When Martin Luther King arrived in Charlotte in May 1963 to address graduation ceremonies at the city's black high schools, he applauded the city's actions, calling the desegregation developments "significant."[95] The *Charlotte Observer* ran a highly flattering behind-the-scenes story on the desegregation effort: "In Birmingham, hundreds were marching in the streets. Closer to home, protesters sat all day in the mayor's office in Greensboro, and were carried out by police when the time came to close the office for the day. In Raleigh and Durham they marched and they were arrested. In Wilmington, in Fayetteville, in Lexington, they protested. But Charlotte chose a different way."[96]

The media, led by McKnight's *Observer*, gave wide coverage to the chamber's desegregation resolution.[97] Ultimately, positive news stories on the chamber's actions were carried throughout the nation and even the world.[98] Both Radio Free Europe and Voice of America broadcast special segments on the desegregation of Charlotte's public accommodations.[99] In June, Attorney General Robert Kennedy began a correspondence with Brookshire to seek the mayor's help in facilitating similar racial change in other southern cities through the use of biracial community committees; the *Observer* gave significant play to the interchange.[100] Two months later, President John Kennedy, with an implicit reference to Charlotte, urged U.S. mayors to establish biracial committees to resolve community problems.[101] In August, ABC News traveled to Charlotte to analyze the events of that summer as part of a documentary on civil rights; the network took its cameras to a meeting of the Mayor's Community Relations Committee.[102] Brookshire was flooded with requests for information about how Charlotte had handled the desegregation crisis.[103] This widespread publicity brought the city increased convention business and helped attract new industry to the city. Eastern Air Lines, for example, placed a major computerized reservations center in Charlotte within the next year.[104] Presidents of major out-of-state corporations with existing facilities in Charlotte wrote Brookshire to express their support for the city's actions.[105]

Many contemporaries attributed the desegregation of Charlotte's public accommodations to the city leaders' strong moral convictions on racial issues. To be sure, Mayor Brookshire, who played a major role in the desegregation efforts, was disturbed by the moral injustice of racial discrimination in employment, public accommodations, and education. In June 1963, Brookshire questioned the immorality of American race relations in an address to a civic club: "Why should we members of the white race, because we happen to be in the majority, deny the freedoms, rights and opportunities we enjoy to members of minority groups? And yet, the social and economic patterns long accepted in this country do just that."[106] It was an extraordinary statement for a southern white mayor in the early 1960s. Yet Brookshire, influenced by strong religious convictions, had become personally convinced of the immorality of certain aspects of Jim Crow and sought to nudge his city toward greater integration.

Yet the desegregation of Charlotte's public accommodations must be understood in significant measure as due to the business community's perception that extended public demonstrations would harm the city's moderate reputation and thereby subvert efforts to attract new industry to the city. The primary movers in the desegregation activities conceded as much.

Brookshire explained his views in a June 1963 article he was requested to write for the *New York Herald Tribune*: "[As a result of demonstrations,] the community's pocketbook is placed in jeopardy, as Birmingham and other cities have learned from experience. Whether we like it or not, we are pressed by circumstances to choose either resistance or to break with long accepted social and economic patterns. . . . [D]iscrimination based on the color of a man's skin is legally and morally wrong and economically unsound."[107] Time and time again, Brookshire would explain to civic audiences the motives behind the desegregation of the city's public accommodations: "[Charlotte acted] out of social conscience, civic pride and economic considerations."[108] Editor McKnight, who drafted the chamber of commerce desegregation resolution, commented that the moral motivation was present in the desegregation effort but was "not dominant"—the economic realities were more important. Another chamber board member specifically noted that Little Rock had recruited no new industry for a few years following the school integration turmoil in that city during the late 1950s.[109] By contrast, Charlotte had enjoyed an excellent record of recruiting new business; throughout the early 1960s, an average of over sixty new businesses opened each year in the city, employing almost two thousand new workers.[110] A season of racial unrest might damage that record. One chamber board member urged support for the desegregation initiative because it would encourage "new industry . . . [and] expansion of existing industry."[111]

The African American community also perceived the importance of the economic motivations; as one black leader commented at the time: "I would like to say that there were moral motives [for the changes]. I can't. There is some interested Christian leadership. But for most, I think they were looking at this thing in cold turkey, good business sense. Charlotte needs this good image to bring new industry. . . . And Birmingham is in the back of all this."[112] The experience of Birmingham was clearly a critical factor in Charlotte's response to the demand for integrated public accommodations. According to *Charlotte News* editor Perry Morgan, the desegregation of 1963 would not have taken place "without Birmingham." That view was widely shared by the city's leaders.[113]

Many of Charlotte's business leaders probably did not personally favor racial mixing—Brookshire, for example, opposed interracial marriage and social mixing of the races—but for most, the city's economic health was more important than the maintenance of certain racial traditions.[114] *Arkansas Gazette* editor Harry Ashmore's earlier description of the typical southern chamber of commerce had application in Charlotte: "It is not that the bustling gentlemen at the local Chambers of Commerce . . . are particularly concerned with race as a moral problem; on the contrary, they, like most of their fellow Southerners, wish the matter of integration would quietly go away. . . . But they also recognize that sustained racial disorder would be fatal to their effort to lure new industries and new capital."[115] Charlotte social critic Harry Golden was even more biting, noting in 1964 that Charlotte's business leadership "would elect Martin [Luther] King or Malcolm X mayor if somehow one of them could give them a guarantee of no labor unions and no minimum wage for laundry workers."[116]

The desegregation of the city's public accommodations provided an important lesson for the African American community of Charlotte. Accommodation brought good personal relationships, but confrontation brought results. Mayor Brookshire, who was largely responsible for securing the support of Charlotte's business community for desegregation, acknowledged at the time that he would have preferred "peaceful gradualism" on the public accommodations issue but that the pressure tactics of Hawkins had pushed him along faster than he might have wanted to go.[117] Litigation and demonstrations were confrontational and alienated the white power structure — Hawkins was deliberately left off the Mayor's Community Relations Committee because of his actions — but they forced changes in the racial status quo.[118] There is no question that the desegregation of Charlotte's public accommodations would not have happened as soon as it did without the pressure tactics of Hawkins.

In June 1963, a few weeks after the Charlotte Chamber of Commerce issued its desegregation resolution, Hawkins threatened additional demonstrations directed at the denial of hospital privileges to African American physicians at Memorial Hospital. He urged the city's black doctors to boycott Good Samaritan to protest their exclusion from Memorial and threatened to seek assistance from the Kennedy administration to halt construction of a new addition at Memorial if the hospital persisted in its discriminatory practices.[119]

Hawkins's threat infuriated Brookshire, who immediately sent a telegram of protest to Hawkins. Brookshire announced that he would hold Hawkins responsible for any ill effect that might flow from such action and charged that Hawkins had defaulted on his promise to bring all racial complaints to the Mayor's Committee.[120] Once again, however, the threatened protest worked. Within days, hospital privileges were extended to black physicians.[121]

In the meantime, Hawkins filed yet another complaint with the federal government, stating that some black patients had been denied admission to Memorial because of their race. Investigators from the U.S. Public Health Service concluded that Memorial was indeed discriminating against black patients, in violation of federal law. Subsequently, in August 1963, Memorial pledged to open "all hospital services to Negroes on the same basis as for whites."[122] Two years later, the NAACP complained to the federal government that two private Charlotte hospitals that received federal aid — Mercy and Presbyterian — discriminated on the basis of race. In May 1965, the Public Health Service announced that both hospitals would cease to receive federal aid because of their discriminatory practices. Eventually, the hospitals agreed to operate on a nondiscriminatory basis.[123]

Finally, in 1964, Hawkins used a combination of public demonstrations and litigation to desegregate the downtown YMCA. Although the YMCA had begun operating its cafeteria and meeting rooms on a nondiscriminatory basis in response to the 1960 sit-ins, it continued to exclude African Americans from membership. In May 1964, Hawkins initiated demonstrations at the facility, challenging its exclusionary policies; the organization's general secretary criticized the picketing, claiming that it would only hurt black interests.[124] Three months later Hawkins, with NAACP legal representation, filed suit pursuant to the newly enacted federal Civil Rights Act.[125] One month later, the YMCA board caved in and enacted a resolution providing for the complete desegregation of the facility.[126] The litigation had proved decisive.

In time, Hawkins faced his own legal troubles. In 1964, a local prosecutor indicted Hawkins for alleged fraud in connection with Hawkins's efforts to register new black voters.[127] After four years of legal wrangling, superior court judge Pou Bailey dismissed the charges, claiming that the state's evidence did not support the claim of fraud.[128] Nevertheless, the extensive publicity given the allegations damaged Hawkins's standing in the community. In 1967, the North Carolina Board of Dental Examiners charged Hawkins with malpractice in connection with dental services provided as part of a Head Start program administered by the Charlotte-Mecklenburg School Board.[129] Hawkins charged that he could not get a fair hearing before the dental board because of his long and bitter and eventually successful struggle to force the desegregation of the North Carolina Dental Society.[130] The board rejected that claim and concluded that Hawkins had rendered inadequate dental care. The North Carolina courts eventually upheld the board's decision to suspend Hawkins's dental license for one year.[131] Despite these legal troubles, Hawkins was the most effective African American leader pressing for greater racial desegregation in Charlotte in the early 1960s.

In the late 1950s and early 1960s, Charlotte earned a national reputation as one of the most racially progressive southern cities. In 1957, the Charlotte School Board had been one of the first school boards in the South to admit a handful of black students to white schools and, in 1962, one of the first to assign students to schools on the basis of geography rather than race. Moreover, the city's restaurants and hotels were some of the first in the South to serve black patrons, one year before Congress required such action with the Civil Rights Act of 1964.

This early desegregation was largely due to the willingness of the African American community to use public demonstrations to apply pressure on the white establishment. Public demonstrations threatened to disturb the city's carefully nurtured image of racial moderation and to expose the city to unfavorable publicity, the cost of which Little Rock and

Birmingham had made all too clear. Charlotte's white business community, intimately linked with the city's power structure, understood the economic necessity of avoiding racial conflict even though this meant initiating token integration, an understanding that business leaders in many other southern cities lacked. Although much of the city's white leadership probably did not personally favor racial mixing, hesitations about desegregation were trumped by the desire to retain the city's favorable business climate.

The handful of black students attending Charlotte's white schools in the early 1960s did not constitute significant desegregation, but their arrival came early and without court order and helped establish the city's image as a different kind of southern city. Likewise, the desegregation of the city's restaurants did not mean that blacks and whites would now socialize together, but it did signify to the country, on the eve of a visit by Martin Luther King, that Charlotte was a city willing to adapt to changing racial mores. Charlotte would ultimately be tested far more severely in the late 1960s and early 1970s on the school busing issue. But patterns of leadership established during the first decade after *Brown* would help the city survive the far more tumultuous second decade.

We believe that an integrated school will best prepare young people for responsibility in an integrated society. Having lived practically all of his life in India, [our son] James has never known the meaning of racial segregation. We have been happy to watch him grow and develop with an unaffected openness to people of all races and backgrounds and we feel it our duty as parents to insure that this healthy development continue.

— Reverend Darius Swann, letter to Charlotte-Mecklenburg Board of Education, September 2, 1964

CHAPTER 5
The Beginnings of the *Swann* Litigation

During the first ten years after the Supreme Court's *Brown* decision, few southern school districts admitted African American schoolchildren to white schools, even in "moderate" North Carolina. By the early 1960s, however, federal courts in North Carolina and in other parts of the South began to strike down race-based pupil assignment schemes and to require the creation of race-neutral assignment plans.[1] In response, many southern school districts established pupil assignment plans ostensibly based on "freedom of choice"; a smaller number of districts, such as Charlotte-Mecklenburg, established pupil assignment systems based at least in part on residence through the creation of geographic attendance zones. In a city as residentially segregated as Charlotte, however, the use of geographic attendance zones left most students in single-race schools. Although the first judicial challenge to school segregation in Charlotte — initiated in 1959 — had met with failure, a small group of parents returned to federal court to try again in 1965. This time the results would be strikingly different. Within a few years, this little band of parents had captured the nation's attention and helped revolutionize the meaning of *Brown* for America's cities.

When schools opened in Charlotte in August 1964, only about 3 percent of the more than twenty thousand African American children in the school system were assigned to a majority-white school.[2] The school board still assigned about half of the African American students to schools on a racial basis, and most of the rest — assigned to schools on the basis of geography — attended single-race schools because of the city's extensive residential segregation.

In addition to this high degree of racial separation, many of the school system's black schools — particularly the twelve-grade "union" schools — were noticeably inferior to their white counterparts. Torrence Lytle School, for example, a rural union school in northern Mecklenburg County, had twice as many students as the school was designed to hold, requiring the use of the gym, cafeteria, and school auditorium as classrooms.[3] Similarly, Second Ward High School, located in the inner city, was, according to a grand jury report, "old and in need of repairs" in addition to being overcrowded.[4]

Dissatisfied with the desegregation efforts of the school board, on December 9, 1964, over 130 black parents petitioned the Charlotte-Mecklenburg School Board to "cease operating the public schools . . . on a racial basis."[5] In response, the board announced plans to close certain grades at some of the all-black union schools and to allow those students to transfer to a white school.[6] The board's proposal did not mollify the parents. One month later, Julius L. Chambers, a young black attorney, filed suit on behalf of ten sets of parents challenging the school board's pupil assignment plan.[7]

Chambers was a new arrival to Charlotte, having just graduated from the University of North Carolina Law School in 1962. Though only twenty-nine years old at the time, over the course of the next decade Chambers would establish himself as the preeminent civil rights lawyer in the South. Chambers had grown up in the town of Mount Gilead, east of Charlotte, where his father owned and operated an auto repair shop. Chambers's parents instilled in their children from an early age an appreciation for the importance of education. The message took root; all of the Chambers children eventually attended both college and graduate school. Yet the schools of Chambers's childhood were thoroughly segregated and inferior to their white counterparts. His elementary school had no indoor plumbing; his high school had no library.[8]

Chambers attended the North Carolina College for Negroes in Durham, where he graduated summa cum laude, was president of both the student government and his fraternity, and was named the college's most outstanding student.[9] Chambers went on to earn a master's degree in European history at the University of Michigan and entered law school in 1959 at the University of North Carolina, which only eight years earlier had admitted its first African American student, having been ordered to do so by a federal court.[10] While in law school, Chambers compiled an extraordinary record, earning the top rank in his class and becoming the first African American to serve as editor-in-chief of the *North Carolina Law Review* — a feat widely noted in the state press.[11] Chambers also became the first African American to win membership in the Order of the Golden Fleece, the highest honorary society at the university.[12] Yet these academic achievements did not remove the indignities of segregation; during his time in Chapel Hill, Chambers was excluded from a school-sponsored dance because of his race.[13]

After his 1962 graduation from law school and a postgraduate year at Columbia Law School, Chambers joined the legal staff of the NAACP Legal Defense Fund in New York City, handling race discrimination cases. After one year in New York, Chambers moved to Charlotte to open a civil rights law practice, working in close cooperation with the Legal Defense Fund's New York lawyers.[14] From the beginning, Chambers demonstrated an extraordinary capacity for work: during his first year in Charlotte, he filed thirty-four school desegregation lawsuits, ten public accommodations lawsuits, ten suits challenging discrimination by public hospitals, and several other lawsuits seeking to save the jobs of black teachers faced with dismissal.[15] Yet Chambers also discovered in his first year that many white southerners deeply resented his efforts to challenge the racial status quo; while Chambers delivered a speech in the coastal city of New Bern, North Carolina, his car was destroyed by a bomb.[16] It would not be Chambers's last experience with violence.

A few years later, Chambers was joined by Adam Stein, a white lawyer from Washington, D.C. The establishment of the law firm of Chambers and Stein, which enjoyed the financial backing of a New York foundation committed to the establishment of integrated southern law firms, marked the first time in the history of North Carolina and one of the first times in the history of the South that a black and a white lawyer had joined forces.[17] Over the course of the next decade, the Chambers law firm would handle hundreds of civil rights cases in North Carolina for the NAACP Legal Defense Fund. In 1984, Chambers returned to New York to head the NAACP Legal Defense Fund, where he remained until 1993 when he became chancellor of his alma mater, now known as North Carolina Central University.

Within months of Chambers's arrival in Charlotte, a large group of black parents, with the assistance of State NAACP President Kelly Alexander, had approached him to represent them in the Charlotte-Mecklenburg school case.[18] Darius and Vera Swann agreed to serve as lead plaintiffs in the litigation. The Swanns, both Smith graduates and

Civil rights attorney Julius Chambers, 1981. (Courtesy of the *Charlotte Observer*)

college classmates with Reginald Hawkins, had spent much of their adult life as missionaries for the United Presbyterian Church. Darius Swann — the first African American Presbyterian missionary ever assigned outside of Africa — had initially served in China, arriving shortly after the Communist revolution. Thereafter, the Swanns had spent eleven years in India, from which they had only recently returned for a sabbatical.[19] Ironically, while in India, the Swanns had seen a photograph of Dorothy Counts in a foreign newspaper that showed her being harassed during her brief stint at Charlotte's Harding High School in 1957.[20] It was a poignant moment for the Swanns. Dorothy's father, Herman, had taught the Swanns at Johnson C. Smith and had pastored Darius's childhood church in Amelia County, Virginia. Dorothy had been a flower girl in the Swanns' wedding.[21]

The Swanns returned to Charlotte from the mission field in 1964 so that Darius could join the faculty of Johnson C. Smith University. During their three-year stay in Charlotte, the Swanns were actively involved in an array of civil rights issues. Darius helped coordinate a voter-registration effort in rural eastern North Carolina while Vera organized black domestic workers in public housing projects in Charlotte.[22] In 1967 the Swanns left Charlotte for New York and then Hawaii to pursue further graduate study. Although the Charlotte school desegregation case would forever bear their name, the Swanns never returned to Charlotte to live.[23]

The Swann family had a personal complaint with the Charlotte-Mecklenburg School Board. At the beginning of the 1964–65 school year, the Swanns had enrolled their son James in Seversville Elementary, which was both integrated and closest to their home. At the end of the first day, however, the Swanns were notified that James must attend Biddleville Elementary, an all-black school.[24] Vera Swann, accompanied by Reginald Hawkins, met personally with School Superintendent Craig Phillips to request that James be allowed to return to Seversville, explaining that James had grown accustomed to a desegregated environment while living in India.[25] Subsequently, Darius Swann made the same request to the school board. The board rebuffed the Swanns, however, who in turn refused to file a formal transfer request as required by the Pearsall Plan, dismissing the transfer system as "evil."[26] Instead, they asked Chambers to file suit against the school board. Both Swanns well understood the importance of litigation in the struggle for racial equality.[27]

A few months later, the North Carolina Teachers Association, the state's black teacher organization, entered the litigation to challenge the school board's assignment of teachers on a racial basis.[28] At that time, only 3 of the system's 109 schools had integrated faculties due to an "implicit policy" of the school board to assign teachers to teach children of their own race.[29] The association's decision to join the litigation was significant because one month earlier, the U.S. Court of Appeals for the Fourth Circuit had limited the ability of schoolchildren to challenge racially discriminatory assignment of teachers unless they could show that being taught by teachers of their same race caused them injury.[30]

The entry of the African American teachers into the litigation was not a foregone conclusion. African American educators had historically been divided about the wisdom of desegregation. During the pre-*Brown* era, some of the strongest black opposition to integration had come from educators such as James Shepard of the North Carolina College for Negroes in Durham. After *Brown*, many black teachers had opposed desegregation on the grounds that they might lose their jobs in the process.[31] Teachers' fears of job loss were not groundless. Shortly after the *Brown* decision, all but three of the North Carolina school superintendents predicted that they would find it "impractical" to use African American teachers in desegregated schools.[32] Those predictions proved prescient; during the first decade after *Brown*, many African American teachers in North Carolina lost their jobs as all-black schools were closed and the teachers were not reassigned.[33] Jack Greenberg, director of the NAACP Legal Defense Fund in New York, complained in 1965 that school boards throughout the South, including in North Carolina, were threatening to dismiss African American teachers to secure their support for the retention of segregated schools.[34]

The North Carolina Teachers Association filed forty-six lawsuits in 1964 and 1965 alone—many with Chambers's assistance—on behalf of African American teachers who were dismissed in the wake of school closures and desegregation.[35] The *Charlotte Observer* estimated that another 182 black teachers would lose their jobs during the 1965–66 school year in Charlotte due to the closure of black schools.[36] Black principals were vulnerable to job loss as well; almost a quarter of the black principals in Charlotte would be dismissed following the 1965–66 school year while the number of white principals increased.[37] Notwithstanding these concerns about job loss, the organization decided to join the Charlotte litigation.[38]

The plaintiffs' lawsuit complained of the continuation of race-based pupil assignments for half of the system's black students, the configuration of school attendance lines gerrymandered to minimize integration, the allowance of pupil transfers away from desegregated schools, and the assignment of teachers on a racial basis. The school board answered by denying the allegations and by stating that the board was currently devising a new assignment plan that would resolve many of the concerns articulated by the plaintiffs.[39]

Yet the school board was confronted by more than just the NAACP-backed litigation. In July 1964, Congress had passed the most sweeping civil rights legislation in the nation's history—the Civil Rights Act of 1964—which prohibited racial discrimination in a broad range of activities. For purposes of school desegregation, the most important section of the act was Title VI, which banned racial discrimination in any public or private entity that received federal funding.[40] The statute required every federal agency that administered a program involving the dispensation of federal funds to issue regulations stipulating that the recipient of those funds did not discriminate on the basis of race.[41] When Congress enacted the Elementary and Secondary Education Act in April 1965, providing over $1 billion of federal aid to elementary and secondary schools throughout the country, Title VI assumed enormous importance because the ability of southern school districts to receive federal funding depended on the nondiscriminatory operation of their schools.[42]

In early January 1965, the U.S. Office of Education of the Department of Health, Education, and Welfare (HEW) released a preliminary version of its awaited set of guidelines, defining for school officials minimum desegregation standards; these guidelines were formally released three months later. The 1965 guidelines required all school districts with a history of school segregation to formulate a voluntary desegregation plan if they were not already subject to a court-ordered plan. The guidelines made clear that dual attendance zones with the right to request a transfer—which were still in place in much of the South—would not satisfy the new administrative standards. If a school board failed to comply, it could lose its federal funding.[43]

With the passage of Title VI and its fund cutoff provision, the courts were no longer the primary enforcer of the school desegregation requirements of *Brown*. The White House report accompanying the Civil Rights Act of 1964 underscored this point: "It was the Congressional purpose, in Title VI of the Civil Rights Act of 1964, to remove school desegregation efforts from the courts, where they had been bogged down for more than a decade."[44]

Within a few weeks of the filing of the complaint in the *Swann* case, the North Carolina Attorney General's Office announced that Title VI required "total and complete desegregation of the public schools," a statement described by the *Charlotte Observer* as the "broadest interpretation of federal laws on segregation ever issued by the attorney general's office in North Carolina."[45] Subsequently, the North Carolina attorney general announced that to comply with Title VI, all North Carolina school systems would have to submit either a proposed voluntary desegregation plan or a statement indicating that the school system had already desegregated its schools. In February, the State Board of Education signed a compliance statement indicating that the state board would work with HEW to secure the necessary compliance statements from local boards of education.[46]

Confronted with pressure from both the Office of Education and the plaintiffs, the Charlotte-Mecklenburg School Board began work on a new pupil assignment plan that would ensure greater desegregation. School Board Chair David Harris dismissed the lawsuit as a "waste of time," claiming that the board and the plaintiffs both desired the same thing and that it was just a "matter of scheduling." In February, under pressure from HEW and the plaintiffs, the board abandoned plans to enlarge an existing black high school in the southwestern part of the county in favor of a new high school — Olympic High School — that would serve that section of the county on a nonracial basis.[47] In March, the school board unveiled its new pupil assignment plan, to take effect the following school year. The plan established nonracial geographic attendance zones for 99 of the system's 109 schools. The other ten schools, however, would continue to educate only African American students and would not be included in the general geographic attendance plan.[48] The board justified the exclusion of the ten black schools from the 1965–66 assignment plan on the grounds that it planned to replace most of these schools with newly constructed ones within the next two years. The board noted that these students would be required to move to a new school when the anticipated school construction was complete and that multiple reassignments would be disruptive to their education.[49] The board pledged to include every school in the geographic assignment plan by the 1967–68 school year.[50] The plan also gave every student the right to transfer to another school pending available space.[51] The plan was silent on the board's long-standing practice of assigning teachers on a racial basis, although one month later the board agreed to the "ultimate" desegregation of teachers.[52]

The exclusion of the ten black schools from the overall attendance plan troubled the plaintiffs, since this meant that about 25 percent of the African American schoolchildren in Charlotte-Mecklenburg would continue to receive school assignments on an explicit racial basis. Several of the ten schools were in residentially desegregated rural areas in the county and hence would have operated as integrated schools had they been included in the general geographic attendance scheme.[53] Many of the students assigned to these schools were required to ride a school bus as far as ten miles, across several white attendance zones, to attend an inferior single-race school.[54]

The plaintiff group also opposed certain aspects of the transfer provision of the school board's plan. Although black students assigned to all-black schools were free to request a transfer to a white school, bus transportation was not provided to students who chose not to attend their regularly assigned school, making such a transfer impractical for many students.[55] Moreover, the transfer provision allowing white students assigned to a desegregated school to return to an all-white school meant that schools desegregated by the geographic attendance plan could revert to single-race schools as a result of pupil transfers. Indeed, thirteen schools that were scheduled for desegregation during the 1965–66 school year on the basis of initial assignments reverted to a single-race status when all of the white students assigned to those schools exercised their transfer rights.[56] Finally, the plaintiffs charged that several of the attendance zones had been gerrymandered with the deliberate intent of minimizing pupil mixing and that teachers were still assigned on the basis of their race.

Although the plan did not eliminate all racially based school assignments, it did mark a significant change from the school board's previous pupil assignment plan. During the prior school year, almost half of the system's black students had received school assignments based on their race. Under the new plan, only about a quarter of the system's black students would be assigned to schools on a racial basis, with a promise to eliminate all racial assignments within two years. The Office of Education guidelines and the litigation had prompted the board to undertake a significant revision of its traditional reliance on race-based pupil assignments.

Federal district court judge Braxton Craven heard the case in July 1965. Craven, who had been appointed to the federal bench in 1961 by President John F. Kennedy, was not new to the question of desegregation. In a widely publicized speech five years earlier Craven, while a state judge, had urged the state's school districts to undertake "token integration" as a means of forestalling "total integration" under the direction of the courts.[57] Now Craven would determine whether the degree of desegregation undertaken by the Charlotte-Mecklenburg School Board was constitutionally sufficient.

Craven held two days of hearings; on the third day, he issued his decision. Craven made it clear at the outset that the school board had no obligation to devise school attendance zones for the purpose of maximizing integration: "It is undoubtedly true that one could deliberately sit down with the purpose in mind to change [school attendance] lines in order to increase mixing of the races and accomplish the same with some degree of success. I know of no such duty upon either the School Board or the District Court."[58]

Regarding the issue of whether the school board had gerrymandered school attendance lines for the purpose of minimizing integration, Craven articulated a deferential level of review: "The question before the District Court is *not* whether a 'better' zone might be established but simply whether the zone which was established is an arbitrary and unreasonable one based on race."[59] There were two ways in which the plaintiffs could show unlawful gerrymandering: first, participants in the line-drawing process could testify that race had been considered when the attendance zones had been created in closed-door meetings; or second, the court could infer, from the configuration of attendance zones, that race must have been considered in certain instances. The first method was unavailing; no witness would testify that the attendance zones had been drawn in such a way as to minimize desegregation.[60] This left it to the plaintiffs to prove, by inference, that race had been a factor in the drawing of attendance lines.

The best case for inferring that attendance zones had been created with the purpose of minimizing desegregation was the Billingsville Elementary School attendance zone. Billingsville School was located in Grier Heights, a small black subdivision tucked into white southeast Charlotte. Grier Heights was something of an anomaly; it was a black neighborhood in an otherwise almost completely white section of the city, and it adjoined one of Charlotte's highest-income white neighborhoods, Eastover. The school board's attendance lines had placed all of Grier Heights in the Billingsville school district; none of the surrounding white neighborhoods were placed in that district. Although Craven could easily have inferred racial intent in the drawing of the Billingsville school district, he refused to do so, noting that the district lines followed certain natural boundaries.

Craven's refusal to find a constitutional violation on the gerrymandering claim was undoubtedly motivated in part by the difficulty of framing a remedy had he found otherwise. Craven noted the difficult remedial task he would have confronted had he found a constitutional violation: "[The plaintiffs' expert] was commendably candid in stating that he had not spent enough time to be able to recommend generally a new and better zoning pattern. If [the plaintiffs' expert], competent and experienced in the field of education, does not feel able to intelligently alter the general zoning pattern, it seems unlikely to me that a District Judge could intelligently do so based upon information made available to him in only a day and a half [of testimony]."[61]

The most controversial part of Craven's opinion pertained to the ten black schools that the school board had excluded from the school attendance zones. This aspect of the plan appeared clearly unconstitutional. At least twice within the prior four months, the U.S. Court of Appeals for the Fourth Circuit had expressly found the continued use of race-based pupil assignments to be unlawful.[62] Craven, however, credited the school board's promises that these students would be assigned to schools on a nonracial basis within two years when new schools were built. The judge in effect concluded that the school board would eventually afford these students their constitutional right to a nonracial school assignment; a delay of one or two years was not unreasonable. Left unaddressed was the general unwillingness of courts to delay the vindication of constitutional rights on grounds of administrative expediency.

Regarding the assignment of teachers, Craven approved the school board's resolution to provide for such desegregation, except that he ordered the board to change its use of the phrase "ultimate desegregation" of teachers to "immediate desegregation." Craven did not define the word "immediate" but did note, "Assignment of teachers may be expected to follow the racial pattern established in the schools."[63]

Craven was clearly eager to find the board's assignment plan constitutional. Had he done otherwise, he would have been forced to supervise the board's assignment activities, a task he obviously wanted to avoid. Craven showed his reluctance to interfere with the school board's determinations of pupil assignments: "This is another school case. Our adversary system of justice is not well-adapted for the disposition of such controversies. . . . Administrators, especially if they have some competence and experience in school administration, can more likely work out with School Superintendents the problems of pupil and teacher assignment in the best interests of all concerned better than can any District Judge operating within the adversary system."[64]

The plaintiffs appealed Craven's decision and sought an injunction pending appeal on the issue of the ten black schools; that request was denied.[65] On appeal, the case received *en banc* consideration by the U.S. Court of Appeals for the Fourth Circuit. Regarding the gerrymandering claim, the plaintiffs argued that the school board should have been *required* to draw the school attendance lines "with the conscious purpose of eliminating as many [one-race] schools as possible and of achieving a maximum intermixture of the races," a proposition that Craven had expressly rejected.[66] It was a bold claim and one that had not yet won judicial acceptance. To be sure, a few federal judges had suggested that in certain circumstances school boards should be required to do more than merely establish a racially neutral assignment plan, although those comments had come in "freedom of choice" cases in which there were serious questions about whether black students were truly "free" to choose a white school.[67] But the plaintiffs were asking for a constitutional requirement that school boards manipulate geographic attendance zones in order to maximize desegregation.

Chief Judge Clement Haynsworth, writing for the court, rejected that view and reaffirmed the notion that school boards were required only to make assignments on a nonracial basis and had no affirmative duty to try to maximize desegregation: "Whatever the Board may do in response to its own initiative or that of the community, we have held that there is no constitutional requirement that it act with the conscious purpose of achieving the maximum mixture of races in the school population. . . . So long as the boundaries are not drawn for the purpose of maintaining racial segregation, the School Board is under no constitutional requirement that it effectively and completely counteract all of the effects of segregated housing patterns."[68]

Regarding the exclusion of the ten black schools from the geographic attendance zones, the court recognized that school assignments based on race were unconstitutional but concluded that given the short-term nature of the problem, the school board's plan was acceptable, particularly since the black students in these ten schools presumably could request a transfer to a white school if they so desired.[69]

Judges Simon Sobeloff and Spencer Bell joined the court's decision but, as they frequently did in school desegregation cases, wrote a separate concurring opinion. In this opinion, Sobeloff and Bell suggested that school boards possessed a greater responsibility for achieving desegregation than the mere creation of a race-neutral attendance plan. Quoting from an earlier opinion, Sobeloff and Bell noted, "It is now 1965 and high time for . . . administrators of schools to proceed actively with *their* nontransferable duty to undo the segregation which both by action and inaction has been persistently perpetuated."[70] The idea that school boards possessed an affirmative responsibility to undo the effects of past segregation had not yet captured a majority of votes on the Fourth Circuit, but it signaled the direction in which the courts would move over the course of the next two years. The plaintiffs decided not to appeal the case to the U.S. Supreme Court, fearing that the Court would affirm, giving greater weight to the decision of the court of appeals.[71]

The crowning irony of the plaintiffs' effort to challenge the constitutionality of the Charlotte-Mecklenburg School Board's assignment plan was that it prevented the Office of Education from using its considerable influence to require a more favorable plan. When the school board had submitted its March 1965 pupil assignment plan for approval, the Office of Education had indicated that it might disapprove the plan and initiate a funding cut because of the race-based assignment of pupils to the ten black schools and what appeared to be racially gerrymandered attendance zones. Indeed, in June, the Office of Education had notified the board that the plan was "not acceptable at this time." But when Judge Craven approved the board's plan on July 14, the Office of Education was obliged by its own guidelines to defer to the court's decision and hence in August 1965 approved the board's plan. That approval cleared the way for the Charlotte-Mecklenburg Board of Education to receive over $2 million in federal funds, a fourfold increase from the prior year.[72]

Moreover, when the 1966 Office of Education guidelines imposed even tougher desegregation obligations on school districts, the Charlotte-Mecklenburg school system was immune from administrative challenge because the new guidelines exempted units whose desegregation plans had been approved by a court.[73] The same applied to a 1968 HEW policy statement that required a school system to adopt an assignment plan that best promoted "elimination of its dual school structure."[74] The litigation strategy of the NAACP had unwittingly insulated the Charlotte-Mecklenburg school system from further administrative or judicial challenge. For almost three decades the federal courts had been the chief ally of the NAACP in its attack on segregated education; now the organization's reliance on the courts had prevented the executive branch from forcing further desegregation of the Charlotte schools.

Pursuant to the school board's new plan, the Charlotte-Mecklenburg schools opened the 1965–66 school year with approximately 10 percent, or 1,950, of the system's 20,341 black students attending majority-white schools, a threefold increase from the year before.[75] Moreover, pursuant to a school board decision in mid-August, a few teachers spent the new school year teaching in schools attended only by students of the opposite race.[76] Shortly before the opening of the schools, Governor Dan Moore announced that all disruptions in the newly desegregated schools would be promptly quelled, by the National Guard if necessary.[77] No such response was necessary; the Charlotte schools opened in the fall of 1965 without incident.[78]

But racial violence would come to Charlotte a few months later. In the early morning hours of November 22, 1965, the homes of four of the city's most prominent black leaders—NAACP attorney Chambers, State NAACP President Kelly Alexander, Kelly's brother and city council member Frederick Alexander, and community activist Reginald Hawkins—were bombed under the cover of darkness.[79] Although miraculously no one was hurt, the four homes suffered substantial damage.

The bombings received national news coverage, with articles appearing in newspapers in New York, Washington, Baltimore, Philadelphia, and Chicago and with segments airing on the television network news reports.[80] The *New York Times* appropriately noted that the bombings "shattered the pride of this racially progressive city."[81] The *Charlotte Observer* lamented the national publicity:

> In the eight years since Dorothy Counts was spat on as she entered old Harding High School, Charlotte has slowly built a national reputation as an enlightened and tolerant city.
>
> How badly that reputation was damaged by Monday morning's bombings may never be fully known.
>
> But the city is reaping an ugly harvest of national publicity certain to tarnish the image so painstakingly cultivated in the years since the internationally publicized ordeal of Dorothy Counts.[82]

The paper's editors worried about the effect the bombings might have on the city's continued prosperity, expressing deep concern about "the possible economic repercussions, about how the headlines might influence those [with] plans to build and money to spend in North Carolina." Proud of the city's progressive image on racial matters, the *Observer* noted that the *New York Times*, in its report, had called Charlotte "a leader among Southern cities in racial desegregation" and that the *Washington Post* had written that North Carolina, and especially Charlotte, were "regarded as superior to many parts of the South in respect for civil rights."[83] The paper, with no support for the claim but eager to defend the city's reputation, suggested that the bombings had been the work of people from outside the community and that Charlotte had "been victimized."[84]

The city responded to the bombings with an outpouring of regret. The *Observer* offered a reward for information leading to the arrest and conviction of the bombers. More than 150 carpenters, masons, bricklayers—more than could be accommodated—volunteered to repair the damage to the four homes. A relief fund organized by Mayor Stanford Brookshire raised more money than was needed to repair the damage.[85] Six days later, twenty-five hundred citizens, both black and white, gathered at the city's Ovens Auditorium to protest the bombings and to hear speeches by a whole array of civic and political leaders, including NAACP Executive Director Roy Wilkins.[86] The *Observer*, in its lead editorial two days before the meeting, exhorted the entire community to attend and noted, "The good name of North Carolina is at stake in this outbreak of lawlessness."[87] Mayor Brookshire called on the people of Charlotte to attend the rally: "Tell the world that Charlotte will not be deterred in its efforts to promote racial harmony and community progress through the fullest possible development of responsible citizenship."[88]

The city's churches joined in the rush to support the bombing victims. About two weeks later, more than one hundred clergy of various denominations—Protestant, Catholic, and Jewish, both black and white—held a worship service across the street from the two damaged homes of the Alexander brothers. The local Christian Ministers Association formed a committee, under the direction of Thomas Blair, rector of the prominent white Christ Episcopal Church, to deal with racial injustice and prejudice.[89] Once again, Charlotte showed itself to be a city eager to protect its image from charges of racism. Memories of the extensive and unfavorable publicity surrounding Dorothy Counts's attempt to integrate Harding High School in 1957 were fresh in the minds of white civic leaders.

The perpetrators were never identified, and hence it was never learned what specifically motivated the violence. Yet the choice of the four victims was not surprising. Chambers, Kelly Alexander, and Hawkins were the three most outspoken black leaders in Charlotte; Fred Alexander was the only elected black official in the city. In early November, the county police chief had told a newspaper reporter that Klan membership in Charlotte seemed to be on the increase.[90] Moreover, just ten days before the bombings, Chambers, with the vocal support of Kelly Alexander and Hawkins, had initiated another desegregation lawsuit that touched a different set of regional passions: football. This lawsuit sought to integrate the Shrine

At a November 28, 1965, rally expressing outrage over the bombings of the homes of four black Charlotteans. Left to right: Roy Wilkins, executive director of the NAACP; Stanford Brookshire, mayor of Charlotte; and Kelly Alexander, president of the North Carolina chapter of the NAACP. (Courtesy of the *Charlotte Observer*)

Bowl, an annual high school football all-star game that was held in Charlotte and that pitted the best high school players from North and South Carolina.[91]

No African American had ever been selected to play in the Shrine Bowl. This racial policy had denied a spot to Charlottean Jimmie Kirkpatrick, described by a local sportswriter as perhaps the finest running back in North Carolina and possibly the best player in the history of Charlotte high school football.[92] Kirkpatrick's exclusion had prompted the litigation. Two days before the bombings, Judge Craven had permitted the 1965 game to go forward as scheduled—denying Kirkpatrick an opportunity to play—but had announced that the sponsors of the game had agreed in the future to allow black players into the game.[93] At least one observer, Charlotte author and social critic Harry Golden, concluded that the Shrine Bowl lawsuit had triggered the bombings. Golden, who had received anonymous threats himself following his outspoken support for the Shrine Bowl desegregation effort, facetiously wrote a friend one week after the bombings, "I sent word by my operative in the local Klan that before each meal I . . . say three times: I love Football, I love Football, I love Football."[94] Chambers agreed that the Shrine Bowl litigation had probably triggered the bombings.[95]

Charlotte would survive the November bombings with its progressive image largely intact, but the incident energized the black community to take more forceful steps to challenge various aspects of racial discrimination in the city. Although no demonstrations, marches, or public disorders followed the bombings, a few weeks later six black ministers, including Swann and Hawkins, organized the Ad Hoc Committee of Concerned Citizens, which called for an end to all discrimination against blacks in Charlotte, including discrimination in pupil assignments.[96] The committee held a number of meetings during December 1965, protesting economic, social, and political conditions in the black community in Charlotte.[97]

The committee complained that the city's outpouring of regret in the wake of the bombings was primarily motivated by a desire to maintain its national image, not a desire for true racial progress.[98] In truth, the city's response was driven by a convergence of factors: genuine outrage at the midnight violence and an intense desire to preserve the city's carefully cultivated reputation for racial moderation. One of the committee's demands was immediately met; on December 14, Charlotte School Superintendent Craig Phillips announced that white and black high schools would compete with one another in sports for the first time, beginning with the 1966–67 school year.[99]

Over the course of the next three years, the number of black students attending desegregated schools in Charlotte steadily increased as the school board in April 1966 finally eliminated all race-based pupil assignments. Several white residents pressured the board to delay the end to all racial assignments, but the board, with only one dissent, declined. The possibility of judicial intervention weighed heavily in the minds of the board members. The school board attorney Brock Barkley advised the board that the odds were against the court allowing the board an extra year to eliminate racial assignments.[100]

The school board eliminated racial assignments by closing seven all-black schools and spending $10 million on new schools.[101] Much of the African American community reacted to the school closures with indignation.[102] A few of the closed schools were still adequate and served as important institutions in the black community. In the view of many African Americans, the school board had closed these schools in response to pressure from white parents who did not want their children sent to schools in black neighborhoods.[103] School Board Chair Harris admitted as much: "The big factor is community acceptance of former Negro schools. [White] People in these communities approve by an overwhelming majority the closing of these schools."[104]

When schools opened in the fall of 1968, 28 percent of the system's 24,241 black students attended a majority-white school, pursuant to a geographic attendance plan encompassing every school in the system.[105] That level of desegregation might have been higher if not for the highly segregated residential patterns in the city; by the end of the 1960s, Charlotte was still one of the most residentially segregated cities in the United States.[106] Nevertheless, Charlotte had a higher percentage of its students attending desegregated schools than did most other southern cities.[107] Although the NAACP would continue to charge that the school board's attendance lines retained segregated schools, further legal challenges to the school system's attendance lines were foreclosed by the unfavorable decisions from Judge Craven and the Fourth Circuit in the *Swann* case. Further desegregation in Charlotte would require a change in the courts' understanding of the constitutional obligation of school boards to achieve school desegregation.

But those changes would soon come. Whereas the 1965 Office of Education guidelines were primarily directed at simply securing initial plans for school desegregation from local school boards, in 1966 the emphasis shifted to evaluating the effectiveness of these plans. In March 1966, under new leadership, the Office of Education issued a second and much tougher set of guidelines.[108] The most significant section of the new guidelines imposed stringent standards on the widely utilized "free choice" plans: "The single most substantial indication as to whether a free-choice plan is actually working to eliminate the dual school structure is the extent to which Negro or other minority group students have in fact transferred from segregated schools. . . . [W]here a free choice plan results in little or no actual desegregation . . . there is reason to believe that the plan is not operating effectively and may not be an appropriate or acceptable method of meeting constitutional and statutory requirements."[109] The guidelines specified the percentage of African American students who must attend a desegregated school in order for the school system to retain its federal funding. For example, if 9 percent of the black students in a free-choice plan had transferred to a desegregated school during the 1965–66 school year, twice that percentage would be expected to do so the following year; if only 5 percent had transferred to a desegregated school during the 1965–66 school year, triple that percentage would be expected to do so the following year. The guidelines authorized the commissioner of education to require local school systems that failed to meet these desegregation levels to either revise their assignment plans or else lose their federal funding.[110]

The 1966 Office of Education guidelines were important for three reasons. First, they constituted the first significant attempt by any branch of government to measure desegregation in terms of the actual percentage of black children attending mixed-race schools. Second, they implicitly rejected the notion, prevailing among southern school officials at the time, that school boards were required only to give black children the opportunity to attend white schools under freedom-of-choice plans, with no attention given to the actual number of children who chose to do so. Third, and perhaps most important, they provided an objective benchmark that courts could use in evaluating the desegregation progress of particular school systems.

The guidelines ultimately had a dramatic effect on southern school desegregation. Faced with a potential cutoff of federal funds, hundreds of southern school districts altered their pupil assignment plans to conform to the demands of the guidelines. Although every southern state would eventually have at least one school system lose federal funds under the Title VI fund cutoff, most southern school systems sought to comply with the guidelines in order to preserve their funding.[111]

Even more significantly, the guidelines moved the courts. If the courts decided that the Constitution required something less than the guidelines, then school boards could avoid the guidelines through litigation, since a pupil assignment system approved by a court did not have to comply with the guidelines. Anxious not to be a refuge for recalcitrant school boards, many courts eventually concluded that the desegregation requirements of the guidelines established the constitutional minimum. Since the guidelines contained certain numerical targets for evaluating desegregation plans, the guidelines objectified desegregation law in a way that a decade of judicial decisions had not.

Not surprisingly, many southern politicians, including North Carolina Governor Moore, urged reconsideration of the new standards, but with no success.[112] As a result, between 1965 — the date of the first set of guidelines—and 1969, the percentage of black children attending desegregated schools in the South increased tenfold, from 2 to 20 percent.[113]

Following the issuance of the 1966 guidelines, a few federal courts in the South began insisting on a greater degree of pupil desegregation in order to satisfy constitutional standards. Before the issuance of the 1966 guidelines, many southern courts had used Judge John Parker's dictum in the *Briggs* case—that *Brown* did not require integration but merely forbade discrimination—to legitimate assignment plans that were facially nondiscriminatory, such as free-choice plans, but that resulted in little or no pupil mixing.[114] Between 1965 and 1968, however, a transformation occurred in the federal courts on the question of whether school boards had a duty to attempt to increase desegregation levels. Critical to this transformation were three opinions by Judge John Minor Wisdom of the U.S. Court of Appeals for the Fifth Circuit.[115] Wisdom, a member of the New Orleans aristocracy, had been appointed to the bench in 1957 by President Dwight Eisenhower and was one of the most racially liberal judges in the South.[116] His three opinions, issued in 1965 and 1966, embodied the most important change in school desegregation doctrine since *Brown*.[117] That such a significant change would come from the pen of a lower-court judge reflected the minimal role of the Supreme Court in the development of school desegregation law in the fourteen years after *Brown*.

In *Singleton v. Jackson Municipal Separate School District*, a lawsuit to desegregate the Jackson, Mississippi, schools, Wisdom wrote in June 1965 that public school authorities had "the duty to provide an integrated school system."[118] Furthermore, Wisdom noted that he attached "great weight to the standards established by the Office of Education" and that judicial standards should be no lower than those set by the guidelines.[119] In December 1966, Wisdom wrote his longest and most significant school desegregation opinion in *United States v. Jefferson County Board of Education*, a sixty-page tour de force that was the most important school desegregation decision since *Brown*.[120] In his *Jefferson County* opinion, which considered on a consolidated basis the desegregation efforts of seven rural Alabama and Louisiana school systems, Wisdom again affirmed the constitutionality of the guidelines: "We hold that the HEW standards are substantially the same as this Court's standards. They are required by the Constitution."[121] In March 1967, the Fifth Circuit sitting *en banc* in the *Jefferson County* case embraced Wisdom's reasoning: "The Court holds that boards and officials administering public schools in this circuit have *the affirmative duty* under the Fourteenth Amendment to bring about an integrated, unitary school system *in which there are no Negro schools and no white schools—just schools.* Expressions in our earlier opinions distinguishing between integration and desegregation must yield to this affirmative duty we now recognize."[122] The *Jefferson County* decisions signaled a dramatic change in school desegregation law, at least as applied in the Fifth Circuit. Henceforth, school boards had an obligation to do more than merely create what appeared to be a race-neutral assignment plan. Now, school boards had an "affirmative" obligation to make sure that facially race-neutral assignment plans actually resulted in significant desegregation.

In the meantime, the majority of judges on the U.S. Court of Appeals for the Fourth Circuit—which covered North Carolina—moved more slowly than the Fifth Circuit and refused to follow Judge Wisdom's view that school boards had an affirmative duty to promote desegregation. Contrary to the Fifth Circuit, the Fourth Circuit held that free-choice plans satisfied constitutional requirements regardless of the level of pupil mixing achieved under those plans.[123]

The *Jefferson County* opinions, which dealt with free-choice plans in the rural South, were silent on one significant issue: a school board's obligation to achieve significant desegregation in urban areas with substantial residential segregation. At several places in these opinions, Wisdom indicated that the Constitution did not require school boards to engage in cross-district busing, and he did not indicate how school boards in urban areas with high levels of residential segregation could fulfill their affirmative obligation to eliminate school segregation without such a remedial tool. The implications of the *Jefferson County* cases for urban America remained unclear.

In the meantime, the U.S. Supreme Court neither embraced nor rejected the Fifth Circuit's new standard. The Court did, however, emphasize that the time for deliberate speed was over. In two 1965 cases—*Bradley v. School Board of Richmond* and *Rogers v. Paul,* involving desegregation plans in Richmond, Virginia, and Fort Smith, Arkansas—the Court issued brief per curiam decisions holding that further delays in school desegregation cases were no longer "tolerable."[124] At the same time, the NAACP Legal Defense Fund continued its strategy of bringing desegregation cases throughout the South, with an eye toward pushing the Supreme Court to define with more precision the desegregation obligations of southern school boards.[125]

The Legal Defense Fund concluded that the pupil assignment plan of New Kent County, Virginia, presented a particularly good opportunity for the Supreme Court to consider whether school boards that previously operated dual school systems had a duty to achieve a certain level of pupil integration. In this rural, lightly populated school district southeast of Richmond, the school board's free-choice plan had resulted in the retention of racially identifiable schools. The Supreme Court decided to take the New Kent County case and heard oral argument one day after the assassination of Martin Luther King in April 1968. One month later, the Court issued its decision in *Green v. County School Board*, its most significant school desegregation opinion since *Brown*.[126] The Court embraced the notion that school boards had an affirmative duty to desegregate schools beyond the establishment of a racially neutral assignment plan. The Court declared constitutionally suspect any freedom-of-choice plan that did not actually result in substantial racial mixing. Borrowing from language in Judge Wisdom's *Jefferson County* opinions, the Court concluded that the ultimate test was whether a school board's desegregation plan promised "realistically to convert promptly to a system without a 'white' school and a 'Negro' school, but just schools."[127] The Court, with its skepticism toward freedom of choice, insistence on results, and imposition of an affirmative duty on school boards, had changed the face of school desegregation law.

The application of *Green* to freedom-of-choice plans was clear. Free choice was out if it did not result in substantial racial mixing. Since most southern school systems used a free-choice assignment plan and since most of these school systems remained largely segregated, *Green* opened a floodgate of challenges to southern pupil assignment plans. But the application of *Green* to an urban school system, such as Charlotte's, whereby students were assigned to schools on the basis of residence, was less clear. The Court in *Green* had considered only free-choice plans that failed to desegregate; it had not considered geographic attendance plans that failed to desegregate due to residential segregation. Moreover, although the Court in *Green* did not specify a remedy for New Kent County's unlawful free-choice system, it did suggest that a geographic attendance plan might pass constitutional muster. As a result, it was unclear whether urban school boards had a duty to do more than establish a race-neutral geographic attendance plan in order to satisfy their "affirmative obligation" to desegregate their schools.

Some observers argued that *Green* would have no impact on cities such as Charlotte, where students were assigned to schools on the basis of residence. The city's leading television station, WBTV, for example, claimed that the Charlotte-Mecklenburg School Board's race-neutral geographic attendance plan satisfied the *Green* decision's demand for "just schools."[128] Others, however, disagreed. Within twenty-four hours of the decision, Chambers announced that his organization would reopen twenty-six desegregation suits in North Carolina—including one in Charlotte—seeking additional relief on the basis of *Green*. Federal district court judge Woodrow Jones, who would be called on to preside over some of these North Carolina cases, understood the potential implications of the *Green* decision as well. Jones predicted that *Green* would open a "Pandora's box" of school desegregation litigation.[129]

As it turns out, Jones was right. *Green* unleashed a flurry of desegregation suits and in time dramatically affected nearly every urban school system in the United States. But it would be a few years before that consequence of *Green* became widely understood.

Since this case was last before this court in 1965, the law (or at least the understanding of the law) has changed. . . . The difference between 1965 and 1969 is simply the difference between *Brown* of 1955 and *Green v. New Kent County* of 1968. The rules of the game have changed, and the methods and philosophies which in good faith the Board has followed are no longer adequate to complete the job which the courts now say must be done "now."

—Federal District Judge James McMillan, *Swann v. Charlotte-Mecklenburg Board of Education*, 1969

CHAPTER 6

The Meaning of *Green* for Charlotte

The Supreme Court's 1968 decision in *Green v. County School Board* unleashed a flurry of school desegregation litigation in the South.[1] The decision completely undermined school board reliance on free-choice assignment plans that resulted in only modest levels of desegregation. The Court's decision was less clear, however, about the fate of geographic assignment plans that resulted in minimal desegregation due to extensive residential segregation. What did *Green* mean for urban America?

One of the first cities to confront that question was Charlotte. Four months after the *Green* decision, the NAACP attorneys reopened the *Swann* case and asked the court to order the Charlotte-Mecklenburg School Board to desegregate completely every school in the system.[2] Yet the only way the board could do so in a city as residentially segregated as Charlotte was to utilize extensive bus transportation to move students across the city. Is that what *Green* required?

The task of deciding whether *Green* required such extensive pupil movement to overcome residential segregation fell to the newly appointed federal district court judge, James B. McMillan. Over the course of the next five years, McMillan would resolve that issue in a manner that affected not only Charlotte but virtually every city in America.

Following the *Green* decision, the leaders of the NAACP Legal Defense Fund—including Julius Chambers—met to determine the best locales for pressing the integrationist vision of *Green* in urban America. The group ultimately decided to pursue litigation in several cities simultaneously—including Charlotte, Memphis, Mobile, and Norfolk—in the hope of developing at least one strong case that could be taken to the Supreme Court. For his part, Chambers agreed to reopen the Charlotte case.[3]

Judge Craven no longer sat as a federal district judge for the Western District of North Carolina; he had been elevated to the U.S. Court of Appeals for the Fourth Circuit in 1967 and had been replaced by Woodrow Jones, a conservative jurist from the western part of the state. Subsequently, the other federal district court judge for the Western District, Wilson Warlick, who had ruled in 1961 on the first challenge to segregated schools in Charlotte, announced his retirement. By this time, no Charlotte attorney had served as a federal district court judge for almost half a century, notwithstanding the city's prominent role as the state's largest city. One year earlier, when Craven had moved up to the U.S. Court of Appeals, the Mecklenburg County Bar Association had declined to endorse a candidate for the vacancy. This time, North Carolina's senior senator, Sam Ervin, let the local bar know that he would consider a Charlottean only if the bar united behind one candidate.[4]

Two leading candidates emerged for the position — Joseph W. Grier, Jr., and James B. McMillan — and the local bar association held a vote among its members to select between the two. Their credentials were similar. The two men had been classmates at the University of North Carolina and Harvard Law School, and McMillan had succeeded Grier as president of the local bar association.[5] Both had held important local and statewide offices in community organizations, had been active members of the Democratic Party, and had served as elders of Charlotte's First Presbyterian Church.[6]

Grier had been head of the city's Parks Commission during the desegregation of Charlotte's park system in the late 1950s and early 1960s, during which Charlotte became the first city in the state and one of the first in the South to integrate a public swimming pool.[7] Many in the local bar may have perceived Grier to be too liberal to win the post in light of his work in that regard.[8] Ultimately, the local bar association chose the more affable McMillan over his close friend Grier.[9] McMillan later commented, "I've always thought of the irony that some people at least voted for me because they thought that Joe [Grier] was going too far [on racial issues]."[10] It was Grier's second missed opportunity at a federal judgeship. Two years earlier, some Charlotteans had unsuccessfully urged President Lyndon Johnson to appoint Grier to the judgeship that ultimately went to Woodrow Jones.[11]

McMillan had grown up in the unusual triracial world of Robeson County, North Carolina, where the population was part white, part Af-

rican American, and part Lumbee Indian. Many of his childhood play-
mates were African American and Lumbee children. McMillan's family
were farmers; his two grandfathers had farmed with slave labor and—in
McMillan's words—had "fought on the 'right' side in the Civil War
against Yankee oppressors."[12]

With his father disabled by arthritis and with family finances strained
by the depression, McMillan worked his own way through Presbyterian
Junior College. He joined the school boxing team, and in 1933, a *Charlotte Observer* sportswriter singled him out for his spirit and courage in
the ring despite his small stature. Almost forty years later, at the height
of the Charlotte busing controversy, an old friend would compare
McMillan's courage as a judge to his earlier courage as a boxer.[13]
McMillan went on to the University of North Carolina at Chapel Hill,
where he excelled and was elected to membership in the Order of the
Golden Fleece. He was set to attend the university's law school until a
history professor loaned McMillan money so that he could go to Harvard
Law School instead.[14]

At Harvard, the southern farm boy distinguished himself in oral ad-
vocacy, capturing the prestigious Ames moot court competition. After
graduation from Harvard and service as a lieutenant in the U.S. Navy
during World War II, McMillan entered private practice in Charlotte in
1946.[15] Over the next twenty years, McMillan emerged as a leading member of the Charlotte bar, eventually assuming the presidency of the North
Carolina Bar Association. At the same time, McMillan took leadership
roles in the local Democratic Party, the Charlotte Chamber of Commerce,
and various charitable and religious organizations.[16] By the time of his
nomination to the court, McMillan was widely regarded by his peers as
"an establishment lawyer."[17]

McMillan sailed through the nomination process. Whereas the previous North Carolina judicial appointment of Woodrow Jones had been
held up by the Johnson administration because of Jones's perceived segregationist views, McMillan's nomination barely caused a ripple of concern. The American Bar Association found him "exceptionally well qualified," its highest mark, and there was no opposition to the nomination
in either North Carolina or Washington.[18]

What were McMillan's views on racial discrimination before he took
the judicial oath? Although McMillan had earlier identified with the
more liberal, nonsegregationist wing of the state Democratic Party, race
was an issue that McMillan had not had to deal with directly, and there

was little to suggest that his racial views were much different from those of the typical southerner. Before *Brown*, McMillan, by his own account, accepted segregation: "I accepted for all of my early life the proposition that the ways of white people and the ways of black people were ordained to be different."[19] Moreover, McMillan initially disagreed with the Supreme Court's *Brown* decision outlawing segregated schools: "Such memory as I have of my reaction when *Brown* was decided was that [lower-court] Judge [John] Parker was close to being right and the Supreme Court was wrong. I had not absorbed enough information and been involved in those issues enough to really understand. . . . I guess you'd say I sort of sat out the whole civil rights revolution."[20] In 1963, speaking to the Law Review Association of the University of North Carolina, McMillan made clear his views about school desegregation. Commenting on a New York school board's desegregation efforts, McMillan said: "School boards should be encouraged rather than discouraged to draw school districts and make pupil assignments without substantial regard to race. At the same time, may we be forever saved from the folly of the New York authorities who have reportedly gone to the wild extreme of requiring that pupils be transported far away from their natural habitat so that some artificial 'average' of racial balance might be maintained."[21] The New York school system to which McMillan was probably referring had engaged in an insignificant amount of pupil reshuffling compared with McMillan's later actions.[22]

Yet certain indications in McMillan's precourt years suggested that he would be sensitive to racial and other civil rights issues that came before him. In the summer of 1961, in his final address to the North Carolina Bar Association on his retirement as president, McMillan criticized lawyers for their failure "to speak with clarity in the area of race relations" and urged them to take a much more active role. More significant, McMillan criticized the failure of school boards to deliver on the promise of *Brown*: "After many years, these requirements [to desegregate] remain more honored in the breach than in the observance. Our local school boards often shrink from serious effort to recognize valid requests for assignment to unsegregated schools. . . . [T]he constitutional validity of the system grows weaker with each passing school assignment system."[23] While serving as president, McMillan also lobbied for the admission of black lawyers to the North Carolina Bar Association.[24] A few years later, when the North Carolina General Assembly enacted a speaker ban prohibiting members of the Communist Party from speaking on state university campuses, McMillan served as coordinator of a University of North Carolina alumni group that fought for repeal.[25] On his appointment, the *Charlotte News* editorialized that McMillan would be sensitive to civil rights issues: "At a time when the federal courts are being called upon increasingly to decide some very sticky civil rights questions it is fortunate that the Western District will get a man with such a deep interest in freedom and fair play."[26]

Shortly before his nomination, some members of the Charlotte bar questioned McMillan about his views on judicial activism. McMillan ducked the question: "You will have to judge in time whether I am a judicial activist or traditionalist. Perhaps neither label fits."[27] McMillan did comment, shortly before his Senate confirmation, that courts could "be the vehicle to allow change without disrupting the established order."[28] The ramifications of that statement would become clear during the first few years of McMillan's judgeship.

NAACP attorney Julius Chambers had a good feeling about McMillan, predicting to his law partners that McMillan would be "another Spencer Bell," the Charlotte judge who had identified with the liberal wing of the U.S. Court of Appeals for the Fourth Circuit during the 1960s. Chambers had served with McMillan on the board of a local legal services organization and sensed that McMillan, as judge, would be sensitive to claims of racial injustice.[29]

In one of his first cases on the bench, McMillan gave notice that he would not be reluctant to challenge governmental agencies he thought had engaged in unconstitutional behavior. In 1968, the American Civil Liberties Union (ACLU) sued the Charlotte police department for allegedly harassing a group of youths living in what was referred to as a "hippie house." According to the ACLU, the Charlotte police had repeatedly searched the house for drugs and other illegal activity without first securing a warrant. McMillan held that the Charlotte police had violated the youths' constitutional rights and enjoined the police department from further visits without a search warrant. "Hippies," wrote McMillan, "are entitled to the protection of the constitution, and the court would be remiss if it allowed the length of a man's hair . . . to affect the measure of his civil rights."[30]

A few of McMillan's comments in this "hippie house" decision were telling as to his judicial philosophy. McMillan recognized that the police were following certain customary practices in their treatment of the "hippies," but he noted: "The law, like science, grows. . . . [C]oncern for individual liberty under law may require that measures long thought permissible be abandoned or improved to conform to changed and sharpened constitutional interpretations."[31] McMillan had given notice that he intended to make good on his confirmation hearing statement that courts could be "the vehicle to allow change."

Still, McMillan's handling of the "hippie house" case was no clear indicator of what he would do with the motion filed by the plaintiffs to reopen the Charlotte school desegregation case. By his own admission, McMillan found the plaintiffs' request perplexing.[32] McMillan thought that the Charlotte-Mecklenburg School Board had already fulfilled its desegregation duties; he wrote a few months later, "[The school board has] achieved a degree and volume of desegregation of schools apparently unsurpassed in these parts, and . . . exceeded the performance of any school board whose actions have been reviewed in appellate court decisions."[33] McMillan well knew that Charlotte had been one of the first school systems in the South to integrate its schools and that a higher percentage of African American students in Charlotte attended a desegregated school than in almost any other city in the United States. According to the U.S. Office of Education, only two other urban school systems in the whole country — San Francisco and Toledo — had achieved a greater degree of pupil desegregation than had Charlotte by 1968.[34] Years later, McMillan reflected on his initial impressions of the case: "The Charlotte schools for many decades had been . . . models of excellence. Many black children were going to 'white schools.' In the rural areas, . . . a few schools were genuinely desegregated. I could not understand how anybody should complain about the Charlotte-Mecklenburg schools or insist that stronger measures were necessary to afford equal opportunity to the black children."[35] After the litigation ended in 1975, McMillan confirmed that he had "started the case with the uninformed assumption that no active segregation was being practiced in the Charlotte-Mecklenburg schools, that the aims of the suit were extreme and unreasonable, and that a little bit of push was all that the Constitution required of the court."[36] It was with some reluctance that McMillan set hearings on the plaintiffs' motion.[37]

McMillan thus entered the litigation not as a judge determined to restructure the Charlotte-Mecklenburg schools but rather as a judge dubious of the plaintiffs' request for more extensive desegregation. McMillan's law clerk at the time, Fred Hicks, initially believed that the judge would deny the plaintiffs' motion for additional relief.[38] The meaning of *Green* for urban America would be given one of its initial interpretations by a judge skeptical of its reach.[39]

McMillan held six days of hearings on the plaintiffs' motion in March 1969. There were two basic questions to be resolved in the hearing. First, did the existence of a large number of single-race schools in Charlotte establish a constitutional violation that the school board was obliged to correct? And second, if so, what actions must the board take to eliminate those single-race schools?

On the first issue, the school board took the position that the case was controlled by Judge Craven's 1965 decision upholding the board's use of geographic attendance zones.[40] Although the Supreme Court had held in *Green* that school boards had an affirmative obligation to eliminate racially identifiable schools, the board argued that its conversion from race-based pupil assignments to race-neutral geographic attendance zones in 1965 satisfied those obligations. According to the board, the presence of single-race schools in Charlotte was due to residential segregation, not school board policy, and the board could not be held responsible for the various personal choices people made about where to live. The board also emphasized that during the three years since Judge Craven had approved geographic attendance zones for Charlotte, the number of black children attending majority-white schools had dramatically increased. School Board Chair William Poe later commented that he had not thought the *Green* decision would have any effect on Charlotte.[41]

The plaintiffs, on the other hand, contended that *Green* imposed on school boards an affirmative duty to do whatever was necessary to eliminate segregated schools. Chambers argued that if geographic attendance zones resulted in single-race schools because of residential segregation, and if the residential segregation was due at least in part to discriminatory acts engaged in by the school board and other government agencies, then the board had a constitutional obligation to adjust those attendance zones to eliminate the segregated schools. Accordingly, Chambers proceeded to attempt to demonstrate that Charlotte was one of the most residentially segregated cities in the United States because of various forms of private and governmental discrimination.[42]

McMillan told Chambers that evidence about residential segregation was irrelevant to the issues at hand: "I don't see that an historical study of why people bought, built, sold and rented houses is going to help us any. . . . I don't think we can sit here and try the whole community and go into all the forty thousand reasons people built houses where they did. . . . I don't think it matters at all for the purpose of the present community problem we're dealing with why people are living now where they are living."[43] Indeed, some courts had previously held that school boards were not obliged to overcome residential segregation so long as the board adopted a nondiscriminatory pupil assignment plan such as one based on residence.[44] However, four days after the Supreme Court's 1968 *Green* decision, the U.S. Court of Appeals for the Fourth Circuit, in a school desegregation case involving the city of Norfolk, had held that the use of geographic attendance zones that resulted in single-race schools due to residential segregation was impermissible if the residential segregation had been caused by racial discrimination.[45] The Fourth Circuit's Norfolk decision bore tremendous potential for the desegregation of urban systems, suggesting that school boards did indeed have the responsibility to alter attendance zones to overcome residential segregation caused by past discrimination.[46] In addition, a few days after the close of the March 1969 hearings in the *Swann* case, the U.S. Office of Education ordered the Raleigh School Board to frame a pupil assignment plan to overcome residential segregation that had resulted from racial discrimination.[47]

McMillan admitted his lack of familiarity with school desegregation law at the time of the March hearing. He ultimately decided to give both parties broad latitude in presenting evidence to the court, thereby opening the door to considerable testimony about the many different reasons for residential segregation in Charlotte.[48] McMillan's decision to allow Chambers to present evidence of the cause of segregated housing patterns later proved critical. McMillan would ultimately conclude that the school board had an obligation to overcome the city's residential segregation. In so doing, he would rely on Chambers's evidence showing that the residential segregation was due at least in part to past acts of discrimination by both private actors and government agencies, including the Charlotte-Mecklenburg School Board.[49]

Since the *Brown* decision fifteen years earlier, Charlotte's population had almost doubled. Although some of this population increase was due to an expansion of the city's limits, much of it was due to an influx of new residents. As new neighborhoods were built to accommodate the expanding population, the residential segregation that characterized Charlotte in 1954 was exacerbated. By 1969, Charlotte's neighborhoods were more segregated than they had been in 1954.[50] Much of the new white development of the 1950s and 1960s occurred in the southern and eastern sections of the county, far removed from the city's traditionally black neighborhoods. At the same time, Charlotte's urban-renewal efforts in the 1960s contributed to the city's residential segregation.

Between 1960 and 1967, the Charlotte Redevelopment Authority, aided by significant federal funding, razed the center-city Second Ward neighborhood, displacing over one thousand black families. Instead of rebuilding the destroyed housing, the city built a new Government Plaza and a downtown park and substantially widened existing thoroughfares; several private office buildings were also located on the site of the old Second Ward neighborhood. Virtually all of the black families displaced by the razing of Second Ward relocated to traditionally black neighborhoods in the northwest section of the city and to traditionally white working-class neighborhoods—Belmont, Villa Height, and Optimist Park—just north of the downtown area, which quickly converted to black neighborhoods. Subsequently, in 1967, the Redevelopment Authority bulldozed a substantial black neighborhood in First Ward, just northeast of the center city. Many of these families relocated to black neighborhoods north and west of the downtown; others moved into a new public housing project, Earle Village Homes, which had been built on part of the newly cleared land. Some black leaders, such as City Councilman Fred Alexander, criticized the removal of black families from center-city neighborhoods into the northwest section of the city, claiming that such actions served only to further segregate the city's black residents from the rest of the city. Alexander's pleas, however, went unheeded. As a result of urban renewal, the residential separation of blacks and whites had significantly increased.[51]

In response to the city's expanding population, the Charlotte-Mecklenburg School Board engaged in an aggressive school-building effort. During the fifteen years following the *Brown* decision, the school board built almost fifty new schools to accommodate a public school population that had doubled in size. Because the board located the vast majority of these new schools in single-race neighborhoods, most of them quickly became identifiable as either black or white schools.[52] In 1969, twenty-five of the thirty-one newly constructed elementary schools had a student population at least 98 percent single race; eight of the thirteen new junior high schools were at least 95 percent single race; and four of the five new senior high schools were at least 91 percent single race.[53]

During the fifteen years following the *Brown* decision, the board took two additional actions that contributed to both residential and school segregation. First, the board continued to assign students to schools on the basis of race until the mid-1960s, thereby encouraging families to settle in neighborhoods that already had schools for children of their color. Second, the board closed a number of schools in areas near both black and white neighborhoods and reassigned those students to other racially identifiable schools. During the March hearing, the school board attorney Brock Barkley conceded that the board had placed schools in single-race neighborhoods but discounted the significance of that action: "We say that the Board of Education cannot be held responsible just because in certain areas where the population is overwhelmingly of one race we have located a school in that area."[54] Both McMillan and ultimately the Supreme Court would disagree, holding the board responsible for contributing to the patterns of residential segregation, and hence school segregation, in the city.[55]

At the March hearing, McMillan further considered the question of what actions the school board must take to overcome the city's extensive residential segregation. Did every majority-black school have to be eliminated? In time, a number of other district court judges charged with interpreting the *Green* decision would say no.[56] Chambers, however, asked McMillan to order the board to eliminate every majority-black school in the system, an order that would require extensive pupil reshuffling away from neighborhood schools.[57] McMillan asked Chambers whether the law either permitted or required him to issue such a sweeping order:

> *McMillan:* So what you're really saying is that you want the Court to hold that any predominantly black school in Charlotte is unlawful.
> *Chambers:* That's correct, and any predominantly white school.
> *McMillan:* That would be going pretty far, wouldn't it?
> *Chambers:* I don't think so, Your Honor.
> *McMillan:* Has anybody ever held that?
> *Chambers:* The Court might differ with me, but that's the way I read *Green*.[58]

Yet there was a dramatic difference between New Kent County, Virginia, the county in question in the *Green* case, and Charlotte-Mecklenburg. New Kent County, Virginia, had only two schools, with approximately thirteen hundred students. Black and white children were scattered somewhat evenly throughout the county, making desegregation by attendance zone a relatively simple task.[59] Charlotte-Mecklenburg, on the other hand, was one of the largest school systems in the nation, with over one hundred schools and eighty-three thousand schoolchildren.[60]

Eliminating the racial identifiability of every school in the Charlotte-Mecklenburg school system could not be accomplished without extensive reshuffling of students. Is this what *Green* required in the urban setting? The Supreme Court had not yet said.

Chambers went further; he also asked McMillan to order the school board to establish a seventy-thirty ratio of white students to black students in every school in the Charlotte-Mecklenburg system.[61] Yet Chambers recognized that this ratio was probably not obtainable in every school; in a conversation with a news reporter, Chambers acknowledged that ratios would probably vary widely and that he was primarily interested in a system in which each school was majority white.[62] When the case reached the U.S. Supreme Court, Chambers would ask only for the elimination of all racially identifiable schools — defined as schools with a majority-black population or with a white population of more than 90 percent — as opposed to a seventy-thirty racial ratio in each school.[63]

One month later, on April 23, 1969, McMillan issued his opinion. The centerpiece of McMillan's decision was a discussion of the Supreme Court's *Green* opinion and how it had dramatically changed school desegregation law by imposing on school boards an affirmative duty to eliminate segregated schools. Quoting long passages from the *Green* decision, McMillan emphasized that the school board's previous legal obligation of merely refraining "from active legal racial discrimination" had been replaced with an affirmative duty to eliminate "the lasting effects of . . . historical *apartheid*." For Charlotte, this meant that the school board must eliminate all remaining racially identifiable schools — a daunting task. McMillan noted that the Charlotte-Mecklenburg school system may previously have been a "model" school system, but he concluded, "The rules of the game have changed."[64]

McMillan's order was open-ended, leaving it to the school board to devise an appropriate pupil assignment plan eliminating the racial identifiability of all of the system's schools. Four years earlier, Judge Craven had expressed the view that the courts should not be in the business of framing pupil assignment plans for school systems. McMillan dealt with that concern by making it clear that the school board, not the court, bore the responsibility for drafting an acceptable plan. "*It is still to this day the local School Board, and not the court, which has the duty to assign pupils and operate the schools, subject to the requirements of the Constitution,*" McMillan wrote. "The Board has assets and experience beyond the reach of a judge to deal with all these problems." Even though one of the plaintiffs' experts, Dr. John A. Finger of Providence, Rhode

Island, had submitted a lengthy report outlining several possible desegregation plans, McMillan decided to leave the actual formulation of the plan up to the discretion of the board. McMillan specifically noted that neither Finger nor the other plaintiffs' experts were "as familiar with the local situation as the local Board and school administrators."[65] In time, McMillan would be severely tested on this issue of deference to the school board.

McMillan gave the board three weeks to submit a plan for the desegregation of both students and faculties but offered no specific guidelines as to how that plan should be devised. McMillan did express his preference for a plan that would provide for a seventy-thirty ratio of white students to black students in each school but stated that he did not have "the power to make such a specific order." Instead, he instructed the board to provide for the complete desegregation of teachers by the 1969–70 school year and for the partial desegregation of the student population by the fall of 1969, to be completed by the following school year.[66] McMillan invited the board to consider a variety of desegregation devices, including the busing of students, to satisfy its obligations.

Even with this initial opinion, McMillan understood the impact his decision would have on the entire city and sought to legitimate his order by reference not only to the law but also to educational policy. Aware of the popular appeal of the "neighborhood school" concept, McMillan criticized neighborhood schools from an educational policy perspective. McMillan noted with irony, "When racial segregation was required by law, nobody evoked the neighborhood school theory to *permit* black children to attend white schools close to where they lived." McMillan further attempted to legitimate his decision by arguing that segregated schools retarded the educational progress of black students: "One point on which the experts all agree (and the statistics tend to bear them out) is that a racial mix in which black students heavily predominate tends to retard the progress of the whole group, whereas if students are mingled with a clear white majority, such as a 70/30 ratio (approximately the ratio of white to black students in Mecklenburg County), the better students can hold their pace, with substantial improvement for the poorer students."[67] These would be only the first of many attempts by McMillan to convince the community of the wisdom, from an educational perspective, of the elimination of single-race schools.

In a community completely unprepared for the legal standard that McMillan articulated, however, the outcry was immediate and forceful, far more forceful than McMillan might have anticipated. Within hours of the decision, School Board Chair William Poe, a widely respected attorney and community leader, announced that the court order had "revolutionary implications" and was "utter folly."[68]

Poe was the son of a Baptist minister. Like McMillan, he was also a Harvard Law School graduate, a long and active member of the Democratic Party, and a leading member of the Charlotte bar.[69] Poe had first been elected to the school board in 1964 — with the endorsement of Reginald Hawkins and his political organization — and was subsequently elevated to the position of board chair.[70] A man of forceful personality, powerful intellect, and fiery temper, Poe served throughout the desegregation controversy as the board's leader and chief spokesperson.[71] Although Poe would disagree vociferously with McMillan about the wisdom and legality of busing to overcome residential segregation, the school board chair was no segregationist. In 1948, as editor of the Wake Forest College student newspaper, Poe had editorialized in favor of integrated congregations in the Southern Baptist Church, a position at odds with church practice and policy.[72] Moreover, Poe understood that the school board's earlier desegregation efforts had been driven by the desire to avoid litigation. "Looking back, everything we've done in integration has been done because of the threat of a court suit," Poe told a reporter in 1966. "And I'm not especially proud of it."[73]

Poe announced that he favored school desegregation but that he was committed to a pupil assignment plan based on residence; Poe also insisted that the Constitution did not require extensive pupil reshuffling in the face of large-scale residential segregation.[74] Yet Poe did not urge defiance of McMillan; instead, he repeatedly argued that the judge had gone far beyond what the Supreme Court had intended in *Green* and that the school board should therefore seek appellate review of McMillan's actions. For the next several years, the popular school board chair and the federal judge would lock horns in a struggle that eventually turned personal.[75] Indeed, Poe would function as McMillan's primary antagonist for the duration of the school desegregation litigation.

Poe was not the only outspoken critic of McMillan. Gibson Smith, a popular candidate in the upcoming mayoral election, attacked the decision as "wrong, uncalled for, and disruptive" and urged the school board to fight it.[76] Several other school board members sharply criticized McMillan as well. Within days, pickets protesting the order appeared outside the Education Center; within weeks, about twenty thousand parents had signed petitions opposing "involuntary" busing of students to

School Board Chair William Poe addresses a school board meeting, October 1967.
(Courtesy of the *Charlotte Observer*)

achieve desegregation.[77] There was a sense that Jim McMillan, stalwart of the Charlotte community for more than two decades, had betrayed his community. As noted by Sam McNinch, a school board member and staunch busing foe, "I was disappointed that a man who lived here with us could order us to do this by force."[78]

To voice opposition to busing, critics held mass meetings, all of which were extensively covered in the print and television media, giving fuel to a growing antibusing coalition.[79] A meeting of angry parents at Quail Hollow Junior High School in the southern section of the county drew two thousand participants and led to the formation of a group calling itself the Concerned Parents Association (CPA), which became the city's leading antibusing organization.[80] At CPA-sponsored rallies throughout the county, speeches were given, donations collected, patriotic songs sung, and prayers delivered.[81] The CPA drew its support from all sections of the county and from all classes of white society. Although the organization did not capture the full public support of the city's business and civic leadership, over one-third of the county's white population would ultimately sign CPA petitions.

Unlike in other cities confronted with desegregation controversies, such as Boston, the white opposition to school busing was not localized in Charlotte, either by class or by geographic region.[82] Many of the CPA leaders were business leaders and professionals, including William Booe, an attorney, Thomas Harris, an insurance salesman, and Don Roberson, a dentist. Nevertheless, the CPA would enjoy its greatest support in the middle- and lower-middle-class white neighborhoods of the city and county.

CPA members were careful to articulate their concerns not as opposition to racial integration but rather as opposition to sending their children to schools in distant black neighborhoods. Open opposition to racial desegregation exceeded the bounds of mainstream political discourse in a "moderate" city like Charlotte. As CPA leader Harris repeatedly stated: "We're not segregationist. We're not a radical racist group. But we do believe that our basic freedoms are being taken away from us."[83] Another parent explained, "They can bring in anybody they like to [my] school, but I don't want my child taken away from there."[84] Those concerns were not new. White community pressure had forced the closure of several traditionally black schools in 1966 when it had become apparent that white students would be required to attend those schools pursuant to geographic zoning.[85]

Underlying much of the white opposition was the belief that educational quality would suffer if blacks and whites were taught in the same classrooms. One antibusing white explained: "We've been taught all our lives that blacks are inferior to whites, and how could you put an inferior person with an above average person without pulling him down?" Other whites, mired in old stereotypes, feared, in the words of one white teacher, "that blacks were going to contaminate their children with all kinds of drugs and diseases and alcohol and profane language."[86]

"No Forced Busing" emerged as the rallying cry of those opposed to McMillan's desegregation order. Yet transporting children by school bus had a long tradition in the South and particularly in North Carolina. North Carolina first provided bus transportation for students in 1911; by the late 1920s, more than 20 percent of the schoolchildren in the state rode buses to school.[87] This extensive use of bus transportation resulted from a widespread school consolidation movement; as schools grew larger, more and more children attended schools located a considerable distance from their homes, requiring some type of transportation. Increasing numbers of children were transported from rural areas to town schools in pursuit of a better education. McMillan himself had ridden a school bus twenty-six miles a day as a child in the late 1920s and early 1930s to attend school in rural Robeson County. By the time of the *Brown* decision in 1954, almost half of the children in North Carolina rode a bus to school, earning the state the proud label "the school busingest" state in the nation.[88]

To be sure, busing had occasionally engendered controversy during the pre-*Brown* era. In the early years of consolidation and school busing, some rural parents expressed opposition on the grounds that it took too much time away from home and might expose their children to negative cultural influences.[89] In time, however, most parents came to understand the educational advantages of school consolidation, notwithstanding the need to travel a considerable distance by bus to reach a school. Indeed, by the time of the 1954 *Brown* decision, the most typical busing controversy involved an effort by black students to secure the opportunity to ride a school bus, the same opportunity that white children enjoyed.[90]

The opposition to school busing to overcome racial imbalance, particularly in the white community, was strangely ironic, given the fact that busing had been extensively used throughout the state to keep schools racially segregated. For decades, thousands of black children in North Carolina, including NAACP attorney Chambers, had been required to ride buses past nearby white schools to attend distant black schools. When HEW required school districts during the 1960s to abandon dual attendance plans, the number of children riding school buses in some southern states actually declined.[91]

The Charlotte-Mecklenburg School Board had successfully defended the 1961 court challenge to its practice of busing black children to distant segregated schools by arguing that there was no particular virtue in neighborhood schools and that busing enjoyed a long and distinguished history in North Carolina education.[92] McMillan himself, in a letter to an antibusing parent, noted the irony of the opposition to the use of buses "to comply with the Constitution," stating that buses had been used "for two generations to evade the Constitution."[93]

Yet by 1969, "neighborhood schools" had become a sacred talisman in Charlotte. The difference between 1961 and 1969 can be understood only in racial terms. In 1961, busing was used to maintain segregated schools and hence was acceptable to the white community; after 1969, busing would be used to foster extensive racial mixing. Pupil integration, particularly when it took place at inner-city black schools, was entirely unacceptable to much of the white community.

Recognizing the impact his decision had had on the city, McMillan took the unusual course of publicly defending it. Within a week of the April 1969 order, McMillan addressed the Charlotte Kiwanis Club, delivering a speech that received front-page coverage in the local papers.[94] Although judges typically avoid public discussion of pending litigation, this was not the typical case. Unlike most cases, in which a judge's decision affects only the actual parties to the lawsuit, the *Swann* case would have a profound effect on every parent and child in Mecklenburg County. Hence, McMillan used his civic club address as an opportunity to explain to the public why he had decided the school case the way he had. It was a tactic that the judge would use again and again throughout the litigation.[95]

Aware that most Charlotteans could not understand how it was that the Constitution required the extensive reassignment of schoolchildren to overcome residential segregation, McMillan sought to explain what he characterized as "judge-made" law. "Judge-made" law, according to McMillan, arose when a court gave meaning to general constitutional language. He offered the First Amendment as an example, which, as a result of "judge-made" law, gave citizens the right to publish letters in the newspaper claiming "that the decision of the local federal court in the local school [desegregation] case" was "Communist in origin."[96] To

McMillan, the desegregation demands of the Supreme Court articulated in the *Green* decision had arisen from "judge-made" law.

In his Kiwanis Club speech, McMillan directly challenged the sanctity of the neighborhood school, aptly noting that ten years earlier, black children could not attend their neighborhood school if that school happened to be white.[97] McMillan would continue to question the value of neighborhood schools; in a later address McMillan claimed, "True education doesn't begin until we *leave* the neighborhood school."[98] McMillan concluded his speech to the Kiwanians with what appeared to be a rebuke of Poe. No one, said McMillan, could evade the Constitution's mandates, "whether he be an insurance salesman, a federal judge, or a school board chairman."[99]

McMillan understood that the city of Charlotte would need to be "educated" concerning the requirements of the Supreme Court in the school desegregation area, the way he had been educated during the March court hearing. As a result, he sought to make himself personally available to the community to explain his decision. Over the next few years, McMillan would grant frequent interviews with news reporters, meet in his chambers or over lunch with community leaders, field phone calls at his home from interested—and often intemperate—citizens, and engage in extensive correspondence with citizens throughout the county and state.[100]

Not everyone in Charlotte opposed McMillan's desegregation order. Many African Americans voiced their support for the judge and complained bitterly of the negative response in the white community. One black educator, noting that African Americans had long been bused to attend segregated black schools, expressed her anger at a school board meeting in May 1969: "I'm getting pretty sick and tired of everybody being uptight about busing. I was bused and my husband was bused . . . and I didn't hear a word from any of you nice white Southern liberals."[101]

One of the primary supporters of the desegregation order was the *Charlotte Observer*. Throughout the litigation, the *Observer*, under the editorship of C. A. McKnight, urged the community to comply with the judge's orders. Only a few other southern judges, most notably in Little Rock and St. Petersburg, enjoyed such unflagging support from a local newspaper.[102] To help readers appreciate the difficulties facing the court, the *Observer* ran the text of McMillan's various orders, accompanied by commentary explaining the precedent on which the judge had relied.[103] Shortly after McMillan's initial order, for example, McKnight offered his readers a rather generous interpretation of *Green*: "Anyone who takes the time to read [*Green v.*] *New Kent County* . . . will be impressed [that] . . . the Supreme Court . . . left [McMillan] very little room to maneuver."[104] The *Observer*, through the editorials of David Gillespie, supported McMillan's every move.[105] Moreover, from the outset, the paper criticized school board members, particularly Board Chair Poe—who "should know better," according to the paper—for their attacks on the judge.[106]

The *Observer*'s support was critical. One of the major tasks confronting McMillan was the legitimation of his decisions in the eyes of the community, particularly in the face of the widespread belief that the judge had misapplied existing law. The *Observer* performed that legitimating role. In the later oral arguments before both the U.S. Court of Appeals and the U.S. Supreme Court wherein McMillan's actions were reviewed, the plaintiffs' attorney Chambers was queried as to whether the busing orders had any support in the community. Chambers on both occasions cited the *Observer*'s support.[107] Social scientists would eventually conclude that newspaper support for busing plans during the 1970s had a demonstrable impact on reducing white flight from urban school systems.[108]

Yet the *Observer*'s involvement in the controversy proved costly. Opponents of desegregation identified the newspaper as one of their chief targets. *Observer* reporters covering school board and antibusing community meetings were harassed, sometimes by board members themselves.[109] In June 1969, for example, *Observer* reporter L. M. Wright complained to his editor that School Board Chair Poe had castigated him for what Poe perceived to be Wright's probusing editorials and news coverage and, according to Wright, had labeled him "a prostitute" who had "sold out."[110] Later, following McMillan's controversial February 1970 order that mandated extensive busing, circulation at the paper declined by over five thousand copies. Gillespie, for his part, was ultimately removed from his editorial position, blamed for having "involved the paper too deeply in controversy by entering the trenches as a combatant instead of remaining above the strife and commenting on it."[111]

The *Observer* was the only major media institution to offer consistent support for the judge: the city's two television stations more often than not editorially opposed the judge's orders, as did the city's evening paper, the *Charlotte News*. The *News*, under the editorship of Perry Morgan, consistently criticized both McMillan and the *Observer*.[112] The *News* would repeatedly argue that McMillan's interpretation of the law differed from that of other federal judges called on to supervise the desegregation of urban school systems and that Charlotte had suffered at the hands of

Charlotte Observer editor C. A. McKnight (left) confers with associate editors Reece Cleghorn (center) and David Gillespie (right), September 1971. (Courtesy of the *Charlotte Observer*)

McMillan's liberal views. In the same way that the *Observer* legitimated McMillan's orders, the *News* editorials served to legitimate opposition to those orders.

In addition to the *Observer*, the judge did enjoy some other support. Four members of the school board urged compliance with the judge's order.[113] One such member, Carlton Watkins, a white pediatrician, noted that the complete desegregation of the schools would probably alienate a large proportion of the city's residents but expressed confidence that the city would go along if ordered to do so by the higher courts.[114] For the next few years Watkins would be an important voice favoring cooperation with McMillan.

Five days after McMillan released his opinion, the school board informally decided not to appeal the decision, concluding that the right to appeal an order to propose a plan was doubtful.[115] Instead, the board instructed School Superintendent William Self to devise a plan, as required by the court order. Within a week, Self returned with a plan that required full faculty desegregation, partial redrawing of attendance zones to increase pupil desegregation, and the elimination of all student transfers that had the effect of increasing segregation.[116] In effect, Self's plan provided for greater desegregation without a complete abandonment of the board's existing geographic attendance plan. On May 8, however, the board voted 5-to-4 to reject Self's plan and to accept McMillan's invitation to ask the court for an extension of time to devise a new plan.[117] In light of the board's lack of consensus, McMillan granted the requested extension.[118]

In the meantime, the school board attorney William Waggoner telephoned McMillan, requesting a meeting with the judge along with Board Chair Poe. McMillan understood Waggoner as seeking "some kind of commitment that would amount to watering down the [desegregation] order" and told him to bring Chambers to the meeting if that was what he wanted to discuss. Waggoner eventually notified McMillan that Poe did not want to meet with the judge.[119]

On May 28, the school board finally approved an extremely limited plan for faculty and pupil desegregation, one that constituted a complete rejection of McMillan's April 23 order. The plan called for faculty desegregation only on a voluntary basis, far removed from what McMillan had ordered or the superintendent had initially proposed. By the time of the mid-June hearing on the plan, less than 2 percent of the system's teachers had volunteered to transfer to a desegregated school. School attendance zones remained virtually unchanged, offering no hope of achieving additional pupil desegregation. The only change from the existing pupil assignment plan was the provision of transportation for students who wanted to transfer voluntarily to another school. The board expressly denied that it had any duty to engage in more pupil desegregation than that which it had accomplished under its existing geographic attendance plan.[120]

Throughout this time, the board remained sharply divided. Most of the votes on any issue related to the desegregation controversy were 5-to-4, making consensus impossible. At the same time, rumors about internal conflicts on the board flowed freely and were readily printed by the *Observer*. Reports circulated that Poe had threatened Superintendent Self's job if he pushed for compliance and that procompliance board member Carlton Watkins had unsuccessfully attempted to unseat Poe as board chair.[121]

In yet another 5-to-4 vote, the board decided to cancel long-standing plans to build a new high school in the center of the city; the school would have greatly facilitated desegregation because it bordered black and white residential areas. According to McMillan, it would have been "the easiest high school in town to desegregate."[122] McMillan allowed the cancellation of the new high school to stand, but he later reflected that this decision had been a mistake and that it had "complicated and tremendously increased the cost and inconvenience of all subsequent activity to desegregate high schools."[123]

In June 1969, McMillan held hearings to review the board's proposed desegregation plan. At the outset, the school board lawyers announced that the board wanted to maintain a neighborhood school system, noting that neither the Supreme Court nor the U.S. Court of Appeals for the Fourth Circuit had "at this time explicitly proclaimed the abolition of the neighborhood school system."[124] It was a direct rebuke of the judge. McMillan acknowledged that the board had decided in effect to disobey his order: "The school superintendent was instructed to prepare a desegregation plan. . . . However, the views of many members [of the board] expressed at the meeting were so opposed to serious and substantial desegregation that everyone including the superintendent could reasonably have concluded, as the court does, that a 'minimal' plan was what was called for, and that the 'plan' was essentially a prelude to anticipated disapproval and appeal."[125]

Poe testified on the board's behalf, justifying the board's inaction on the grounds that most Charlotteans opposed the elimination of neighborhood schools.[126] Poe conceded that the board had a duty to obey the court, but he added, "That duty is coupled with a responsibility to the people to maintain their support."[127] The idea that the board could balance its legal obligations against community sentiment irritated McMillan. To McMillan, the board had an obligation to fully desegregate the school system, notwithstanding the views of the community. It was an issue that would divide the judge and the school board chair for the next five years.

Poe was an articulate proponent of the view that McMillan had misconstrued the law in his April order. Suggestions that the school board chair was motivated by personal considerations, however, weakened his position. Chambers, in his cross-examination of the school board chair at the June hearing, suggested that Poe was unwilling to alter the attendance lines of the all-black Second Ward High School to include more white students because one of the closest white neighborhoods to Second Ward was Poe's own Myers Park neighborhood. Board member Betsey Kelly later testified that Poe had told her that he did not want his children sent to Second Ward because he did not believe the educational opportunity would be the same. Although Poe denied that his actions had been influenced by personal considerations, the attacks served to exacerbate tensions among board members.[128]

At the end of the June hearing, McMillan issued an order finding the board's desegregation plan legally deficient. He ordered the board to present another desegregation plan to the court by August 4, to take effect in the fall. The plaintiffs renewed their request that McMillan either adopt the desegregation plan prepared by the plaintiffs' expert John Finger or appoint a panel of experts to devise a plan.[129] McMillan, reluctant to impose a desegregation plan on the board, rejected that request, emphasizing that the responsibility to develop a plan lay with the local school administrators rather than with a "visiting fireman" such as Finger.[130]

At the same time, McMillan was cognizant of the extreme political pressures on the board. At the end of the June hearing, McMillan, given to an informal style, leaned against the back wall of the courtroom and addressed the overflow audience: "Thank you for your patience. This has been a tense sort of hearing. . . . Obviously, the community has a major problem to solve. And we won't solve it either by berating those who have to do it or by bragging on what has been done in the past."[131] McMillan refused to find the board in contempt of court, as the plaintiffs urged him to do, despite the board's explicit unwillingness to obey his April desegregation order. In a written order on the contempt issue, McMillan noted that the board had been badly divided and that "on an issue of such significance, the amount of foot-dragging" that had taken place "should not be considered as contempt of court." McMillan shrugged off the attacks on him by several school board members: "The members of the board have had uncomplimentary things to say . . . about the court, and many of them obviously disagree with the legality and propriety of the order of the court; but these latter sentiments may be regarded by the court as evidence of disagreement with rather than contempt for the court who is himself not far removed from active participation in the time-honored custom of criticizing a judge who has ruled against him."[132]

The community furor over the prospect of widespread integration continued during the weeks following McMillan's June order. On June 24, the North Carolina General Assembly enacted into law a bill, sponsored by Representative James Carson of Mecklenburg County, that prohibited the use of state funds to bus students to achieve "a balance or ratio of race" in any school.[133] Because the Charlotte-Mecklenburg School Board relied on state funds to provide bus transportation for students, the statute threatened to thwart the desegregation efforts of the court, although the school board attorney Barkley announced that he thought the statute would probably be found unconstitutional.[134]

In July, Vice-President Spiro Agnew visited Charlotte. Speaking to a black-tie Republican dinner, Agnew attacked the use of school busing to achieve racial balance.[135] The attack was consistent with earlier statements made by President Richard Nixon. One year earlier, during the presidential campaign of 1968, candidate Nixon had delivered from Charlotte a major television address on school desegregation in which he criticized overzealous federal judges and HEW bureaucrats in their handling of school desegregation matters.[136] Moreover, during the summer of 1969, Nixon's Department of HEW took two actions that marked a departure from its traditional support for desegregation efforts. First, the department suspended its policy of cutting off funds to recalcitrant school districts, and second, it sought, for the first time in its history, a delay in the implementation of a desegregation plan.[137]

Agnew's speech in particular and the Nixon administration's attitude in general annoyed McMillan.[138] Dealing with a badly divided school board and a confused community was difficult enough without the vice-president coming to Charlotte and legitimizing the views of those people who claimed that the judge had misinterpreted the law. McMillan's opponents would draw increasing support from various Nixon administration officials, particularly Vice-President Agnew, who placed himself firmly on record as opposing school busing to achieve school desegregation.[139]

In the meantime, the badly divided school board struggled to resolve its internal conflicts over the desegregation question. Ultimately, in a compromise bid, the board made an effort to come up with a desegregation plan to satisfy the court's August 1969 deadline. The board appointed a subcommittee of five members to study desegregation plans that had been devised by various other school systems and to recommend a plan for Charlotte-Mecklenburg. On July 22, the subcommittee presented to the board a modest desegregation plan, which was adopted and filed with the court on July 29. In a policy statement accompanying the plan, the board acknowledged for the first time its "affirmative constitutional duty to desegregate pupils, teachers, principals and staff members 'at the earliest possible date.'"[140]

The board's plan for accomplishing further desegregation consisted of closing seven all-black schools and assigning those three thousand students to outlying white schools, a scheme that had been used in Buffalo and Syracuse, and reassigning another twelve hundred African American students from overcrowded black schools to white schools. The board justified placing the desegregation burden exclusively on African American children by claiming that in other cities, "one-way busing of Negroes was generally acceptable to all segments of those communities."[141] In addition, the schools slated for closing were among the oldest in the system, each having been built between 1912 and 1935.[142]

Not surprisingly, announcements of the school closings provoked strident protests from the African American community. Black leaders charged that the plan singled out minority children to bear the burden of desegregation, a burden created by past segregationist actions.[143] George Leake, a prominent A.M.E. Zion minister who had been an unsuccessful candidate for mayor three months earlier, organized a Black Solidarity Committee to challenge the school closings. Leake led rallies, marches, and a petition drive, which garnered nineteen thousand signatures, and threatened an economic boycott of white businesses. He asked for the reopening of the African American schools until they could be replaced by new schools that would be constructed in the black community and that could then receive incoming white students.[144] Other African American ministers joined Leake in his protest of the desegregation plan, as did the *Star of Zion* of Charlotte, the denominational publication of the A.M.E. Zion Church, which decried integration efforts that unfairly burdened black children.[145]

There were two strands to the African American opposition to the board's school closing plan. One group, represented by Chambers and the NAACP, favored integration but strongly objected to burdening exclusively African American children with the extensive pupil reassignments that desegregation required.[146] A second group simply favored the retention of African American schools, minimizing the value of integrated schools. This was not the first time such divisions in the African American community had arisen over the conflict between integration and the preservation of traditionally black schools. In 1965, for example, when the school board had converted most of the school system to a geographic assignment plan, many African American parents had objected, stating that they wanted their children excluded from the geographic attendance plan so that their children could continue to attend all-black schools.[147] Moreover, every year since the adoption of the geographic attendance plan, more than half of the African American students assigned to a desegregated school had exercised their right to transfer to a school that was either all black or virtually all black.[148] In some measure this conduct was due to fears about the treatment of African Americans in white schools, but it underscored the fact that not everyone in the black community favored the NAACP's integrationist agenda.

This split in the Charlotte African American community reflected a larger split within the national civil rights community over the wisdom of school busing. Although the national office of the NAACP remained steadfast in its commitment to integration through busing, other black civil rights groups argued in favor of retaining neighborhood schools. In Atlanta, for example, the local NAACP chapter would ultimately diverge from the national office and favor the retention of majority-black neighborhood schools in lieu of widespread busing.[149] A 1969 survey by *U.S. News and World Report* revealed that many civil rights leaders believed that blacks could "benefit more from an improvement of schools in their own neighborhoods than . . . from being bused to white schools." The Congress of Racial Equality (CORE) in particular took this view, favoring the retention of neighborhood schools. "Busing is not relevant to high-quality education," CORE President James Farmer announced in March 1969. "It works severe hardships on the people it affects."[150] Eventually CORE would interject itself into the Charlotte litigation on the side of neighborhood schools.

The split in the African American community complicated Chambers's position. In early August he called McMillan's law clerk, Fred Hicks, to see if the judge had begun work on an order in response to the school board's plan. Chambers confided to Hicks that "his people" were sharply divided, "with [Reginald] Hawkins leading a segment that [felt] the educational advantages resulting from approval of the [board] plan far out-weigh[ed] the disadvantages" and with Leake, on the other hand, "look-ing at the plan only from an emotional point of view" and pressing for rejection of the board's one-sided plan.[151]

Ultimately in Charlotte, the NAACP's integrationist view would pre-vail as most of the black community rallied behind Chambers's push for a fully desegregated school system. By 1974, over 80 percent of the black parents surveyed in Charlotte indicated that they preferred integrated schools in significant measure because of the perceived improvement in educational quality.[152] To some extent, the increased black support for integration was due to the work of Chambers; throughout the ten years of the *Swann* litigation, Chambers frequently addressed local black com-munity and church groups, explaining his position and seeking sup-port.[153] The extraordinary respect that Chambers enjoyed within the Af-rican American community and his extensive efforts to convince this community of the wisdom of desegregation were critical to this increased support for his integrationist agenda.[154] Nevertheless, for the next five years, a significant minority of black parents would continue to favor neighborhood schools.

The division within the black community over the wisdom of integra-tion steeled the resolve of many whites to oppose McMillan's order. If neither blacks nor whites wanted school integration, many whites ar-gued, then McMillan was completely out of touch with community wishes, and his desegregation orders should be resisted.[155]

Faced with hostility from both the black and the white communities, McMillan held hearings on the new proposed board plan on a hot August day. The courtroom was packed with onlookers, most of whom were par-ents of black schoolchildren slated for reassignment to schools in white neighborhoods.[156] McMillan took the unusual step of calling a few of his own witnesses during the August hearing. Although judges possess the right to call and examine their own witnesses, most choose not to, relying instead on witnesses called by the parties themselves. McMillan, however, keenly aware of the impact his rulings had had on the entire city, perceived the need to depart from traditional judicial practice. Accordingly, McMillan called as witnesses both Leake and Paul Whitfield, a white par-ent from the Paw Creek neighborhood in the northwest section of the county who had publicly criticized the school board's pupil reassignment plan because of its impact on his neighborhood. McMillan called these witnesses for two purposes: to convey to disgruntled elements of both the white and the black communities a sense that they had been heard, and to educate the community concerning the requirements of the law in school desegregation cases. McMillan, for example, questioned Whitfield:

> *McMillan:* Mr. Whitfield, . . . why is this hearing being conducted in a court?
> *Whitfield:* My answer, Judge, would be that the community has failed in its responsibility to meet the problem head on.
> *McMillan:* We are here because we are all subject to some law.
> *Whitfield:* Yes, sir.
> *McMillan:* To wit, the Constitution. . . . Do you think that the Court's consideration of the legality, the constitutionality or unconstitutionality of the [board] plan ought to be affected by 21,000 signatures who say don't bus us into town and 19,000 signatures that say don't bus us out of town and 800 signatures that say don't split up the Paw Creek school?
> *Whitfield:* I think not, sir.
> *McMillan:* That's not the stuff of which the rights of man are made, is it?
> *Whitfield:* That's right, sir.[157]

The questions may have been directed at Whitfield, but the audience was clearly the city of Charlotte.

The bulk of the August hearing, however, consisted of an examination of Superintendent Self. Self defended the board's decision to reassign black students away from their neighborhood schools, citing the positive educational benefits achieved by school consolidation in the earlier part of the century: "I think from the standpoint of an educator moving youngsters from one geographic area to another has been defended down through history on the basis of improving educational opportunity."[158] Although Self sought to defend the board's one-way desegregation plan, his reasoning raised the obvious question of whether such benefits might not also follow from the reassignment of white students to black schools.

The board's limited busing plan had placed the superintendent in a difficult posture. As an educator, Self understood the value of assigning children away from their neighborhood schools in the pursuit of certain educational objectives. As a high-profile public figure, however, which Self had become during the past three months, the superintendent understood that reassigning white students to black schools was politically explosive. Chambers pressed Self to acknowledge that "two-way" busing was educationally acceptable and that the board had rejected it solely because of white opposition. Self conceded that the plaintiffs' two-way busing proposal was administratively feasible if politically acceptable. Self explained that the board planned to redraw student attendance zones over the course of the coming year in a manner that would increase pupil desegregation in some unspecified amount but had declined to do so for the 1969–70 school year because of community opposition.[159]

Chambers attacked the board plan, arguing that the board could have developed a more extensive desegregation plan for the 1969–70 school year, that the plan unfairly burdened black students, and that the freedom-of-choice provision would allow those twelve hundred white students assigned to black schools to transfer back to white schools. He urged McMillan to order the board to adopt the desegregation plan drawn up by the plaintiffs' expert John Finger. McMillan, however, "with great reluctance" held the board plan acceptable on an interim basis, even though it was less than what the law required. He acknowledged the unfair burden that the one-way busing placed on black students and noted, "[It] can legitimately be said and has been eloquently said that this plan is an affront to the dignity and pride of the black citizens." McMillan made it clear that he would not "endorse or approve any future plan" that put "the burden of desegregation primarily upon one race."[160]

At the same time, McMillan sympathized with the board's plight. He explained to Chambers:

> The fact that the Supreme Court ruled as it did [in *Green*] and that it's the duty of the School Board and the court to desegregate the schools now doesn't mean that they need to be hung if it doesn't happen this week. It takes a little time and a little patience and, frankly, I find in the policy change and in the somewhat disappointing one-way proposition a lot of action and a lot of implications which I think are most favorable for the completion of this job in fairly short order. . . .
>
> It will be helpful if we remembered that we are not just here grading papers on some rule that's been in existence forever, but we are here taking part in a change that nobody here started and nobody here will see the end of.[161]

McMillan reiterated his view that "the choice of how to do the job of desegregation" was for "the School Board — not for the court."[162]

At the same time, McMillan underscored that the difficult political pressures confronting the board could not be used to avoid the demands of the Constitution. Using special typeface for emphasis, McMillan wrote in his August order: "*The question is not whether people like desegre-*

gated public schools, but what the law requires of those who operate them. THE DUTY TO OBSERVE THE CONSTITUTION AND DESEGREGATE THE SCHOOLS CANNOT BE REDUCED OR AVOIDED BECAUSE OF SOOTH-ING SAYINGS FROM OTHER GOVERNMENT OFFICIALS NOR OUTCRIES FROM THOSE WHO WANT THE LAW TO GO AWAY." Borrowing from the rhetoric of the Nixon-Agnew campaign of the previous fall, McMillan sardonically noted: "The issue is one of law and order. . . . A community bent on 'law and order' should expect its school board members to obey the United States Constitution, *and should encourage them in every move they make toward such compliance.* The call for 'law and order' in the streets and slums is necessary, but it sounds hollow when it issues from people content with segregated public schools."[163] Noting the extensive criticism he had received from the community, McMillan wrote: "A correspondent who signs 'Puzzled' inquires: 'If the whites don't want it and the blacks don't want it, why do we have to have it?' The answer is, the Constitution of the United States."[164]

McMillan understood the importance of convincing a skeptical and angry community that his actions were dictated by law. McMillan's public statements, his private conversations with citizens, and his written opinions all reinforced that theme. Although in most cases judges can simply issue orders and expect the parties to comply, McMillan perceived a need to explain to the community that he was compelled to act in accord with legal principles as he understood them, even if his actions ran contrary to community sentiment. The *Observer* supported the judge in those efforts, noting, "Opponents of the plan must be reminded that the court cannot be bound by mere public acceptance or by what will make either a majority or minority of the people happy."[165]

Although McMillan justified his order primarily on the grounds that it was required by the constitutional mandates of higher federal courts, he also tried again to justify his decision on educational grounds. The plaintiffs had presented evidence that showed that white students performed significantly better on achievement tests than did African American students. Technically, the evidence had no relevance: the constitutional infirmity of de jure segregation had already been established in the *Brown* case, and hence there was no need to prove that segregation was actually harmful to African American students. Notwithstanding that fact, the plaintiffs' attorneys decided to present the evidence anyway. As the plaintiffs' counsel Adam Stein later explained: "We had had enough experience trying discrimination cases to know that many district judges were going to do less than the law required unless they could be persuaded that there was something particularly bad going on that needed to be corrected."[166] Convinced that the significant disparity in achievement levels lent greater credence to their argument that extraordinary efforts to overcome residential segregation were justified, the plaintiffs presented McMillan with evidence documenting the disparities between white and black students.

The evidence undoubtedly moved McMillan. He included in his August opinion a chart of the average achievement test scores of students. The chart indicated a dramatic disparity between black and white students: the twenty-one elementary schools, seven junior high schools, and two high schools with the poorest achievement test scores were predominantly or all black; white schools consistently topped the charts.[167] McMillan commented: "This alarming contrast in performance . . . was not fully known to the court before he studied the evidence in the case. It can not be explained solely in terms of cultural, racial or family background without honestly facing the impact of segregation. . . . Segregation produces inferior education."[168] William Sturges, one of the attorneys who would later represent the school board, conceded the importance of this evidence: "McMillan ultimately felt that black students had been given a bad deal."[169] McMillan himself would later acknowledge that he relied in part on this significant gap in achievement test scores to justify his insistence on full desegregation of the Charlotte schools.[170]

McMillan believed that the Supreme Court's *Green* decision compelled his actions. Nevertheless, his conclusion that desegregation would enhance the educational achievement of African American children clearly hardened his resolve to integrate fully the Charlotte-Mecklenburg schools. In his August order, McMillan cited the testimony of plaintiffs' experts that transferring "underprivileged black children from black schools into schools with 70% or more white students produce[d] a dramatic improvement in the rate of progress and an increase in the absolute performance of the less advanced students, without material detriment to the whites."[171] The broad disparities in educational achievement between black and white students triggered in McMillan a moral disquiet influenced by his strong religious convictions. As McMillan explained to a skeptical parent a few months later, "The best parts of our law and Constitution . . . reflect Christian principles."[172]

Yet predicting enhanced black performance as a justification for a desegregation order was a complicated move. On the one hand, it might make desegregation more palatable if the community understood that desegregation would improve black education. On the other hand, it left McMillan open to the claim that he was attempting to impose, by judicial fiat, his own educational views on a skeptical public. Indeed, some of the judge's critics would later level precisely that charge.[173] Moreover, social scientists were by no means united in their view of the effects of desegregation on pupil achievement, making reliance on such data a risky venture. Indeed, during the early 1970s, an increasing number of social scientists would question the extent to which integrated schools did in fact improve the achievement levels of African American students.[174]

In early September 1969, the Charlotte-Mecklenburg schools opened under the board's new desegregation plan. Although the plan did not satisfy constitutional requirements as interpreted by McMillan, the judge remained confident that the board would eventually satisfy its constitutional obligation to eliminate racially identifiable schools. As it turned out, that confidence was sorely misplaced.

CHAPTER 7

The School Busing Storm
Comes to Charlotte

Although for the first several months of the desegregation litigation, Judge James McMillan resisted the plaintiffs' request that he impose a desegregation plan on the school board, the judge eventually relented and in February 1970 ordered into effect one of the most sweeping
school desegregation plans ever devised. But a city that had adapted relatively easily to earlier changes in racial expectations suffered an explo-
sion of community opposition to McMillan's order. To many Charlotteans, it seemed terribly unfair that Charlotte, the city that had led the
South by integrating its schools in 1957 and that had a higher percentage
of black children attending integrated schools than did most other urban
school systems, should be forced to do so much. Charlotte had previously
proven itself willing to adapt to changing racial expectations when the
stakes were lower—admitting a handful of black children to a white
school or permitting a few black families to take a meal in an integrated
restaurant—but the reassignment of young children to distant schools
tested the city's resilience in an unparalleled manner. By the spring of
1970, Charlotte had become a focal point in the national debate over
busing.

The Charlotte-Mecklenburg schools opened in the fall of 1969 with
many African American students assigned for the first time to schools in
distant white neighborhoods. Although the desegregation plan was one-
sided and left many schools overwhelmingly segregated, McMillan de-

termined that it was an acceptable first step. Yet the plan did not achieve even the modest level of desegregation that the board had promised. Although the board closed seven all-black schools and reassigned those students to white schools, over two-thirds of the affected students exercised their right to transfer to another black school.[1] Furthermore, the board failed to transfer twelve hundred additional African American students from overcrowded black schools to white schools as promised, citing unforeseen space problems. As a result, during the 1969–70 school year, only 8,517 out of 24,714 African American students in the Charlotte-Mecklenburg school systems attended majority-white schools; over 75 percent of the schools in the system remained racially identifiable.[2] In short, the board had promised minimal desegregation and delivered even less.

In October 1969, McMillan's patience with the board underwent a dramatic transformation in response to the U.S. Supreme Court's decision in *Alexander v. Holmes County*.[3] In that case, the U.S. Court of Appeals for the Fifth Circuit had allowed, at the urging of the Nixon Justice Department, a postponement of the desegregation of thirty Mississippi school districts by extending those school districts' deadline for filing desegregation plans from August 11, 1969, until December 1, 1969. The Fifth Circuit had earlier ordered the defendant school boards, in conjunction with the Department of HEW, to develop desegregation plans by August 11, to take effect by the beginning of the 1969–70 school year. HEW had prepared the appropriate desegregation plans by the August deadline, stating, "Each of the enclosed plans is educationally and administratively sound." Several days later, HEW Secretary Robert Finch, reflecting the Nixon administration's lukewarm posture in desegregation cases, took the extraordinary step of asking the Fifth Circuit to ignore the plans submitted by his department and delay desegregation. When the Fifth Circuit granted the delay, the plaintiffs immediately appealed to the U.S. Supreme Court.[4]

HEW's action marked the first time that the federal government had ever attempted to delay implementation of a desegregation order. The delaying action created a crisis in the Justice Department; as a result, the solicitor general refused to defend the government's position before the Supreme Court, and several attorneys resigned in protest.[5] The Supreme Court acted with unusual speed, setting the case for an early argument and rendering an opinion on October 29 — only twenty days after deciding to hear the case and six days after oral argument. In a short opinion, the Supreme Court announced that the court of appeals had erred: "[The lower court] should have denied all motions for additional time because continued operation of segregated schools under a standard allowing 'all deliberate speed' for desegregation is no longer constitutionally permissible. Under explicit holdings of this Court, the obligation of every school district is to terminate dual school systems at once and to operate now and hereafter only unitary schools." The Court ordered every affected school district to "begin immediately to operate as unitary school systems."[6]

The *Alexander* decision signaled an unprecedented sense of urgency in school desegregation cases. After allowing local school boards to desegregate at a slow pace for much of the prior fifteen years, the Court had now indicated that further delays would not be tolerated—even delays until the end of a school semester or school year. In some sense, the *Alexander* decision constituted the Court's atonement for its "all deliberate speed" language in the second *Brown* decision, language that had allowed another generation of African American children to remain in segregated schools. More important, faced for the first time with Justice Department recalcitrance in a desegregation case and an administration with a questionable commitment to school integration, the Court felt compelled to emphasize, in dramatic fashion, that the time for delay and deliberate speed had come to an end. As had happened in 1958 with the Little Rock litigation, the politicization of school desegregation enforcement prompted the Court to take extraordinary action reaffirming its commitment to school integration.[7]

If *Green* altered the substantive demands on school boards, *Alexander* changed the time period within which those demands were to be met. The implications of the decision were immediately understood. The *Charlotte Observer* reported the decision with banner headlines: "All Public Schools Must Desegregate At Once, Supreme Court Rules."[8] Not surprisingly, the decision unleashed a frenzied period of desegregation activity throughout the South.

The *Alexander* decision had a profound impact on McMillan. In a bit of overstatement, given the *Green* decision of the previous year, he termed it "the most significant in this field since *Brown v. Board of Education*."[9] The *Alexander* decision, with its insistence on immediate desegregation, transformed McMillan's role in the litigation. No longer would he sit and wait patiently for the school board to move gradually toward a desegregated school system. If the school board persisted in its refusal to draft an acceptable desegregation plan, then the judge would have to see to it that the draft was done and that it was done immediately.

The same day as the *Alexander* decision, the board petitioned Mc-Millan for yet another extension to prepare a new desegregation plan. The board indicated that its computer consultant was hard at work on a new assignment plan but that the plan would not be completed for a few more months. McMillan denied the request, explaining that the *Alexander* decision tied his hands: "The Supreme Court's prohibition against extension of time as laid down in *Alexander v. Holmes County* is binding upon this court and this School Board, and bars the exercise of the court's usual discretion in such matters. . . . [T]o allow the request of the defendants for extension of time to comply with this court's previous judgments would be contrary to the Supreme Court's decision and should not be done."[10] McMillan further noted that the computer analysis that the board was developing would not achieve full desegregation at the elementary school level because it limited attendance at each school to students living within one and a half miles of the school. In a city as residentially segregated as Charlotte, such a plan could not possibly eliminate the racial identifiability of every elementary school in the system. The majority of the board, in its submission to McMillan, conceded the plan's limitations: "[The plan] *will not produce desegregation of all schools by September, 1970.* . . . It is *hoped* that the number of all white and all black schools will be substantially *reduced.* . . . [T]he restructuring of attendance lines . . . *may* satisfy constitutional requirements."[11] Since McMillan was insisting that every school have a majority of white pupils, it was apparent that the board's plan would not satisfy the court.

To McMillan, it had become clear that a majority of the board's members did not "accept the duty to desegregate the schools at any ascertainable time." Although McMillan still maintained that "a Mecklenburg plan ought if possible to be prepared by the Mecklenburg School Board and its large and experienced staff, rather than by outside experts," he indicated that he was prepared to do whatever was necessary to comply with the Supreme Court's demands. "Withholding or delaying the constitutional rights of children . . . is not the province of the School Board nor of this court." He announced that the board had ten days, until November 17, to devise a desegregation plan that would satisfy the court.[12]

As expected, the board's limited November 17 plan did not satisfy McMillan's requirements. The board majority stood by its long-standing commitment to neighborhood schools and refused to depart from the concept of contiguous school districts. Yet in a city as residentially segregated as Charlotte, contiguous school districts could never eliminate the racial identifiability of every school. The board majority, under the leadership of Board Chair William Poe, remained convinced that the Supreme Court did not require school boards to engage in a radical restructuring of school attendance lines, with extensive busing of students, to satisfy desegregation requirements. Hence, the board majority explicitly rejected other methods of desegregation, such as the pairing of noncontiguous school districts: "*A majority of the Board of Education believes that the constitutional requirements of desegregation will be achieved by the restructuring of attendance lines, the restricting freedom of transfer, and other provisions of this plan. The majority of the Board has, therefore, discarded further consideration of pairing, grouping, clustering and transporting.*"[13] Under the board's proposed plan, seven elementary schools would remain all black, and an undetermined number of other elementary schools would retain a black majority.[14]

The *Charlotte Observer* attacked the board for its failure of leadership:

> This is one of the few times in the past two decades that a local public body has so badly failed a test of leadership in resolving community problems.
>
> The tragedy is not so much that the board has failed to come up with a plan that Federal Judge James McMillan can look upon with favor, but that the board majority has sought to make the judge and the court an adversary of the system and the people.[15]

Chambers renewed his request that McMillan hold the board in contempt of court. He noted, "The board now unequivocally, defiantly and contumaciously advises the court that it will not now, nor in the future, carry out its constitutional responsibilities."[16] McMillan, however, again declined to hold the board in contempt: "This is a changing field of law. Despite the peremptory warnings of [*Green* and *Alexander*], strident voices, including those of school board members, still express doubt that the law of those cases applies to Mecklenburg County. This district court claims no infallibility."[17]

Nevertheless, the board's actions clearly frustrated McMillan. One day after the board announced its limited plan, McMillan expressed his exasperation: "The School Board by its latest non-plan seems to have left the court with little to do except accept the School Board's retirement from the duties for which it was elected, and to try to have somebody else prepare a plan and get on with the job."[18] On December 1, he formally rejected the board's limited desegregation plan and became one of the first judges in the nation to appoint his own "consultant" to devise a new de-segregation plan, a move he had hesitated for months to make despite the plaintiffs' insistence that he do so.[19] The refusal of the board to eliminate all predominantly black schools and the Supreme Court's insistence in *Alexander* on immediate desegregation convinced McMillan of the need to oversee directly the creation of an acceptable plan through an expert consultant.[20] "I sweat blood in the wording of these orders," McMillan told a news reporter, "and then [the board members] pretend as if the whole thing had never happened."[21]

McMillan appointed one of the plaintiffs' expert witnesses, John Finger, as his consultant. The choice of Finger was not ideal because of his prior association with the plaintiffs.[22] Nevertheless, the urgency of the *Alexander* decision convinced McMillan that he had little choice. Finger had previously drafted other urban desegregation plans and was already familiar with the Charlotte-Mecklenburg school system.[23] Hence, he could devise a plan more quickly than an expert unfamiliar with the case and the school system. McMillan ordered the board to cooperate fully with Finger, including paying all of his expenses and providing all of the support staff that he might need.[24] The *Charlotte Observer* lamented Finger's appointment as again signaling a failure of school board leadership: "It is a humiliating moment for the members of the board and this community. Here we had an opportunity to work out our own problems as the court saw them and as the community could have understood them given better leadership. The judge sought to use some patience and understanding. He twice chose to take the board's slowness not as defiance but as difficulty in working out the mechanics of full desegregation. Now he has virtually discarded leniency as a lost cause."[25]

In response to the appointment of Finger, the board set about to complete another desegregation plan. Four members of the board, who had consistently favored desegregation, sought a resolution that "every school in the Charlotte-Mecklenburg system [would] reflect approximately the racial proportions found in the population of the district as a whole," a concept that would have easily satisfied McMillan. Lacking the support of a fifth member, the motion failed.[26]

In the meantime, the board majority remained frustrated with Mc-Millan's interpretation of the constitutional demands on urban school boards faced with extensive residential segregation. Charlotte already had a higher level of pupil desegregation than almost every other urban school system in the United States, a fact that McMillan found irrele-

Judge James McMillan (right) meets with special consultant John Finger in
McMillan's chambers to discuss desegregation plan, December 4, 1969.
(Courtesy of the *Charlotte Observer*)

vant.[27] Moreover, other judges around the South were approving desegregation plans that left majority-black schools in place, even in cities that
had less residential segregation than Charlotte. The *Charlotte News* captured the board's frustration in a lengthy editorial attacking McMillan
for ignoring what was being permitted by "legal and educational leaders
. . . around the country." The *News* wrote: "Although the court's right to
hand down its interpretation of the law is indisputable, also indisputable
is that Judge McMillan's interpretation is by no means universally shared.
There is thoughtful opposition to the theory that racial balance is the ultimate and only talisman of quality education. There is from impeccable
sources disagreement that the constitution requires racial balance in defiance of housing patterns." Noting that other judges had not required as
much desegregation as had McMillan, the *News* urged the board to appeal McMillan's orders.[28]

In December 1969, federal judge Walter Hoffman issued a decision in
a Norfolk, Virginia, school desegregation case wherein he approved an
assignment plan that left some schools educating only African Americans.
Hoffman noted that the costs of busing outweighed its benefits: "Where

Antibusing protester marching outside the U.S. courthouse as Finger arrives to meet with McMillan, December 4, 1969. (Courtesy of the *Charlotte Observer*)

a school board presents a reasonable plan grounded upon sound educational principles, there remains room for the adoption of a plan with reasonable prospects for success even though there may remain, for a period of several years, some school buildings which will be occupied only by blacks or by whites."[29] Hoffman's views were sharply at odds with McMillan's. When Hoffman, under pressure from the Fourth Circuit, later ordered extensive busing, he termed such action "ridiculous."[30] The fact that Norfolk was a similar city to Charlotte in terms of population and the extent of residential segregation made the different views of the two judges particularly disturbing to many Charlotteans.

The *Charlotte News* featured the Norfolk decision in a front-page story that contrasted Hoffman's treatment of school desegregation with McMillan's and noted that McMillan had ordered the elimination of all single-race schools, whereas Hoffman had not.[31] The prominent play given by the *News* to the Norfolk comparison helped fuel the feeling that McMillan had misconstrued the demands of the Constitution. The *News* would continue to compare McMillan's actions with those of other federal judges, giving the school board additional incentive to resist full compliance with the judge's orders.

Even the board members sympathetic to McMillan's desegregation demands agreed that the views of a higher court were needed. Carlton Watkins, a board member who had consistently supported the judge, told a reporter in early December, "[An appeal] may be the only way to convince the community that McMillan is correct in the directions he has given the board."[32] Ironically, McMillan himself privately favored an appeal so as to give the higher courts the opportunity to give further direction. In early December, in response to a letter from the chair of the State Democratic Executive Committee, who had criticized McMillan's orders, the judge wrote, "I would like to see an appeal because we have gone long enough with so many people falsely pretending that this is a matter of local opinion and that I have forsaken the course of the law in the rulings that I have made."[33] McMillan explained to another correspondent, "If as I believe I have been correct and the appellate courts say so, it may go a long way towards stifling some of the Bilbos and bringing the moderates out of the woodwork where most of them have been hiding for many months."[34]

At the same time, McMillan remained steadfast in his insistence that *Green* required the elimination of the racial identifiability of every school in the system, regardless of the views of school boards and judges in other parts of the South: "The fact that other communities might be more backward in observing the Constitution than Mecklenburg would hardly seem to support denial of constitutional rights to Mecklenburg citizens."[35]

In the meantime, the U.S. Court of Appeals for the Fourth Circuit decided two cases that contributed to the sense of urgency that the *Alexander* decision had created and increased the pressure on McMillan to order immediate desegregation. On December 2, 1969, the Fourth Circuit, in *Nesbit v. Statesville City Board of Education*, ordered five school districts in North Carolina and Virginia to file desegregation plans within six days and ordered the district judges in those cases to approve or modify such plans in time to take effect by January 1, 1970.[36] The *Nesbit* decision stunned the Charlotte-Mecklenburg School Board.[37] Although the board had been contemplating an appeal from McMillan's latest order, the *Nesbit* decision raised the prospect that if the board appealed, the Fourth Circuit might require midyear desegregation, a result unlikely from McMillan. Fearing such a decision, the board decided not to file an appeal.[38] McMillan, hoping to utilize the *Nesbit* decision to his advantage, sent copies of the decision, along with the Supreme Court's earlier *Alexander* decision, to a few lawyers in Charlotte, urging them to help "clarify public thinking" by explaining to the community that the higher courts were insisting on immediate desegregation.[39]

The Fourth Circuit continued its demands for immediate action. On January 19, 1970, the court, in *Stanley v. Darlington County School District*, ordered two South Carolina school districts to file desegregation plans within four days, with implementation by February 9. The court noted, "Whatever the disruption which will be occasioned by the immediate reassignment of teachers and pupils in mid-year, there remains no judicial discretion to postpone immediate implementation [of desegregation plans]."[40] The *Stanley* decision carried a special irony. The author of the opinion was Chief Judge Clement Haynsworth; one of the two school districts ordered to desegregate midyear was Haynsworth's own Greenville, South Carolina, school system. The previous November, the U.S. Senate had rejected Haynsworth's nomination to serve on the U.S. Supreme Court. Civil rights groups, including the NAACP, had opposed the nomination, in part because of Haynsworth's school desegregation decisions. The opposition of those groups, along with that of organized labor, had been critical to Haynsworth's defeat.[41] Chambers had been one of Haynsworth's attackers, labeling the judge "an outright admittedly segregated jurist" who was "unfit to serve on the United States Supreme

Court."[42] Less than two months after his rejection by the Senate, this "seg-regated jurist" had ordered his own school system to integrate its schools within three weeks.

In the meantime, the U.S. Supreme Court kept up the pressure for mid-year desegregation. On January 14, 1970, in *Carter v. West Feliciana Parish School Board*, the Supreme Court vacated without oral argument an order of the Fifth Circuit permitting pupil desegregation in several Deep South school districts to be deferred until September 1970.[43] Once again, the Nixon Justice Department had joined the defendant school board in seeking a delay in the implementation of a desegregation order. The Court held that the Fifth Circuit had misconstrued its decision in *Alexander* by allowing the postponement and ordered the school districts in question to desegregate within eighteen days. A few of the justices sought to specify the time period within which a school board must institute a new deseg-regation plan after a finding of noncompliance with the *Green* decision; Justices John Harlan and Byron White suggested eight weeks. That pro-posal drew a sharp rebuke from Justices Hugo Black, William Douglas, William Brennan, and Thurgood Marshall, who characterized the Harlan-White view as a "retreat" from the Court's insistence, in *Alexander*, that desegregation take place "now."[44] After years of deliberate speed, the Supreme Court had changed course with a fury.

In response to the *Carter* decision, the *Swann* plaintiffs asked Mc-Millan, on January 20, 1970, to have Finger bring in his plan so that de-segregation could begin immediately.[45] McMillan had already indicated that he took seriously the Supreme Court's demand for immediate deseg-regation. On December 19, 1969, McMillan had held a hearing to con-sider a desegregation plan submitted by the school board in Statesville, North Carolina, in accord with the Fourth Circuit's *Nesbit* decision. The school board's proposed plan desegregated every school in the system but kept a few schools majority black. On the morning of the first day of the hearing, Chambers, who represented the Statesville plaintiffs, argued that the board's plan was deficient. McMillan agreed and ordered the States-ville School Board to break for lunch and return in the afternoon with a new plan. Over lunch, the board drafted another desegregation plan that eliminated every majority-black school. That afternoon, McMillan ac-cepted the board's new plan, which was implemented following the Christmas recess.[46]

On February 1, 1970, both Finger and the school board submitted plans to McMillan to desegregate the Charlotte-Mecklenburg schools.

Finger's plan, prepared in significant measure by the Charlotte-Mecklenburg school staff under Finger's direction, eliminated every majority-black school in the system. Initially Finger, at the judge's instruction, had excluded certain rural areas of the school system from the desegregation plan; ultimately, at the urging of certain school staff members, Finger revised the plan to include the entire school system.[47] The Finger Plan, as it became known, desegregated every high school in the system pursuant to the creation of new attendance zones. Nine of the junior high schools were desegregated through the pairing of noncontiguous black and white residential areas in different parts of the city. The elementary schools were desegregated through a combination of new attendance zones, the creation of noncontiguous attendance zones, and with thirty-three of the schools, a special coupling of inner-city and suburban schools. Pursuant to this coupling, black students from grades one through four would be transferred to a white suburban school, whereas white fifth- and sixth-graders would attend inner-city black schools. The school staff offered assurances that it was feasible to implement the plan during the current school year.[48]

The board plan used elongated, contiguous districts encompassing both black and white residential areas. The board refused to use any noncontiguous school districts and, as a result, left nine elementary schools and one junior high school predominantly black and eight elementary schools all white.[49] Ironically, the board plan required longer bus trips for junior and senior high school students than did the Finger Plan.[50] The board plan gained the support of only six of the nine board members. One member, Sam McNinch, opposed any redistricting efforts to increase desegregation. Two other members, Julia Maulden and Coleman Kerry, the latter of whom was one of the plaintiffs in the litigation, favored the more extensive Finger Plan.[51]

On February 2, 1970, McMillan held hearings on the two plans. Community interest ran high; the courtroom once again overflowed with onlookers. At the beginning of the hearings, McMillan took the unusual step of informally addressing the onlookers.[52] Seated at the front of the elegant, walnut-paneled courtroom below a portrait of Judge John Parker, the renowned Fourth Circuit judge who had written that *Brown* did not require integration but only the elimination of state-mandated segregation, McMillan spoke for almost half an hour. His comments ranged from the poignant to the humorous. The judge first expressed sympathy for the man who for months had been his adversary, School Board Chair Poe: "I've sometimes wondered what I would have thought if I'd been in

Bill Poe's place operating the schools for four years under a court order approved in 1965 allowing freedom-of-choice and geographic assignments and along came a new judge who says you've got to do it all over again." Observing that the audience comprised primarily disgruntled mothers of young schoolchildren, McMillan mused, "I want to say something to disappoint some of you mothers, but my old friend Jim McMillan who died the other day was not the judge."[53]

Yet the central thrust of McMillan's address to the courtroom, and by inference to the community of Charlotte, was that his actions were compelled by the Constitution, a consistent theme in the judge's various public statements and judicial orders issued since the previous April: "I want to say a word to these members of the school board who are here. This is a court of law. Questions of constitutionality are raised and whatever the Constitution says as it relates to the problems of the [school] board and schools is what we must follow as a court."[54] McMillan's claim that his actions were dictated by what "the Constitution says" was eminently understandable, but his comments sidestepped the fact that there was considerable controversy at the time concerning what the Constitution required for the desegregation of an urban school system. The Supreme Court, in interpreting the relevant constitutional language, had not said whether an urban school system denied black children the equal protection of the laws if it left some schools majority black in the face of extensive residential segregation. Moreover, a number of other district court judges had expressly found that in fact the Constitution did not so require.

The bulk of the two-day hearings consisted of an examination of Superintendent William Self. Through Self's testimony, the board sought to convince McMillan that the Finger Plan, with its extensive busing components, was too disruptive, particularly for elementary school children. McMillan was equally determined to counter any suggestion that community opposition should affect his decision. At one point during the direct examination of Self by School Board attorney William Waggoner, McMillan showed a flash of anger, one of the few times this happened during the entire litigation. In response to a question by Waggoner, Self testified about the Finger Plan, "[It may] be so traumatic that what you were hoping would happen in a desegregated classroom would be beyond the realm of possibility." McMillan, conscious of the overcrowded courtroom and the repeated efforts of the board to focus on the desires of the wider community, interrupted the testimony:

McMillan: You're talking now about whether people like it or not, aren't you? . . . Let's confine ourselves not to whether we like what the law requires but to the educational questions involved.

Waggoner: Can we get his testimony in the record?

McMillan: I don't think it's pertinent and I told you Monday [February 1] that we're not holding a popularity hearing on this question, and I'm not going to do it today.

Waggoner: If the Court please, what he is stating is that the opinion of children and parents can so affect the educational system that the benefits to be derived from desegregation can be submerged because of lack of popular support or acceptance. . . .

McMillan: I have instructed you not to call for any more evidence on the question of whether the people of Mecklenburg County like or don't like what the law requires. . . . I'm instructing you, Mr. Waggoner, not to proceed any further with comment on what people like or don't like about the law of the land.[55]

McMillan bitterly noted that he realized the Constitution was not held in very high esteem in Mecklenburg County but that this fact was not relevant to the court's duty to enforce the Constitution's demands.[56]

McMillan issued his decision on the two plans on February 5, 1970. He approved the board's senior high school desegregation plan with a few minor changes. Regarding the system's twenty-one junior high schools, McMillan characterized the board plan as "inferior in design and results to Dr. Finger's plan" because it left three of these schools with black populations of less than 3 percent. Nevertheless, McMillan concluded that because the board plan for junior high schools was "a purely 'home grown' product," he would approve it provided certain changes were made in the assignments to the one junior high school—Piedmont—that the board had left with a majority-black population.[57]

The most controversial aspect of McMillan's order pertained to elementary schools. Because of the small size of most of the system's elementary schools, they could not be desegregated without extensive pairing of noncontiguous attendance zones and substantial busing. The board had refused to adopt such a plan, expressing concern about young children riding buses to schools far from home, and had therefore left about half of the African American elementary school students attending predominantly black schools, a few of which had almost no white students. The Finger Plan, on the other hand, provided that every elementary school would be predominantly white, as required by the judge. Mc-Millan rejected the board's plan for the elementary schools and approved the Finger Plan.[58]

McMillan ordered that the elementary school desegregation be accomplished no later than April 1, 1970, and that the junior and senior high school desegregation be accomplished no later than May 4, 1970. Although recognizing that there would be an appeal of his order, McMillan, consistent with Judge Haynsworth's decision three weeks earlier in the *Stanley* case, indicated that he would not stay his order pending appeal and ordered the board to take immediate action to begin compliance.[59] McMillan did not favor midyear desegregation because of the disruption to students but believed that the recent decisions from the Supreme Court and Fourth Circuit left him no choice. As he told a news reporter: "The higher courts have said desegregate now — they're breathing down my neck. I had hoped we'd be able to wait until next fall."[60]

McMillan's order provided for the complete desegregation of one of the largest school systems in the United States. No other federal judge had ever ordered a school system to adopt as extensive a busing plan as had McMillan for Charlotte.[61] Although the national media did not immediately grasp the legal significance of McMillan's order, within weeks the importance of the Charlotte busing order was widely appreciated.[62] As the case moved into the higher courts, observers throughout the country came to understand that the courts would use Charlotte to define the desegregation obligations of urban school boards.

Since the *Brown* decision, Charlotte had prided itself on its ability to adapt to changing expectations in matters of race. McMillan's February 5 order, however, tested the community's resilience in an unparalleled manner. Within days of the issuance of the order, a wave of opposition swept the community, soon spreading throughout the state and even the nation. Charlotte quickly became a national symbol for school busing.

On the evening on which the decision was announced, and continuing for many evenings thereafter, antibusing picketers marched outside McMillan's home; included among them were some of his neighbors.[63] Within days, picketing had spread to the courthouse and the offices of the *Charlotte Observer*.[64] Hundreds of angry citizens telephoned the judge's home and wrote letters to express their displeasure with his ruling.[65] There was an ugly side to many of these communications. Both McMillan and Chambers received anonymous threats. For example, one such letter to Chambers — addressed to "Julius Chambers, Negro, Charlotte, North

Carolina"—suggested that he would reach the same violent end as had John and Robert Kennedy and Martin Luther King.[66] McMillan received similar letters.[67] Many letters demanded that impeachment proceedings be initiated against the judge.[68] Others complained of the influence of "Anti-Christ Jews" on the litigation, a pointed reference to NAACP attorneys Adam Stein and Jack Greenberg.[69] The flow of threatening letters and phone calls to the judge eventually became so intense that federal marshals provided him around-the-clock protection and McMillan took to carrying a gun.[70] During the bitter months of 1970, McMillan joined the long list of southern federal judges whose insistence on the strict enforcement of the Supreme Court's desegregation demands had come at considerable personal cost.[71]

Other people wrote to support McMillan, including Frank Porter Graham, who had taken many unpopular stands during his tenure as president of the University of North Carolina and as U.S. senator. McMillan replied: "Dear Dr. Frank: Since the first day I saw you walking across the campus in Chapel Hill in 1934 I have admired and respected you in what you stand for. My life has fallen in ways which have brought me recently up against questions which you had faced and fought long before you reached my age."[72] Another supporter appropriately likened McMillan to South Carolina federal judge Waties Waring, who twenty years earlier had been contemptuously scorned by Charleston white society for his pro–civil rights opinions.[73]

Notwithstanding the harassing phone calls, the judge refused to get an unlisted telephone number. To do so, in McMillan's view, would have unduly isolated him from the community. Similarly, McMillan promptly replied to those critics who wrote to express their displeasure with his busing order.[74] McMillan developed over the course of the litigation the view that he should remain accessible to the community, even if that meant subjecting himself to considerable personal abuse.[75]

Within days of McMillan's order, the Concerned Parents Association (CPA), established the prior spring, sought to arouse public opposition to McMillan's actions. Holding rallies in school auditoriums, the CPA organized an eighty-thousand-signature petition drive seeking a boycott of the court's order.[76] The CPA's calling card—"NO FORCED BUSING" bumper stickers—appeared throughout the city.[77] Thomas Harris, an insurance salesman and the CPA chair, explained his group's views:

If what our civic leaders are counseling is calmness and deliberation, I agree. If, on the other hand, what they are counseling is that we give up our convictions and accept it as an unalterable fact that our freedom of choice and decision is gone forever, then I do not agree.

And if our civic leaders are trying to lead us down the path of surrendering our liberties in this vital area, then I think they are going to be strongly repudiated.[78]

One busing opponent was more direct: "I am against bussing. I am willing to die if necessary to keep it from happening."[79]

Much of the CPA's effort focused on petitioning political leaders in Washington, Raleigh, and Charlotte to take action to prevent implementation of the McMillan order. The White House, in particular, was flooded with telegrams: "Faced with forced busing. Desire freedom of choice. Request intervention as per campaign promise."[80] Follow-up contacts were made with Vice-President Spiro Agnew's office, seeking his help.[81] One Nixon administration official later commented that the president had received more mail from Charlotte in response to McMillan's order than it had ever received from any other locality on any issue. The CPA leaders' primary goal was to win in the court of public opinion what they could not win in the court of law. Charlotte attorney John Golding explained to one CPA gathering: "This might sound funny for a lawyer to say but in the final analysis, this case will be tried, won or lost, in the court of public opinion. No law can stand against the will of the people."[82]

Within the CPA, competing viewpoints emerged as to the appropriate focus of the organization. Some favored using the antibusing effort as a platform for attacking a whole array of liberal positions that troubled many conservative white Charlotteans, whereas others preferred to keep the focus on the busing issue. In some measure, this division was inevitable in as large and amorphous an organization as the CPA. Ultimately, the CPA chose to focus on the extensive use of school busing.[83]

Without question, the resistance to McMillan's busing order would have been intense even if the order had come directly from the U.S. Supreme Court. The displeasure with the order was magnified, however, because of the perception that Charlotte had been singled out unfairly to bear a burden that other communities had escaped. Once again, the *Charlotte News*, under the editorship of Perry Morgan, attacked McMillan on this issue. To Morgan, the desegregation order was doubly unfair. First, McMillan's desegregation order subjected Charlotte to an unprecedented level of school busing, notwithstanding its history as a racially moderate southern city and its record as having one of the most desegregated urban school systems in the country. "It is ironic and to some it seems unfair that one of the three North Carolina school systems that led the South in early compliance with court requirements of school desegregation now faces almost incalculable difficulty in complying with the latest. Charlotte, together with Winston-Salem and Greensboro, undertook voluntary desegregation 13 years ago, when most of the political leadership of the South was on the fool's errand of trying to thwart and defy the nation's courts."[84]

Even more troubling to Morgan was the fact that a growing number of southern judges were interpreting the *Green* decision in a manner that allowed the retention of majority-black schools. Morgan complained of a judicial double standard: one for Charlotte and another for other cities where federal judges had permitted the retention of majority-black schools.[85] To be sure, in the first few months of 1970, federal judges throughout the South approved urban desegregation plans that left some schools with a majority-black population. In city after city—Atlanta, Fort Lauderdale, Fort Worth, Jackson, Knoxville, Memphis, Miami, Mobile, Norfolk, Orlando, Winston-Salem—federal judges required less desegregation than had McMillan, troubling evidence that McMillan had required Charlotte to take more extensive action than the law required.[86] A number of these decisions permitting the retention of black schools would ultimately be appealed and reversed by appellate courts, but in the frenzy of February 1970, the contrast between McMillan and these other federal judges served only to further antagonize those opposed to school busing. Morgan noted quite accurately in early 1970 that McMillan had been called on to implement judicial policy that had not "been articulated clearly" by the higher courts and that was "not understood by the citizens."[87]

In the meantime, leading state and national politicians joined the attack on school busing. North Carolina's senior senator Sam Ervin offered his support to the CPA by attacking McMillan: "I am incapable of comprehending why any American is opposed to a freedom of choice plan which grants equality of freedom to all parents of children of all races. Once again, we are confronted in America with the old issue of governmental tyranny versus liberty. I am glad that the Concerned Parents of Mecklenburg County stand on the side of liberty."[88] Senator Ervin continued his attack on McMillan on the floor of Congress: "These policies and rules to bus students and to force integration which are being enforced in such a harsh manner are . . . rules and policies made out of the head and from the imagination of Federal judges exercising the most unbounded discretion that any judges have ever exercised at any time in the history of this Nation, and exercising a discretion which might be becoming to totalitarian countries."[89] Ervin, the senator responsible for McMillan's appointment to the bench, would be a bitter critic of the judge for the next several years. Ervin later commented, "I am not infallible and . . . conclusive evidence of that fact is to be found in my recommendation of Jim McMillan for the District Judgeship."[90] McMillan, in turn, would tell a Senate committee in 1981: "I love and respect Senator Ervin. I had his views [on race] 20 years ago. I have had to learn something about it, and I have changed mine. He has not changed his."[91]

The governor of North Carolina, Robert Scott, entered the fray as well. One week after McMillan's order, Scott issued a press release in which he directed the Department of Administration not to release any funds in violation of the state's antibusing statute, which the general assembly had enacted the previous summer.[92] As a result, the state superintendent of public instruction, Craig Phillips, wrote the Charlotte-Mecklenburg superintendent, Self, that no state monies would be available to Charlotte for busing, contrary to an earlier promise of financial support.[93] At the same time, Scott pledged his continued support for neighborhood schools: "I am personally committed to doing everything lawful to preserve our neighborhood schools. The neighborhood-school concept has been the strength of our public education system in North Carolina and our state has been committed to that policy for some time. It is sound educational policy and must be preserved." Shortly thereafter, Scott joined the chorus of leaders seeking President Richard Nixon's intervention, reminding Nixon of his campaign pledge to limit school busing.[94]

Ultimately, the Nixon administration responded. In mid-February, Secretary of HEW Robert Finch announced his opposition to the Charlotte desegregation plan.[95] Finch's statement was particularly significant given the primary role HEW had played during the previous five years in promoting school desegregation throughout the South. Chambers recognized the damage that Finch's opposition could cause and accused Finch of "materially contribut[ing] to the possibility that a federal court's orders [would] be defied."[96] Indeed, the statements by Ervin, Scott, and Finch all received extensive news coverage and gave legitimacy to those favoring resistance to the court. At the same time, Leon Panetta, the director of the Office of Civil Rights in the Department of HEW, was forced to resign in mid-February because of his aggressive support for desegregation remedies, an event that received extensive publicity and prompted a firestorm of protest among HEW employees.[97]

Finally, on March 24, 1970, President Nixon delivered a major televised address, setting forth his administration's policy on school busing: "The neighborhood school will be deemed the most appropriate . . . system." He added, "Transportation of pupils beyond normal geographic school zones for the purpose of achieving racial balance will not be required."[98] Nixon implicitly criticized McMillan's February order, labeling some recent court decisions "untypical" and "beyond . . . generally accepted principles." He noted that unless these decisions were affirmed by the Supreme Court, he would not "consider them as precedents to guide administration policy elsewhere."[99] The Nixon statement, more than anything else, symbolized the isolation of federal judges such as McMillan who took seriously the Supreme Court's desegregation demands.

Congress eventually took action itself, enacting legislation that prevented HEW from requiring school districts to bus children in order to remain eligible for federal funds.[100] The legislation did not, however, restrict the remedial powers of federal judges, the constitutionality of which would have been highly questionable, and hence did not affect McMillan's order. Shortly thereafter, in an extraordinary gesture, a federal district court judge in Louisiana responded to the storm of opposition to school busing by reversing his earlier desegregation order that had required extensive pupil reshuffling and by allowing the city of Monroe, Louisiana, to revert to the use of neighborhood schools. The judge explained his actions by noting: "Things have changed substantially in light of . . . congressional action and presidential action. Things are now in a state of flux."[101]

At the same time, certain national civil rights groups criticized the growing movement toward extensive pupil reshuffling to meet desegregation goals, once again reflecting the split within the African American community over school desegregation. Shortly after McMillan's February 1970 busing order, the Congress of Racial Equality (CORE) issued a major policy statement on school segregation, calling for the creation of "community school districts" formed "along natural, geographic lines" as the "best possible way of destroying segregation and insuring equal education for Black children."[102] Without specifically naming the NAACP, the report sharply criticized those who promoted integration as a way of achieving equality, labeling such actions "insidiously racist." The report concluded:

> Blacks who subscribe to this theory are suffering from self-hatred, the legacy of generations of brainwashing. They have been told — and they

believe — that it is exposure to Whites *in and by itself* that makes Blacks equal citizens. . . .

[T]he court can offer Black children, teachers and administrators very little protection from the crippling abuses which arise daily in an *integrated* setting when whites don't favor union.[103]

CORE would continue work at cross-purposes with Chambers and the NAACP. When the *Swann* case finally made its way to the U.S. Supreme Court several months later, CORE filed an amicus brief urging the retention of black schools: "Integration, as it is designed, places the Black child in the position of implied inferiority. Not only is he asked to give up much of his culture and identity, but with the dispersal of Blacks he loses many of the communal ties which have traditionally been the cornerstone of the Black community."[104] CORE would continue to complain bitterly about the NAACP's "monopoly" in speaking on behalf of the black community.[105]

In the face of growing community and national hysteria over the busing issue, the Charlotte-Mecklenburg School Board tried to walk a middle line. On the one hand, the board urged calm. Board Chair Poe, for example, asked parents to respond to the court's order "without open defiance and disrespect for the law as pronounced by the courts." Only one of the nine board members — Sam McNinch — endorsed the CPA's call for a school boycott. On the other hand Poe repeatedly argued, "Legitimate judicial remedies ought to be pursued until they are exhausted."[106] Poe remained convinced that the Constitution did not require all that McMillan had ordered, particularly the bus transportation of elementary schoolchildren, and that the appellate courts would eventually so state.

To be sure, a few community groups supported McMillan's busing order. The local chapter of the League of Women Voters, for example, issued a report concluding that segregated schools led "to cultural deprivation of all children" and sought to encourage community acceptance of McMillan's order.[107] Similarly, a biracial group of citizens organized an Interested Citizens Association to encourage the board to implement the Finger Plan.[108] Although the group did not favor the movement of children away from their neighborhood schools, it argued that such movement was the only way to desegregate the schools.[109] As usual, the *Charlotte Observer* endorsed the judge's order and called for the community to accept it.[110] Throughout the difficult days of the winter and spring of 1970, the paper remained the judge's primary supporter. But those who supported the judge earned the wrath of the antibusing forces. During

February 1970, many Charlotteans canceled their *Observer* subscriptions, and one newspaper reported that white churches whose ministers supported the busing order experienced a decline in contributions.[111]

In a departure from earlier patterns, the city's civic and political leadership did little to encourage community acceptance of McMillan's February 1970 order. The Charlotte Chamber of Commerce, for example, so vital to the city's earlier successes with racial problems, remained silent, a fact noted by the *Charlotte Observer*: "Unfortunately, community leadership has not functioned in the sound tradition of the past decade's experience where the school desegregation crisis is concerned. The greatest sin among community spokesmen has been silence in this instance."[112] One business leader later commented on the significance of the chamber's silence: "Had the Chamber gotten involved earlier, it would have made a big difference. . . . Had the Chamber and the presidents of the city's major corporations come in and acted as a mediating force, there would have been an easier resolution of the problem."[113]

But in the early 1970s, no chamber leader emerged to facilitate a resolution of the desegregation controversy as had Stanford Brookshire several years earlier. In some measure, the chamber's differing reaction to the 1970 busing crisis and the 1963 public accommodations controversy was due to the very different demands that each placed on the city. Pupil mixing, particularly at distant inner-city schools, proved far more difficult for the white community to accept than had integrated restaurants. As one business leader later commented, "It was one thing to go to lunch with a Johnson C. Smith professor; it was quite another to send one's child to school in a black neighborhood."[114]

Mayor John Belk, another former chamber president, said little about the desegregation controversy. The difference between Mayor Belk and his predecessor, Brookshire, is striking. Brookshire used his considerable influence in 1963 to help desegregate the city's public accommodations. Belk, on the other hand, remained virtually silent throughout the entire busing controversy. Yet Belk's silence was propitious; the mayor opposed school busing, and by remaining silent, he avoided fanning the flames of opposition even further.

The local bar said little as well. The *North Carolina Law Record*, in a brief article entitled "Where Are You, Charlotte?" criticized Charlotte lawyers for their refusal to defend McMillan against the personal attacks on his character: "We have few attorneys rallying to the defense of a man crucified simply because he interpreted the law as he thought was right."[115] To be sure, some lawyers wrote to McMillan to express their support, but few spoke publicly in his defense, notwithstanding Mc-Millan's private pleas that his fellow lawyers help explain to a confused community the demands of the Constitution.[116] McMillan wrote letters to several attorneys during the winter of 1970, seeking their help. He told one correspondent, for example, "[CPA leader] Dr. Roberson and a lot of other people could understand this situation better if you lawyers would talk to them about law."[117]

In the meantime, the CPA did more than encourage community opposition to school busing. In the weeks before and after the February 5 busing order, the organization carried on an extensive litigation campaign in the state courts to subvert McMillan's actions. The CPA correctly understood that state judges, subject to periodic elections, would be much more responsive to community sentiment than would McMillan.

Shortly before McMillan entered his busing order, several CPA members, including Chairman Tom Harris, secured from state judge Francis Clarkson a temporary restraining order preventing School Superintendent Self from paying Finger.[118] Both the board and the plaintiffs opposed this interference in the desegregation process. Two weeks later, on February 9, state judge William McLean ruled that Finger could be paid if the board approved the payment; McLean's decision ended the dispute.[119]

In the meantime, the CPA requested an injunction invoking the state antibusing law, which prohibited the use of state money to bus students for purposes of racial desegregation. The CPA specifically sought an order enjoining the school board from using any public funds to purchase, rent, or operate a school bus for the purpose of transporting students pursuant to a desegregation plan.[120] On February 12, Judge McLean granted the CPA's request for a temporary restraining order and set the matter for a full hearing on the question.[121]

The CPA group filed yet another state court action on February 22 seeking an injunction preventing the school board from implementing any desegregation plan that required children to attend a particular school because of their race. This suit went much further than the first two suits; this one sought to prevent the school board from taking *any* action to implement the desegregation plan, not just the expenditure of money to pay Finger or buy school buses. Late on Sunday evening, February 22, Judge Frank Snepp entered a temporary restraining order granting the relief requested. In so doing, Snepp effectively thwarted Mc-Millan's February 5 order.[122]

As both a state legislator and an attorney, Judge Snepp had a long history of involvement with racial issues. In 1957, Snepp had been one of the primary opponents in the North Carolina General Assembly to legislation that would have required the NAACP to disclose its membership lists. Two years later, Snepp represented the Mecklenburg County School Board in the NAACP desegregation suit that resulted in a victory for the board in 1961.[123] In that case, Snepp had successfully defended the exclusion of black students from a white school by arguing that busing had a long tradition in North Carolina education and that proximity to a school had "never been a determinative factor in the assignment of pupils."[124]

On February 27, five days after Snepp granted the temporary restraining order, the school board voted to comply with Snepp's order and directed Superintendent Self to stop compliance with McMillan's February 5 order.[125] The CPA's strategy of seeking relief from a more sympathetic judge had, at least temporarily, derailed the desegregation process in Charlotte.

Chambers quickly struck back. He first asked McMillan to dissolve both McLean's and Snepp's restraining orders and to direct all parties to cease interfering with the federal court's mandates. He then asked McMillan to fine each board member $10,000 for contempt of court for directing Superintendent Self to cease working on the implementation of the February 5 order. McMillan dissolved the two state court orders and requested Chief Judge Clement Haynsworth of the Fourth Circuit to designate a three-judge court to consider the constitutionality of the state antibusing statute, since the state court litigation turned on the application of that statute. These actions effectively ended the state court challenges to McMillan's desegregation order. Once again, however, McMillan refused to hold the board members in contempt of court.[126]

In the meantime, the board appealed McMillan's busing order. On March 5, the U.S. Court of Appeals for the Fourth Circuit ordered McMillan to make further factual findings on the issue of the ability of the county and state to provide the bus transportation necessary to implement the plan. The Fourth Circuit's more significant action, however, came in a second order. In a major blow to McMillan, the Fourth Circuit stayed all portions of McMillan's order that required the busing of students, pending full consideration of his busing order by that court.[127] Eleven days later, on March 16, the U.S. Supreme Court left the Fourth Circuit's stay in effect.[128]

The Supreme Court's refusal to overturn the Fourth Circuit stay sent troubling signals as to the Court's intentions in school desegregation cases. Earlier in the 1969 term the Court, in its *Alexander* and *Carter* decisions, had underscored the importance of immediate desegregation, notwithstanding the disruption of midyear assignment changes. Now, in March, the Court had hesitated, allowing a stay of the desegregation plan in Charlotte to stand unchallenged. The Court had never in its history issued its own stay of a school desegregation order and had on many occasions reversed lower-court stays of desegregation orders.[129]

It was the second time in a matter of days that at least some of the justices had hinted at their uneasiness with the prospect of extensive school busing in southern cities. One week earlier, the Supreme Court had reversed the U.S. Court of Appeals for the Sixth Circuit's finding that the city of Memphis no longer operated a dual system. Chief Justice Warren Burger, however, concurred separately, noting that the time was coming for the Court to consider the question of whether school boards must engage in extensive pupil reshuffling coupled with busing to overcome residential segregation in America's cities.[130] The Burger concurrence sent a signal that the Court was uncertain about the need for urban school boards to engage in widespread school busing.

Urban desegregation clearly presented the Supreme Court with a problem of far greater magnitude than nonurban desegregation, which had been the subject of the *Green, Alexander,* and *Carter* decisions. The urgency communicated by the Supreme Court's recent decisions that desegregation must be accomplished immediately and presumably at all costs had been called into serious question. The *Charlotte News,* in an editorial, captured the mood: "The issue of school desegregation is in a shambles of confusion and will remain that way until the Supreme Court faces this fact and points the way."[131]

On the day after the Supreme Court's refusal to set aside the stay of his desegregation plan, McMillan held a hearing on the issue of the school board's ability to provide the requisite bus transportation. Both the school board attorneys and the plaintiffs' attorneys presented extensive evidence on the question of the feasibility of obtaining the requisite bus transportation. Plaintiffs' attorney Stein had for weeks been working overtime trying to find available buses to implement the Finger Plan.[132]

During the weeks before the hearing on the feasibility of the Finger Plan, McMillan had contacted the plaintiffs' attorneys to discuss the case. Although such ex parte contacts between a judge and a party are often regarded as questionable by 1990s standards of judicial conduct, in the late 1960s and early 1970s they were more common. McMillan ran his court in an informal style, and throughout the *Swann* litigation he met privately with various school board members and other people from the community to discuss the case. In one such conversation, the judge and the plaintiffs' attorneys discussed the evidence that would support a finding that the Finger Plan could indeed be implemented.[133] McMillan had gone out on a limb in ordering that the extensive Finger Plan be implemented by April 1, as requested by the plaintiffs. Now, the judge had to rely on the plaintiffs to produce evidence showing that in fact the plan was feasible.

Four days after the hearing, McMillan issued extensive findings of fact concluding that the state could indeed provide the necessary buses required by his February 5 order. McMillan found that his order would require 138 additional buses, notwithstanding the school board's claim that his order would require 422 additional buses. McMillan emphasized that the North Carolina Board of Education had 775 buses in stock awaiting order from local school boards and that therefore the plan could be implemented with no great difficulty.[134] McMillan commented, "The problem is not one of availability of buses but of the unwillingness of Mecklenburg to buy them and of the state to furnish or make them available until the final decision in this case."[135]

On March 22, the school board asked McMillan to stay the entire order, not just those aspects of his order that the Fourth Circuit had previously stayed, until the following school year. All nine members of the board joined that request, even the board members that supported McMillan's order in its entirety. The board justified its request as a means of avoiding the considerable disruption that would flow from a piecemeal implementation of the desegregation plan in the final month of the school year.[136]

The plaintiffs objected to the board's request for a stay. Although in a motion filed with the court in September 1969 the plaintiffs had labeled as "unconscionable" the prospect of transferring students to new schools in the middle of the school year, now in March the plaintiffs were asking for exactly that.[137] The educational benefits of implementing a desegregation plan during the final month of the school year seemed elusive. Yet the plaintiffs understood the importance of going to the higher courts with the new desegregation plan in effect. If the school system was already operating with the new plan, objections to its feasibility would be far weaker.[138]

On the day before new pupil assignments were to be mailed to students, McMillan granted the board's request to stay his desegregation order in its entirety until the following September.[139] It was unquestionably a bitter moment for McMillan. For one year, the judge had endured overwhelming community hostility because of his adherence to the rigorous desegregation standards of the Fourth Circuit and the Supreme Court. Now, both courts had undercut him on the stay issue. McMillan explained his decision:

> The Fourth Circuit Court of Appeals and the Supreme Court have now demonstrated an interest in the cost and inconvenience and disruption that the order might produce — factors which, though bussing was not specifically mentioned, appear not to have been of particular interest to either the Fourth Circuit Court or the Supreme Court, when [the] *Holmes County, Carter, Greenville* and *Statesville* [cases] were decided.
>
> The only reason this court entered an order requiring mid-semester transfers of children was its belief that the language of the Supreme Court and the Fourth Circuit . . . required district courts to direct desegregation before the end of this school year.
>
> The urgency of "desegregation now" has now been in part dispelled by the same courts which ordered it.[140]

In his opinion granting the stay, McMillan made clear that he had "never . . . at any time considered wholesale mid-year or mid-term transfers of pupils or teachers desirable."[141] In a candid moment a few weeks earlier, McMillan had confided to a friend, "If I had been making the law I would have stopped short of the orders that I have entered in this case, but I probably would have started the process earlier."[142] As a lower-court judge, however, McMillan was obliged to follow, as best he could, the various, and often confusing, dictates of the higher courts.

School Board Chair Poe thought Nixon's statement on busing, issued two days earlier, had influenced McMillan.[143] It is much more likely that McMillan went back to his original preference — no implementation of the desegregation plan until the following school year — because of the Supreme Court's treatment of the stay issue.

By the end of March 1970, Charlotte had received a temporary reprieve from a midyear, systemwide reassignment of students. McMillan had ordered the school board to eliminate every majority-black school and to do so immediately. But extensive urban busing, opposed by the president, many members of Congress, and a plethora of state officials, appeared to give the Supreme Court pause. Perhaps McMillan had indeed misinterpreted the *Green* mandate as requiring the elimination of the racial identifiability of *every* school in an urban system. Over the course of the next twelve months, the Fourth Circuit and ultimately the Supreme Court would provide the long-awaited answer. McMillan's busing order was understood throughout the country as providing the context by which the Supreme Court would finally resolve the meaning of *Green* for urban America.[144]

All things being equal, with no history of discrimination, it might well be desirable to assign pupils to schools nearest their homes. But all things are not equal in a system that has been deliberately constructed and maintained to enforce racial segregation. . . . In these circumstances, we find no basis for holding that local school authorities may not be required to employ bus transportation as one tool of school desegregation. . . .

The order of the District Court . . . is affirmed.

— U.S. Supreme Court Chief Justice Warren Burger, *Swann v. Charlotte-Mecklenburg Board of Education*, April 20, 1971

CHAPTER 8

The Supreme Court Settles the Issue

By March 1970, Charlotte was a city deep in turmoil, perhaps the greatest turmoil in its long history. Virtually the entire leadership of the city agreed that the views of the higher courts were desperately needed to defuse the situation. Over the course of the next twelve months, both the U.S. Court of Appeals for the Fourth Circuit and the U.S. Supreme Court would evaluate Judge James McMillan's actions. As the city and the nation waited for the high courts' judgment, the city's schools proceeded to open under one of the most extensive desegregation plans ever imposed on a public school system. A city that had smoothly adjusted to the various racial demands of the past fifteen years confronted its most difficult test.

During the spring of 1970, the opponents of McMillan's busing order took their grievances to two separate courts: a three-judge federal court to determine the constitutionality of the state antibusing statute and the full U.S. Court of Appeals for the Fourth Circuit to consider McMillan's February busing order on its merits. On March 24, 1970, the three-judge court, consisting of McMillan and two Fourth Circuit judges — Braxton Craven, who had ruled on the 1965 desegregation challenge in Charlotte, and John Butzner of Richmond — convened to consider the constitutionality of the antibusing statute. The hearing had been triggered by the CPA's efforts to use the statute to secure a state court injunction preventing the school board from complying with McMillan's February 5 busing order. Both North Carolina Attorney General Robert Morgan, who defended the statute on behalf of the state, and the CPA attempted —

unsuccessfully—to have McMillan disqualified from the case on account of bias.[1]

One month later, on April 28, the three-judge court found the state antibusing statute unconstitutional on the grounds that it could potentially "interfere with the school board's performance of its affirmative constitutional duty" to desegregate the schools. The court noted that because the Supreme Court in *Green* required school boards to dismantle dual school systems, legislation that prevented a school board from utilizing any reasonable method to carry out that responsibility was unconstitutional.[2] The court thereby thwarted the CPA's efforts to use the antibusing statute to circumvent McMillan's busing order.

Yet the decision of the three-judge panel was by no means an endorsement of McMillan's order. The court expressly noted, "Although we hold these statutory prohibitions unconstitutional . . . , it does not follow that 'bussing' will be an appropriate remedy in any particular school desegregation case."[3] The question of the appropriateness of McMillan's busing order would be decided separately by the full Fourth Circuit. The three-judge court expressly referred to Chief Justice Warren Burger's concurring opinion in the Memphis case issued only a few weeks earlier, in which Burger noted that the Supreme Court had yet to resolve whether the Constitution required extensive bus transportation to overcome residential segregation.[4]

More troubling was a comment made by Judge Craven to the plaintiffs' attorneys. The day after the oral argument in the case, Craven, in an unusual gesture, summoned plaintiffs' counsel to his chambers for an informal discussion of the case. Craven, who had already disqualified himself from participation in the Fourth Circuit's consideration of the February busing order because of his prior involvement with the case as a district court judge, encouraged the plaintiffs to settle the litigation, forecasting an unfavorable reception for McMillan's order in the Fourth Circuit.[5]

It was a bad omen, but it fell on deaf ears. The NAACP had selected Charlotte in the summer of 1968 as one of several cities particularly well suited to test the meaning of *Green*, and the NAACP attorneys had litigated the case with a high degree of skill and aggressiveness, coaxing from a newly appointed judge one of the most extensive desegregation orders ever entered.[6] Although McMillan had proceeded more slowly than the NAACP attorneys might have liked, he had interpreted *Green* in a manner that offered tremendous promise for the integration of city school systems throughout the nation. Moreover, notwithstanding its March action on the stay request, the Supreme Court had signaled during the fall and winter of 1969–70 a new intensity on the issue of school desegregation. Compromise at this point was out of the question.

On April 9, 1970, the entire Fourth Circuit heard argument on the propriety of McMillan's February busing order. At the Fourth Circuit's invitation, the Nixon administration intervened in the case, its first such school desegregation involvement since President Richard Nixon's antibusing speech two weeks earlier.[7] The administration had previously sought to intervene at the district court level by means of a personal phone call from Attorney General John Mitchell to McMillan. McMillan later commented: "I told [Mitchell] that if he filed a formal request I would allow it, but if he simply wanted to use the case as another political platform to make inflammatory statements, I did not give a * * * * * whether they ever showed up. That was the last I heard from him about intervention."[8]

Both the school board and the Nixon administration argued that the Supreme Court did not require the degree of busing that McMillan had ordered. Once again, the Nixon Justice Department joined a local school board seeking to resist more extensive integration.[9] The Justice Department labeled the elementary school portion of McMillan's order "extreme" and "an abuse of discretion."[10] The school board, for its part, emphasized that its proposed plan, though retaining a few majority-black schools, still achieved a greater degree of desegregation than any other plan ever drafted by a major city school board.[11]

On May 26, 1970, the court of appeals rendered its much awaited decision. The court affirmed McMillan's order for the junior and senior high schools but reversed his order for elementary schools on the grounds that the school board "should not be required to undertake such extensive additional bussing" of young children.[12] Aware that McMillan had ordered such extensive busing of elementary school children in order to eliminate every majority-black school, the court concluded that not every school in a unitary school system had to be desegregated. At the same time, however, the court found the board's elementary school plan deficient because, in leaving about half of the students in racially identifiable schools, it did not accomplish enough desegregation.

The Fourth Circuit invited the school board to devise a new elementary school desegregation plan in consultation with the Department of HEW and directed McMillan to evaluate the new elementary school desegregation plan under a "reasonableness" standard. Under this reasonableness test, the court advised McMillan to "take into consideration the ages of the pupils, the distance and time required for transportation, the effect on traffic, and the cost in relation to the board's resources."[13]

The Fourth Circuit's opinion marked a compromise of competing views. On the one hand, it expressly affirmed the school board's obligation to take extensive measures, including the use of noncontiguous attendance zones accompanied by the provision of bus transportation, in order to eliminate racially imbalanced schools resulting from residential segregation. On the other hand, the court noted that there was a limit on the amount of pupil reshuffling that school boards were required to undertake, defined by the court's "reasonableness" standard. Under this standard, some school districts would need to eliminate every racially identifiable school, whereas other school districts could lawfully retain such schools. The court explained: "All schools in towns, small cities, and rural areas generally can be integrated. . . . Some cities, in contrast, have black ghettos so large that integration of every school is an improbable, if not an unattainable, goal."[14]

The Nixon administration's presentation had heavily influenced the Fourth Circuit's decision. The court's reasonableness test was similar to the "rule of reason" articulated by Nixon in his March speech on school desegregation and by the Justice Department in its brief to the court. Furthermore, the court agreed with the administration that the junior and senior high school desegregation ordered by McMillan was reasonable but that the elementary school desegregation plan should be reversed and reformulated with HEW assistance. Finally, the court concluded, as the administration had urged, that not every school in a unitary school system need be integrated.

The Fourth Circuit's decision, however, served only to magnify the confusion in the minds of the people of Charlotte as to what exactly the Constitution required. Both the school board and the plaintiffs had urged the appellate court not to remand the case but to resolve decisively the question of what the school board must do to satisfy its constitutional obligations. "Reasonableness" was an amorphous standard that would surely invite future disagreements and uncertainty. As Simon Sobeloff, one of the dissenting Fourth Circuit judges, noted: "The concept [of reasonableness] is highly susceptible to delaying tactics in the courts. Everyone can advance a different opinion of what is reasonable."[15] Sobeloff had been involved with school desegregation cases for over fifteen years; before joining the Fourth Circuit in 1956, he had argued, as solicitor general, the second *Brown* case for the U.S. government. Soboloff well understood the price that had been paid as a result of judicial ambiguity in defining legal standards applicable to school desegregation cases.[16]

Privately, McMillan expressed his disapproval of the Fourth Circuit's actions. A few weeks after the Fourth Circuit announced its decision, McMillan wrote a friend and complained that the appellate court had agreed that the Charlotte schools were unconstitutionally segregated but had limited the remedy available to the affected schoolchildren: "The Court accepted all the law and all the facts on which I had proceeded, but apparently could not stomach the amount of transportation which it would require to implement such an order. The anomaly is that we now have a group of 8,000 or 10,000 children unconstitutionally segregated and a decision by the Court which says that only a 'reasonable' number of these people are entitled to relief. . . . What a district judge can do with that kind of pronouncement only a circuit judge can know."[17]

In July 1970, McMillan held hearings to assess the reasonableness of the various elementary school desegregation plans before him as required by the Fourth Circuit. Although the Fourth Circuit had ordered the school board to file a new elementary school desegregation plan with McMillan for his consideration, a majority of the badly divided board failed to agree on what action to take and hence offered no new plan to the court. The board argued that there was no reasonable alternative to its February plan.[18] Yet the Fourth Circuit had already rejected that plan as not satisfying basic constitutional mandates. By failing to offer a new plan, the board in effect invited McMillan to implement whatever plan he wanted without the board's input.

A minority group of four board members, however, led by Carlton Watkins, filed their own ambitious desegregation plan that eliminated every majority-black school in the system.[19] The plan involved slightly less busing than did the Finger Plan and used a lottery to determine which students would be reassigned.[20]

The Department of HEW, whose participation in the remand proceedings before McMillan had been expressly invited by the Fourth Circuit, submitted a plan as well. The HEW plan left several elementary schools majority black and placed approximately 60 percent of the school system's African American elementary children in schools with at least a 40 percent black population and hence at risk of becoming predominantly black.[21] Schools in Charlotte with a high black population had a history of losing white students. During the previous few years, ten predominantly white schools that had obtained a 40 percent black population had quickly become majority African American as white students transferred to other schools or left the public school system altogether. Moreover, the HEW plan grossly overutilized some schools; the plan slated Villa Heights Elementary School, for example, to educate twice as many students as it was designed to hold.[22]

At the July hearings, McMillan considered the reasonableness of the original board plan, the Finger Plan, the plan presented by the board minority, and the HEW plan.[23] All parties agreed that the HEW plan was the least desirable of the four plans; even the HEW official who had drafted the plan, Henry Kemp, testified that he could not recommend his plan as "educationally sound." Kemp explained that he had been instructed by his superiors to devise a plan using contiguous school zones and minimal busing, which made meaningful desegregation difficult.[24] Kemp's task had probably been made more difficult by the forced resignation of James E. Allen, assistant secretary of HEW and commissioner of education, on June 10, allegedly because of his liberal views on school desegregation.[25]

The original board plan had been expressly rejected by the Fourth Circuit, leaving McMillan only two plans to evaluate: the Finger Plan and the board minority plan, both of which eliminated every majority-black elementary school. In early August, McMillan issued a lengthy opinion in which he concluded that both plans were reasonable and invited the school board to implement either the Finger Plan, which he favored, or the board minority plan, which was also acceptable. Recognizing the difficulty the badly split board would face in having to implement a desegregation plan that five of its members firmly opposed, McMillan appended to his order an unusual section entitled "Suggestions for Plan Implementation." Among the judge's suggestions was the establishment of a biracial community advisory committee both to advise the board on implementation of the desegregation plan and to seek community support.[26] In some ways, McMillan was inviting the board to return to Stanford Brookshire's model of enlisting civic leaders to help the city navigate troubled waters — a model that had well served the city in the early 1960s. The school board, however, rejected the advice.

In his opinion, McMillan went to great lengths to emphasize the reasonableness of the Finger Plan. He included a detailed list of thirty-five reasons why the Finger Plan was reasonable in terms of cost, length of bus ride, and availability of buses. Central to McMillan's conclusions about the reasonableness of the plan was the fact that elementary schoolchildren already took lengthy bus rides to schools throughout the state. The judge noted that 55 percent of the North Carolina school population rode a bus to school; the average travel time for those students was longer than what the Finger Plan required.[27] Thus, to require a few thousand elementary schoolchildren in Charlotte to leave their immediate neighborhood in order to eliminate racially imbalanced schools could hardly be termed unreasonable. To a judge who himself had ridden a school bus twenty-six miles a day as a youngster in the 1920s and 1930s, the bus trips faced by Charlotte schoolchildren were quite reasonable.

Although McMillan had from the beginning justified his extensive desegregation demands on the grounds that the Constitution, as interpreted by the Supreme Court in the *Green* decision, required such action — "a black child in urban Charlotte whose education is being crippled by unlawful segregation is just as much entitled to relief as his contemporary on a Virginia farm"[28] — the judge took the opportunity once again to justify his decision on educational grounds. In McMillan's previous discussions of the school board's constitutional obligations, he had addressed the educational benefits of a desegregated education, and during the July hearing on the various plans, McMillan returned to that theme. McMillan stated, "The reason we are here is the dictum of the Supreme Court sixteen years ago that segregated education is inferior education for the black students."[29] McMillan requested that the school board attorneys provide information about educational achievement test scores for the 1969–70 school year, which McMillan then released, over the board's objection.[30] The achievement test scores continued to show a wide gap between black and white students. Yet the achievement scores indicated that black students in desegregated schools performed better than did black students in segregated schools.[31] McMillan cited the achievement test scores as evidence that desegregation was worth the inconvenience to those students required to leave their neighborhoods to attend school.[32]

Once again, McMillan's efforts to justify his busing requirements in terms of improved education were, from a constitutional perspective, unnecessary. The U.S. Supreme Court, in its *Brown* decision, had already determined that segregated schools were inherently detrimental to African American children. Yet in Charlotte, as in many southern cities, a certain dissonance existed between the Supreme Court's certitude about the value of an integrated education and the views of much of the community, particularly the parents of white schoolchildren. Some white parents, moved by paternalism, might concede a benefit to a few African American children attending a white school; far fewer perceived any corresponding benefit to a white child. As long as African American children traveled to white schools and their numbers remained at a "tolerable" level, most white Charlotteans found desegregation acceptable and perhaps of some modest social benefit. But, in the view of many white parents, such benefits vanished when their children were required to attend school in distant black neighborhoods. This was the conflict that would continue to bedevil the Charlotte-Mecklenburg School Board for the next four years.

By the same token, an increasingly vocal part of the African American community questioned the value of an integrated education. As noted, in February 1970 the Congress of Racial Equality had issued a highly critical report of extensive school integration efforts. One year later, at U.S. Senate hearings on school desegregation, various African American leaders questioned the value of extensive pupil mixing. Charles Hamilton, an African American professor from Columbia University, for example, told the Senate, "We should be concerned essentially with quality education, and not with the superficial bringing together of black and white students."[33] Increasingly, the integration-oriented NAACP would be placed on the defensive on the school busing issue. In those same 1971 Senate hearings, NAACP attorney Julius Chambers attempted to defend school integration as a necessary evil to ensure that African American children received equal educational facilities and programs: "I don't think that those who are now in power would provide the facilities and services that would be necessary in order to accomplish equal educational programs. As I view it, the only way that we can obtain quality education for all children, black and white, is to accomplish racial mixing of students in the various schools. And I think that busing is the necessary means for accomplishing this result."[34] Several months later, in an address to a national policy conference on black education, Chambers underscored the importance of school integration: "If blacks fail to bring down the barriers of racial isolation, we will remain a substantially inferior class of human beings."[35]

McMillan well understood the nationwide attention on the Charlotte case as it worked its way up through the courts and the widespread perception that it might function as the defining case for future desegregation activity in the nation's cities. In his August opinion, McMillan emphasized that his orders affected only Charlotte. Even though he had mandated the elimination of every majority-black school, that did not mean that every urban school system had to do the same: "This court has not ruled and does not rule that 'racial balance' is required under the Constitution; nor that all black schools in all cities are unlawful; . . . *nor that the particular order entered in this case could be correct in other circumstances not before this court.*"[36] Instead, McMillan emphasized that the circumstances in various cities around the country would vary widely and that his actions would not dictate what must be done in another urban context: "This is a local suit involving actions of the State of North Carolina and its local governments and agencies. The facts about the development of black Charlotte may not be the facts of the development of black Chicago or black Denver or New York or Baltimore. Some other court will have to pass on that problem. The decision of the case involves local history, local statutes, local geography, local demography, local state history including half a century of bus transportation, local zoning, local school boards—in other words, local and individual merits."[37] It was a shrewd gesture. This case was on its way to the U.S. Supreme Court, and McMillan's order would fare much better if the Court could affirm it without necessarily concluding that every urban school system must do likewise.

It had been a painful year for the new federal judge. Picketed at home by his neighbors, burned in effigy, and generally reviled by much of the city and state, McMillan had been courageously steadfast in his adherence to his understanding of the Supreme Court's desegregation demands. McMillan used this August opinion as an opportunity to reflect on his unpopular rulings: "A judge would ordinarily like to decide cases to suit his neighbors. . . . To yield to public clamor, however, is to corrupt the judicial process and to turn the effective operation of courts over to political activism and to the temporary local opinion makers. This a court must not do. . . . [If] courts [fail to adhere to] the stable bulwarks of the Constitution itself, we lose our government of laws and are back to the government of man, unfettered by law, which our forefathers sought to avoid."[38] The question was whether the "stable bulwarks of the Constitution" required the full extent of the actions taken by McMillan. The Supreme Court would soon put that issue to rest.

Both the plaintiffs and the school board sought review by the Supreme Court of the Fourth Circuit's decision upholding McMillan's order for junior and senior high school students and remanding that portion of his order that pertained to elementary school students. On June 29, the Supreme Court issued a writ of certiorari accepting the case for full consideration.[39] The significance of the *Swann* appeal was widely understood.

Chief Judge John R. Brown of the U.S. Court of Appeals for the Fifth Circuit, in the only press release he ever issued, announced that the Fifth Circuit would freeze all but its most essential school desegregation activity until the Court issued a decision in the Charlotte case.[40]

In a striking and decisive move, the Supreme Court reinstated McMillan's February 5 busing order pending his further consideration of the reasonableness of the elementary school portion of the plan and the Court's eventual consideration of the order on its merits.[41] It is not entirely clear why the Court reinstated McMillan's order, particularly after it had refused to set aside the Fourth Circuit's stay of his order in March. The justices' internal correspondence pertaining to the *Swann* case sheds no light on the issue.[42] In some measure, the reinstatement may have been an effort by the Court to signal once again the urgency of school desegregation, a perspective that had been clouded by the Court's earlier action on the Fourth Circuit's stay.

Hugo Black, the Court's only southerner and the justice who would prove least favorably disposed to McMillan's busing order, dissented from the reinstatement order, favoring instead a special summer court session to consider the case before the opening of schools in the fall.[43] The justices had traditionally deemed few cases of sufficient importance to cause them to forgo their summer recess; the last summer session had come twelve years earlier in the extraordinary Little Rock school desegregation case, in which the very authority of the Supreme Court had been at stake.[44] No justice joined Black in his call for a special summer court session to consider the *Swann* case.[45]

In the meantime, the Charlotte-Mecklenburg School Board, the Charlotte City Council, and the Mecklenburg County Board of Commissioners passed a joint resolution requesting the Supreme Court to reconsider its decision not to hear the case before the start of school in the fall.[46] Sounding a familiar theme, the resolution emphasized that the city was confused as to what exactly the Supreme Court required: "Past experience shows that Charlotte-Mecklenburg will face up to its problems and will respond to the leadership of its elected officials once its citizens understand what must be done and why. However, the present posture of our local school desegregation case is such that neither the community nor its leaders know what ultimately will be required of them when the United States Supreme Court rules on our case."[47] The three groups initially planned to ask the Supreme Court to stay implementation of McMillan's order pending the Court's consideration of the case, but black city council member Fred Alexander dissented on the stay issue, and the three boards dropped that aspect of the resolution in the interest of unanimity.[48] One month later, School Board Chair William Poe, Charlotte Mayor John Belk, and Charles Lowe, chair of the Mecklenburg County Board of Commissioners, led a delegation of community leaders to Washington to seek Justice Department assistance in gaining early Supreme Court consideration of the Charlotte case.[49]

Ironically, the Nixon administration opposed early consideration of the case, fearing that the Court's decision in the *Swann* case might require immediate and extensive busing in other school systems, thereby disrupting the 1970–71 school year.[50] Hence, Assistant Attorney General Jerris Leonard rebuffed the delegation's efforts to gain Justice Department support for an early court date.

Subsequently, other community groups tried to secure a stay of McMillan's order pending consideration by the Supreme Court. The CPA sent a petition to President Nixon with tens of thousands of signatures reminding him of his earlier opposition to busing and requesting that he direct Attorney General John Mitchell to seek a stay of McMillan's order from the Supreme Court. The CPA petition had no effect.[51] The Charlotte Chamber of Commerce petitioned Fourth Circuit chief judge Clement Haynsworth to stay McMillan's order. Although not a party to the litigation, the chamber told Haynsworth that the busing controversy had divided the city "in a way in which it [had] never been divided" and urged the judge to postpone implementation of the Finger Plan until the Supreme Court had had the opportunity to consider the case.[52] Shortly thereafter, the school board approached Haynsworth with its own request for a stay. A few days later, the South Carolina jurist denied the stay requests, correctly noting that a stay would constitute a reversal of the Supreme Court's reinstatement order, which exceeded his authority as a lower-court judge.[53]

In the meantime, both the Mecklenburg County state legislative delegation and North Carolina Governor Robert Scott contacted Chief Justice Burger directly, requesting a stay of McMillan's order pending the Court's consideration of the case. The governor's telegram to Burger promised that once the Supreme Court ruled on the issue, the people of Charlotte would abide by the decision.[54] On August 25, Burger denied all stay requests, dashing any remaining hope that the busing order might be avoided.[55] A few days later, the Court announced that it would not consider the *Swann* appeal until October 12, the first day of the Court's new term. Justice Black again requested that the Court hear the case before October 12 but enjoyed no support.[56] The state's newspapers announced Burger's stay decision in screaming headlines: "Schools Face Huge Busing Problem."[57]

The refusal of the Supreme Court to consider the *Swann* case during its summer recess, coupled with its reinstatement of McMillan's order, constituted a significant blow to the school board's case, a fact that did not escape Poe and the school board lawyers. Poe well understood that the board's appeal would be substantially weakened if McMillan's plan had already been implemented by the time the Supreme Court considered the case.[58] If the schools opened and operated reasonably successfully under McMillan's busing order, the plaintiffs would be in a much stronger position to argue that the plan was not so unreasonable as to be objectionable.[59] The Supreme Court had never reversed a lower-court judge in a school desegregation case for demanding too much pupil mixing. Moreover, a Supreme Court intent on remaining strong on desegregation would be unlikely to overturn an operational desegregation plan in favor of something less extensive. The Supreme Court's actions in the summer of 1970 proved to be a precursor of what was to come the following spring.

In the meantime, the board faced the decision of whether to proceed with the Finger Plan or the board minority plan for the 1970–71 school year. In early August, McMillan had notified the board that either plan was acceptable. The board minority plan involved less busing than did the Finger Plan, and board member Carlton Watkins led a move to win its acceptance.[60] Poe, who opposed adoption of the board minority plan, explained, "It's another psychological move on the part of the judge who . . . would like to label the plan the board plan."[61]

On August 6, the board held a meeting to decide what to do. The meeting was well attended by busing opponents and was one of the most raucous meetings in the school board's history. In the absence of two of its members most supportive of McMillan—Coleman Kerry and Betsey Kelly—the board voted 4 to 3 to reject the minority plan and to "acquiesce in" the Finger Plan.[62] Poe moved that the board adopt a statement that it would do all that it could to implement the Finger Plan unless the Supreme Court granted a stay. He explained, "I simply want it to appear that we are not defying the court." Several members of the audience yelled, "Why not?" Others announced their willingness to go to jail before allowing their children to be bused against their will. Ultimately, the board voted down Poe's motion.[63] The August 6 meeting reflected the depth of the white community's feelings about McMillan's busing order.

In the meantime, the CPA continued to lead the antibusing opposition. During the spring and summer of 1970, the organization sent sixty thousand pamphlets to parents, urging them to send telegrams to Board Chair Poe and voice opposition to the busing order.[64] The CPA enjoyed popular support in much of the white community. During the school board election of May 1970, CPA-backed candidates won all three open seats, capturing 53 percent of the total vote in a thirteen-candidate field.[65] The organization's chair, Tom Harris, and its attorney, William Booe, captured seats without a runoff; the third CPA-backed candidate, Jane Scott, won election after prevailing in a runoff with Coleman Kerry, the board's one African American and a strong supporter of desegregation efforts.

The head-to-head runoff contest between Kerry and Scott, which Scott won by less than one thousand votes out of forty-six thousand cast, provided a telling proxy of community views on school desegregation. Kerry carried all of the city's African American precincts; more significant, he carried about 60 percent of the vote in white southeast Charlotte, the wealthiest section of the city and home to most of the city's civic and political leaders. Scott, a housewife living in the western section of the county, won the election by carrying lower- and middle-income white neighborhoods in the eastern and western sections of the county by wide margins.[66] Those precincts that most strongly supported the CPA candidates had provided strong support two years earlier for George Wallace in his 1968 presidential election bid and would do so again in 1972.[67]

Scott's strong support in the eastern and western sections of the county was not surprising. These were the sections where the busing burden on white children was the greatest and where representation on the county's elected boards had traditionally been minimal. Resentment of busing as well as resentment of the absence of a political voice in the political affairs of Charlotte fueled Scott's candidacy. This polite daughter of Pennsylvania schoolteachers initially became engaged with school issues in response to the reassignment of her own children away from nearby schools that had been racially integrated for several years. In time, these personal concerns transformed into a political candidacy as Scott emerged as a strong voice for white discontent.[68]

The support of white southeast Charlotte for Kerry rather than CPA candidate Scott was also not surprising. Southeast Charlotte was the area of the city least affected by the busing order, mitigating the effect of the

School buses are prepared for the opening of school under the Finger Plan, September 1970. (Courtesy of the *Charlotte Observer*)

CPA's antibusing appeals. Moreover, the aggressive tactics of the CPA offended the sensibilities of many of the southeast's more prominent and established residents. These voters valued the preservation of good race relations and a strong public school system and many feared that the CPA's boisterous opposition to school busing and its promotion of a school boycott would harm the city. Indeed, southeast Charlotte would continue to support black candidates, giving its support to city council member Fred Alexander in his 1972 and 1974 bids for the state senate and to Phil Berry in his 1972 school board election.[69]

With the stay efforts foiled by the Supreme Court, the school board prepared to open schools in the fall of 1970 under the Finger Plan. The board, however, lacked a sufficient number of buses to implement the plan in its entirety. Earlier in the summer, the school board had petitioned the Mecklenburg County Board of Commissioners, which appropriated all local monies for the school system, for additional revenues to purchase buses. The commissioners, however, had declined the request.[70] A renewed request in late August had also failed.[71]

Ultimately, the state agreed to loan the Charlotte-Mecklenburg School Board a number of secondhand buses, and a last-minute lawsuit filed in state court in Raleigh to stop the shipment of the buses was dismissed.[72] Even with the state's buses, however, the school board was forced to delay the opening of schools from August 31 until September 9 and thereafter to operate many schools on half-day schedules for several weeks as transportation problems were ironed out.[73] Ultimately, over forty-three thousand students, about half of the school system, rode a bus to school, an increase of twenty thousand over the prior year.[74] Despite these transportation problems, the Charlotte-Mecklenburg school system opened in September 1970 as the most fully desegregated urban school system in the nation's history.[75] Indeed, few other desegregation plans would ever accomplish as much racial balance throughout a metropolitan school system as did McMillan's 1970 Finger Plan.[76]

In the meantime, the election of the three CPA members in May 1970 had reinforced a feeling among many in the white community that McMillan's busing order could be stopped. As one civic leader later noted, many antibusing whites believed they now "had someone in authority" who could "stop [busing] or at least delay it." Those in the black community who favored the busing plan viewed the election the same way. As one black teacher explained, "A lot of blacks thought the Lord had died that day."[77]

Frustrated by the Supreme Court's refusal to grant a stay, the CPA urged its supporters to boycott the schools. The boycott never materialized, however, since few parents wanted to deny their children an education or to defy the authorities by illegally withholding their children from school.[78] "There was a sense it would be self-destructive," one observer noted. "It wouldn't hurt the judge, it wouldn't stop the buses. It would just hurt the kids."[79]

Many parents, however, did place their children in private schools. Ultimately, over two thousand of the system's eighty-three thousand students left the school system for private schools in the fall of 1970, increasing private school enrollment in Mecklenburg County from fifty-four hundred to seventy-four hundred.[80] Of those students leaving for private school, 30 percent were fifth- and sixth-graders, the two grades in which white students were most frequently assigned to schools in black neighborhoods. Indeed, six makeshift private schools opened in the fall of 1970 to serve only grades five and six.[81] In addition, a few students left Charlotte for public schools in neighboring counties, although the massive physical size of the school district made such relocations difficult for parents who held jobs in Charlotte.[82] The consolidation of the Charlotte City schools and the Mecklenburg County schools in 1960 — an effort in which McMillan had played a significant role as a civic leader — had created one of the largest school districts in the United States.[83] Ultimately, the percentage of students who left the Charlotte-Mecklenburg schools was much smaller than that in most urban school systems confronted with similar busing demands in the early 1970s.[84]

Notwithstanding the tremendous community agitation over Mc-Millan's busing order, schools opened in Charlotte with less strife than in most other southern cities, a fact noted in the national press.[85] To be sure, there were a few distressing incidents. Vandals, for example, struck three schools shortly before they opened, scrawling "NO FORCED BUSING" on the walls and causing thousands of dollars in damage.[86] One school bus had its windows shattered while carrying a group of elementary schoolchildren to their first day of school.[87] A large number of schools experienced bomb threats. Indeed, six schools were temporarily closed on the first day of school due to bomb threats; such temporary closures became a fact of life over the course of the next few years.[88] Nevertheless, given the turmoil of the prior six months and the more severe troubles in other southern school districts, the school opening in Charlotte was remarkably peaceful.

The failure of the CPA boycott and the relatively tranquil opening of the schools under the Finger Plan were due in large measure to the fact that Charlotte remained a city committed both to obeying as opposed to defying legal authority and to preserving the city's strong public school system. Critical to this response was the unwillingness of the city's political leaders to embrace school boycotts and extralegal resistance. Even opposition leaders such as Board Chair Poe believed that the judge's order should be tested in the higher courts, not in the streets.[89] The Charlotte Chamber of Commerce criticized the CPA's call for a school boycott and urged all citizens to "obey the law."[90] Other prominent civic leaders joined in, urging the CPA leaders to cancel the boycott.[91] The local chapter of the League of Women Voters was particularly energetic in encouraging community acceptance.[92] Disregard for properly constituted authority still exceeded the parameters of acceptable political discourse in Charlotte. Moreover, a significant number of Charlotteans did not want to sacrifice their strong public school system in the cause of hopeless defiance.

At the same time, most civic and political leaders stopped short of embracing the desegregation order. Instead, most privately if not publicly contended that the order was wrong and that all available legal appeals should be taken. This continuing questioning of the legitimacy of McMillan's actions would help keep the city in turmoil for the next few years.

Over the course of the 1970–71 school year, the city would be tested once again by the strains of violence. On February 4, 1971, Chambers's law office burst into flames in the middle of the night, suffering extensive damage. Arson was suspected. It was the third fire in the Chambers family in six months; two previous fires of suspect origins had caused substantial damage to the automobile repair shop belonging to Chambers's father in Mount Gilead, a small town east of Charlotte.[93]

As it had with the 1965 bombings, the city responded to the fire with an outpouring of regret. Local fund-raisers were held for the law firm, and temporary office space was donated.[94] Various lawyers, including those representing the school board, made their legal files available to the Chambers firm to replace those that had been destroyed. The *Charlotte Observer* decried the violence, emphasizing that Chambers and the NAACP had always worked within the system: "Chambers and his associates are not symbols of the radicalized young black. They are advocates for that part of the Negro community that seeks to work within society's orderly processes to win equality and justice by peaceable, legal means."[95] Nevertheless, the fire was a reminder that there were many elements in the city of Charlotte: a political and business leadership committed to orderly change and a less predictable element whose frustrations could occasionally lead to violence.

In the meantime, in October 1970, the Supreme Court heard oral argument on the challenge to McMillan's various desegregation orders. Chambers, in his first visit to the U.S. Supreme Court, argued the case for the plaintiffs along with James Nabrit of the NAACP Legal Defense Fund in New York. According to Chambers, the issue was whether a school board could "continue to perpetuate segregated schools . . . when a feasible plan [was] available to disestablish the segregated schools."[96] Chambers contended that the currently operational Finger Plan constituted such a plan and that therefore it was reasonable to require the board to eliminate every racially identifiable school in the system. Chambers defined a racially identifiable school as one that was majority African American or more than 90 percent white.[97]

Justice Black expressed alarm at the degree of pupil reshuffling required to eliminate every single-race school in Charlotte: "It disturbs me to hear we should try to change the whole lives of people around the country. You're challenging the place people live. You want to haul people miles and miles and miles in order to get an equal ratio in the schools. It's a pretty big job to assign us, isn't it?"[98] Black's comments signaled that at least one member of the Court was deeply troubled by the sweeping desegregation orders entered by lower-court judges, such as McMillan, attempting to overcome well-entrenched patterns of urban residential segregation.

Solicitor General Erwin Griswold argued for the Nixon administration. Griswold conceded, in response to a question from Justice John Harlan, that busing for purposes of overcoming racial imbalance was indeed a permissible remedial device in school desegregation cases. The real issue, Griswold noted, was "the amount, and the distance, of the busing" that a federal court judge could reasonably order.[99] In Griswold's view, McMillan had demanded too much busing at the elementary school level.

Charlotte lawyers William Waggoner and Benjamin Horack argued for the school board, since the board's attempts to retain a seasoned Supreme Court advocate to present its argument to the Court had failed.[100] The board attorneys, cognizant of the fact that the Charlotte-Mecklenburg schools had already engaged in more desegregation than most other urban school systems, argued that the board had exceeded its constitutional duty to eliminate segregated schools and urged the Court to so find.

Five days after oral argument, the justices met to discuss the case. Four justices — Harlan, William Brennan, William Douglas, and Thurgood Marshall — expressed strong support for McMillan's order, emphasizing that district judges must be given broad discretion in framing desegregation remedies. Justice Black, on the other hand, emerged as McMillan's sharpest critic, expressing the view that McMillan's order had required far too much pupil reshuffling in the pursuit of racial balance. The other justices, including Chief Justice Burger, were more measured in their views, expressing concern with what they perceived to be McMillan's insistence on a specific racial ratio in each school. The chief justice assigned the task of drafting the opinion to himself. Burger's insistence on keeping the opinion, notwithstanding his reservations about the propriety of McMillan's actions, would make the Court's deliberative process more difficult, since a majority of the justices eventually favored a stronger opinion than what Burger wanted to write.[101]

Burger's initial draft, circulated in early December 1970, expressed serious qualms about McMillan's order. At the outset, Burger gave a narrow construction to the *Green* decision, emphasizing that it had been incorrectly read "by some as a mandate for integration." The clear implication was that McMillan had pursued an integrationist agenda that exceeded his power as a district court judge. Moreover, Burger noted that although "the scope of equitable remedies to redress past wrongs" was "broad," judicial remedial powers in school desegregation cases were more limited. Burger noted that in many equity cases, the remedy was clear-cut, such as the removal of an illegal dam, but in school desegregation cases, the remedy was not so obvious: how do you "undo" decades of pupil assignments based on race? Burger concluded, "The objective should be to achieve as nearly as possible that distribution of students that would have normally existed had the school authorities not previously practiced discrimination." Under such a standard, however, remedial orders would invariably be more limited than was McMillan's because of the impossibility of concluding with any certainty that every school would have been integrated had there never been a history of racial discrimination in pupil assignments. Burger's opinion ordered McMillan to reconsider his actions on remand in light of the Court's opinion.[102]

Four of the justices—Brennan, Douglas, Marshall, and Potter Stewart—immediately expressed opposition to Burger's draft opinion, with Marshall and Stewart preparing their own draft opinions. These justices criticized Burger's interpretation of *Green* as not requiring integration and his restrictive reading of the scope of judicial remedial power in desegregation cases. Each of the four justices concluded that district court judges, in exercising their remedial powers in desegregation cases, should seek to achieve the greatest amount of pupil mixing possible, a far cry from Burger's more limited view of the scope of the district court's remedial power. Brennan, Douglas, and Marshall emphasized the importance of a clear affirmance of McMillan's actions without a remand for further consideration.[103]

In mid-January 1971, Burger circulated a second draft of his opinion; in a cover memorandum accompanying the opinion, Burger claimed to have addressed the articulated concerns of the other justices. In fact, the changes in the second draft were minor; in particular, Burger continued to take a restricted view of the district court's remedial powers in desegregation cases and to insist that McMillan reconsider his actions in light of the Court's opinion. In response to Burger's second draft, Douglas wrote a dissenting opinion that contained a strong affirmation of McMillan's actions. Subsequently, Douglas and Brennan persuaded Stewart to draft his own dissent, reasoning that the centrist Stewart would be more likely to capture the votes of a majority of the Court. In February 1971, Stewart drafted a dissenting opinion containing a clear affirmance of McMillan's actions. Stewart had initially been reluctant to affirm McMillan outright because of his perception that McMillan had mandated a specific racial ratio of 71 percent white students and 29 percent black students in each school. Now, Stewart took the view that McMillan had not actually required a particular racial balance but had used racial ratios as a desegregation goal from which he had ultimately departed.[104]

By now, Burger understood that a majority of the Court favored an outright affirmance of McMillan and that he was therefore in danger of losing control of the opinion. In response, in early March 1971, Burger circulated a third draft that retained most of the language of the earlier drafts but that affirmed McMillan's actions. Although Burger had finally agreed to the result that a majority of the justices desired, his opinion still contained much language that several justices found objectionable. As a result, over the course of the next few weeks, the other justices continued their efforts to modify the opinion. Harlan, for example, insisted that Burger's notion that district judges must endeavor to re-create the assignment system that would have existed had the school authorities not operated a dual system was an unworkable standard. Burger ultimately excised that language from the opinion, replacing it with another statement: "A district court has broad power to fashion a remedy that will assure a unitary system." Harlan also persuaded Burger to delete the statement that the Constitution did not require integration but only the elimination of segregation. But Burger held fast to some of the language to which some of the other justices objected; he retained, for example, the following statement: "The limits on time of travel will vary with many factors, but probably with none more than the age of the students." Thus he left open the possibility that future courts might decline to order extensive busing of elementary school students.[105]

In the meantime, Black, the justice who had been most troubled by McMillan's busing order, informed Burger of his disagreement with much of the language in the opinion and threatened to file a dissenting opinion. In particular, Black objected to the extensive use of busing to achieve what he perceived to be a particular racial balance: "I strongly disagree with any implication that may be found in the Court's opinion that federal courts may order school boards to transport students across cities to balance schools racially or to eliminate one-race schools which have resulted from private residential patterns rather than school-board imposed segregation. . . . The Constitution, in my judgment, does not require racial balance."[106] Because of the Court's tradition, dating from the *Brown* decision, of issuing only unanimous opinions in school desegregation cases, Burger sought to use the threat of a Black dissent to retain certain language that the other justices wanted deleted from the opinion and also to add a few additional qualifications to the Court's affirmation of Mc-

Millan. Burger, presumably to mollify Black, qualified his discussion of the remedial power of federal judges by writing: "Conditions in different localities will vary so widely that no rigid rules can be laid down to govern all situations."[107]

On April 20, 1971, the Court announced its decision. Speaking for a unanimous court, Chief Justice Burger noted at the outset that the Court had decided to hear the case in part to define the limits on the remedial powers of federal district court judges charged with implementing the Supreme Court's mandate "to eliminate racially separate public schools."[108] The Court divided the problem into four separate questions: whether a judge was permitted to use racial quotas in devising a remedy for segregated schools; whether a judge was required to eliminate every single-race school; whether there were any limits on a judge's power to rearrange school attendance zones; and whether there were any limits on a judge's authority to order the use of bus transportation.

On the question of whether the board was required to maintain a particular racial balance at each school, the Court concluded that a district court judge was permitted to use such ratios as a "starting point" but that strict adherence to racial ratios would be unconstitutional.[109] The justices concluded that although McMillan had expressly referred to a 71–29 racial ratio in several of his orders, he had used that ratio merely as a starting point and that strict adherence to that ratio was not required. Indeed, McMillan had approved a desegregation plan that provided for wide variations from that ratio.

Regarding the question of whether the school board was obliged to eliminate every single-race school, as McMillan had insisted, the Court indicated that there might be circumstances in which a desegregated system could retain schools with pupils of only one race. Nevertheless, the Court noted that there would be a presumption against single-race schools and that school authorities would bear the burden of showing that such schools were not the result of present or past discriminatory action on their part.[110]

Finally the Court turned to the thorny question of the limits on a judge's power to rearrange school attendance zones coupled with the extensive use of busing. The Court expressly legitimated the use of drastically gerrymandered attendance zones, noncontiguous attendance zones, and the busing of students, all of which the Finger Plan encompassed. The key question, however, was whether there were any limits on the amount of busing that a court could order. This aspect of the opinion contains considerable ambiguity. The Court affirmed McMillan's order in every regard but noted, "An objection to transportation of students may have validity when the time or distance of travel is so great as to either risk the health of the children or significantly impinge on the educational process."[111] District judges possessed considerable discretion to order busing to overcome residential segregation, but there were some undefined limits to the amount of such busing that could be ordered. Burger and Black had successfully insisted that the Court leave open the question of the limits on the use of busing. School Board Chair Poe immediately complained that the Court had left the most important issue to the trial court's discretion and without proper definition: "We had hoped that [the Supreme Court] would . . . lay down some rules that we could live by, rather than leaving the matter to the discretion of the judge."[112]

The Court concluded its opinion with a discussion of the ongoing responsibility of district court judges in monitoring school desegregation cases. The Court noted that once a school board established a unitary school system, further intervention by the courts would not be necessary in the absence of deliberate attempts by school authorities to alter the racial composition of the schools.[113] Yet the Court failed to specify when a school district reached unitary status, a failure that would continue to bedevil the Charlotte-Mecklenburg School Board.

The Supreme Court's opinion, although ambiguous in some of its language, contained a strong affirmation of the use of extensive school busing to overcome residential segregation in America's cities. In the Court's view, McMillan had properly interpreted its mandate in *Green* concerning the affirmative obligation of school boards to eliminate the racial identifiability of urban schools. McMillan's busing order may have been extensive, but according to a unanimous Supreme Court, it was not an unreasonable order given the degree of residential segregation in Charlotte. At the same time, the Court did not hold that its *Green* decision *required* the elimination of every majority-black school. McMillan, the Court concluded, had acted within his discretion in requiring the Charlotte-Mecklenburg School Board to do so. Had McMillan concluded that it was not feasible to eliminate every majority-black school and had he approved a plan that left some such schools in place, some of the language in the Court's opinion suggests that it would have affirmed that decision as well. For almost two decades the Supreme Court had relied on the discretion of lower-court judges in school desegregation cases; the *Swann* decision was but the latest affirmation of that continuing deference.

The affirmation of McMillan's exercise of discretion in the *Swann* case legitimated the exercise of power by district court judges to reshape urban school systems.[114] School desegregation cases — along with other types of institutional reform litigation, such as challenges to prison overcrowding — permitted and indeed required lower-court judges on occasion to issue orders affecting the lives and pocketbooks of thousands of people with no direct involvement in the litigation at hand. In affirming that exercise of judicial power, the Court helped fuel the growing public controversy over the role of unelected federal judges in American politics.

Yet the Court was clearly conscious of the political implications of its decision. One month before the Court announced its decision, Justice Brennan urged his fellow justices to issue a strong opinion that would "avoid saying anything that might be seized upon" by the South to legitimate resistance to future desegregation efforts. In a comment suggesting that Supreme Court justices are not so isolated as some might think, Brennan noted that recent newspaper surveys had indicated a lessening of opposition to desegregation and that he wanted to make sure the opinion did not contain any language that would give comfort to those still seeking to resist pupil mixing.[115]

The Supreme Court's *Swann* decision had an immediate impact across the South. Many lower-court judges ordered school boards to adopt McMillan's desegregation techniques, which the Supreme Court had legitimated. Within a few months of the decision, more than forty judges had entered new desegregation decrees. The overwhelming majority of these judges ordered the elimination of all majority-black schools and allowed only minimal variations in each school from the overall black-white student ratio.[116] Even though the Supreme Court had not required other lower-court judges to issue decrees similar to that issued by McMillan, McMillan's order became a benchmark that many other federal judges sought to emulate. Moreover, within four months of the decision, HEW negotiated thirty-seven new desegregation plans, including some that for the first time created noncontiguous school attendance zones.[117] Over one hundred school districts across America opened their schools in September 1971 with new pupil assignment plans.[118]

The Supreme Court's clear affirmance of McMillan's order constituted a major vindication for the beleaguered judge. Letters, phone calls, and telegrams congratulating McMillan flooded his chambers in the days following the Court's decision. Solicitor General Griswold, who had opposed McMillan's order before the Supreme Court on behalf of the Nixon administration, wrote a warm letter of appreciation: "It seems to me that you are the one person who has come through this best. You have acted courageously, it is true, but your every action has been wholly professional and in the highest traditions of our calling. One does not thank a judge for doing his duty, but one can be grateful that we have such fine and able people on the bench as you are."[119] McMillan acknowledged the Court's vindication. Writing to a friend a week after the Court's decision, McMillan noted, "These haven't been the easiest of days and months, but I must confess that in retrospect they don't look so bad in view of the Court's reaffirmation that law involves principles and not just public opinion."[120]

The *Swann* decision was also yet another major triumph for Chambers and the NAACP lawyers. Just three years earlier in the *Green* decision, the NAACP had established that school boards had an affirmative duty to desegregate their schools. Now in the *Swann* case, they had established that this duty must be exercised in urban areas even at the cost of extensive pupil reshuffling. Although McMillan had proceeded more slowly than Chambers might have liked, the judge ultimately agreed with Chambers on every major issue in the litigation, and the Supreme Court had affirmed McMillan's actions. For Chambers, it was his second landmark victory in a month. In March 1971, in *Griggs v. Duke Power Co.*, the Supreme Court in another unanimous Burger opinion had significantly expanded the ability of employees to prove unlawful racial discrimination in the workplace.[121]

The *Swann* decision was greeted with varying responses in Charlotte. Many in the African American community were euphoric. Elo Henderson, a local Presbyterian minister, called the decision "the best news" he had heard "since Jesus Christ rose from the dead."[122] Much of the white community, though considerably less enthusiastic, resigned itself to the fact that the Supreme Court had definitively settled the busing issue. School Board Chair Poe, who had urged the appeal to the Supreme Court and in fact had predicted a victory for the school board, counseled acceptance of the Supreme Court's decision.[123] As the *Observer* editorialized, "All citizens who have based their opposition to Judge McMillan's orders on the grounds that they couldn't take the word of one man, now have the highest authority in the land saying the same thing."[124] Even some of the CPA leaders appeared to acknowledge the Court's final resolution of the busing issue. The day the decision was announced, CPA Chair Thomas Harris announced: "I've taken an oath to abide by the laws. I don't see myself with any other opportunity [to challenge the busing order]."[125] The *Charlotte News*, which had consistently criticized

McMillan's busing order, called for an end to resistance: "Massive resistance is both impractical and ultimately futile. Attempts to ban busing per se are pointless."[126]

The Supreme Court's decision in the *Swann* case marked the beginning of the end of resistance to school desegregation in Charlotte. The school board had received what it had requested—an interpretation from the nation's highest court—and now it was time to adapt. But the desegregation controversy was far from over. Many members of the community, with considerable representation on the school board, still could not abide the assignment of their children to schools in black neighborhoods. On a motion of board member William Booe and contrary to the advice of its attorneys, the board voted to ask the Supreme Court to reconsider its decision, an utterly futile gesture.[127] Moreover, one week after the decision, a board majority voted to ask Congress for a constitutional amendment banning the use of busing in school desegregation cases.[128] The Supreme Court of the United States had settled the question of busing for the city of Charlotte and had given Judge McMillan an enormous vote of confidence. But it would take the school board three years to fully accept that fact.

People all over the Charlotte-Mecklenburg community are so anxious to develop a quiet, smoothly operating school system that I think they'd be willing to do almost anything.

—Chamber of Commerce President C. C. Cameron, *Charlotte Observer*, June 24, 1973

CHAPTER 9

The Search for Stability

The U.S. Supreme Court had settled the question of whether Judge James McMillan had acted properly in ordering the school board to eliminate every majority-black school. Some members of the board, however, had difficulty accepting that judgment, and congressional efforts to enact antibusing legislation steeled their resolve to continue to fight. At the same time, other members of the board believed that many white parents — particularly in the high-income neighborhoods in southeast Charlotte — would pull their children from the public schools rather than allow them to attend inner-city black schools and that therefore the busing burden should fall most heavily on African American students and lower-income white students.

Those attitudes angered certain black and white parents, who demanded the creation of a stable and fair assignment plan that would spread the burden of busing evenly throughout the school system. Yet for three years, despite considerable prodding from McMillan, the school board remained unwilling to do so, fearing white flight. Resolution of the standoff would come only with the emergence of a broad-based community group that forged consensus around an assignment plan that both the judge and most of the community could accept. This citizen initiative helped resolve the city's desegregation crisis. Unwittingly, it also helped transform the city's politics.

Once the dust had settled from the Supreme Court's momentous decision in the *Swann* case, the school board — particularly Board Chair William Poe — set about to find ways of reducing incentives for white parents to pull their children from the public schools. The previous fall, over two thousand white children had enrolled in private schools, and Poe feared a wide-scale abandonment of the public school system by white parents in the wake of the Supreme Court's decision affirming McMillan's actions.[1] The example of other southern cities such as Richmond and Atlanta, which had converted from a majority-white to a majority-black school system in just a few short years, loomed large in the minds of the school patrons.[2] Accordingly, two months after the *Swann* decision, the school board requested McMillan to allow it to abandon the court-imposed Finger Plan, which the Supreme Court had approved, and to substitute in its place the board's own newly devised plan.[3]

The board plan involved a significant underutilization of schools in African American neighborhoods and overutilization of schools in white neighborhoods. Two schools in African American residential areas would be closed altogether, continuing the long-established pattern of closing traditionally black schools and shifting those students to distant white schools. The board further proposed reducing by one-half the student population at fifteen other elementary schools in predominantly African American neighborhoods. Those fifteen schools would be used only for sixth-graders. African American students in grades one through five would attend schools in white neighborhoods; white students would then travel to these underutilized schools for the sixth grade. In addition, the board proposed a substantial reduction in the student population at the one remaining traditionally black high school—West Charlotte High School—to about 60 percent of its capacity.[4]

West Charlotte would emerge as a central point of conflict between the judge and the board. The school board had built West Charlotte in 1961—seven years after the *Brown* decision—in the middle of an African American neighborhood in northwest Charlotte, with the clear intention of using the school to educate only black students. Now, ten years later, many members of the board believed that white parents simply would not permit their children to attend the school. Within a week of McMillan's original April 1969 order, Poe had identified the desegregation of West Charlotte as an insurmountable problem: "There is no city on the face of the earth that has ever solved the West Charlotte problem. No city. To me this is the real issue before us."[5] The board would struggle with the "West Charlotte problem" for the next three years.

To compensate for the underutilization of the schools in African American neighborhoods, the board proposed increasing the student population at several schools in white neighborhoods to accommodate the in-

Students in northwest Charlotte ride a school bus to junior high school, February 1972. (Courtesy of the *Charlotte Observer*)

coming black students. To house these students, the board planned to purchase 172 new mobile classroom units at a cost of over $1.4 million, a figure that more than doubled the total operational costs of the Finger Plan.[6] Ultimately, the board used 232 mobile units during the 1971–72 school year at schools located primarily in suburban white neighborhoods. Although the school board had bitterly criticized the extensive busing required under the Finger Plan, this new board plan increased by about 20 percent the number of students bused away from their neighborhood schools and increased the distances students traveled to attend school.[7]

Although African American students bore the greatest busing burden under the board's new plan, many white students, particularly those who lived in the northern and western parts of the county, faced lengthy bus rides to attend schools in distant black neighborhoods. At the same time, many white students who lived in southeast Charlotte—the wealthiest section of the city—were exempted from the busing requirement altogether.

Board Chair Poe defended the board's plan on the grounds that it brought stability to the school system by minimizing the likelihood of "white flight." In Poe's view, the board plan reduced the incentives for white parents—particularly those in southeast Charlotte—to flee the school system in favor of private schools.[8] Because African American students and lower-income white students would be the least likely to flee the public school system, the board determined that they should bear the greatest busing burden. A local television station, WBTV, agreed, raising the specter that the school system could become "almost totally black" without such a plan.[9] At approximately the same time that the board proposed its new plan, a federal judge in Atlanta declined to order extensive school busing for that city's school system due to concerns about white flight.[10] Poe's instincts about white flight were on target. Social scientists would later demonstrate that white flight from urban school systems generally did increase when white students were assigned to schools in black neighborhoods and that white flight was more likely among parents with income levels sufficient to support private education.[11] Moreover, a 1975 study of white flight found a positive correlation between income and white flight in Charlotte.[12]

Judge McMillan, however, objected to the unfairness of the uneven distribution of the desegregation burden under the board plan, noting that the plan "unlawfully discriminate[d] against black children." McMillan specifically rejected the board's "white flight" justification for its plan, concluding that the facts would not "support a finding that 'white flight' [was] a serious threat to the public schools of Mecklenburg."[13] McMillan, citing the Supreme Court's 1968 decision in *Monroe v. Board of Commissioners*, noted that white flight was "still not acceptable as a reason to shrink from constitutional obligations."[14] For the next several years, McMillan and the board would struggle over the perceived threat of white flight. In significant measure, the sheer size of the Charlotte-Mecklenburg school system made white flight difficult. Unlike many southern cities, such as Richmond and Atlanta, Charlotte had no nearby suburban school districts to which white students could easily flee. Social scientists would later find that in large countywide school districts, such as Charlotte, the decline in white enrollment in response to busing plans was about one-half that of city-only school systems because of the geographic barriers to white flight.[15] Thus, although some white students would continue to leave the school system for private schools, Charlotte experienced significantly less white flight than did most other southern cities and even today is one of the few large American cities to retain a majority-white school system.

McMillan let it be known in the June 1971 hearings on the board's plan that he would not approve it because of the underutilization of the black schools. Members of the board disagreed about what action to take in light of that disapproval. Board Chair Poe, although clearly unhappy with McMillan's position on the white flight issue, favored drafting another plan that the judge would accept. Poe disagreed with McMillan's perception of the potential for white flight and its legal significance but recognized that the Supreme Court two months earlier had given the judge a sweeping affirmation of his exercise of discretion.

On the other hand, board member William Booe, the strongest opponent of both busing and cooperation with McMillan, challenged Poe, urging his colleagues to resist the judge more aggressively.[16] Booe, a lawyer who had represented the CPA in its earlier efforts to thwart implementation of the Finger Plan, had been elected to the board as part of the CPA's slate in May 1970. Booe was the board's most combative member, with little interest in forging consensus.[17] Possessed of a fiery temper and belligerent manner, Booe would on occasion challenge his colleagues to resolve their differences by resort to fisticuffs.[18] A major split eventually developed between Booe and Poe, causing significant problems for the board. Both men were united in the view that McMillan had exceeded the requirements of the Constitution and had undermined public confidence in the school system. Yet the pragmatic Poe, fully cognizant of the fact that the Supreme Court had ratified McMillan's actions, would prove more willing than Booe to seek a workable solution with the judge. Booe could not countenance Poe's willingness to compromise and repeatedly called for Poe's resignation. On one occasion, Booe called Poe "incompetent" and recklessly claimed that Poe headed "the list of those who have attempted to tear down education in this county."[19] Described by one of his colleagues as a "pre–Civil War conservative," Booe preferred to fight the good fight rather than give in to the judge on any issue.[20] Such a spirit would repeatedly serve to antagonize the judge, Booe's fellow board members, and much of the community.

The board majority ultimately agreed with Poe and decided to withdraw its plan and to submit a new one to the judge. The board's revised plan remedied some of the problems McMillan had identified. Pursuant to this revised plan, all but three of the elementary schools located in African American neighborhoods would operate at near-capacity, educating both fifth- and sixth-graders.[21] Of the three elementary schools excluded from this arrangement, the board proposed closing one and utilizing two others only for sixth-graders.[22] The board continued, however, to exclude several sections of southeast Charlotte from busing obligations altogether.[23]

McMillan found the plan discriminatory, since most African American children were required to attend schools in distant white neighborhoods ten of their twelve years, whereas some white children never had to leave their neighborhood at all. Moreover, the judge found that the plan tended to perpetuate segregation through the underutilization of schools in African American neighborhoods and the overutilization of schools in white neighborhoods. Nevertheless, in late June, McMillan approved the board's plan with certain modifications: that the board neither close nor underutilize any traditionally African American school and that the board not allow students to transfer from their assigned schools if such transfers tended to increase the racial identifiability of any school. McMillan indicated that if the board would comply with each of these requirements, and would ensure that no school operated for any period of the school year with a predominantly African American population, he would allow the board to abandon the court-ordered Finger Plan and to proceed with its own plan beginning in the fall of 1971.[24]

In McMillan's view, the board's plan, even as revised, was plainly inferior to the Finger Plan. It imposed an uneven busing burden on African American children, it necessitated substantial increased busing for the system as a whole, and it required the expenditure of $1.4 million to purchase new mobile units. Yet McMillan was keenly interested, as he had been throughout the litigation, in letting the board assume full authority for pupil assignments: "The court welcomes the situation in which, for the first time, in all details, the pupil assignments are entirely the work of the local board rather than being, even in theory, the work of court appointed consultants." Accordingly, McMillan ratified the board's plan. At the same time, however, McMillan was clear that the plan did not satisfy constitutional standards: "Racial discrimination through official action has not ended in this school system. Racial discrimination through official action has not ended when a school board knowingly adopts a plan likely to cause a return to segregated schools and then refuses to guard against such re-segregation."[25] In an aside, the judge addressed the question of the exclusion of certain higher-income white children from their share of the busing burden. McMillan indicated that this might be "a type of class discrimination which courts some day may undertake to consider as a constitutional question," but he noted that he would allow the creation of such white "protectorates" for the time being.[26]

In the meantime, in August 1971, shortly before the start of the new school year, the parents of a group of white children in northeast and west Charlotte, part of an organization calling itself Citizens United for Fairness, petitioned the court to allow them to intervene in the *Swann* litigation. These parents asked McMillan to address the "class discrimination" issue that he had avoided in his June decision. They complained that the board's plan required northeast and westside white children to go to schools outside their neighborhoods an average of six or seven years out of twelve, whereas white children in the wealthier communities of southeast Charlotte were required to leave their neighborhood schools only one or two years out of twelve if at all.[27] Two days later, Chambers charged that the board was freely allowing transfers in violation of the court's June order and that the effect of the board's actions would be the resegregation of some of the traditionally African American schools.[28]

McMillan held a hearing on the two matters at the end of September 1971. Regarding the complaint of the white parents, McMillan acknowledged that the replacement of the Finger Plan with the board plan had involved a shift in the busing burden away from the city's wealthier white southeast neighborhoods: "It is apparent that the [board] plan puts increased burdens of transportation upon black children and upon children in certain low- and middle-income white communities; that it relieves the vast majority of students of the wealthier precincts in southeast Mecklenburg from any assignment or transportation to formerly black schools; and that, compared to these wealthier white people in southeast Mecklenburg, many more of the children of the intervenors are going to formerly black schools." Conceding that "the evidence no doubt show[ed] economic and class discrimination," McMillan nevertheless concluded that this type of discrimination against lower-income whites was a political and not a constitutional issue and hence declined to award the intervenors any relief.[29] Over the course of the next two years, McMillan would come to see this issue of "economic and class discrimination" differently.

Regarding the plaintiffs' concern about the resegregation of certain schools due to student transfers, McMillan noted that the board in fact had allowed so many transfers that three elementary schools had become predominantly black, three more were on the verge of a black majority, and West Charlotte High School had a 48 percent black population, despite a projected black population of between 23 and 28 percent.[30] This resegregation was due to the board's decision to allow students who changed residences to transfer to another school, which encouraged student movement to new neighborhoods. McMillan directed the board not to allow any more student transfers, but that order came too late; for the second straight year, about half a dozen schools had become majority black despite promises from the school board that it would prevent such action.[31]

In the meantime, the board appealed McMillan's June 1971 order that had required certain modifications to the board's plan. Poe unsuccessfully tried to persuade his colleagues not to appeal, noting that the Supreme Court had given McMillan broad discretion in supervising pupil assignments.[32] The board, in its presentation to the Fourth Circuit, emphasized once again the unfairness of McMillan's demands: Charlotte-Mecklenburg had a greater degree of pupil desegregation than almost every other large urban school system in the country.[33] Moreover, other federal judges — in Atlanta, Dallas, and Chattanooga — continued to permit the retention of majority-black schools.[34]

Yet McMillan's insistence on the elimination of all majority-black schools in Charlotte had been affirmed by the Supreme Court the year before as a proper exercise of his discretion. As a result, the Fourth Circuit sitting *en banc* gave the school board only summary consideration. In a two-sentence opinion released in February 1972, the court unanimously concluded that McMillan had not abused his discretion in modifying the board's proposed plan.[35] McMillan might be requiring more extensive desegregation than other federal judges, but the Supreme Court's *Swann* decision gave him broad discretion to modify pupil assignment plans as he saw fit in order to achieve desegregation. The school board, however, would have serious difficulty accepting that fact. As a consequence, over the course of the next few years, it would expend much energy pursuing fruitless appeals.

In the meantime, antagonism toward school busing to overcome racial imbalance had spread throughout the nation in response to the Supreme Court's *Swann* decision. In early 1972, both houses of Congress held widely publicized hearings that addressed the issue of school busing and that included consideration of a proposed constitutional amendment prohibiting busing for purposes of achieving racial balance. Although the Nixon administration did not formally endorse the constitutional amendment, President Richard Nixon did suggest on several occasions his desire to find a way to restrict the use of busing.[36] In March 1972, George Wallace won a significant victory in the Florida Democratic presidential primary, attacking President Nixon for his inability to put a halt to "forced busing."[37] Two days later, Nixon asked Congress, in a nationally televised speech, for legislation that would impose a moratorium on court-ordered busing and that would provide for a return to neighborhood schools.[38]

In the wake of its defeat in the Fourth Circuit in February 1972, the school board vowed to go to Washington to support congressional efforts to pass a constitutional amendment making it illegal to assign children to schools solely on the basis of their race.[39] One of Charlotte's leading television stations supported the amendment efforts, endorsing the "right of the people . . . to correct what the great majority" felt to be "judicial excesses."[40] Board Chair Poe and board members Jane Scott and Sam McNinch traveled to Washington during the spring of 1972 to testify before the House Judiciary Committee in support of the proposed constitutional amendment. Board member Julia Maulden, with McMillan's encouragement, appeared in opposition.[41] Poe spoke as the designated representative of the board majority, complaining that the Supreme Court's deference to district court judges permitted broad discrepancies across the country in terms of the amount of busing required. Poe, with a veiled reference to McMillan, told the congressmen, "Some of the Federal judiciary, if left unbridled, are capable of destroying public support for our schools."[42]

Although Congress did not pass the proposed constitutional amendment, the antibusing backlash would continue for the next few years and was partly responsible for a realignment in southern politics. The busing issue helped Nixon gain reelection in 1972 with strong southern support and contributed to the election of the first Republican governor and U.S. senator in North Carolina since the nineteenth century. "I can tell you what's brought [the Republican Party this success] — and any man that knows politics knows," one state Republican leader noted. "The race question brought it."[43] In an appeal to white Anglo-Saxon voters — and to distance himself from his Greek-American Democrat opponent, Nick Galiafanakis — the successful Republican candidate for senator in 1972, Jesse Helms, campaigned under the slogan: "Jesse: He's One of Us."[44] Helms's success demonstrated the tremendous potential of a "send them a message" campaign around racial issues in North Carolina in the early 1970s.

Yet ironically, in Charlotte, community dissatisfaction with the staunch antibusing members of the school board had increased. Charlotte might be laboring under an extensive desegregation plan, but the community rejected those candidates for public office who campaigned on a promise of finding new ways of avoiding school desegregation. In May 1972, three of the nine seats on the board were up for election. Two years earlier, the three CPA-backed antibusing candidates—William Booe, Tom Harris, and Jane Scott—had won resounding victories, capturing 53 percent of the total vote. This time, the three CPA-backed candidates captured only 18.6 percent of the vote, and not one was elected.[45] The CPA candidates strongly supported both Nixon's proposed antibusing legislation and the constitutional amendment prohibiting the use of busing for desegregation purposes.[46] But by 1972, antibusing posturing was no longer a winning political issue in Charlotte-Mecklenburg School Board elections. A 1972 poll revealed that only one-third of Charlotte parents found busing to be the most troubling aspect of the public schools.[47] The CPA's failure in the 1972 elections did not signal community enthusiasm for school desegregation but rather a community realization that desegregation could not be avoided and that continued obstruction served only to undermine the public school system and the city's long-term interests. The city had fought McMillan's busing order through the legal process, but when the Supreme Court had affirmed McMillan's actions in 1971, the desire to resist had substantially lessened. As one government official noted, the 1972 school board election was "a public recognition" that the city was "headed in the direction of acceptance."[48] Every antibusing candidate would lose in the 1974 and 1976 school board elections as well. But the voters in 1970 had elected three strong antibusing candidates to six-year terms and, particularly in the case of William Booe, had thereby ensured several years of school board conflict.

Significantly, Board Chair Poe won reelection in May 1972 with the largest vote of all of the candidates by deliberately avoiding busing as a campaign issue and focusing instead on early childhood education.[49] "I did not talk at all about busing in that campaign," Poe later commented. "I talked about the need to provide quality education."[50] Although Poe strongly opposed the extensive busing requirements imposed by the court, Poe understood that the board operated under certain legal constraints and that some school busing could not be avoided. Certain of his colleagues could never accept that fact.

The 1972 elections also marked the first time in the city's history that an African American candidate won a school board election.[51] Phil Berry, a local banker running with the support of the city's business community, captured one of the three open seats. Ironically, Berry had been a tenth-grader at Plato Price, an all-black school in the western section of the county, when the Supreme Court had issued its *Brown* decision in 1954. Berry had greeted the *Brown* decision with great anticipation, assuming that he would be assigned to nearby West Mecklenburg, a white high school. That assignment never came.[52] Berry would ultimately become board chair in 1976 when Poe retired.[53]

Notwithstanding Charlotte's unwillingness to elect staunch antibusing candidates to the school board, the continuing turmoil in Washington during the spring and summer of 1972 around the busing issue affected Charlotte. Several of the school board candidates noted that they would seek to reopen the *Swann* litigation if the efforts in Congress to pass an antibusing measure were successful. Thus, although the electoral results indicated that a majority of Charlotteans had reconciled themselves to the fact of busing, the possibility of congressional action encouraged many who hoped that McMillan's busing order might be overturned by statute or constitutional amendment. As Superintendent William Self explained to a news reporter in May 1972, "Just when we thought we had all that behind us and could get on with our educational targets, the political pot is astir with it again and threatens to set us back."[54]

In the meantime, the school system continued to experience the same type of racial disturbances that had marred the previous school year. The disturbances served to undermine white support for desegregated schools and caused many in the black community to question the value of an integrated education.

During the fall of 1971, three of the city's high schools — Myers Park, South Mecklenburg, and Olympic — experienced significant disturbances that forced the temporary closure of each school. The school system suspended or expelled almost four thousand students in the wake of those disturbances, and criminal charges were brought against seventy-seven students.[55] Moreover, during the 1971–72 school year, the school system suffered an average of four bomb threats each week, a slight reduction from the year before.[56] By 1973, student disturbances would necessitate the temporary closure of every high school in the system.[57]

The staff of the Charlotte-Mecklenburg schools prepared a report in December 1971 on the student disruptions and, in a highly significant gesture, placed much of the blame with the school board itself: "The prevailing attitude on the part of members of the Board of Education has been one of attempting to meet the letter of the court order rather than finding ways to implement the spirit of the orders. This attitude has generally been reflected throughout the community. There is an apparent need for more positive community leadership and support for the schools."[58] Three months later, the mayor's Charlotte-Mecklenburg Community Relations Committee, a successor to Stanford Brookshire's earlier committee, which now functioned under the leadership of Presbyterian minister Warner Hall, issued its own report, concluding that the school board had failed the community in its leadership and that the "verbal assaults on each other" by board members had helped divide the community.[59] The report called for responsible leadership from the city's elected and civic leaders.

Without question, the frequent and public squabbling among board members had helped undermine community morale and had made constructive action extremely difficult. And these disputes would continue; one year later, for example, three of the board's antibusing members filed suit against their colleagues for excluding them from an informal gathering of board members at Poe's home.[60]

In the meantime, the African American community complained that their children bore the brunt of the disciplinary action taken in the wake of the student disruptions. Since the initial court-ordered desegregation during the 1969–70 school year, the number of African American students suspended from school had dramatically increased. School officials had suspended about 1,500 students the year before McMillan's first desegregation order. The following year, that number doubled to about 3,200 students and then doubled again during the 1970–71 school year to more than 6,500 students. Almost 90 percent of the students suspended during this time were African American.[61] Moreover, of the 77 students arrested during the serious high school disturbances of the fall of 1971, all but 2 were African American.[62]

The school discipline issue ultimately wound up before McMillan. In December 1969, two African American elementary school students who had been expelled from the school system after a fight with a teacher brought suit, challenging the process by which their expulsion decisions had been reached. At that time, board procedures afforded a suspended or expelled student no right to be heard before the exclusion.[63] In November 1971, McMillan conducted a hearing at which the plaintiffs presented considerable testimony concerning large numbers of African American students who had been denied any opportunity to respond to allegations against them before their expulsion. McMillan ordered the school board in June 1972 to devise a new set of disciplinary procedures that guaranteed a presuspension right to a hearing with counsel and the right to present evidence and confront adverse witnesses.[64] In the fall of 1972, the school administration adopted such procedures.[65]

Yet the perception that African American students were being discriminated against in school discipline matters continued. In October 1972,

Police officers subdue two students following a disturbance at East Mecklenburg
High School, October 1972. (Courtesy of the *Charlotte Observer*)

twelve students were suspended from East Mecklenburg High School after a racial disturbance that caused a temporary shutdown of the school.[66]
Almost all of the suspended students were African American.[67] Frustrated
by a perceived discriminatory application of the disciplinary rules, a
group of African American students in January 1973 presented to the
school board a list of grievances in which they asked for an end to au-
tomatic suspensions of students involved in fights, the removal of police
officers from school campuses, and a return to neighborhood schools.[68]
The final request reflected a growing feeling, in much of the African
American community, that school desegregation was not worth the high
cost paid by black students. In a 1973 study, the U.S. Commission on
Civil Rights concluded that resentment toward school desegregation in
Charlotte was widespread within the African American community because of the unequal busing burden.[69]

In March 1973, a group of black and white students brought suit challenging their assignment to schools outside of their neighborhoods.[70] The
lawsuit had no hope of success — and was later dismissed by McMillan —
since the Supreme Court in *Swann* had established that the assignment
of students outside of their neighborhoods was an appropriate remedial

The Search for Stability | 227

device in school desegregation cases, but it highlighted the deep resentment among many in the city's African American community toward the school board's unequal assignment practices.[71]

Following his October 1971 order approving the board plan as modified, McMillan adopted a "hands off" approach to the schools. In the summer of 1972, when the white intervenors from the northeastern and western sections of the county again complained to the court about the unequal burdens of the board's busing program, McMillan declined to take action, expressing the view that at least one year should pass without major changes in pupil assignments. McMillan did note, however, that the burdens of school busing continued to fall most heavily on young African American children.[72] In November 1972, Chambers asked McMillan to reopen the case, charging that West Charlotte was in danger of once again becoming a majority African American high school.[73] McMillan declined to take action, again preferring to minimize court intrusion and to give the board more time to create a stable assignment plan.

Over the course of the next several months, however, it became increasingly apparent that the board, as currently constituted, would not adopt an acceptable plan without further intervention from the court. In September 1972, the board commissioned a school staff committee to restudy the entire desegregation plan and make recommendations, a step McMillan had encouraged the board to take as early as June 1971. The staff, under the direction of Assistant Superintendent John Phillips, completed its study six months later, in March 1973. The staff report sharply criticized the board's distribution of the busing burden: "[Black children] are bearing the dominant burden of assignment change and time of transportation both in hours and years. . . . The [board] plan calls for the extensive assignment of the *youngest* black children out of their home neighborhood for ten (in some cases, all) of their school years."[74] The report concluded that the unequal busing burden created not only resentment in the African American community but also instability in the city's housing patterns as residents sought to move to neighborhoods where the busing burden was less severe.[75] The staff report was significant for two reasons. First, it marked the first time that the school staff had formally recognized the unfairness of the pupil assignment plan. Second, it contributed to a shift in public mood on the busing issue. After the report's release, an increasing number of citizens in Charlotte-Mecklenburg began to identify the board, not the judge, as the central problem and to demand a fair assignment plan.[76] Notwithstanding the strong views expressed in the staff report, the board ignored the report's conclusions and recommendations.

In the meantime, the board continued to search for ways to avoid McMillan's supervision of its pupil assignment plan. In the spring of 1973, encouraged by the ongoing national debate over school busing, the board enacted yet another resolution supporting a constitutional amendment prohibiting the busing of schoolchildren for purposes of desegregation. Such efforts again served to raise false hopes that the demands of desegregation could be avoided. At the same time, the board considered a resolution asking McMillan to declare the schools a unitary system and hence beyond his supervisory control. In the board's favor was the fact that federal district court judge Eugene Gordon had recently found the Greensboro, North Carolina, school system unitary, notwithstanding the fact that two schools remained predominantly black. The proponents of the resolution realized that McMillan would decline to follow Gordon, but they hoped to create an immediate appeal issue. Poe and Booe bitterly disputed the wisdom of seeking an additional appeal on this issue. Poe argued that the board had not "come close" to establishing a unitary system as defined by McMillan and that the Fourth Circuit would undoubtedly back the judge on that point.[77] Poe told Booe: "You went to the Supreme Court in 1971 and you lost nine-zip, too, so you can't tell us you know more about the law than our legal counsel. No one here has the power to reverse the Supreme Court." The resolution ultimately failed by a 5-to-4 vote.[78]

The board ultimately submitted a new pupil assignment plan to McMillan for the 1973–74 school year, but not surprisingly, the board's proposed plan did not satisfy the judge. The new plan provided for yet another reduction in the population of West Charlotte High School, to approximately 60 percent of its capacity, a move that McMillan had explicitly rejected in June 1971. Moreover, the plan placed most of the busing burden on African American children and lower- and middle-income white children while minimizing the burden on southeast Charlotte.[79]

Having allowed the board to operate its own plan for two years without his intervention, McMillan decided to examine with more care the board's new plan. The central issues remained, as they had for three years, the racial instability of certain schools in black neighborhoods and the unfairness and instability of the board plan because of the uneven distribution of the busing burden. During hearings on the new assignment plan in May 1973, McMillan advised the board that it must undertake "a complete revision of the plan," encompassing in the West Charlotte attendance area white students from southeast Charlotte neighborhoods. After hesitating for two years, McMillan had finally decided that the board must distribute the busing burden more evenly throughout the school system.[80]

In the meantime, residents of the northeast section of the county became increasingly vocal about the unfairness of the busing plan. A group of these residents, including several associated with the nearby University of North Carolina at Charlotte, had been meeting for a couple of years to coordinate strategy. The group had made regular appearances before the school board to press its claims concerning the unfairness of the busing burden. At the May hearing, Julian Mason, a white English professor and one of the leaders of the northeast group, approached Chambers and requested the opportunity to address the court. Skeptical at first, Chambers permitted Mason to take the stand.[81] Mason explained the unfairness of the board's plan to his section of the county: "We have developed a good situation in our area. But it has already begun to deteriorate because everyone . . . is angry. The people feel that the desegregation of schools is not being fairly shared. They feel more and more that the southeast is sheltered, and suspect more and more correlation between where the school board lives and what areas escape."[82] Afterward, Mason followed up on his concerns with an open letter to the school board: "Until all of the community is involved in busing there will be no stability in our school system. I call for fair sharing of busing by all. The black community and the northern part of the community have already done their share. Look to those who have not done theirs (the south) before adding yet more busing to areas which already have enough."[83] Meanwhile, a group of dissatisfied white parents, including Mason, published a newspaper advertisement implying a connection between the residences of six of the nine board members in southeast Charlotte and the burdens of desegregation.[84] At a June school board meeting, other white parents criticized the board for its unstable and inequitable plan, praising McMillan as the "last and only hope of sanity in our schools."[85]

Ironically, much of the white community had come to view McMillan as a potential champion of the interests of residents who lived outside of southeast Charlotte. By 1973, a majority of Charlotteans accepted the inevitability of busing; most were now concerned with establishing a desegregation plan that spread the burden of busing more evenly. In a strange twist, many white parents, including scores of former CPA members from the eastern and western sections of the county, now understood that their interests would be best protected by the very judge who for so long had been the object of their scorn.

In the meantime, a few of the more recalcitrant board members indicated that they understood the need to spread the busing burden more equally throughout the county. During hearings on the board's plan in May 1973, staunch antibusing board member Sam McNinch, while testifying, engaged in an unusual colloquy with McMillan:

> *McNinch:* It's not our school system, Judge. It's not yours. It belongs to the people out there. I would hope that you would not dictate what we do because that does not get the feelings of the people involved.
>
> *McMillan:* I share that hope. . . . If I am satisfied that the Board has taken the football and run with it, it ought to become irrelevant as soon as possible whether you have twenty-eight or fifty-four percent black in a school. . . . I'm not at any time unmindful of the fact that we've come a lot further toward desegregation than any city I know of.[86]

A few days later, McNinch arranged to have a private lunch with the judge to follow up on their courtroom conversation. The meeting appeared to have a strong effect on McNinch; he commented to a reporter afterward: "I have to put my trust in the judge at this point."[87] After that lunch, McNinch proposed that a board subcommittee meet with McMillan informally in his chambers to discuss further the judge's expectations. The board approved the meeting over the strong objection of its attorneys.[88] To be sure, the notion of a judge holding a private meeting with one set of litigants in a case before him was highly unusual. Yet McMillan understood that this was not a typical lawsuit; if a meeting with several members of the school board could facilitate the ultimate settlement of the case, then a departure from typical patterns was warranted.

On June 14, 1973, four members of the board—antibusing activists McNinch and Jane Scott, along with Phil Berry and Carlton Watkins—met with McMillan to discuss the prospects of ending the judge's involvement in the pupil assignment process.[89] McMillan reiterated the position he had taken in the hearings: he would not approve a pupil assignment plan unless the white students assigned to West Charlotte came from the southeast section of the city, which to date had largely escaped the burdens of busing.[90] The board members left the meeting in an upbeat mood.

McNinch had already signaled his willingness to come to terms with the need to spread the busing burden throughout the county; Scott indicated that it was no longer a question of whether there would be busing but who would be bused and for how long. Both McNinch and Scott, two of the board's strongest opponents of busing, favored additional meetings with the judge.[91] The *Charlotte Observer* enthused that the meeting might have "marked a turning point in the search for a settlement."[92]

This enthusiasm following the in-chambers meeting between the judge and the board members crumbled a few days later when McMillan released his opinion on the board's latest assignment plan. McMillan's opinion contained perhaps the strongest indictment of the school board's actions that he had ever written, including the implication that certain board members were motivated by the desire to keep their own children safe from busing:

> Six of the ten high school feeder areas, mostly in east and southeast Mecklenburg, continue to enjoy substantial immunity from having children transported to "black" schools. . . .
>
> Six of the nine members of the Board and numerous key staff members live in the "no bussing" country in the east and southeast parts of the county. With peripheral exceptions only, white children from that area have not been "bussed" to formerly black schools.[93]

McMillan noted that the West Charlotte situation remained both unstable and unfair. First, the feeder schools for West Charlotte were almost half black, thereby creating a likelihood that the high school itself would eventually become a predominantly black school again. Second, although white students from southeast Charlotte were much closer to West Charlotte than were students in the northeast section of the county, the southeast whites had been allowed to attend nearby high schools, whereas the northeast students had been assigned to West Charlotte.[94] McMillan acknowledged that the board took the position that parents in the southeast section of the city would not allow their children to attend formerly black schools, but he declined to accept that rationale as either an accurate predictor of parental behavior or a legally significant position.[95]

McMillan ordered the board to replace the white students from the northeast assigned to West Charlotte with white students from the southeast, explaining that principles of fairness required such action: "Even though *perfect* fairness in desegregating schools may still be impossible, fairness is still the prime guide of a court of equity; and *gross unfairness*, such as still exists in the current situation, is the legitimate target of a court of equity which was originally called to act because of the unfairness (lack of equal protection of laws) in the operation of the schools."[96] McMillan was aware that his order challenged the sensibilities of much of southeast Charlotte but was now convinced that it would be impossible to create a fair and stable assignment system if a large portion of the county continued to be exempt from the busing requirements.

Under pressure from the court, the board assigned six hundred white students — selected at random — from the southeastern section of the city to West Charlotte.[97] Although the board permitted students who changed their residence to attend the school designated for the student's new residential area, McMillan reversed that aspect of the board's plan.[98] McMillan's hard line on the transfer issue was clearly necessary. One reason several schools had become majority black during the past few years was because many white students assigned to schools in African American neighborhoods had changed their residence and hence their school assignment. Allowing such transfers encouraged students seeking to avoid an unfavorable assignment to change their residence. McMillan determined that the board's transfer provision left the assignment plan too unstable.[99]

The *Charlotte Observer* concluded, probably correctly, that McMillan had undermined whatever progress had been made in the June 14 meeting with the four board members by ruling as quickly and as forcefully as he did after that meeting.[100] By the same token, certain board members, particularly Booe, Harris, and Poe, none of whom had attended the informal meeting, were opposed to including southeast Charlotte students in the busing plan. Poe could accept McMillan's insistence on the elimination of every majority-black school; the Supreme Court had settled that issue. But to Poe, McMillan was now engaged in a very different enterprise. "The Supreme Court has not talked about socio-economic integration," Poe complained. "It's just the judge's idea of how society ought to be."[101] To Poe, McMillan's insistence on the inclusion of southeast Charlotte children in the busing plan was deeply troubling: "This is the next grand step in a master plan that I don't like. It's unfortunate when we are placed in that position by the tremendous amount of power in the hands of one man. I don't think that's how this country ought to be governed."[102] At the heart of Poe's opposition to the assignment of southeast students to West Charlotte remained his fears of white flight. Compared with other urban school districts, Charlotte had experienced minimal white flight from the school system. Between 1968 and 1973, Charlotte had lost about 10 percent of its white enrollment, one of the lowest totals of all urban school districts.[103] But Poe feared that those numbers would significantly increase if white children in southeast Charlotte were reassigned to schools in black neighborhoods.

Yet McMillan's insistence on including southeast Charlotte in the desegregation plan was clearly defensible. McMillan bore the responsibility for overseeing the transition from an unconstitutionally segregated school system to a unitary system. In the judge's view, that transition could not take place unless the system's pupil assignment system was reasonably stable. As long as the board continued to exclude one section of the city from the busing burden, the plan would remain unstable, since white parents could avoid assignments to schools in black neighborhoods by simply moving their residence.[104]

By the summer of 1973, significant elements of the community agreed with McMillan. As the board deliberated the question of whether to appeal, the *Charlotte News*, which had editorially criticized the judge throughout much of the controversy, wrote that an appeal would not resolve the problems with the board's feeder plan and that the real problem was the "perceived discrimination" in favor of southeast Charlotte.[105] Whereas the dominant cry of 1970 had been "no forced busing," by 1973 "fairness and stability" had become the most commonly heard refrain in the community.[106] Significantly, an August 1973 antibusing rally drew only 150 partisans, notwithstanding a prediction of thousands.[107] The days of antibusing rallies that attracted thousands of Charlotteans had long past.

W. T. Harris, chair of the Mecklenburg County Board of Commissioners and one of the most powerful business and political leaders in the city, also took issue with the board: "I think the Supreme Court has already ruled that Mecklenburg County is going to carry out Judge McMillan's order. I think we should get down and carry out the educational program." C. C. Cameron, president of the Charlotte Chamber of Commerce, sounded a similar theme. Cameron, a resident of southeast Charlotte, told a reporter that people in his area would accept an increase in busing in return for a permanent and stable school plan.[108] Cameron ultimately called about thirty-five or forty business leaders to his office for a meeting to figure out how the city could "take its medicine and get on with it."[109] Cameron's actions were significant; they signified that the business community would use its influence to resolve the stalemate between the judge and the board.[110]

The board sharply divided on the question of whether to appeal McMillan's latest order. Although many community leaders called on the board to accept McMillan's dictates regarding West Charlotte, the board decided in early July, by a 5-to-4 vote and contrary to the advice of its attorney, to once again seek review in the Fourth Circuit.[111] Several members of the board, in particular Poe, hoped to place before the appellate court the propriety of McMillan's insistence on eliminating "class" discrimination by requiring the board to include southeast Charlotte in its busing proposals.[112]

At the same time, Booe moved, with the support of McNinch and Scott, to withdraw the board's assignment plan altogether and force the judge to draft his own assignment plan, a move designed to strengthen the board's appeal prospects. Although the motion failed, it signaled the fact that a significant minority of the board remained steadfast in its opposition to McMillan.[113] In August, in the face of an order from McMillan that the board devise a timetable for the creation of a new desegregation plan for the 1974–75 year, Booe, McNinch, and Scott unsuccessfully sought to have the board engage in no such preparations.[114] These actions of McNinch and Scott, though not surprising, indicated that the promise of the June 14 meeting in McMillan's chambers had indeed been fleeting. By the end of the summer of 1973, the board was hopelessly divided between the antibusing trio of Booe, McNinch, and Scott and the rest of the board. McNinch recommended in September that the entire board resign because of its extreme division.[115]

Ultimately the board's appeal efforts would fail yet again. At the January 1974 oral argument on the appeal, the school board's attorney, William Sturges, conceded that the board did not want to change its assignment plan midyear. Relying on that concession, the Fourth Circuit dismissed the board's appeal on ripeness grounds. In so doing, the Fourth Circuit avoided a decision on the question of whether McMillan had properly insisted on a balancing of the burdens of desegregation throughout the city.[116] The Fourth Circuit's refusal to even review McMillan's latest order constituted another implicit affirmation of the judge's discretion.

In the fall of 1973, the board majority proceeded with the difficult task of devising a new desegregation plan. In November, the board invited a large number of community organizations reflecting a whole range of perspectives on the desegregation issue to come before it and offer input on pupil assignments. Margaret Ray, head of an organization calling itself the Quality Education Committee, brought representatives of the various organizations together ahead of time for a series of potluck dinners.[117]

Although those attending these informal gatherings represented a variety of constituencies from throughout the city and county with their own specific concerns about desegregation, each participant shared the view that school busing was unavoidable, that the burdens of busing should be distributed more fairly, and that a stable plan that would eliminate the year-to-year upheavals in pupil assignments was of critical importance.

As a result of these informal gatherings, the various group representatives decided to form their own group, the Citizens Advisory Group, for the purpose of forging a pupil assignment plan that met the fairness and stability goals the various members had articulated. The Citizens Advisory Group, a biracial collection of twenty-five citizens, reflected every conceivable viewpoint on the busing issue, from busing champions to busing opponents.[118] Ray, a former high school teacher in the Charlotte-Mecklenburg schools and a resident of southeast Charlotte, emerged as the group's leader and spokesperson. Ray personally knew a number of the key players in the community, including McMillan, several of the board members and school staff, and a number of other elected officials. Those relationships would prove useful as the fledgling organization struggled for legitimacy.[119]

The Citizens Advisory Group first addressed the school board in November 1973. Following that meeting, the board gave the advisory group permission to work with the school staff to develop its own desegregation plan.[120] A few weeks later, the advisory group received a boost when the Mecklenburg County Board of Commissioners unanimously approved a resolution calling for a stable plan that would equalize the busing burdens — one of the advisory group's primary goals.[121] Subsequently, the chamber of commerce released the results of a survey of community attitudes toward desegregation; the survey had found that although two-thirds of the respondents opposed busing, almost 90 percent favored the creation of a community group to assist the board in making pupil assignments.[122] Charlotte's civic and business leadership now appeared poised to help resolve the city's desegregation dilemma, recognizing, as it had in earlier years, that the continued strength and stability of the public education system, and hence the city itself, depended on such action.

In early 1974, Ray met privately with McMillan and told him that her group would propose a plan that would distribute the burden of busing as evenly as possible, allow students in integrated neighborhoods to attend neighborhood schools, build new schools with racial impact in mind, keep each school in the system between 25 and 40 percent black, and prohibit student transfers that threatened to upset the racial balance in any school. McMillan encouraged Ray to proceed along those lines.[123]

In a February 11, 1974, report to the school board, the Citizens Advisory Group set out in general language the conditions that Ray had proposed in private to McMillan.[124] In a rebuff to the advisory group, the board declined to act on the group's proposal and instead proceeded with discussions about making West Charlotte an "open school" with no fixed pupil assignments. The optional school idea was clearly an attempt to deflect the thorniest desegregation issue of all: how to attract enough white students to West Charlotte High School to eliminate its status as a racially identifiable black school. Ironically, John Finger, McMillan's special master, had privately proposed to Chambers the previous year the idea of closing West Charlotte and reassigning its students to the other nine high schools; Chambers had sharply disagreed.[125] To close West Charlotte would increase the busing burden on a large number of African American students and underscore yet again the notion that Charlotte's schools would be desegregated at the expense of black schoolchildren.

Not surprisingly, the optional school proposal drew strong attacks from the African American community. Within days, Phil Berry, the board's only African American, presented his colleagues with a petition signed by three thousand individuals and a number of organizations asking the board to drop the idea.[126] The board ultimately rejected the optional school plan, and on March 1, 1974, submitted to McMillan an assignment plan similar to that which the judge had rejected the year before. Once again, no students from the southeast would attend West Charlotte; white students from the northeast section of the county would do so instead.[127] Two of the board members—Scott and Booe—had suggested that the board submit no plan whatsoever to the court, forcing McMillan to adopt his own plan.[128] Booe in particular continued to attack his fellow board members for their cooperation with McMillan in the desegregation process.[129]

In the meantime, McMillan requested that the board provide him with additional information about student transfers to assist him in evaluating the board's plan. The board had continued to allow students who were assigned to West Charlotte and who changed their residence to transfer to a different high school, a practice that had reduced that school's white population. McMillan had long objected to this practice as destabilizing and thus made the informal request of the board for information about transfers. Contrary to the advice of board attorney Sturges, a majority of the board voted, for the first time in the nine-year history of the litigation, to deny the judge's request for information.[130]

The board majority argued, yet again, that the Supreme Court had not clearly mandated the elimination of every majority-black school, nor had it expressly required school boards to make yearly adjustments in pupil assignments in order to retain majority-white schools. In the board's favor was the fact that in early 1974, the U.S. Supreme Court had declined to review school desegregation cases from Memphis and Knoxville in which lower-court judges had allowed the retention of majority-black schools.[131] The board would receive further support in May when federal judge Frank Johnson, one of the South's most liberal judges, found a pupil assignment constitutionally sufficient even though it left several schools predominantly black.[132] Yet the school board still failed to appreciate that both the Supreme Court and the Fourth Circuit had consistently granted McMillan broad discretion in supervising the desegregation of the Charlotte-Mecklenburg school system and that the judge's determination to keep West Charlotte a majority-white school was well within that discretion.

With the Citizens Advisory Group frustrated in its attempt to provide input on the board's assignment plan and the board clearly moving toward a major confrontation with the court, McMillan entered an additional order on April 3 requesting the advisory group to comment on the board's plan and to state how its own recommendations could be substituted for the board's proposal. McMillan further directed the school board to cooperate with the advisory group by making available all "technical and other assistance" that members of the group might need "in familiarizing themselves with the school system and in developing solutions."[133] McMillan invited the advisory group to appear at the mid-April hearing on the board's plan, explaining that the board's default made the move necessary:

> It is a possible interpretation of [the board's] response that defendants are more interested in litigation than in fairness and stability. In any event, they have again defaulted in an obligation to the community and to the school patrons (in addition to the long-standing default in compliance with the orders of the court).
>
> It is also apparent that with the Board thus dedicated it would be an idle exercise to direct defendants to require their staff, unaided, to produce effective plans to eliminate the discrimination which remains, and to address themselves to the unfairness which on the presently in-

complete record, appears manifest in many phases of the proposed pupil assignment plan.[134]

McMillan did not appoint the Citizens Advisory Group to serve as a special master, as he had done five years earlier with Finger, but the biracial group functioned in a similar manner. Recognizing that a plan drawn by the advisory group would have the substantial benefit of coming from a local community organization, McMillan decided to make the group a participant in the proceedings. McMillan perceived a growing desire in the community to find a stable and fair plan that spread the desegregation burden throughout the county, but he realized that the board majority remained steadfast in its opposition to such action. The *Charlotte News* understood the broad support the advisory group enjoyed: "A key part of the pressure to stabilize and equalize assignment plans is coming not from the court, but the community."[135] Although the *News* regretted the formal participation of the advisory group in the litigation, it noted that the board's extreme conduct was "making matters more difficult and unsettling for everyone."[136] Booe, fearing that McMillan would use the advisory group to bypass the board, led an effort to secure an order from the Fourth Circuit staying McMillan's order. By a 5-to-4 vote, the board declined to seek a stay.[137]

In mid-April 1974, McMillan conducted hearings on the board's pupil assignment plan. Ray testified at these hearings and presented the Citizens Advisory Group's written report outlining a tentative assignment plan that would spread the desegregation burden throughout the county. McMillan praised the group for its "thoroughness, intelligence and motivation" and requested Ray to submit additional information to him about the advisory group's plan within ten days.[138] McMillan's comments boosted the prestige of the new community group and further indicated that the judge viewed the group as the mechanism for securing an acceptable plan without the court's direct involvement.

The advisory group formulated a more detailed pupil assignment proposal, which it presented to McMillan. Under this proposal, large numbers of southeast Charlotte students, including those in Board Chair Poe's neighborhood, would attend West Charlotte High School. Poe attacked the proposal as "potentially disastrous" and predicted that the proposal, if adopted, would cause extensive white flight from the public school system.[139] "I don't believe that report represents a cross-section view of the citizens of this community," Poe announced. "A cross-section would not have come up with those suggestions. The point they missed is that without public support there won't be any public school system."[140]

Yet the PTA presidents at the schools most affected by the proposal disagreed, predicting that southeast Charlotte would accept the plan.[141] Moreover, County Commission Chair Harris weighed in with his support, announcing that he thought the city would support a fair and stable assignment plan that eliminated the inequities and instabilities of the past four years.[142] Harris had met privately with McMillan after the April hearing and had asked the judge what was required to put the desegregation controversy to rest. McMillan had told Harris that the matter could not be resolved until the board agreed to include southeast Charlotte in the busing plan.[143] Harris proceeded to contact key community leaders, urging their support for the advisory group's plan.[144] At Harris's urging, the Charlotte Chamber of Commerce announced its support for the Citizens Advisory Group's desegregation plan.[145]

In late May 1974, the community weighed in by casting ballots for three open seats on the school board. Three moderate candidates—Robert Culbertson, an insurance salesman, Marilyn Huff, a homemaker, and John McLaughlin, a postmaster—captured the open seats. Each favored a more conciliatory approach toward McMillan.[146] Three antibusing candidates, including incumbent McNinch, were defeated in the election.[147]

In the meantime, despite Poe's concerns about white flight, the board voted to enter into negotiations with Ray and the advisory group over an acceptable plan. The board designated a school administrator, Ed Sanders, to meet with Ray. Sanders had a long involvement with school desegregation, dating back to his tenure as principal of Central High School, which had desegregated in 1957.[148] As Ray and Sanders met daily for the next five weeks, school assignments to West Charlotte proved to be the most difficult hurdle. McMillan had made it abundantly clear that he would reject any plan that did not require the wealthier white neighborhoods in southeast Charlotte to send their children to West Charlotte. The West Charlotte issue had taken on enormous symbolic significance; the perceived fairness of the plan to both the judge and the community depended on having white students from the southeast attend West Charlotte High School.

In early June, Ray and Sanders completed their desegregation plan. The Ray-Sanders plan provided for the establishment of satellite zones similar to the old feeder plan, with only one school projected to have more than a 44 percent black student population. The new plan spread the burden of busing more evenly than ever before; significantly, the plan provided that one of the most exclusive southeast Charlotte neighborhoods, East-over, would send its children to West Charlotte High School. As Poe would explain the proposal a few months later: "This year we have frankly sought stability by consciously giving to every neighborhood some reason to be unhappy about its school assignment at some point between kindergarten and graduation. It's an odd way to gain stability, but it does show some promise."[149] In addition, the plan sharply circumscribed the right to transfer after initial assignment, a departure from past board practice. About the same number of students would be bused as under previous desegregation plans, but for much shorter distances.[150] The board was directed to review the racial ratios at the various schools every three years.[151]

The plaintiffs had initially regarded the Citizens Advisory Group with some skepticism, still favoring a desegregation plan drafted by a court-appointed master such as Finger. In June, however, Chambers announced that the plaintiffs supported the Ray-Sanders plan.[152] One month later, in July 1974, the board considered the work of Ray and Sanders. Board member Booe strenuously objected to the plan, arguing that it exceeded the board's "legal requirements." He noted, "What we are talking about is going way beyond what the Supreme Court said we have to do."[153] Yet much of the city had grown tired of such blandishments, understanding that these pronouncements had served only to exacerbate community conflict. With just two dissenting votes, the board approved the plan and filed it with the court the next day.[154]

McMillan welcomed the new plan and the policies and guidelines that accompanied the plan:

> Adoption of these new guidelines and policies is understood as a clean break with the essentially "reluctant" attitude which dominated Board actions for many years. The new guidelines and policies appear to reflect a growing community realization that equal protection of laws in public education is the concern of private citizens and local officials and is not the private problem of courts, federal or otherwise. . . .
>
> It will be assumed that the sizeable continuing problems yet remaining will be resolved by spontaneous action by staff or board, with input as needed from the Citizens Advisory Group and other community "ombudsmen."[155]

Even though the Ray-Sanders plan left one school—Hidden Valley Elementary—with a majority-black population, McMillan departed from his prior posture on majority-black schools and ratified the plan in its entirety. The Hidden Valley assignment reflected the fact that the neighborhood surrounding the northeast Charlotte school was substantially integrated; Ray and Sanders wanted to encourage such residential integration by allowing the Hidden Valley children to attend their neighborhood school for all six years.

The board's acquiescence in the advisory group proposal foreclosed appellate review of McMillan's continued insistence that the busing burden be shared by wealthier white neighborhoods, and hence the Fourth Circuit never considered the issue of "economic discrimination." Nevertheless, given the opportunity, the Fourth Circuit most likely would have found McMillan's insistence on a shared busing burden to be within his discretion. One year later, in July 1975, having seen the new desegregation plan operate successfully for one year, McMillan officially closed the case of *Swann v. Charlotte-Mecklenburg Board of Education* and turned the operation of the schools completely over to the school board.[156]

The Citizen Advisory Group's emergence as a legitimate community coalition committed to finding an acceptable assignment plan helped resolve the city's school desegregation controversy. McMillan later commented that the advisory group, "more than any other single factor, bridged the gap [between the court and the school board] and brought the controversy to a close."[157] This success is all the more significant in light of the fact that such groups in other cities were generally ineffective in framing desegregation plans during the 1970s.[158] The advisory group's effectiveness was due, first, to the support the group enjoyed from the judge and the city's business and civic leaders and, second, to the group's inclusion of representatives from nearly every constituency in the school system. The court's support of the advisory group was particularly critical, since it gave the group much-needed legitimacy. Moreover, the advisory group's ability to speak with one voice on behalf of a broad array of interests — black and white, antibusing and probusing — enabled it to capture the needed support of the school system's diverse constituencies for its assignment plan.

In the resolution of the busing crisis, unlike in earlier moments of racial conflict in the city's history, the active involvement of Charlotte's civic and business leadership had been slow to come. As School Board Chair Poe later conceded, there was "almost a complete default on the part of . . . community leaders" in the face of the busing controversy.[159] In significant measure, this silence was due to the fact that the reassignment of white children to schools in black neighborhoods proved far more difficult to accept than the token admission of black children into white schools or than the integration of hotels, restaurants, and hospitals. Moreover, by 1973, some business leaders had already pulled their children from the public schools and enrolled them in private schools.[160] By the spring of 1974, however, community leaders such as County Commission Chair Harris were lobbying aggressively in support of the advisory group's efforts to create a fair and stable assignment plan. Although the white business leadership had not initiated the final move toward the resolution of the busing crisis, it offered important support for the advisory group's activities.

The emergence of the advisory group, drawing on citizens from throughout the county, helped initiate a transformation in political power in Charlotte. During the 1950s and 1960s, Charlotte's politics had been dominated by a small group of white businessmen, most of whom lived in southeast Charlotte. Indeed, throughout that time period, the vast majority of the city's school board members, city councilmen, county commissioners, and members of the general assembly resided in the southeast section of the city.[161] Yet during the early 1970s, scores of community and neighborhood groups sprang up throughout the city and county, prompted by both the desegregation controversy and broader neighborhood preservation concerns.

This emergence of political activists throughout the city and county eventually led in 1977 to the creation of a partial ward system for electing members of the city council in place of the at-large system. The days of the city's political domination by a small group of chamber of commerce leaders from the southeast had ended. The election of 1985 was indicative of this new state of affairs. That year, an African American, Harvey Gantt, won his second term as mayor, and the eleven-member city council consisted of six white women, two African American men, one Jewish man, and two other white men; none of the members came from the old business elite of southeast Charlotte.[162]

The ultimate resolution of the city's school desegregation crisis resulted from a convergence of forces: the persistence of a few African American leaders unwilling to compromise in the face of perceived injustice, the emergence of a group of citizens who understood that continued recalcitrance undermined community interests, and the perseverance of a judge who remained steadfast in his interpretation of constitutional requirements. Board Chair Poe's comments made in 1975 after the closure of the litigation probably captured the sentiments of many Charlotteans:

I don't like the ratio concept, but it does bring into focus what's fair, what's equitable. I thought at the outset that Judge McMillan was going entirely too far, and in many ways, I still think so. Much of the community has been alienated by what he has done. But . . . I'd hazard a guess that desegregation was clearly necessary and bound to come, and he speeded up the pace of it, and I think he'll be vindicated on that score. Things are smoother now, and working better than I thought they would be. There would be no way to undo all of what we've done, not even with a constitutional amendment, and I'm not sure there would be the will to do that.[163]

The *Swann* case will be one of the most important components in the . . . history of this city. It really went beyond racial equity in the schools. The case raised the question of racial equity in the entire community, and . . . that has produced such a clear distinction between our city and a great many others.

—Charlotte banker Dennis Rash, *Charlotte Observer*, March 26, 1989

Epilogue

When Judge James McMillan closed the *Swann* case in July 1975, the monumental effort to desegregate the Charlotte-Mecklenburg schools came to an end, twenty-one years after the *Brown* decision.[1] In a remarkable about-face, the Charlotte-Mecklenburg School Board would, for the next several years, aggressively pursue a policy of retaining integrated schools. Although no longer under the supervision of the court, the board voted in 1977 to overhaul its pupil assignment plan to compensate for the fact that eight schools had become majority black due to changing residential patterns.[2] Even though the U.S. Supreme Court had ruled the previous year that school boards were not required to continue to adjust pupil assignments to account for residential changes, the board reassigned 4,850 students to new schools in order to maintain a fully desegregated system.[3] It was a dramatic reversal from eight years earlier. The board that had once resisted McMillan's order that it reassign students to overcome residential segregation was now doing precisely that with no pressure from the court. Two years later, in 1979, the board returned to court to *defend* its prointegration policies in the face of a challenge from white parents — many of whom were recent arrivals to the city — who objected to the 1977 assignment changes.[4] This time, the school board attorneys and Julius Chambers would join forces to preserve the board's extensive busing plan. The school board would continue to make regular changes in its pupil assignment plan in order to retain a fully desegregated school system. Even as other cities, such as Norfolk, Austin, and Oklahoma City, sharply modified their desegregation plans during the late 1980s, Charlotte retained its commitment to a fully integrated school system.[5]

During the past two decades, numerous scholars have examined in considerable detail the school desegregation experiences of urban school systems throughout the nation.[6] A large number of these studies have concluded that the busing experience in urban America has been a failure, measured in terms of the level of integration actually achieved, white flight, educational achievement, and community support for public education.[7] What can be said about Charlotte?

First of all, the Charlotte-Mecklenburg school system achieved an unparalleled degree of pupil integration as a result of its desegregation plan. A 1987 report prepared for the U.S. Commission on Civil Rights concluded that of the nation's 125 major school systems analyzed, the Charlotte-Mecklenburg school system had achieved the greatest amount of pupil mixing between 1967 and 1985.[8] That high level of pupil integration was due to several factors. First, both the court and later the school board maintained a commitment to the complete integration of nearly every school in the system, notwithstanding a high level of residential segregation and shifting residential patterns.[9] Second, although many white parents pulled their children out of the public schools, the degree of white flight in Charlotte was considerably less than that in most other cities, enabling the school board to maintain a high degree of racial mixing throughout the system. A 1977 study of thirty of the country's largest school systems concluded that only one — Tampa, Florida — had achieved as much pupil mixing as had Charlotte with less white flight.[10]

To be sure, white enrollments in the public schools did decline following the implementation of the busing plan. Between 1969 and 1983, about 20 percent of the white student population left the Charlotte-Mecklenburg public schools. Moreover, during that same time period, the percentage of the student population that was white declined from 71 percent in 1969 to 62 percent in 1983.[11] But most other urban school systems fared far worse over the same time period. The average southern school system under a court-imposed desegregation order lost 38 percent of its white population between 1970 and 1984, and the percentage of the student population that was white declined by almost 16 percent. In northern school systems, the white flight was even greater. The average northern school system under a court-ordered desegregation plan lost 53 percent of its white population between 1970 and 1984, and the percentage of students who were white in those schools declined by over 19 percent.[12] Although most of this white flight is probably attributable to the desegregation efforts, some whites abandoned public schools for other reasons, such as concerns about urban decay. Indeed, urban school systems in the late 1960s and early 1970s that were not subject to desegregation decrees also lost large numbers of white students.[13]

The dearth of white flight in Charlotte compared with that in other urban school systems, particularly those in the North, was due in significant measure to the enormous physical size of the Charlotte-Mecklenburg 550-square-mile school district, a district more than half the size of the state of Rhode Island. The boundaries of the school system encompassed most of the Charlotte-Mecklenburg metropolitan area, making white flight difficult. Moreover, by virtue of including suburban and rural children in the same system with inner-city children, the Charlotte-Mecklenburg School Board was able to retain a higher percentage of white students than could many other urban school systems — particularly in northern cities — of a smaller physical size.[14] Throughout the country, school districts that encompassed both urban and suburban areas, as in Charlotte and many cities in Florida, proved far easier to desegregate than urban school districts composed exclusively of city dwellers.[15] Particularly in the aftermath of the Supreme Court's 1974 decision in *Milliken v. Bradley*, which sharply limited multi-school-district desegregation plans, many big-city school boards simply could not achieve any degree of meaningful pupil integration, and efforts to do so prompted significant white flight.[16] As a result, by 1980, only one of the ten largest cities in the United States had a student population that was more than one-third white.[17]

A comparison of Charlotte and Richmond illustrates the advantages of Charlotte's geography. In the late 1960s, both cities had virtually identical metropolitan-area populations.[18] Nearly all of Charlotte's metropolitan area was encompassed in one school district, whereas Richmond was divided between a city school district and two large suburban school districts. Whereas white enrollments in the Charlotte-Mecklenburg school district held relatively steady during the late 1960s and early 1970s, by contrast Richmond's city school district experienced a dramatic decline in white enrollment as white families easily moved into one of the surrounding suburban county school districts.[19]

Other factors contributed to the relatively small amount of white flight in Charlotte as well. Since the *Brown* decision, the city has understood the value of maintaining a strong public school system. In the early 1970s, despite the considerable turmoil surrounding the busing controversy, an extraordinary number of parents — more than eight thousand, or one for every ten students — volunteered time in the public schools.[20] A 1972 study of school desegregation in forty-three southern cities concluded that community acceptance of school desegregation in Charlotte was "probably superior to that of almost any other city in the South."[21] The Charlotte Chamber of Commerce would later use the city's strong public school system and the successful settlement of the school controversy as a key selling point in the recruitment of new industry to the city.[22]

Not only did Charlotte desegregate its schools with less white flight than other cities, but the desegregation plan also prompted an increase in residential integration.[23] This change was due in some measure to a policy decision by the city council in 1975 to locate new public housing units throughout the city so as not to disturb the integrated patterns in the schools. In so doing, Charlotte became one of the first cities in the United States to coordinate its public housing and school desegregation policies.[24] Public housing placement in the city had historically served to solidify residential segregation; scattered-site public housing helped reverse the city's entrenched residential segregation. As School Board Chair William Poe commented, "It took school desegregation to make us see you don't build new slums with concentrated public housing."[25] The increase in residential integration may also have been helped by the fact that the pupil assignment plan rewarded those families who lived in integrated neighborhoods by allowing their children to attend neighborhood schools.[26]

In the wake of school desegregation, Charlotte-Mecklenburg students also experienced a significant increase in educational achievement levels. In 1968, before McMillan's first desegregation order, sixth-graders in the Charlotte-Mecklenburg public school system had reading and math skills about one grade *below* the national average; these test scores were also below regional averages. Between 1970, the first year of the busing order, and 1973, achievement test scores declined throughout the school system. In 1974, however, those scores stabilized, and in 1975 they increased for the first time since before McMillan's initial desegregation decree. By 1981, achievement test scores were the highest in the school system's history. That year, for example, the city's sixth-graders possessed, on average, reading and math skills about one grade *above* the national average, a gain of two years since 1968. These increases in achievement test results were duplicated at the third- and ninth-grade levels. For the first time in the school system's history, student test scores exceeded both regional and national averages.[27]

To be sure, white students in 1981 still performed far better than did black students, although the gap had narrowed, particularly in the younger grades. In 1981, white sixth-graders were about one and one-half

An adult volunteer helps children at Hidden Valley Elementary School in northeast Charlotte, September 1970. (Courtesy of the *Charlotte Observer*)

grades above the national average in math skills, whereas black sixth-graders were just below the national average.[28] Nevertheless, both white and black students were performing at higher levels in the early 1980s than they had in the late 1960s before widespread pupil integration. As one longtime school administrator, Chris Folk, would later comment, the rise in achievement test scores "would never have happened . . . without integration."[29]

Black achievement test scores would continue to climb until the mid-1980s, slightly narrowing the gap between black and white achievement levels. After 1986, however, the achievement test scores of both black and white students dipped — perhaps in response to a new form of achievement test. This drop was greater, however, for black students. By 1992, the gap between white and black achievement test scores was still substantial, with white students consistently performing about 35 to 40 percentage points higher than their black peers.[30] Achievement levels in Charlotte-Mecklenburg — particularly for black students — significantly increased following the implementation of school busing, but pupil mixing did not eliminate the gap in performance between the two racial groups.

Although many Charlotteans opposed reassigning students to schools outside of their neighborhoods, most took pride in the fact that the city had successfully adapted itself to a demanding set of racial expectations in a manner that few other American cities had been capable of doing. In 1984, when President Ronald Reagan made a campaign stop in Charlotte and told the audience that busing was a "failed" social experiment, he was met with a strange silence. The *Charlotte Observer* reprimanded the president the next day on its editorial page: "You Were Wrong, Mr. President." The *Observer* claimed that Charlotte's "proudest achievement" was "its fully integrated public school system."[31] Other community leaders have echoed that view.[32] Even School Board Chair Poe, who had consistently opposed the extensive busing ordered by McMillan, understood the significance of the *Swann* litigation for Charlotte. "The desegregation order was the key to most of our interracial relations here. It was the biggest single thing we have done in terms of race relations," Poe later commented.[33] "It may even be that the only viable cities in years to come will be cities like Charlotte which have settled the race issue."[34] Significantly, in 1981, in the middle of a Senate fight led by North Carolina Senator Jesse Helms to prevent the Justice Department from requiring the use of busing in the resolution of school desegregation cases, the Charlotte-Mecklenburg School Board canceled a scheduled meeting so that all of its members could attend a dinner honoring Chambers and McMillan on the tenth anniversary of the Supreme Court's *Swann* decision. That the school board would pause to honor two of its most persistent critics of the early 1970s captured the attention of the national press.[35]

Charlotte's resolution of the busing issue not only was a source of local pride but also became a mechanism for civic promotion. As in 1957 and 1963, observers throughout the country in the 1970s perceived that Charlotte had peacefully and effectively resolved its racial problems; city leaders exploited that perception by fashioning a public persona for Charlotte as "The City That Made It Work."[36] After McMillan's withdrawal from the case in 1975, the *New York Times*, the *Washington Post*, *Newsweek*, and CBS television all offered positive portrayals of Charlotte's school desegregation experiences, contrasting Charlotte with more troubled American cities such as Boston.[37] In a gesture that took on enormous symbolic importance, a group of black and white students at West Charlotte High School raised money to bring several Boston high school students to Charlotte in the fall of 1974 to witness firsthand the city's successful desegregation experience; several Charlotte students then traveled to Boston to offer support to their peers in a city faced with school desegregation problems of an entirely different magnitude.[38] Just as Mayor Stanford Brookshire had gone to considerable lengths in 1963 to publicize Charlotte's successful desegregation of its public accommodations, so in the mid-1970s the city's leaders publicized Charlotte's successful resolution of the busing controversy.

In the view of one of the city's leading journalists, Frye Gaillard, the successful resolution of the *Swann* litigation ushered in a "Golden Decade" in the city's history, marked by expanded political participation, rising student achievement scores, and continued economic prosperity.[39] During the decade following the end of the school litigation, Charlotte elected its first black school board chair, Phil Berry, and its first black mayor, Harvey Gantt, both with broad biracial support. Indeed, Gantt captured about 40 percent of the white vote in his first mayoral bid in 1983 and an even higher percentage in 1985.[40] Gantt's election was particularly noteworthy: few African Americans had ever been elected mayor in cities with a majority-white population.[41] Unquestionably, these political successes were due in significant measure to the city's peaceful resolution of the desegregation issue. As white political leader W. T. Harris commented after Gantt's election as mayor, "I would say to you that prior to school integration, we couldn't have done that, regardless of how good he was."[42]

West Charlotte High School students (right) welcome students from Boston (left), October 1974. The stuffed lion, representing the West Charlotte mascot, is a gift from the Charlotte students. (Courtesy of the *Charlotte Observer*)

At the same time, Charlotte's economic prosperity continued unabated. By the mid-1980s, the city could boast of being the financial center of the southern United States as well as one of the nation's leading distribution centers; by the 1990s, Charlotte was the third-largest banking center in the United States and a national leader in new job growth.[43] Between 1974 and 1984, more than twelve hundred new businesses located in Charlotte, bringing twenty-seven thousand jobs and over $1 billion in investment. For at least one business, the decision to move to Charlotte was influenced by the city's school desegregation experience. A spokesperson for Royal Insurance Company, which relocated to Charlotte from New York City in 1985, noted that Charlotte's strong—and successfully integrated—public schools had been an important factor in his company's selection of Charlotte.[44]

To be sure, during the past few years, many Charlotteans have questioned anew the continued wisdom of mandatory school busing.[45] In 1990, an antibusing school board candidate who characterized his election bid as "a referendum on busing" captured 42 percent of the vote.[46]

A 1992 survey of community attitudes revealed that 40 percent of black respondents and 60 percent of white respondents believed that school busing had adversely affected educational quality.[47] In recent years, Charlotte has extensively utilized voluntary magnet schools in the inner city as an alternative means of integrating the schools, prompting a community-wide debate over the best way to achieve educational equality. School Superintendent John Murphy, who came to Charlotte in 1991, favors the increased use of voluntary magnet schools, observing in 1994, "The promise of court-ordered busing has fallen short where it matters most: in improving learning for African American students."[48]

Many of the city's black leaders, however, fear that a complete abandonment of mandatory busing will ultimately lead to the resegregation of the city's schools, to the disadvantage of black schoolchildren.[49] The city will likely struggle with this issue during the next several years. But regardless of what course Charlotte takes in the 1990s, Charlotte's extensive school desegregation efforts of the 1970s undoubtedly improved educational opportunities for many African American students, and the city's successful adaptation to that desegregation is undeniably one of the major factors in the city's ongoing prosperity.

What does the desegregation of the Charlotte schools tell us about the manner in which racial change occurred in the post-*Brown* South? The desegregation of southern schools during the two decades after the *Brown* decision resulted from both direct-action protest that helped build public and political support for desegregation initiatives and a litigation campaign that steadily moved the courts in the direction of requiring greater pupil mixing. During the first decade of the post-*Brown* era the courts, reluctant to move too far ahead of public sentiment, offered little relief. In the absence of explicit direction and support from the Supreme Court for desegregation efforts, only a handful of federal judges required meaningful pupil mixing until the mid-1960s. As a result, political pressure proved far more effective than litigation in securing integration gains at both the local and the national level. The various forms of racial desegregation in Charlotte in the 1950s and early 1960s took place as a result of public pressure, not litigation, as the two primary lawsuits—the 1961 and 1965 school desegregation cases—met with failure. This pattern is consistent with the national context, since significant pupil integration did not come to the South until Congress and the Johnson administration took action beginning in 1964. Integration efforts succeeded in Charlotte in these early years because Charlotte showed itself particularly responsive to public protest in ways that many other southern communities did not.

By the late 1960s, the politics of race had become far more complex. As the push for integration confronted deeply entrenched patterns of residential segregation in America's cities, political resistance increased. At the same time, much of black America had become alienated by the slow pace of racial change and skeptical of the ultimate value of racial mixing; in frustration, many African Americans turned inward, in the direction of self-empowerment. As the biracial liberal coalition responsible for the major civil rights legislation of the mid-1960s fell apart, the courts emerged as the central institution capable of producing greater integration. Thus, in the late 1960s and the early 1970s, litigation — particularly in Charlotte — became the most effective means of challenging urban segregation. Aided by a judge who proved willing to withstand the storms of public opposition, the black community in Charlotte gained in the courtroom what they could not possibly have gained in the streets: one of the most thoroughly integrated urban school systems in the United States.

Those observers who have argued that the courts were far less effective at producing racial change in America than were the political branches of government have much support in the early years of the civil rights movement, since significant desegregation did not come to the American South until the legislative and executive branches of government assumed direct responsibility for ensuring that the promise of the *Brown* decision was met.[50] But in the late 1960s, when the push for greater racial integration shifted to urban schools, the courts delivered what the legislature and executive could not — at least until the *Milliken v. Bradley* decision of 1974 effectively thwarted further urban integration.

America in the 1990s has by no means resolved the problem of race. The legacy of three centuries of racial oppression remains with us today. In many ways, critics such as Derrick Bell are correct when they suggest that black demands for racial change in this country have succeeded only when both white and black interests are served by the demanded change.[51] Reinhold Niebuhr's observation in 1932 that it was hopeless to expect meaningful racial change "merely by trusting in the moral sense of the white race" proved sadly correct for much of the ensuing sixty years.[52] Nevertheless, on occasion, both political protest and judicial action have been remarkably effective in forging the convergence of white and black interests necessary to secure the full promise of racial equality.

Notes

INTRODUCTION

1 There are a number of biographies of Martin Luther King, including Garrow, *Bearing the Cross*, and Branch, *Parting the Waters*. For the institutions mentioned, see, e.g., Tushnet, *The NAACP's Legal Strategy against Segregated Education*; Meier and Rudwick, *CORE*; Carson, *In Struggle*; Fairclough, *To Redeem the Soul of America*.

2 Burk, *The Eisenhower Administration*; Brauer, *John F. Kennedy*; Dudziak, "Desegregation as a Cold War Imperative"; Orfield, *The Reconstruction of Southern Education*; Read and McGough, *Let Them Be Judged*; Kluger, *Simple Justice*; Burstein, *Discrimination, Jobs, and Politics*; Peltason, *Fifty-Eight Lonely Men*; Rosenberg, *The Hollow Hope*; Wilkinson, *From Brown to Bakke*.

3 See, e.g., Chafe, *Civilities and Civil Rights*; Colburn, *Racial Change and Community Crisis*; Norrell, *Reaping the Whirlwind*; Lukas, *Common Ground*; Formisano, *Boston against Busing*; Pratt, *The Color of Their Skin*; Freyer, *The Little Rock Crisis*; Dittmer, *Local People*.

4 *Brown v. Board of Education of Topeka, Kansas*, 347 U.S. 483 (1954).

5 See Tushnet, *The NAACP's Legal Strategy against Segregated Education*; Kluger, *Simple Justice*.

6 *Swann v. Charlotte-Mecklenburg Board of Education*, 402 U.S. 1 (1971).

7 See, e.g., Bass, *Unlikely Heroes*; Greenberg, *Crusaders in the Courts*; Kluger, *Simple Justice*; Read and McGough, *Let Them Be Judged*; Yarbrough, *Judge Frank Johnson*.

8 See, e.g., Branch, *Parting the Waters*; Garrow, *Protest at Selma*; Graham, *The Civil Rights Era*; Rosenberg, *The Hollow Hope*.

9 See Chafe, *Civilities and Civil Rights*, who discusses the manner in which the white community of Greensboro used the ethic of "civility" in matters of race to mask the preservation of certain racial roles.

10 Jacoway and Colburn, *Southern Businessmen and Desegregation*.

11 Bell, "*Brown v. Board of Education* and the Interest-Convergence Dilemma"; Dudziak, "Desegregation as a Cold War Imperative."

CHAPTER ONE

1 *Brown v. Board of Education*, 347 U.S. 483 (1954).

2 *Laws of North Carolina* (1838–39), chap. 8, sec. 3, p. 13; North Carolina Advisory Committee, *Equal Protection of the Laws*, p. 99.

3 Lefler and Newsome, *The History of a Southern State*, p. 499.

4 Noble, *A History of Public Schools*, pp. 292–93, 296.

5 Williamson, *The Crucible of Race*, pp. 252–53.

6   Quoted in Knight, *Public School Education*, p. 254.

7   Lefler and Newsome, *The History of a Southern State*, p. 500.

8   Constitution of North Carolina (1875), art. 9, sec. 2.

9   Charles S. Johnson, *Backgrounds to Patterns of Negro Segregation*, pp. 178–79.

10 Logan, *The Negro in North Carolina*, p. 139.

11 Lefler and Newsome, *The History of a Southern State*, pp. 499–503.

12 Whitener, "Public Education in North Carolina," p. 90.

13 Coon, "The Beginnings of the North Carolina City Schools."

14 Lefler and Newsome, *The History of a Southern State*, p. 503.

15 *Charlotte Observer*, "Editorial," January 1, 1883, quoted in Claiborne, *The Charlotte Observer*, pp. 49–50. See also Coon, "The Beginnings of the North Carolina City Schools," pp. 241–42.

16 Blythe and Brockmann, *Hornets' Nest*, pp. 219–20; Logan, *The Negro in North Carolina*, p. 140; *Biennial Report of the Superintendent of Public Instruction, 1879* and *Biennial Report of the Superintendent of Public Instruction, 1880*, both in University of North Carolina Library, North Carolina Collection, Chapel Hill.

17 Lefler and Newsome, *The History of a Southern State*, p. 500; Logan, *The Negro in North Carolina*, p. 140. In 1880, per pupil expenditures in North Carolina were $1.47 per white pupil and $1.38 per black pupil. Logan, *The Negro in North Carolina*, p. 140. By the same token, Mecklenburg County, in 1874, spent $2.55 per white child and $1.63 per black child. Blythe and Brockmann, *Hornets' Nest*, pp. 219–20.

18 Constitution of North Carolina (1875), art. 9.

19 Logan, *The Negro in North Carolina*, p. 140.

20 Ibid., pp. 155–56.

21 Weinberg, *A Chance to Learn*, p. 40; Bond, *The Education of the Negro*, p. 44; Ashmore, *The Negro and the Schools*, p. 8.

22 Coon, "School Support and Our North Carolina Courts," p. 416; Logan, *The Negro in North Carolina*, pp. 155–56; Escott, *Many Excellent People*, p. 184.

23 Logan, *The Negro in North Carolina*, pp. 162–63; Harlan, *Separate and Unequal*, p. 47.

24 Escott, *Many Excellent People*, p. 185; Logan, *The Negro in North Carolina*, pp. 158–59.

25 Leloudis, "'A More Certain Means of Grace,'" p. 206; Logan, *The Negro in North Carolina*, p. 159.

26 Logan, *The Negro in North Carolina*, pp. 140–41; Anderson, *Race and Politics in North Carolina*, pp. 326–27.

27 Elmer D. Johnson, "James Yadkin Joyner," pp. 365–66.

28 Powell, *North Carolina through Four Centuries*, p. 519.

29 Lefler and Newsome, *The History of a Southern State*, p. 503. Even so, the illiteracy rate among whites in North Carolina in 1900 was the highest of all southern states. Woodward, *Origins of the New South*, p. 400.

30 Logan, *The Negro in North Carolina*, pp. 156–57.

31 U.S. Bureau of the Census, *Report on Population of the United States at the Eleventh Census: 1890*, p. 592; Logan, *The Negro in North Carolina*, p. 108.

32 Harlan, *Separate and Unequal*, p. 47.

33 *Puitt v. Commissioners of Gaston County*, 94 N.C. 709 (1886).

34 Ibid., pp. 715–16.

35 The North Carolina Supreme Court applied the *Puitt* holding in a series of later cases: *Markham v. Manning*, 96 N.C. 132, 2 S.E. 40 (1887); *Duke v. Brown*, 96 N.C. 127, 1 S.E. 873 (1887); *Riggsbee v. Durham*, 94 N.C. 800 (1886).

36 *Puitt v. Commissioners of Gaston County*, p. 719 (quoting *Hall v. DeCuir*, 95 U.S. 485, 504 [1877] [Clifford, J., concurring]).

37 See, e.g., *State v. McCann*, 21 Ohio 198 (1871); *Roberts v. City of Boston*, 5 Cush. (Mass.) 198 (1849); *State v. Duffy*, 7 Nev. 342 (1872); *People v. Easton*, 13 Abb. Pr. (n.s.) 159 (1872).

38 The Pennsylvania case was *Allen v. Davis*, 10 WNC 1156 (1881).

39 *Plessy v. Ferguson*, 163 U.S. 537 (1896).

40 Kousser, *Dead End*. The only other favorable decision from a state that had joined the Confederacy was *Maddox v. Neal*, 45 Ark. 121 (1885).

41 The Georgia Supreme Court upheld a statute providing for separate taxation in *Reid v. Mayor of Eatonton*, 80 Ga. 755, 6 S.E. 602 (1888), whereas the Kentucky Supreme Court struck down a separate taxation scheme in *Dawson v. Lee*, 83 Ky. 49 (1885).

42 Harlan, *Separate and Unequal*, p. 47; Logan, *The Negro in North Carolina*, p. 163.

43 Logan, *The Negro in North Carolina*, p. 163.

44 Ibid., p. 162.

45 Harlan, *Separate and Unequal*, p. 10.

46 Weinberg, *A Chance to Learn*, p. 50.

47 Crow, "Cracking the Solid South," p. 341.

48 Greenwood, *Bittersweet Legacy*, pp. 195–96.

49 Claiborne, *The Charlotte Observer*, p. 106.

50 Luebke, *Tar Heel Politics*, p. 6.

51 Quoted in Greenwood, *Bittersweet Legacy*, p. 200; Crow, "Cracking the Solid South," pp. 340–42.

52 North Carolina Advisory Committee, *Equal Protection of the Laws*, p. 203.

53 Lefler and Newsome, *The History of a Southern State*, pp. 527–28.

54 Edmonds, *The Negro and Fusion Politics in North Carolina*, pp. 198–217; Harlan, *Separate and Unequal*, pp. 53–55, 66–68.

55 Harlan, *Separate and Unequal*, pp. 130, 250.

56 Ibid., pp. 265–66, 118–19.

57 See *McLeod v. Commissioners of Carthage*, 148 N.C. 77, 61 S.E. 605 (1908) (legitimating state statute permitting creation of special white district in town of Carthage); *Bonitz v. Board of Trustees*, 154 N.C. 375, 70 S.E. 735 (1911) (legitimating state statute permitting creation of special white district in town of Ahoskie).

58 Harlan, *Separate and Unequal*, pp. 40, 104–5.

59 Du Bois and Dill, *The Common School and the Negro American*, p. 50.

60 Greenwood, *Bittersweet Legacy*, pp. 216–17.

61 *Biennial Report of the Superintendent of Public Instruction of North Carolina for 1908–1909* and *1909–1910*, both in University of North Carolina Library, North Carolina Collection, Chapel Hill.

62 Harlan, *Separate and Unequal*, p. 131.

63 These figures apply to those items for which a separate accounting by race was conducted. Harlan, *Separate and Unequal*, p. 131.

64 Quoted in Crow, Escott, and Hatley, *A History of African Americans in North Carolina*, p. 123.

65 Kellogg, *NAACP*, p. 188; Murray, *History of the North Carolina Teachers Association*, p. 29. See generally Henry Bullock, *A History of Negro Education in the South*, pp. 117–146.

66 Coon, *Public Taxation and Negro Schools*, pp. 7–8.

67 *Hooker v. Town of Greenville*, 130 N.C. 472, 42 S.E. 141 (1902).

68 Ibid., p. 474 (emphasis in the original).

69 Orr, *Charles Brantley Aycock*, p. 225.

70 Justices David M. Furches and Robert M. Douglas, both Republicans, had been impeached in 1901 but were acquitted by the senate. Lefler and Newsome, *The History of a Southern State*, p. 533. One of the leaders of the impeachment move had expressed concern that Furches and Douglas would invalidate the suffrage amendment of 1900 that had disfranchised black voters. Orr, *Charles Brantley Aycock*, p. 218.

71 In 1902, Henry G. Connor and Platt D. Walker replaced Justices David M. Furches and Charles A. Cook. 132 N.C. Reports, frontpiece (1903). In 1904, George H. Brown, Jr., and William A. Hoke replaced Justices Robert M. Douglas and Walter A. Montgomery. 137 N.C. Reports, frontpiece (1905).

72 *Lowery v. School Trustees of Kernersville*, 140 N.C. 33, 46, 52 S.E. 267, 272 (1905).

73 Ibid., p. 46, 52 S.E. 272.

74 Ibid., p. 47, 52 S.E. 272.

75 Also between 1905 and 1912, the Supreme Court of North Carolina considered several challenges to local school financing schemes that arguably harmed black schools, rejecting all of them: *Smith v. School Trustees of Robersonville*, 141 N.C. 143, 53 S.E. 524 (1906); *McLeod v. Commissioners of Carthage*, 148 N.C. 77, 61 S.E. 605 (1908); *Bonitz v. Board of Trustees*, 154 N.C. 375, 70 S.E. 735 (1911); *Whitford v. Commissioners of Craven County*, 159 N.C. 160, 74 S.E. 1014 (1912). The only exception was *Williams v. Bradford*, 158 N.C. 36, 73 S.E. 154 (1911), in which the court struck down legislation permitting an additional school tax to be spent solely for a white school, on the grounds that the statute left the local school board with no discretion in the expenditure of the tax revenues.

76 Quoted in Du Bois and Dill, *The Common School and the Negro American*, p. 49 (emphasis supplied).

77 *McLeod v. Commissioners of Carthage*, pp. 77, 87, 61 S.E. 605, 608.

78 *Lowery v. School Trustees of Kernersville*, p. 48, 52 S.E. 272.

79 U.S. Bureau of the Census, *Thirteenth Census of the United States* 4:500, and *Twelfth Census of the United States*, p. 352.

80 Smith, *Emancipation*, pp. 205–6.

81 Lewis, "The History of Black Lawyers in North Carolina"; Smith, *Emancipation*, p. 202.

82 See generally Harlan, *Separate and Unequal*.

83 See generally Tushnet, *The NAACP's Legal Strategy against Segregated Education*.

84 Ware, "*Hocutt*: Genesis of *Brown*," p. 227.

85 Tushnet, *The NAACP's Legal Strategy against Segregated Education*, pp. 52–53.

86 Finch, *The NAACP*, pp. 96–97; "Hocutt to Lose Suit to Enter University for Lack of Records," *Greensboro Daily News*, March 28, 1933, p. 1.

87 Greenwood, *Bittersweet Legacy*, pp. 225–26.

88 Burns, "North Carolina and the Negro Dilemma," p. 118; "Hocutt to Lose Suit to Enter University for Lack of Records," *Greensboro Daily News*, March 28, 1933, p. 1. Moreover, in large measure due to Shepard's influence, the local NAACP chapter opposed the litigation. Tushnet, *The NAACP's Legal Strategy against Segregated Education*, pp. 52–53.

89 Crow, Escott, and Hatley, *A History of African Americans in North Carolina*, p. 160.

90 Tushnet, *The NAACP's Legal Strategy against Segregated Education*, p. 53. The NAACP did consider filing suit against the medical school at the University of North Carolina in 1936 on behalf of a black applicant who had been denied admission, but it ultimately declined to do so in part because of the poor qualifications of the student. Ibid., p. 82.

91 Marshall, "An Evaluation of Recent Efforts," p. 318.

92 McNeil, "Charles Hamilton Houston."

93 Quoted in Murray, *History of the North Carolina Teachers Association*, p. 48.

94 Shepard, "Racial Relationships in North Carolina," p. 6, University of North Carolina Library, North Carolina Collection, Chapel Hill; Burns, "North Carolina and the Negro Dilemma," p. 137.

95 Other accommodationist black leaders included Alfonso Elder, Shepard's successor as president of the North Carolina College of Negroes, and J. N. Seabrook, president of another state-supported college for black students in Fayetteville. "Hearings End in Law Schools Case," *Carolina Times*, September 2, 1950, p. 1; Burns, "North Carolina and the Negro Dilemma," p. 147.

96 Burns, "North Carolina and the Negro Dilemma," pp. 120–21, 131.

97 *Missouri ex rel. Gaines v. Canada*, 305 U.S. 337 (1938).

98 Burns, "North Carolina and the Negro Dilemma," pp. 131, 145; *Epps v. Carmichael*, 93 F. Supp. 327 (M.D.N.C. 1950).

99 Sosna, *In Search of the Silent South*, pp. 85–86.

100 *Alston v. School Board*, 112 F.2d 992 (4th Cir. 1940).

101 In the late 1930s and early 1940s, black teachers won equalization suits in six southern states — Virginia, Florida, Louisiana, Kentucky, Tennessee, and Texas. Charles S. Johnson, *Into the Main Stream*, pp. 137–51; Franklin, *From Slavery to Freedom*, pp. 536–37.

102 Newbold, "Some Achievements," pp. 456–65; Murray, *History of the North Carolina Teachers Association*, p. 50.

103 Crow, Escott, and Hatley, *A History of African Americans in North Carolina*, p. 136; North Carolina Advisory Committee, *Equal Protection of the Laws*, p. 102; Paul and Coates, *The School Segregation Decision*, p. 19; Ashmore, *The Negro and the Schools*, pp. 158–59; Swanson and Griffin, *Public Education in the South*, p. 59.

104 Ashmore, *The Negro and the Schools*, p. 159.

105 Department of Public Instruction, Raleigh, "Report of Governor's Commission," p. 96, University of North Carolina Library, North Carolina Collection, Chapel Hill; Newbold, "Some Achievements," pp. 458–59; Murray, *History of the North Carolina Teachers Association*, pp. 46–47.

106 Tushnet, *The NAACP's Legal Strategy against Segregated Education*, p. 58.

107 "Editorial — The Teachers' Salary Crime," *Carolina Times*, November 13, 1943, p. 4.

108 "Negroes Seeking Better Schools," *Raleigh News and Observer*, June 12, 1946, p. 11; Burns, "North Carolina and the Negro Dilemma," pp. 88–89.

109 Address of Kelly Alexander to Annual North Carolina Conference of NAACP Branches, June 1, 1950, p. 3, Box 1-3, Kelly Alexander Papers, Charlotte.

110 *Blue v. Durham Public School District*, 95 F. Supp. 441 (M.D.N.C. 1951).

111 Burns, "North Carolina and the Negro Dilemma," pp. 100–101; Cecelski, *Along Freedom Road*, pp. 28, 180 n. 30; Donald Ramseur to Kelly Alexander, February 3, 1955, Box 37-18, Kelly Alexander Papers.

112 For example, the suits in Washington County, Lumberton, and Old Fort failed. *Winborne v. Taylor*, 195 F.2d 649 (4th Cir. 1952); *Joyner v. McDowell County Board of Education*, 244 N.C. 164, 92 S.E.2d 795 (1956); Tushnet, *The NAACP's Legal Strategy against Segregated Education*, p. 106. The suits in New Hanover County and Pamlico County succeeded. Cecelski, *Along Freedom Road*, pp. 28, 180 n. 30.

113 "North Carolina," *Southern School News*, September 3, 1954, p. 10. Between 1940 and 1952, per pupil expenditures on black pupils in North Carolina increased 462 percent, whereas per pupil expenditures on white pupils increased 285 percent. Ibid.

114 Ashmore, *The Negro and the Schools*, p. 153.

115 These Supreme Court decisions included *Sweatt v. Painter*, 339 U.S. 629 (1950); *McLaurin v. Oklahoma State Regents*, 339 U.S. 637 (1950); *Sipuel v. Board of Regents*, 332 U.S. 631 (1948); *Missouri ex rel. Gaines v. Canada*, 305 U.S. 337 (1938).

116 Burns, "North Carolina and the Negro Dilemma," pp. 60–62. A 1927 NAACP study of southern school financing concluded that disparities in

terms of expenditures, average class size, and average teacher salaries between black and white schools were smaller in North Carolina than in any
other southern state. NAACP, "The Negro Common School in North Carolina," pp. 79, 117. In 1929, Oswald Garrison Villard made a similar claim
in a *Harpers* article. Villard, "The Crumbling Color Line," p. 156. North
Carolina's better treatment of black education would continue throughout
the pre-*Brown* period. In 1935–36, for example, according to the U.S. Office of Education, the average expenditure for white children in North Carolina was more than twice that for black children, but this gap was the
smallest of all the seven states in the South that were examined. Charles S.
Johnson, *Backgrounds to Patterns of Negro Segregation*, p. 14.

117 Hoey, *Addresses, Letters, and Papers*, p. 38.
118 Address of Kelly Alexander to Annual North Carolina Conference of
NAACP Branches, June 23, 1949, p. 6, Box 1-3, Kelly Alexander Papers.
119 Address of Kelly Alexander, June 1, 1950, p. 6; Address of Kelly Alexander,
October 17, 1952, p. 5, Box 1-3, Kelly Alexander Papers.
120 *Sweatt v. Painter*, 339 U.S. 629 (1950); *McLaurin v. Oklahoma State Regents*, 339 U.S. 637 (1950).
121 *McKissick v. Carmichael*, 187 F.2d 949 (4th Cir.), *cert. denied*, 341 U.S.
951 (1951). After the suit was filed, Elder made the preposterous claim that
black students at his school would receive law training equal to that offered
anywhere else in the United States. Burns, "North Carolina and the Negro
Dilemma," pp. 139–40.
122 *Brown v. Board of Education*, 344 U.S. 1 (1952).
123 Earnhardt, "Critical Years." The organization did, however, reorganize in
the wake of the *Brown* decision as the North Carolina Council on Human
Relations, with a strong prointegration agenda.
124 Sosna, *In Search of the Silent South*, pp. 85–86.
125 Pleasants and Burns, *Frank Porter Graham*, pp. 194–99, 215; Myerson,
Nothing Could Be Finer, p. 33; Bass and DeVries, *The Transformation of
Southern Politics*, pp. 219–20.

CHAPTER TWO

1 *Brown v. Board of Education*, 347 U.S. 483 (1954).
2 By 1964, more than twice as many black students in Virginia attended desegregated schools as in North Carolina, even though North Carolina had
a larger student enrollment. Likewise, by 1964, a higher percentage of black
students in Louisiana attended desegregated schools than in North Carolina, notwithstanding Louisiana's far more defiant response to the *Brown*
decision. Southern Education Reporting Service, *Statistical Summary*, p.
29.
3 Ibid.
4 A companion case, *Bolling v. Sharpe*, 347 U.S. 497 (1954), arose from the
District of Columbia.

5 For cases concerning segregation in graduate education, see, e.g., *Sweatt v. Painter*, 339 U.S. 629 (1950); *McLaurin v. Oklahoma State Regents*, 339 U.S. 637 (1950).

6 *Brown v. Board of Education*, 347 U.S. 494 (1954). There are several excellent narratives of the *Brown* decision and the process leading up to the decision, the best of which is Kluger, *Simple Justice*.

7 Quoted in Goldfield, *Black, White, and Southern*, p. 75.

8 Quoted in Sarratt, *The Ordeal of Desegregation*, p. 1.

9 Muse, *Ten Years of Prelude*, p. 21; Bartley, *The Rise of Massive Resistance*, p. 54.

10 "Umstead 'Terribly Disappointed' Man," *Durham Morning Herald*, May 18, 1954, p. 1; "North Carolina," *Southern School News*, September 3, 1954, p. 10.

11 Umstead, "The United States Supreme Court Reverses Itself on Public Schools," *Public Addresses, Letters, and Papers*, p. 201; "North Carolina," *Southern School News*, September 3, 1954, p. 10. The only desegregated schools in North Carolina during the 1954–55 school year were Catholic schools. All of the state's Catholic high schools and some of the Catholic elementary schools opened on a desegregated basis in September 1954. "North Carolina," *Southern School News*, October 1, 1954, p. 11.

12 "North Carolina," *Southern School News*, September 3, 1954, p. 10.

13 Quoted in Chafe, *Civilities and Civil Rights*, pp. 65–66. Some have suggested that his candor cost Carlyle an appointment to the vacant U.S. Senate seat. Batchelor, "Save Our Schools," p. 24.

14 Chafe, *Civilities and Civil Rights*, p. 66.

15 Interview, James Paul, February 24, 1993.

16 Paul and Coates, *The School Segregation Decision*; Interview, James Paul, February 24, 1993.

17 Paul and Coates, *The School Segregation Decision*, pp. 90–92.

18 Ibid., pp. 118–19.

19 The news media applauded the formation of the committee, particularly the inclusion of the black members, as consistent with the state's measured response to desegregation, a response that would help preserve the public school system. "Editorial — Beginning in Wisdom," *Raleigh News and Observer*, August 13, 1954, p. 4.

20 Batchelor, "Save Our Schools," p. 32.

21 Interview, James Paul, February 24, 1993.

22 "North Carolina," *Southern School News*, September 3, 1954, p. 10.

23 Ibid., October 1, 1954, p. 11.

24 Brief of Harry McMullan, in Kurland and Casper, *Landmark Briefs and Arguments* 49A:983–85.

25 Ibid., p. 985; "North Carolina," *Southern School News*, December 1, 1954, p. 11.

26 Bass and DeVries, *The Transformation of Southern Politics*, pp. 229–30.

27 "North Carolina," *Southern School News*, February 3, 1955, p. 14.

28 Ibid.

29 Kelly Alexander, "Implementation of the United States Supreme Court Decision of May 17, 1954, in North Carolina," p. 11, Box 37-15, Kelly Alexander Papers, Charlotte.

30 Lamanna, "The Negro Public School Teacher and School Desegregation," p. 54.

31 "North Carolina," *Southern School News*, February 3, 1955, p. 14.

32 N.C.G.S. Sec. 115–176 et seq. (1955). The statute gave local school boards "full and complete" authority to enroll schoolchildren and provided that the school board's "decision as to the enrollment of any pupil in any such school" would be "final." In making these decisions, school boards were directed to consider "the orderly and efficient administration" of the schools, "the effective instruction of the pupils," and the "health, safety, and general welfare of such pupils." Sec. 115–177 (1955).

33 Oral Argument, *Brown v. Board of Education*, April 13, 1955, p. 13, in Kurland and Casper, *Landmark Briefs and Arguments* 49A:1227.

34 "North Carolina," *Southern School News*, March 3, 1955, p. 13. Other states would take a different course. Louisiana and South Carolina, for example, enacted legislation in 1955 requiring a fund cutoff for schools that desegregated. "Education: Public Schools—Louisiana," *Race Relations Law Reporter* 1 (1956): 239 (Louisiana); "Education: Public Schools—South Carolina," *Race Relations Law Reporter* 1 (1956): 241 (South Carolina).

35 "North Carolina," *Southern School News*, March 3, 1955, p. 13.

36 Ibid., April 7, 1955, p. 12.

37 Luther Hodges, *Businessman in the Statehouse*, p. 83.

38 "Report of the North Carolina Advisory Committee on Education," *Race Relations Law Reporter* 1 (1956): 582, 585.

39 Ibid., p. 585.

40 "N.C. Advisory Committee Asks 2 Constitutional Amendments," *Southern School News*, May 1956, p. 6; "N.C. Governor Suggests 'Local Option' Plan for Schools," *Southern School News*, November 1955, p. 13.

41 Luther Hodges, "Address on State-Wide Radio-Television Network," *Messages, Addresses, and Public Papers*, p. 210.

42 Luther Hodges, "Message to the Special Session of the General Assembly, July 23, 1956," *Messages, Addresses, and Public Papers*, p. 33.

43 "N.C. Adopts 'Pearsall Plan' by 4 to 1; Challenge Quickly Filed in U.S. Court," *Southern School News*, October 1956, p. 7.

44 John B. Martin, *The Deep South Says "Never,"* p. 11. Those four states were Alabama, Georgia, Mississippi, and South Carolina.

45 Those states were Georgia, Louisiana, South Carolina, and Virginia. "Public Schools—Georgia," *Race Relations Law Reporter* 1 (1956): 421; "Public Schools—Louisiana," *Race Relations Law Reporter* 1 (1956): 239; "Public Schools—South Carolina," *Race Relations Law Reporter* 1 (1956): 241; "Public Schools—Virginia," *Race Relations Law Reporter* 1 (1956): 1111.

46 "Constitutional Law: Interposition and Nullification—Alabama," *Race*

Relations Law Reporter 1 (1956): 437; "Constitutional Law: Interposition and Nullification—Arkansas," *Race Relations Law Reporter* 1 (1956): 1116; "Constitutional Law: Interposition and Nullification—Florida," *Race Relations Law Reporter* 2 (1957): 707; "Constitutional Law: Interposition and Nullification—Georgia," *Race Relations Law Reporter* 1 (1956): 438; "Constitutional Law: Interposition—Louisiana," *Race Relations Law Reporter* 1 (1956): 753; "Constitutional Law: Interposition and Nullification—Mississippi," *Race Relations Law Reporter* 1 (1956): 440; "Constitutional Law: Interposition and Nullification—South Carolina," *Race Relations Law Reporter* 1 (1956): 443; "Constitutional Law: Interposition and Nullification—Virginia," *Race Relations Law Reporter* 1 (1956): 445.

47 Those ten states were Alabama, Arkansas, Florida, Georgia, Louisiana, Mississippi, South Carolina, Tennessee, Texas, and Virginia. Murphy, "The South Counterattacks."

48 "Charlotte Parents Initiate Moves Aimed at Utilizing Pearsall Plan Provisions," *Southern School News*, August 1958, p. 15.

49 Virginia's pupil placement statute was declared unconstitutional in January 1957 in significant measure because of the mandatory school closing provision. *Atkins v. School Board of Newport News*, 148 F. Supp. 430 (E.D. Va. 1957), *aff'd*, 246 F.2d 325 (4th Cir. 1957), *cert. denied*, 355 U.S. 855 (1957).

50 "Lawyer Recalls 'Buying Time' for Integration," *Raleigh News and Observer*, November 7, 1976, p. 1.

51 "Editorial—First Job of Both Races: To Retain Public Schools," *Charlotte Observer*, November 14, 1963, p. 2B.

52 "No Surprise Involved in End to Plan," *Raleigh News and Observer*, April 5, 1966, p. 1.

53 Luther Hodges, "Address before Combined Parent-Teacher Associations of Cabarrus County," April 20, 1956, *Messages, Addresses, and Public Papers*, p. 331.

54 "Lawyer Recalls 'Buying Time' for Integration," *Raleigh News and Observer*, November 7, 1976, p. 1.

55 Public opinion polls are but one indicator of the changing mood. In 1954, 24 percent of southerners approved of the *Brown* decision; by May 1955 that figure had dropped to 20 percent. Tumin, *Segregation and Desegregation*, pp. 105–7. In 1954, 15 percent of white southerners indicated that they would not object to sending their children to an integrated school; by 1959, that figure was 8 percent. Erskine, "The Polls: Race Relations," pp. 140–41.

56 The following are examples of some of this legislation. *Alabama*: Act No. 117, April 14, 1956, *Race Relations Law Reporter* 1 (1956): 717. *Georgia*: Act No. 11, February 6, 1956, *Race Relations Law Reporter* 1 (1956): 418. *Mississippi*: House Bill No. 31, February 24, 1956, *Race Relations Law Reporter* 1 (1956): 422; Chapter 254, 1956, *Race Relations Law Reporter*

2 (1957): 480. *Virginia*: Chapter 56, 71, September 29, 1956, *Race Relations Law Reporter* 1 (1956): 1091.

57 Muse, *Ten Years of Prelude*, p. 66.

58 Goldfield, *Black, White, and Southern*, p. 84. The manifesto read in part:
   We regard the decision of the Supreme Court in the school cases as a clear abuse of judicial power. It climaxes a trend in the Federal judiciary undertaking to legislate, in derogation of the authority of Congress, and to encroach upon the reserved rights of the States and the people. . . .

   We commend the motives of those states which have declared the intention to resist forced integration by any lawful means. . . .

   We pledge ourselves to use all lawful means to bring about a reversal of this decision which is contrary to the Constitution and to prevent the use of force in its implementation.
   Congressional Record 102 (March 12, 1956): 4515–16.

59 Quoting Anthony Lewis in Goldfield, *Black, White, and Southern*, p. 85.

60 Eisenhower also declined to authorize procedures for investigating complaints arising out of desegregation efforts and refused to seek enforcement legislation from Congress. Burk, *The Eisenhower Administration*, pp. 144–45.

61 Ibid., pp. 152–53.

62 Ibid., pp. 160–62.

63 "Dr. Beverly Lake Amplifies upon Position Taken in Asheboro Speech," *Raleigh News and Observer*, July 20, 1955; Charles Dunn, "An Exercise of Choice," p. 120.

64 Luther Hodges, "Address on State-Wide Radio-Television Network," August 8, 1955, *Messages, Addresses, and Public Papers*, p. 206.

65 May 1956 statement to Editorial Writers Conference quoted in "Confidential Memorandum from Harry Golden to George Mitchell" (May 23, 1956), Box 37-15, Kelly Alexander Papers.

66 "Hodges Defends Lake in Squabble," *Charlotte News*, July 18, 1955.

67 "Lawyer Recalls 'Buying Time' for Integration," *Raleigh News and Observer*, November 7, 1976, p. 1.

68 "Editorial—A New Voice for the Extremists," *Charlotte News*, July 15, 1955, p. 6A; "Editorial—Inciting the Extremists," *Raleigh News and Observer*, July 15, 1955, p. 4; "Lawyer Recalls 'Buying Time' for Integration," *Raleigh News and Observer*, November 7, 1976, p. 1.

69 "N.C. Court Upholds Pupil Assignment in Initial Test," *Southern School News*, April 1956, p. 11.

70 "Two N.C. Solons Losers on Issue of 'Manifesto,'" *Southern School News*, June 1956, p. 8.

71 "Pearsall Plan: The Spirit of Moderation," *Greensboro Daily News*, September 2, 1956, p. 6.

72 "Pearsall Plan Is Legal, Joyner Tells Assembly," *Raleigh News and Observer*, July 26, 1956, p. 1.

73 "Editorial—Saturday's Election," *Greensboro Daily News*, September 10, 1956, sec. 1, p. 6.

74 "Carlyle Calls for Defeat of Pearsall Group Plan," *Winston-Salem Journal*, July 3, 1956, p. 1; Charles Dunn, "An Exercise of Choice," p. 69.

75 Trillin, "Remembrance of Moderates Past," p. 85. Vandiver was governor of Georgia from 1959 until 1963.

76 Chafe, *Civilities and Civil Rights*. The discussion of school desegregation throughout the state during this time period bore the same quality.

77 See, e.g., Paul Johnston to Emma Byers, May 29, 1956, Hodges Papers, Raleigh.

78 Charlotte-Mecklenburg Council on Human Relations, "Voices of Moderation," (July 1956), Box 121-86, Frederick Alexander Papers, Charlotte.

79 "Editor Sees Race Relations Hurt," *Durham Morning Herald*, March 12, 1956, p. 8A.

80 Seawell, "North Carolina at a Crossroad," p. 3.

81 Charlotte-Mecklenburg Council on Human Relations, "Role of Business Leaders," (1956), Box 121-86, Frederick Alexander Papers.

82 North Carolina Council on Human Relations, *Human Relations Bulletin*, (March 1956), p. 5, Box 121-86, Frederick Alexander Papers.

83 Anti-Defamation League, *The High Cost of Conflict*, p. 8.

84 *Atlanta Constitution*, February 27, 1959, quoted in ibid., p. 33.

85 Cobb, *The Selling of the South*, p. 123.

86 Ibid., p. 147.

87 Holmes, "Credit in the Development of the South," quoted in Anti-Defamation League, *The High Cost of Conflict*, p. 1.

88 "The Middle Road Is Best," *Charlotte Observer*, July 28, 1957, p. 2B; "3 N.C. Cities Assign 12 Negroes to Previously All-White Schools," *Southern School News*, August 1957, p. 3.

89 Southern Regional Council, Special Report on Charlotte, Greensboro, and Winston-Salem, North Carolina (1957), p. 2, Box III-A-105, NAACP Papers, Washington, D.C.

90 Peebles, "School Desegregation in Raleigh," p. 56.

91 "Administration Measures Are Directed at NAACP," *Raleigh News and Observer*, May 17, 1957, p. 1.

92 Kelly Alexander, statement of North Carolina State Conference of Branches, NAACP, to North Carolina General Assembly, May 28, 1957, Box III-A-279, NAACP Papers, Washington, D.C.

93 North Carolina State Conference of Branches of NAACP, "Press Release," June 8, 1957, Box III-A-179, NAACP Papers, Washington, D.C.

94 "Racial Bill Approved by Group," *Charlotte Observer*, June 6, 1957, p. 5A.

95 NAACP North Carolina State Conference of Branches, Action Letter, June 1, 1957, Box III-A-279, NAACP Papers, Washington, D.C.; "Anti-NAACP Bill in Trouble," *Raleigh News and Observer*, May 31, 1957, p. A3.

96 "Editorial—It Is Not Worthy of This State," *Charlotte Observer*, June 4, 1957, p. 2C.

97 Beyle, "The Paradox of North Carolina," p. 4.

98 Key, *Southern Politics in State and Nation*, p. 214. Following Key's classic work, published in 1949, there has been much discussion about whether in fact Key's characterization of North Carolina as "progressive" was accurate. See, e.g., Luebke, *Tar Heel Politics*, p. 1; Luebke, "Corporate Conservatism and Government Moderation," p. 107; Bass and DeVries, *The Transformation of Southern Politics*, p. 229; Beyle, "The Paradox of North Carolina," p. 1; Edsall and Williams, "North Carolina: Bipartisan Paradox," p. 366. Most would concede, however, that to the extent that "progressive" is defined in terms of promoting industrial expansion, the state has indeed been progressive for much of this century. Luebke, "Corporative Conservatism and Government Moderation," pp. 107–8.

99 Key, *Southern Politics in State and Nation*, pp. 209–10.

100 Harlan, *Separate and Unequal*, p. 40; Du Bois and Dill, *The Common School and the Negro American*, p. 50.

101 Luebke, *Tar Heel Politics*, p. 114.

102 Edsall and Williams, "North Carolina: Bipartisan Paradox," p. 371; Beyle, "The Paradox of North Carolina," p. 4.

103 See, e.g., Black, *Southern Governors and Civil Rights*; Key, *Southern Politics in State and Nation*, p. 229.

104 Key, *Southern Politics in State and Nation*, pp. 217–18; Beyle, "The Paradox of North Carolina," p. 5.

105 Ashmore, *The Negro and the Schools*, pp. 173–204. Even Virginia, which had a smaller black population than did North Carolina on a statewide basis, had a substantially higher percentage of counties with a majority-black population than did North Carolina.

106 Quoted in Black, *Southern Governors and Civil Rights*, p. 218.

107 Ibid., p. 219.

108 *Morrow v. Mecklenburg County Board of Education*, 195 F. Supp. 109 (W.D.N.C. 1961).

109 Most typically this happened in mountain counties with small black populations. *Griffith v. Board of Education of Yancey County*, 186 F. Supp. 511 (W.D.N.C. 1960).

110 North Carolina Advisory Committee, Equal Protection of the Law in Education in North Carolina (1960), Box III-A-288, NAACP Papers, Washington, D.C.

111 Blacks in the mountain town of Bryson City sought to attend a local white school to avoid a forty-five-mile round trip to a black school in another county. The request was denied. "N.C. Pupil Assignment Faces Test," *Charlotte Observer*, July 21, 1957, p. 2D.

112 Charlotte granted five of forty transfer requests, Greensboro granted six of thirteen transfer requests, and Winston-Salem granted one of four transfer requests. "3 N.C. Cities Assign 12 Negroes to Previously All-White Schools," *Southern School News*, August 1957, p. 3.

113 See generally Coogan, "School Board Decisions on Desegregation in North Carolina"; Lamanna, "The Negro Public School Teacher and School Desegregation."

114 "Integration Seen Bolstering Law," *Charlotte Observer*, July 24, 1957, p. 2A.

115 "3 N.C. Cities Assign 12 Negroes to Previously All-White Schools," *Southern School News*, August 1957, p. 3.

116 Ibid.

117 Ibid.

118 Southern Education Reporting Service, *Statistical Summary*, p. 26. In addition to these four states, however, all of the border states had integrated at least some of their schools.

119 North Carolina Advisory Committee, Equal Protection of the Law in Education in North Carolina (1960), Box III-A-288, NAACP Papers, Washington, D.C.; "66 School Applications Rejected," *Charlotte Observer*, August 6, 1957, p. 1B; "Students May Ask for Reassignment," *Charlotte Observer*, August 3, 1957, p. 1B; "All-White School Eyed by Negroes," *Charlotte Observer*, July 10, 1957, p. 6A.

120 "Three Localities Begin Desegregation: Total Now Stands at Seven," *Southern School News*, September 1959, p. 10.

121 American Friends Service Committee, *Newsletter* (October 1959), University of North Carolina Library, North Carolina Collection, Chapel Hill; North Carolina Advisory Committee, Equal Protection of the Law in Education in North Carolina (1960), Box III-A-288, NAACP Papers, Washington, D.C.

122 "Integration Held Slow in N.C.," *Greensboro Daily News*, October 2, 1960, p. A1.

123 Both the North Carolina Supreme Court and the U.S. Court of Appeals for the Fourth Circuit found the North Carolina assignment plan to be constitutional as written. *Carson v. Warlick*, 238 F.2d 724, 728 (4th Cir. 1956); *Constanton v. Anson County*, 244 N.C. 221, 93 S.E.2d 163 (1956). On NAACP litigation in North Carolina, see "N.C. Leads South in Desegregation Cases Pending or Proposed, NAACP Told Here," *Asheville Citizen*, October 10, 1959, p. 10. On unlawful school segregation in other states, see, e.g., *Adkins v. School Board of Newport News*, 148 F. Supp. 430 (E.D. Va. 1957), aff'd, 246 F.2d 325 (4th Cir. 1957), cert. denied, 355 U.S. 855 (1957); *Bush v. Orleans Parish School Board*, 138 F. Supp. 337 (E.D. La. 1956), aff'd, 242 F.2d 156 (5th Cir. 1957), cert. denied, 354 U.S. 921 (1957).

124 In 1960, a court in North Carolina ruled in favor of a handful of black students in Yancey County seeking admission to a white school; these students had been required to make an eighty-mile trip on mountain roads to attend a black school in a neighboring county. *Griffith v. Board of Education of Yancey County*, 186 F. Supp. 511 (W.D.N.C. 1960).

125 *Brown v. Board of Education*, 349 U.S. 294, 297 (1955).

126 "Brief of the United States on the Further Argument of the Questions of Relief," *Brown v. Board of Education*, 1954, p. 27, in Kurland and Casper, *Landmark Briefs and Arguments* 49A:768.

127 Wilkinson, *From Brown to Bakke*, p. 64.

128 *Cooper v. Aaron*, 358 U.S. 1 (1958). See also *Aaron v. Cooper*, 357 U.S. 566 (1958); *Aaron v. Cooper*, 358 U.S. 1 (1958); *United States v. Louisiana*, 364 U.S. 500 (1960); *Faubus v. Aaron*, 361 U.S. 197 (1959); *Shuttlesworth v. Birmingham Board of Education*, 358 U.S. 101 (1958). At the same time, between 1956 and 1958, the Court denied certiorari in at least a dozen school desegregation cases. Greenberg, "The Supreme Court, Civil Rights, and Civil Dissonance," p. 1524 n. 10.

129 Wasby, D'Amato, and Metrailer, *Desegregation from Brown to Alexander*, pp. 166–73.

130 See, e.g., Bickel, "The Decade of School Desegregation," p. 209: "It will be beneficial if the Court gives a new and unified sense of direction to the lower judges, and it will, incidentally, also be helpful if the Court exerts itself to keep the few opposition judges in line." This reluctance continued in the 1960s. The Court issued only two full opinions in southern school desegregation cases from 1960 until 1964.

131 See generally Peltason, *Fifty-Eight Lonely Men*; Bass, *Unlikely Heroes*.

132 See, e.g., L. R. McKnight to Kelly Alexander, September 14, 1954, Box 37-16, Kelly Alexander Papers; Conrad Pearson to Roy Wilkens, November 20, 1959, Box III-A-279, NAACP Papers, Washington, D.C.; Lamanna, "The Negro Public School Teacher and School Desegregation," p. 57.

133 See *Carson v. Board of Education of McDowell County*, 227 F.2d 789, 790 (4th Cir. 1955); *Carson v. Warlick*, 238 F.2d 724, 727 (4th Cir. 1956), *cert. denied*, 353 U.S. 910 (1957); *Covington v. Edwards*, 165 F. Supp. 957, 959 (M.D.N.C. 1958), *aff'd*, 264 F.2d 780 (4th Cir. 1959), *cert. denied*, 361 U.S. 840 (1959); *Holt v. Raleigh City Board of Education*, 164 F. Supp. 853, 862 (E.D. N.C. 1958), *aff'd*, 265 F.2d 95 (4th Cir. 1959), *cert. denied*, 361 U.S. 818 (1959).

134 *Shuttlesworth v. Birmingham Board of Education*, 162 F. Supp. 372, 381–82 (N.D. Ala. 1958).

135 *Shuttlesworth v. Birmingham Board of Education*, 385 U.S. 101 (1958) (per curiam).

136 There had, however, been a number of attempts to desegregate the schools in North Carolina, all of which the courts rejected. See, e.g., *Carson v. Warlick*, 238 F.2d 724, 727 (4th Cir. 1956), *cert. denied*, 353 U.S. 910 (1957); *Covington v. Edwards*, 165 F. Supp. 957 (M.D.N.C. 1958), *aff'd*, 264 F.2d 180 (4th Cir. 1959), *cert. denied*, 361 U.S. 840 (1959); *Holt v. Raleigh City Board of Education*, 164 F. Supp. 853 (E.D. N.C. 1958), *aff'd*, 265 F.2d 95 (4th Cir. 1959), *cert. denied*, 361 U.S. 818 (1959).

137 See, e.g., *Adkins v. School Board of Newport News*, 148 F. Supp. 430 (E.D. Va. 1957), *aff'd*, 246 F.2d 325 (4th Cir. 1957), *cert. denied*, 355 U.S. 855 (1957); *Bush v. Orleans Parish School Board*, 138 F. Supp. 337 (E.D. La.

1956), *aff'd*, 242 F.2d 156 (5th Cir. 1957), *cert. denied*, 354 U.S. 921 (1957).

138 Southern Education Reporting Service, *Statistical Summary*, p. 29.

CHAPTER THREE

1 Hanchett, "Sorting Out the New South City," p. 43; Greenwood, *Bittersweet Legacy*, p. 9; Blythe and Brockmann, *Hornets' Nest*, p. 267.

2 Hanchett, "Sorting Out the New South City," p. 37; Greenwood, *Bittersweet Legacy*, pp. 8–13.

3 U.S. Bureau of the Census, *Twelfth Census of the United States*; U.S. Bureau of the Census, *Thirteenth Census of the United States*.

4 Leach, "Progress under Pressure," p. 4; Greenwood, *Bittersweet Legacy*, p. 114; Hanchett, "Sorting Out the New South City," p. 116.

5 Hanchett, "Sorting Out the New South City," p. 456.

6 Ibid., p. 458.

7 "Tournament Invigorates Charlotte," *New York Times*, April 2, 1994, p. 7A.

8 U.S. Bureau of the Census, *Census of Population, 1950*, p. 33; U.S. Bureau of the Census, *Census of Population and Housing, 1960*, p. 13; U.S. Bureau of the Census, *1990 Census of Population and Housing*, p. 17; "Now We'll Be City," *Charlotte Observer*, June 30, 1991, p. 1D; Hanchett, "Sorting Out the New South City," p. 191.

9 "Tournament Invigorates Charlotte," *New York Times*, April 2, 1994, p. 7A.

10 Hanchett, "Sorting Out the New South City," p. 520; Taeuber and Taeuber, *Negroes in Cities*, pp. 32–34, 40–41.

11 Hanchett, "Sorting Out the New South City," pp. 6, 103, 264.

12 Greenwood, *Bittersweet Legacy*, pp. 69–70.

13 Hanchett, "Sorting Out the New South City," p. 516.

14 Greenwood, *Bittersweet Legacy*, pp. 216–17.

15 A few North Carolina cities did enact such ordinances, most notably Greensboro, Mooresville, Winston-Salem, and Asheville. North Carolina Advisory Committee, *Equal Protection of the Laws*, p. 168; Kellogg, *NAACP*, p. 184.

16 Hanchett, "Sorting Out the New South City," pp. 306–18.

17 *Phillips v. Wearn*, 226 N.C. 290, 37 S.E.2d 895 (1946); *Vernon v. R.J. Reynolds Realty Co.*, 226 N.C. 58, 36 S.E. 2d 710 (1945); *Sheets v. Dillon*, 221 N.C. 426 (1942); *St. Louis Union Trust Co. v. Foster*, 211 N.C. 331, 190 S.E. 522 (1937); *Eason v. Buffaloe*, 198 N.C. 520, 152 S.E. 496 (1930); *Shelley v. Kraemer*, 334 U.S. 1 (1948). In its earlier decision in *Corrigan v. Buckley*, 271 U.S. 323 (1926), the U.S. Supreme Court had expressly found that enforcement of racially restrictive covenants did not violate the Constitution.

18 Hanchett, "Sorting Out the New South City," pp. 200–225, 271–302.

19 *Charlotte Observer*, September 22, 1912, quoted in ibid., p. 303.

20 Orfield, *Must We Bus?*, pp. 79–82; Federal Housing Administration, *FHA Underwriting Manual*, paragraph 935; Myrdal, *An American Dilemma*, p. 625; Hanchett, "Sorting Out the New South City," pp. 468–76.

21 Hanchett, "Sorting out the New South City," p. 469.

22 Weaver, *The Negro Ghetto*, p. 152; Hanchett, "Sorting Out the New South City," pp. 468–76.

23 Hanchett, "Sorting Out the New South City," p. 474.

24 Testimony of William E. McIntyre, *Swann v. Charlotte-Mecklenburg Board of Education*, March 26, 1969, in U.S. Supreme Court Records and Briefs, pp. 282a–83a, Williamsburg, Va.

25 Hanchett, "Sorting Out the New South City," pp, 475–76.

26 A 1936 FHA policy manual noted that if children were "compelled to attend school with . . . an incompatible racial element," the neighborhood would "prove far less stable and desirable than if the condition did not exist." Quoted in testimony of Marion Wright Edelman, Washington Research Group, in U.S. Senate Committee on Labor and Public Welfare, *Hearings before the Subcommittee on Education*, pp. 626–27.

27 Hanchett, "Sorting Out the New South City," p. 475; "Natural Borders Would Stop Extensive City Integration," *Charlotte News*, June 3, 1955, p. 1A.

28 Transcript of Hearing, *Swann v. Charlotte-Mecklenburg Board of Education*, March 10, 1969, in Record on Appeal to United States Court of Appeals, p. 17, U.S. Courthouse, Charlotte.

29 Clayton, *W. J. Cash*, p. 139; Crow, Escott, and Hatley, *A History of African Americans in North Carolina*, p. 130; "She Knew the Man Who Gazed into the Mind of the South," *Charlotte Observer*, February 3, 1991, p. 1C.

30 Claiborne, *The Charlotte Observer*, p. 199.

31 Leach, "Progress under Pressure," p. 207; Hanchett, "Sorting Out the New South City," p. 480.

32 Leach, "Progress under Pressure," p. 208; Hanchett, "Sorting Out the New South City," p. 481.

33 Hanchett, "Sorting Out the New South City," p. 496.

34 Taeuber and Taeuber, *Negroes in Cities*, pp. 32–34; 40–41; "Analysis of Student Enrollment and Professional Instructional Staff of One Hundred Largest School Districts," contained in Chambers Papers, Charlotte. Those thirteen cities were Dallas, Flint, Fort Lauderdale, Jacksonville, Miami, Montgomery, Norfolk, Orlando, Richmond, Shreveport, Tampa, West Palm Beach, and Winston-Salem.

35 Charlotte, 2.2 to one; Asheville, 1.7 to one; Durham, 1.9 to one; Greensboro–High Point, 1.9 to one; Raleigh, 2.1 to one; Winston-Salem, 1.8 to one; Chattanooga, 1.6 to one; Memphis, 2.3 to one; Nashville, 1.8 to one; Norfolk, 1.8 to one; Richmond, 1.9 to one; Roanoke, 1.9 to one. The disparities in the Deep South were worse than in Charlotte: Mobile, 2.4 to one; Montgomery, 3.0 to one; Atlanta, 2.2 to one; Augusta, 2.3 to one; Savannah, 2.5 to one. U.S. Bureau of the Census, *Census of Population, 1950*.

36 U.S. Bureau of the Census, *Census of Population, 1950*, pp. 33–71.

37 Crow, Escott, and Hatley, *A History of African Americans in North Carolina*, p. 135.

38 "North Carolina," *Southern School News*, September 3, 1954, p. 10; North Carolina Advisory Committee, *Equal Protection of the Laws*, p. 104.

39 Charlotte Branch, NAACP, "Implementing an Effective NAACP Program in Charlotte, North Carolina," (July 10, 1961), Box III-C-112, NAACP Papers, Washington, D.C.; "NAACP Urges Charlotte to Provide Equal School Facilities for All," *Charlotte Observer*, July 11, 1948, p. 9B.

40 "Time of Crisis Taught Lessons of Past," *Charlotte Observer*, July 7, 1991.

41 U.S. Bureau of the Census, *Census of Population and Housing, 1960*.

42 Crow, Escott, and Hatley, *A History of African Americans in North Carolina*, p. 130.

43 North Carolina Advisory Committee, *Equal Protection of the Laws*, pp. 205–8, 222–23.

44 Towe, *Barriers to Black Political Participation in North Carolina*, p. 13; Emory, "Some Aspects of the Black Experience in Politics," pp. 90–91.

45 See Greenwood, *Bittersweet Legacy*.

46 Ibid., pp. 214–44.

47 Loftus Carson, "Community Approach toward Implementation of the Supreme Court Decision on Public Education in North Carolina," (1954), Box II-A-227, NAACP Papers, Washington, D.C.

48 North Carolina Advisory Committee, *Equal Protection of the Laws*, p. 178.

49 "Suit to Shut Off All U.S. Funds Prepared," *Charlotte Observer*, June 30, 1969, p. 1B.

50 For example, Claude Broach, minister at St. John's Baptist Church in downtown Charlotte, claimed that the Supreme Court in *Brown* had "echoed the conscience of the church." Claude Broach, "Sermon," p. 2, Box 121-86, Frederick Alexander Papers, Charlotte.

51 *Charlotte Observer*, September 9, 1955.

52 Earnhardt, "Critical Years."

53 Leach, "Progress under Pressure," p. 37.

54 "Membership of Negroes Questioned," *Charlotte News*, April 28, 1955; "N.C. Doctors Admit Negroes," *Raleigh News and Observer*, May 3, 1955; Claiborne, *The Charlotte Observer*, p. 247. The state granted black doctors "scientific" membership but not "social" membership; full membership would not come until 1964. Halperin, "Special Report," pp. 61–62.

55 "N.C. Negroes Are Pushing Desegregation," *Charlotte Observer*, July 19, 1957, p. 9A; Southern Regional Council, "Special Report on Charlotte, Greensboro, and Winston-Salem, North Carolina," (1957), p. 12, Box III-A-105, NAACP Papers, Washington, D.C.

56 "Bathing Pool in Charlotte Integrated," *Greensboro Daily News*, July 28, 1960, p. 1A; Interview, Joseph Grier, July 8, 1992.

57 Claiborne, *The Charlotte Observer*, pp. 245–47.

58 Ibid., p. 246.

59 "Editorial," *Charlotte Observer*, September 13, 1955.

60 Claiborne, *The Charlotte Observer*, pp. 50–51; Greenwood, *Bittersweet Legacy*, pp. 189–90, 193.

61 Quoted in Greenwood, *Bittersweet Legacy*, p. 212.

62 Claiborne, *The Charlotte Observer*, pp. 284–85.

63 The *Observer*, for example, was one of the only major papers in the state to oppose the Pearsall Plan in 1956. "N.C. Editors State Pearsall Plan Views," *Durham Morning Herald*, September 6, 1956, p. 3A.

64 "Editorial—Handwriting on the Wall," *Charlotte News*, June 7, 1950, p. 4A. McKnight did, however, believe that the elimination of segregation would cause "a degree of chaos that probably would be more detrimental to the national welfare and to that of the nation's citizens than a continuation of segregation would be." Ibid.

65 Clayton, *W. J. Cash*, pp. 142–43.

66 Yet the *Observer* did not endorse every effort to secure racial equality. The paper would criticize some of the public demonstration activities of black Charlotteans in the early 1960s, particularly those of Dr. Reginald Hawkins. "Editorial—Memorial's Race Problems Need Calm, Logical Action," *Charlotte Observer*, March 3, 1962, p. 2B. Moreover, the *Observer* initially defended the retention of what amounted to a dual community college system in the late 1950s. "Editorial—Two Colleges? Grounds for Debate," *Charlotte Observer*, May 21, 1959, p. 2B.

67 John Cunningham, "Statement about the Mayor's Committee on Community Relations," June 1963, Box 1-5, Charlotte-Mecklenburg Community Relations Committee Papers, Charlotte (UNCC).

68 Interview, Jack Bullard, December 14, 1994.

69 "Editor Sees Race Relations Hurt," *Durham Morning Herald*, March 12, 1956, p. 8A.

70 Charlotte-Mecklenburg Council on Human Relations, "What Would Public School Desegregation Mean to Charlotte," (1956), and "Role of Business Leaders," (1956), Box 1-5, Charlotte-Mecklenburg Community Relations Committee Papers, Charlotte (UNCC).

71 North Carolina Council on Human Relations, *Human Relations Bulletin*, (March 1956), p. 5 (quoting *New York Times*, March 13, 1956), Box 121-86, Frederick Alexander Papers.

72 "Petition," 1951, Box 1-1, Grier Papers, Charlotte.

73 *Leeper v. Charlotte Park and Recreation Commission*, 242 N.C. 311 (1955); Interview, Joseph Grier, July 8, 1992.

74 "N.C. Negro Parents Go to Court in Challenge of 'Pearsall Plan,'" *Southern School News*, January 1957, p. 8; "N.C. Legislature May Be Asked to Readopt '56 School Measures," *Southern School News*, February 1957, p. 5.

75 "Two N.C. Cities Begin Studies on Compliance with Decree," *Southern School News*, July 6, 1955, p. 6; "North Carolina: The Integration Issue," *Raleigh News and Observer*, March 15, 1956, p. 4; "Pearsall Heads Schools Group; Governor Stresses Task Ahead," *Raleigh News and Observer*, June 22, 1955, p. 1.

76 "NAACP State President, Long Time Civil Rights Leader," *Revealer* (Raleigh, N.C.), December 1975, Box 34-12, Kelly Alexander Papers, Charlotte; "Biographical Sketch of Kelly Miller Alexander," Box IV-C-26, NAACP Papers, Washington, D.C.

77 Leach, "Progress under Pressure," p. 113.

78 "NAACP State President, Long Time Civil Rights Leader," *Revealer* (Raleigh, N.C.), December 1975, Box 34-12, Kelly Alexander Papers; Center for Urban Affairs, *Paths toward Freedom*, p. 129.

79 Address of Kelly Alexander, June 23, 1949, at Annual North Carolina Conference of NAACP Branches, Box 1-3, Kelly Alexander Papers.

80 Burns, "North Carolina and the Negro Dilemma," p. 47; Gavins, "The NAACP in North Carolina during the Age of Segregation," p. 117.

81 "Desegregation Spotty as Schools Open," *Southern School News*, September 1955, p. 1; "N.C. Leads South in Desegregation Cases Pending or Proposed, NAACP Told Here," *Asheville Citizen*, October 10, 1959, p. 10.

82 "Atlanta Declaration," May 23, 1954, Box II-A-227, NAACP Papers, Washington, D.C.

83 "North Carolina," *Southern School News*, September 1954, p. 10; "Immediate School Integration Urged," *Raleigh News and Observer*, August 13, 1954, p. 21.

84 "North Carolina," *Southern School News*, November 1954, p. 13; "Editorial — Patience Is the Best Policy," *Charlotte News*, September 25, 1954, p. 4A. Several of the state's newspapers were critical of the NAACP's petitions, calling them "impetuous." See, e.g., "Editorial — Patience Is the Best Policy," *Charlotte News*, September 25, 1954, p. 4A.

85 "NAACP Will Seek Integration in Fall," *Charlotte Observer*, July 9, 1955, p. 1A.

86 "N.C. School Board Tells Group Initiative Is Up to Individuals," *Southern School News*, May 1957, p. 16.

87 *Carson v. Warlick*, 238 F.2d 724 (4th Cir. 1956).

88 "These Are 5 Negro Children Who'll Go to White Schools," *Charlotte Observer*, July 24, 1957, p. 1A.

89 Ibid.; "On Sept. 4, 1957, Four Young Charlotte Students Braved Fear and Uncertainty to Take Their Place in History as School Desegregation Pioneers," *Charlotte Observer*, April 12, 1992, p. 1C.

90 Charlotte Branch, NAACP, "Implementing an Effective NAACP Program in Charlotte, North Carolina," July 10, 1961, p. 18, Box III-C-112, NAACP Papers, Washington, D.C.

91 Conrad Pearson to Roy Wilkins, November 20, 1959, Box III-A-279, NAACP Papers, Washington, D.C. (to forestall foreclosure, NAACP offered collateral for mortgage of parent who had unsuccessfully sought a transfer for his children).

92 Testimony of Reginald Hawkins, *Swann v. Charlotte-Mecklenburg Board of Education*, July 12, 1965, p. 25, Chambers Papers.

93 Leach, "Progress under Pressure," pp. 57–58; Interview, Reginald Hawkins, October 12, 1992.

94 Leach, "Progress under Pressure," p. 58.
95 "Negro Leaders Differ on Hodges' School Talk," *Charlotte News*, August 9, 1955, p. 1A.
96 Quoted in Leach, "Progress under Pressure," p. 64.
97 Tross, Radio Address, WBT, September 11, 1945, quoted in ibid., p. 63.
98 Quoted in ibid., p. 64.
99 Ibid., pp. 58–62.
100 Interview, Jane Scott, October 15, 1992.
101 Interview, Reginald Hawkins, October 12, 1992. But at the time, Hawkins was critical of Tross: "He has no influence. He helps us more than he hurts us. If he starts opposing us, we know we are headed in the right direction." "Hawkins Still Blocks . . . and 'Wins,'" *Charlotte Observer*, May 4, 1962, p. 4A; Leach, "Progress under Pressure," p. 67.
102 Quoted in Leach, "Progress under Pressure," p. 68.
103 Charlotte-Mecklenburg Council on Human Relations, "What Would Public School Desegregation Mean to Charlotte?," (1956), Box 121–86, Frederick Alexander Papers.
104 "Golden Rule," *Time*, April 1, 1957, p. 62.
105 Thompson, *Presbyterians in the South*, pp. 539–42.
106 "120 Ministers Meet at Site of Bombings," *Charlotte Observer*, December 6, 1965, p. 1C.
107 Interview, Julia Maulden, December 14, 1994.
108 "Episcopal Minister Asserts Integration 'Not God's Will,'" *Charlotte Observer*, September 16, 1957, p. 1B.
109 "North Carolina," *Southern School News*, November 1954, p. 13.
110 "No-Busing Pastor Packs Sanctuary," *Charlotte Observer*, July 20, 1970, p. 1A.
111 Marney, *Structures of Prejudice*, p. 137.
112 Interview, Julia Maulden, December 14, 1994.
113 "North Carolina," *Southern School News*, October 1, 1954, p. 11.
114 "4 Whites Aid Negro Picketers," *Charlotte Observer*, March 11, 1962, p. 6A.
115 *Southern School News*, March 1958, p. 6; Lila Bellar to James McMillan, February 11, 1970, Series 1, Folder 17A, McMillan Papers, Chapel Hill.
116 "More Negro Appointments Urged," *Charlotte Observer*, December 9, 1965, p. 21B.
117 Quoted in Thompson, *Presbyterians in the South*, p. 542.
118 "Ministers: Racial Fight Must End," *Charlotte Observer*, March 16, 1960, p. 1B.
119 "The Paper War," *Charlotte Focus* 1, no. 6 (1970), Box 4, Folder 33, McMillan Papers.
120 "3 N.C. Cities Assign 12 Negroes to Previously All-White Schools," *Southern School News*, August 1957, p. 3.
121 U.S. Commission on Civil Rights, *Civil Rights U.S.A.*, p. 73.
122 "3 N.C. Cities Assign 12 Negroes to Previously All-White Schools," *Southern School News*, August 1957, p. 3.

123 "Negro School Children File Entry Applications in Four N.C. Cities," *Southern School News*, July 1957 p. 6; "3 N.C. Cities Assign 12 Negroes to Previously All-White Schools," *Southern School News*, August 1957, p. 3.

124 "3 N.C. Cities Assign 12 Negroes to Previously All-White Schools," *Southern School News*, August 1957, p. 3; "City Hears School Appeals," *Charlotte Observer*, August 8, 1957, p. 1C.

125 "3 N.C. Cities Assign 12 Negroes to Previously All-White Schools," *Southern School News*, August 1957, p. 3.

126 "Wisdom, Courage, and Law Dictate a School Decision," *Charlotte Observer*, July 24, 1957, p. 2B.

127 "State School Policy Hailed by Speaker," *Charlotte Observer*, August 2, 1957, p. 1B.

128 "N.C. Assembly Approves Referendum on Tuition, School Closing," *Southern School News*, August 1956, p. 16.

129 Southern Regional Council, "Patriots of North Carolina, Inc.," (1956), University of North Carolina Library, North Carolina Collection, Chapel Hill; McMillen, *The Citizens' Council*, p. 111. Quotation is from "Patriot Group Establishes Early Meet," *Charlotte Observer*, August 26, 1955, p. 8A.

130 "Here's an Insight into Integrated Schools in N.C.," *Raleigh News and Observer*, April 11, 1958, p. 17; North Carolina Council on Human Relations, *Human Relations Bulletin*, March 1958, p. 6, Box 121-86, Frederick Alexander Papers.

131 McMillen, *The Citizens' Council*, pp. 111–12.

132 Leach, "Progress under Pressure," p. 21.

133 Ibid., pp. 13–14, 21.

134 "3 N.C. Cities Assign 12 Negroes to Previously All-White Schools," *Southern School News*, August 1957, p. 3.

135 "2 School Boards Get Court Order," *Charlotte Observer*, August 27, 1957, p. 1A.

136 "N.C. Courts Block Effort to Prevent Desegregation," *Southern School News*, September 1957, p. 15.

137 *Charlotte Observer*, October 8, 1936; Burns, "North Carolina and the Negro Dilemma," p. 197.

138 "Charlotte Parents Initiate Moves Aimed at Utilizing Pearsall Plan's Provisions," *Southern School News*, August 1958, p. 15; *Raleigh News and Observer*, July 18, 1958.

139 Pride and Woodard, *The Burden of Busing*, pp. 55–56.

140 Quoted in Pride and Woodard, *The Burden of Busing*, p. 56.

141 "Kasper Raps School Decision; Has Run-In with Littlejohn," *Charlotte Observer*, September 2, 1957, p. 1B.

142 "White Citizens Council Organized by Kasper," *Charlotte Observer*, September 2, 1957, p. 1B.

143 Pride and Woodard, *The Burden of Busing*, p. 56; "Kasper Free Momentarily," *Charlotte Observer*, September 13, 1957, p. 1A.

144 Quoted in Leach, "Progress under Pressure," p. 18.

145 "Kasper Oil," *Charlotte Observer*, September 5, 1957, p. 1C.

146 "N.C. Supreme Court Validates Bonds," *Southern School News*, July 1956, p. 4.

147 Leach, "Progress under Pressure," pp. 25–26; "Officers Waited for Bombing Try," *Charlotte Observer*, February 17, 1958, p. 2A.

148 "Courts Ready 3 N.C. Cases for Action; School Bomb Try Nipped," *Southern School News*, March 1958, p. 6.

149 "Police Quiz Five in Bomb Plot," *Charlotte Observer*, February 16, 1958, p. 1A; "5 Charged in Plot to Dynamite School," *Charlotte Observer*, February 17, 1958, p. 1A; "Klansman Says Cole in Klan for Money," *Charlotte Observer*, February 19, 1958, p. 1B; "Ex-Klansman Says Cole Never Bared Funds," *Charlotte Observer*, February 21, 1958, p. 10C; "5 Klansmen Guilty of Cross Burning," *Charlotte Observer*, February 22, 1958, p. 10B; "3 Klansmen Receive Long Prison Terms," *Charlotte Observer*, March 21, 1958, p. 1A.

150 "Negro Girl Is Jeered at Harding," *Charlotte Observer*, September 5, 1957, p. 1A.

151 "Abusive Language Hurled at Harding Student," *Charlotte Observer*, September 5, 1957, p. 5A; National Education Association, *Three Cities That Are Making Desegregation Work*, p. 24.

152 "Integration: Third and Critical Phase," *New York Times Magazine*, November 27, 1960, p. 24.

153 "School Tension Subsides," *Charlotte Observer*, September 6, 1957, p. 1A; Leach, "Progress under Pressure," p. 22.

154 "Negro Has a Bad Day at Harding," *Charlotte Observer*, September 12, 1957, p. 1A; "Negro Girl Quits White High School," *Charlotte Observer*, September 13, 1957, p. 1A; "Integrated Schools Are Calm," *Charlotte Observer*, September 14, 1957, p. 1B; "On Sept. 4, 1957, Four Young Charlotte Students Braved Fear and Uncertainty to Take Their Place in History as School Desegregation Pioneers," *Charlotte Observer*, April 12, 1992, p. 1C.

155 "Negro Girl Quits White High School," *Charlotte Observer*, September 13, 1957, p. 1A; National Education Association, *Three Cities That Are Making Desegregation Work*, pp. 24–25; Gaillard, *Dream Long Deferred*, p. 8.

156 North Carolina Council on Human Relations, *Human Relations Bulletin*, (October 1957), p. 3 (citing an article on Counts in Lima, Peru, newspaper), Box 121-86, Frederick Alexander Papers; Muse, *Ten Years of Prelude*, pp. 114–15; Interview, Darius Swann, December 6, 1994; Gaillard, *Dream Long Deferred*, p. 8. The NAACP national office in New York City received letters from around the country expressing sympathy for Counts. Box III-A-105, NAACP Papers, Washington, D.C.

157 Watters, *Charlotte*, p. 46.

158 "On Sept. 4, 1957, Four Young Charlotte Students Braved Fear and Uncertainty to Take Their Place in History as School Desegregation Pioneers,"

Charlotte Observer, April 12, 1992, p. 1C; "School Tension Subsides," *Charlotte Observer*, September 6, 1957, p. 1A; Interview, Ed Sanders, October 12, 1992.

159 Interview, Ed Sanders, October 12, 1992.

160 Ibid.; "On Sept. 4, 1957, Four Young Charlotte Students Braved Fear and Uncertainty to Take Their Place in History as School Desegregation Pioneers," *Charlotte Observer*, April 12, 1992, p. 1C.

161 Wright, "Integration and Public Morals."

162 "Charlotte May Be Used as Integration Model," *Charlotte Observer*, December 2, 1959, p. 8B.

163 Charlotte Chamber of Commerce, *Charlotte*, January 1962, January 1963, August 1963, Box 114A-1, Frederick Alexander Papers.

164 "Three Localities Begin Desegregation; Total Now Stands at Seven," *Southern School News*, September 1959, p. 10.

165 Charlotte-Mecklenburg Council on Human Relations, "School Board Must Move toward Full Compliance."

166 "Brief of Respondents," *Swann v. Charlotte-Mecklenburg Board of Education*, 1970, p. 6, in Kurland and Casper, *Landmark Briefs and Arguments* 70:237.

167 Dale, "City-County Educational Consolidation in Charlotte and Mecklenburg," p. 3.

168 Ibid., pp. 107–41.

169 *Morrow v. Mecklenburg County Board of Education*, 195 F. Supp. 109 (W.D.N.C. 1961); "Durham, Greensboro, Mecklenburg Cases Pushed," *Southern School News*, May 1959, p. 10.

170 *Morrow v. Mecklenburg County Board of Education*, pp. 111–12.

171 Quoted in Peltason, *Fifty-Eight Lonely Men*, p. 8.

172 *Morrow v. Mecklenburg County Board of Education*, p. 114 (emphasis supplied).

173 Ibid., p. 112.

174 U.S. Commission on Civil Rights, *Civil Rights, U.S.A.*, p. 87.

175 "N.C. Highlights," *Southern School News*, May 1961, p. 9.

176 "Charlotte Builds Two Community Colleges; No Racial Restriction," *Southern School News*, May 1961, p. 9; "Charlotte to Get Equal Facilities," *Carolina Times*, August 20, 1949, p. 1.

177 "Courts Ready 3 N.C. Cases for Action; School Bomb Try Nipped," *Southern School News*, March 1958, p. 6.

178 *Wynn v. Trustees of the Charlotte Community College System*, 255 N.C. 594, 595, 122 S.E.2d 404, 405 (1961).

179 "Charlotte Builds Two Community Colleges; No Racial Restriction," *Southern School News*, May 1961, p. 9; "Plans for Colleges Target of Protest," *Charlotte Observer*, March 5, 1961, p. 1C; Charlotte-Mecklenburg Council on Human Relations, "The New Negro and Carver College," (August 1961), Public Library of Charlotte and Mecklenburg County, Charlotte; Leach, "Progress under Pressure," p. 87.

180 "Court Asked to Order Construction Halt on One of Two Charlotte College Units," *Southern School News*, June 1961, p. 5; Leach, "Progress under Pressure," p. 88.

181 Interview, Charles Jones, December 16, 1994.

182 "Court Dismisses Suit to Halt College Project," *Southern School News*, July 1961, p. 11.

183 *Wynn v. Trustees*, p. 601, 122 S.E.2d 409.

184 Leach, "Progress under Pressure," p. 89; "Campus Sells for $412,501," *Charlotte Observer*, December 21, 1965, p. 1C; "In the Colleges — Central Piedmont Operating Only as a Night School," *Southern School News*, March 1964, p. 10.

185 "Charlotte Builds Two Community Colleges; No Racial Restriction," *Southern School News*, May 1961, p. 9.

186 U.S. Commission on Civil Rights, *Civil Rights U.S.A.*, pp. 86, 89.

187 "Charlotte Changes Placement Policy; More Negroes Assigned," *Southern School News*, June 1962, p. 7.

188 U.S. Commission on Civil Rights, *Civil Rights U.S.A.*, p. 89; "Chapel Hill Refuses to Change Boundary Putting White Pupils in Negro Schools," *Southern School News*, September 1962, p. 17.

189 "Charlotte Changes Placement Policy; More Negroes Assigned," *Southern School News*, June 1962, p. 7.

190 U.S. Commission on Civil Rights, *Civil Rights U.S.A.*, p. 50; "Charlotte-Mecklenburg Assignment Plan Extended," *Southern School News*, June 1963, p. 13.

191 U.S. Commission on Civil Rights, *Civil Rights U.S.A.*, p. 90.

192 "Charlotte Changes Placement Policy; More Negroes Assigned," *Southern School News*, June 1962, p. 7.

193 "Burlington Inaugurates 4-Year Plan for Desegregating System," *Southern School News*, July 1963, pp. 13–14.

194 "Answer to Complaint," *Swann v. Charlotte-Mecklenburg*, February 5, 1965, p. 12, Chambers Papers.

195 "Complete Desegregation Ordered in Yancey County," *Southern School News*, October 1963, p. 5.

196 "Answer to Complaint," *Swann v. Charlotte-Mecklenburg*, February 5, 1965, p. 12, Chambers Papers.

197 Paul Ervin, "A National Day of Mourning," unpublished speech, June 9, 1968, p. 4, Ervin Papers, Atlanta; Interview, Paul Ervin, Jr., January 23, 1992.

198 Ervin was probably motivated as well by his own personal disagreement with the school board's segregationist policies. Ervin was a member of the North Carolina Advisory Committee on Civil Rights, which was charged with preparing a study of race relations in North Carolina. In the committee's October 1960 report, which Ervin had drafted and which was released just a few months before Warlick's decision, the committee recounted in detail the history of unequal education in North Carolina and concluded,

"Discrimination on account of race in public schools is general in North Carolina." "Integration Held Slow in N.C.," *Greensboro Daily News*, October 2, 1960, p. 1A.

199 *Griffith v. Board of Education of Yancey County*, 186 F. Supp. 512 (W.D.N.C. 1960).

200 *Vickers v. Chapel Hill Board of Education*, 196 F. Supp. 97, 101 (M.D.N.C. 1961).

201 *Wheeler v. Durham City Board of Education*, 309 F.2d 630, 633 (4th Cir. 1962).

202 "Thurgood Marshall Calls for Broader Desegregation Drive," *Southern School News*, June 1961, p. 5.

CHAPTER FOUR

1 Greenwood, *Bittersweet Legacy*, pp. 236–37.

2 Interview, Reginald Hawkins, October 12, 1992.

3 "7 Lunch Counters to Desegregate," *Charlotte Observer*, July 9, 1960, p. 1A.

4 Oppenheimer, *The Sit-In Movement of 1960*, pp. 121–22.

5 Interview, Charles Jones, December 16, 1994.

6 Oppenheimer, *The Sit-In Movement of 1960*, pp. 118–22.

7 Interview, Sidney Freeman, December 15, 1994.

8 "Ministers: Racial Fight Must End," *Charlotte Observer*, March 16, 1960, p. 1B.

9 Interview, Sidney Freeman, December 15, 1994; "By Nature Religious Pastor-Activist Saw Some Tumultuous Times," *Charlotte Observer*, January 29, 1989, p. 1B.

10 Interview, Charles Jones, December 16, 1994; "College Students Lead Lunch Counter Demonstrations," *Southern School News*, March, 1960, p. 3; Oppenheimer, *The Sit-In Movement of 1960*, p. 119.

11 Interview, Charles Jones, December 16, 1994; Oppenheimer, *The Sit-In Movement of 1960*, p. 121 (quotation).

12 Brookshire, "Brookshire Lives," University of North Carolina Library, North Carolina Collection, Chapel Hill.

13 "Mayor Asks Businessmen to Open Jobs to Negroes," *Charlotte Observer*, January 7, 1963, p. 7A; "Mayor: City Has Duty to Negroes," *Charlotte Observer*, October 10, 1962, p. 1E.

14 Stanford Brookshire to J. K. Clontz, February 14, 1963, Box 1-5, Charlotte-Mecklenburg Community Relations Committee Papers, Charlotte (UNCC).

15 "Ministers: Racial Fight Must End," *Charlotte Observer*, March 16, 1960, p. 1B.

16 Brookshire, "Unpublished Address," 1961, Box 26-4, Brookshire Papers, Charlotte.

17 Brookshire, "Charlotte's Response to the Civil Rights Movement," January

22, 1979, Box 36-1, Brookshire Papers; Oppenheimer, *The Sit-In Movement of 1960*, pp. 118–22.

18 Oppenheimer, *The Sit-In Movement of 1960*, pp. 121–23.

19 Brookshire, "Charlotte's Response to the Civil Rights Movement," January 22, 1979, p. 5, Box 36-1, Brookshire Papers.

20 "Editorial — The Merchants Have Made the Only Possible Decision," *Charlotte Observer*, July 10, 1960, p. 2E.

21 Oppenheimer, *The Sit-In Movement of 1960*, p. 179.

22 "NAACP Leader Criticizes Use of Placement Act," *Southern School News*, May 1961, p. 9.

23 Ibid.; "Harding Would Settle for Desegregation," *Charlotte Observer*, April 19, 1961, p. 11A.

24 "NAACP Leader Criticizes Use of Placement Act," *Southern School News*, May 1961, p. 9.

25 Interview, Reginald Hawkins, October 12, 1992; Davis, "A Multi-Disciplinary Critique," p. 86.

26 "King May Postpone NC Tour with Hawkins," *Charlotte Observer*, April 2, 1968, p. 1C.

27 Interview, Sidney Freeman, December 15, 1994.

28 Interview, Raymond Worsley, October 15, 1992.

29 "Only 300 Attend Irwin First Day," *Charlotte Observer*, September 1, 1961, p. 1B; "School-Boycott Leaders Seek More Public Support," *Charlotte Observer*, September 8, 1961, p. 4A.

30 "School Unit Told It Is Evading Desegregation Opportunities," *Charlotte Observer*, April 19, 1961, p. 11A.

31 "Only 300 Attend Irwin First Day," *Charlotte Observer*, September 1, 1961, p. 1B.

32 "Hawkins Heaps Abuse on School Officials," *Charlotte Observer*, September 4, 1961, p. 1C.

33 "Negro Group Ends Boycott of Irwin Ave. Junior High," *Charlotte Observer*, September 14, 1961, p. 1B; U.S. Commission on Civil Rights, *Civil Rights U.S.A.*, pp. 87–88.

34 "School Issue Discussed," *Raleigh News and Observer*, August 3, 1961, p. 31.

35 "NAACP, Schools Vie on Harding," *Charlotte News*, August 2, 1961, p. 1C.

36 "'Old Harding' Fight to Start," *Charlotte Observer*, August 16, 1961, September 4, 1961; Interview, Reginald Hawkins, October 12, 1992.

37 *Hawkins v. North Carolina Dental Society*, 355 F.2d 718 (4th Cir. 1966).

38 "Editorial — First Job of Both Races: To Retain Public Schools," *Charlotte Observer*, November 14, 1963, p. 2B (quotation); "Hawkins' Group Asks School Board for Integration Plan," *Charlotte Observer*, November 13, 1963, p. 7A; "School Bonds Get Support of NAACP," *Charlotte Observer*, November 13, 1963, p. 7A; "Negroes: Desegregate Now," *Charlotte News*, November 12, 1963, p. 1B.

39 "School Bonds Get Support of NAACP," *Charlotte Observer*, November 13, 1963, p. 7A.

40 "Editorial—NAACP Statement Provides Good Answer to 'Black Power,'" *Raleigh Times*, October 15, 1966, p. 4; "Anti-Christian Cult Attempting Southward Move," *Raleigh News and Observer*, September 11, 1960.

41 Greenwood, *Bittersweet Legacy*, pp. 111–12; Leach, "Progress under Pressure," pp. 128–29.

42 "Memorial Hospital Bond Issue Vital," *Charlotte Observer*, May 5, 1957, p. 1C; "Editorial—Hospital Need Overshadows Attempts to Confuse Issue," *Charlotte Observer*, May 7, 1957, p. 2B; Leach, "Progress under Pressure," p. 129; Halperin, "Special Report," p. 58.

43 "Negro Doctors Want Hospitals Desegregated," *Charlotte Observer*, July 18, 1961, p. 5A.

44 "Dickson Says Memorial Can't Admit Negroes," *Charlotte Observer*, October 20, 1959, p. 1B; Leach, "Progress under Pressure," pp. 131–32.

45 "Doctors Stymie Samaritan Project," *Charlotte Observer*, March 17, 1960, p. 1C.

46 "Resolutions Criticized by Dickson," *Charlotte Observer*, March 17, 1960, p. 1C.

47 "Negro Patients Get Additional Memorial Beds," *Charlotte Observer*, February 21, 1962, p. 1B (quotation); Leach, "Progress under Pressure," p. 136.

48 Halperin, "Special Report," p. 61.

49 "Brookshire Says He Regrets Pickets' Use of 'Coercion,'" *Charlotte Observer*, March 4, 1962, p. 16C.

50 "Injunction Is Sought on Rebuilding Funds," *Charlotte Observer*, July 24, 1962, p. 1B.

51 "Probe of Hospital 'Collusion' Asked," *Charlotte Observer*, June 23, 1962, p. 3A; "Memorial Hospital about to Get Second U.S. Investigation," *Charlotte Observer*, August 11, 1962, p. 1B.

52 "Discrimination May Be Cited at Memorial," *Charlotte Observer*, August 16, 1962, p. 1D; Halperin, "Special Report," p. 61.

53 "Chamber Action Significant One," *Charlotte Observer*, May 28, 1963, p. 1A.

54 Waynick, Brooks, and Pitts, *North Carolina and the Negro*, pp. 52–53.

55 Leach, "Progress under Pressure," p. 120.

56 "Picketing Scheduled by Negroes," *Charlotte News*, April 19, 1963, p. 1B.

57 Moye, "Charlotte-Mecklenburg Consolidation," p. 172.

58 "King Addresses 7,500 at Charlotte Commencement," *Southern School News*, June 1963, p. 13; "Charlotte Commencement Exercises Questioned," *Southern School News*, March 1963, p. 13.

59 "Charlotte Picketing Postponed," *Charlotte Observer*, April 21, 1963; "Chamber Action Significant One," *Charlotte Observer*, May 28, 1963, p. 1A; Brookshire to Reginald Hawkins, May 10, 1963, Box 1-5, Charlotte-Mecklenburg Community Relations Committee Papers, Charlotte (UNCC); Interview, Reginald Hawkins, October 12, 1992. Quotation from

"Hotels, Motels Open to Negroes," *Charlotte Observer*, April 24, 1963, p. 1B.

60 "Manger Is Target of Integrationists," *Charlotte Observer*, May 10, 1963, p. 1C; John Cunningham to Brookshire, May 13, 1963, Box 1-5, Charlotte-Mecklenburg Community Relations Committee Papers, Charlotte (UNCC).

61 "State Says Motel within the Law," *Charlotte Observer*, May 15, 1963, p. 1B.

62 "J. C. Smith Students March across Town," *Charlotte Observer*, May 21, 1963, p. 1B. Despite the traditional celebration of the signing of the Mecklenburg Declaration of Independence, the document's authenticity is questionable.

63 "Editorial—Charlotte Needs No 'D-Day' to Combat Discrimination," *Charlotte Observer*, May 22, 1963, p. 2C.

64 Moye, "Charlotte-Mecklenburg Consolidation," p. 165.

65 Blythe and Brockmann, *Hornets' Nest*, pp. 138–39.

66 "Editorial—Between Soup and Nuts, Progress," *Charlotte Observer*, March 13, 1958, p. 2B.

67 "Editorial," *Charlotte Observer*, February 12, 1960, p. 2B.

68 "Charlotte's Soul: An Adding Machine?," *Charlotte Observer*, December 13, 1961, p. 2B.

69 Cash, "Close View of a Calvinist Lhasa," p. 445.

70 Leach, "Progress under Pressure," p. 11.

71 Moye, "Charlotte-Mecklenburg Consolidation," p. 165.

72 "Brookshire May Run for Mayor," *Charlotte Observer*, April 5, 1961; Brookshire, "Brookshire Lives," University of North Carolina Library, North Carolina Collection, Chapel Hill; Interview, William Sturges, October 12, 1992.

73 Cramer, "School Desegregation and New Industry," p. 384.

74 "Business in Dixie: Many Southerners Say Racial Tension Slows Area's Economic Gains," *Wall Street Journal*, May 26, 1961, p. 1.

75 Watters, *Charlotte*, p. 39.

76 "Charlotte C of C Asks Firms to Serve All," *Charlotte Observer*, May 28, 1963, p. 1A.

77 Editorial, "Charlotte Needs No 'D-Day' to Combat Discrimination," *Charlotte Observer*, May 22, 1963, p. 2C.

78 "Charlotte C of C Asks Firms to Serve All," *Charlotte Observer*, May 28, 1963, p. 1A; "8 Hotels, Motels Will Desegregate," *Charlotte Observer*, May 30, 1963, p. 1A.

79 Waynick, Brooks, and Pitts, *North Carolina and the Negro*, pp. 54–57; Watters, *Charlotte*, p. 6.

80 "Charlotte Has Built Its Integration Road," *Charlotte Observer*, July 14, 1963, p. 1A.

81 John Cunningham, "Statement about the Mayor's Committee on Community Relations," June 1963, Box 1-5, Charlotte-Mecklenburg Community Relations Committee Papers, Charlotte (UNCC).

82 "Charlotte Has Built Its Integration Road," *Charlotte Observer*, July 14, 1963, p. 1A.

83 John Cunningham to Stanford Brookshire, Box 1-5, Charlotte-Mecklenburg Community Relations Committee Papers, Charlotte (UNCC).

84 Brookshire to Sherrill, telegram, June 13, 1963, Box 1-5, Charlotte-Mecklenburg Community Relations Committee Papers, Charlotte (UNCC); *Washington (D.C.) Daily News*, July 25, 1963.

85 Chafe, *Civilities and Civil Rights*, p. 169.

86 Ibid., p. 167; James Farmer, "Mass Action Makes N.C. Live Up to Liberal Reputation," *CORE-lator*, (July 1963), p. 1, University of North Carolina Library, North Carolina Collection, Chapel Hill; Meier and Rudwick, *CORE*, p. 217.

87 "Greensboro Race Crisis: A Summing Up," *Greensboro Daily News*, September 15, 1963, p. 1C.

88 "Turning Point 25 Years Ago, Charlotte Began New Era in Race Relations," *Charlotte Observer*, May 29, 1988, p. 1D.

89 Leach, "Progress under Pressure," p. 24.

90 "Editorial — Our State Won't Go Backward," *Charlotte Observer*, September 12, 1962, p. 2B.

91 Goldfield, *Black, White, and Southern*, p. 133.

92 Jacoway, "An Introduction," p. 8.

93 Bailey, *Southern White Protestantism*, p. 148; Sarratt, *The Ordeal of Desegregation*, pp. 285–86.

94 Cobb, *The Selling of the South*, p. 149.

95 "King Addresses 7,500 At Charlotte Commencement," *Southern School News*, June 1963, p. 13.

96 "Charlotte Has Built Its Integration Road," *Charlotte Observer*, July 14, 1963, p. 1A.

97 "Charlotte C of C Asks Firms to Serve All," *Charlotte Observer*, May 28, 1963, p. 1A; "Chamber Action Significant One," *Charlotte Observer*, May 28, 1963, p. 1A.

98 Brookshire, "This Decade of Progress or Peril," 1963, p. 8, Box 26-4, Brookshire Papers.

99 Watters, *Charlotte*, p. 9.

100 Robert Kennedy to Stanford Brookshire, June 24, 1963, and Brookshire to Kennedy, June 28, 1963, Box 1-5, Charlotte-Mecklenburg Community Relations Committee Papers, Charlotte (UNCC).

101 Thomas Francis to Stanford Brookshire, August 13, 1963, Box 1-5, Charlotte-Mecklenburg Community Relations Committee Papers, Charlotte (UNCC).

102 John Cunningham to Mayor's Committee, memorandum, August 23, 1963, Box 1-5, Charlotte-Mecklenburg Community Relations Committee Papers, Charlotte (UNCC).

103 See, e.g., Brookshire to Elwood Sachsenmaier, May 30, 1963, and E. C. Brandon, Jr., to William Veeder, June 4, 1963, Box 1-5, Charlotte-

Mecklenburg Community Relations Committee Papers, Charlotte (UNCC).

104 Watters, *Charlotte*, pp. 9, 22.

105 John Simon, President of APCO, Inc., to Brookshire, June 3, 1963, Box 1-5, Charlotte-Mecklenburg Community Relations Committee Papers, Charlotte (UNCC).

106 "Rights, Responsibility Called '2-Way Street,'" *Charlotte Observer*, July 6, 1963, p. 1B.

107 *New York Herald Tribune*, June 16, 1963, Box 26-4, Brookshire Papers.

108 Brookshire, "Guidelines in Community Relations," May 1963, Box 26-4, Brookshire Papers.

109 "Charlotte Has Built Its Integration Road," *Charlotte Observer*, July 14, 1963, p. 1A.

110 Charlotte Chamber of Commerce, *Charlotte*, January 1962, January 1963, August 1963, Box 114A-1, Frederick Alexander Papers, Charlotte.

111 "Charlotte C of C Asks Firms to Serve All," *Charlotte Observer*, May 28, 1963, p. 1A.

112 "Charlotte Has Built Its Integration Road," *Charlotte Observer*, July 14, 1963, p. 1A.

113 Watters, *Charlotte*, pp. 68, 81.

114 "Intermarriage Stand Attacked by Mayor," *Charlotte News*, February 25, 1963, p. 1B; Brookshire to Charles Jones, March 7, 1963, Box 1-5, Charlotte-Mecklenburg Community Relations Committee Papers, Charlotte (UNCC).

115 Ashmore, *Epitaph for Dixie*, p. 118.

116 Watters, *Charlotte*, p. 76.

117 Brookshire, unpublished speech, 1963, Box 26-4, Brookshire Papers.

118 Brookshire commented that he had left "impatient activists" off the committee. "Turning Point 25 Years Ago, Charlotte Began New Era in Race Relations," *Charlotte Observer*, May 29, 1988, p. 1D.

119 "Hawkins Says He May Ask U.S. Action," *Charlotte Observer*, June 24, 1963, p. 4B.

120 Brookshire to Hawkins, telegram, June 21, 1963, Box 26-4, Brookshire Papers.

121 "Memorial Staff Votes on July 9," *Charlotte Observer*, July 2, 1963, p. 1B.

122 "Open-Door Policy Starts Immediately," *Charlotte Observer*, August 24, 1963, p. 1B; "Hospital Race Bars Fall," *Charlotte News*, August 23, 1963, p. 1B.

123 "Mercy Complies with Rights Act," *Charlotte Observer*, July 21, 1965, p. 1C.

124 "Hawkins-Led Force Slated to Picket Central YMCA," *Charlotte Observer*, May 13, 1964, p. 15A.

125 "FBI Checks 2nd Rights Protest against YMCA," *Charlotte Observer*, August 16, 1964, p. 1C.

126 "YMCA's Integration Steps Are Revealed," *Charlotte Observer*, April 20, 1965, p. 1B.

127 "Hawkins, Special Registrar Indicted," *Charlotte Observer*, July 14, 1964, p. 1B.

128 "Hawkins Case Dismissed," *Charlotte News*, May 24, 1968, p. 1A.

129 "Board Accuses Charlotte Dentists of Malpractice," *Charlotte News*, July 31, 1967, p. 1B.

130 Hawkins had initiated an effort in 1960 to force the desegregation of the North Carolina Dental Society and ultimately filed a lawsuit, with NAACP support, seeking a court order compelling such action by the society. Hawkins prevailed in 1966 when the U.S. Court of Appeals for the Fourth Circuit held that the society's exclusion of black dentists from its membership violated the Constitution. *Hawkins v. North Carolina Dental Society*, 355 F.2d 718 (4th Cir. 1966).

131 "High Court Rejects 3 Dentists' Plea," *Charlotte Observer*, November 6, 1973, p. 2B.

CHAPTER FIVE

1 See, e.g., *Green v. School Board of the City of Roanoke*, 304 F.2d 118 (4th Cir. 1962); *Wheeler v. Durham City Board of Education*, 309 F.2d 630 (4th Cir. 1962).

2 "Desegregation: School Board Sees Some Changes," *Charlotte Observer*, February 3, 1965, p. 1B.

3 "Overcrowded Negro School Poses Problems," *Charlotte News*, December 4, 1964, p. 1B.

4 "Lawsuit against Cabarrus County Asks 1964 School Desegregation," *Southern School News*, November 1963, p. 4.

5 Petition, December 9, 1964, Chambers Papers, Charlotte.

6 "Integration Plan Bared," *Charlotte Observer*, January 7, 1965, p. 1C; "Pineville Area Desegregation Move Planned in Fall," January 8, 1965, p. 1C; "Are Local Schools Prepared for Single Policy on Race?," *Charlotte Observer*, January 15, 1965, p. 2C; "Negroes Offered Option in School Phase-Outs," *Charlotte News*, January 12, 1965, p. 5B.

7 "Complaint," *Swann v. Charlotte-Mecklenburg Board of Education*, January 1965, Chambers Papers.

8 "A Scholar Finds His Books," *Charlotte News*, May 19, 1961, p. 14A (reprinted from *Chapel Hill Weekly*); "He Hopes He's Set Example," *Charlotte Observer*, May 5, 1961, p. 8A; "Julius Chambers Waited a Long Time," *Charlotte Observer*, April 21, 1971, p. 2A.

9 "A Scholar Finds His Books," *Charlotte News*, May 19, 1961, p. 14A (reprinted from *Chapel Hill Weekly*).

10 *McKissick v. Carmichael*, 187 F.2d 949 (4th Cir.), *cert. denied*, 341 U.S. 951 (1951).

11 "He Hopes He's Set Example," *Charlotte Observer*, May 5, 1961, p. 8A;

"Negro Named Editor of Law Publication at State University," *Southern School News*, June 1961, p. 5; NAACP Press Release, "Top Law Student at University of North Carolina Is Lauded by NAACP," Box III-A-288, NAACP Papers, Washington, D.C. Chambers was also the first black student to serve as editor-in-chief of a law review at a southern state law school. Ibid.

12 "UNC Students Honor Negro," *Charlotte News*, April 17, 1962, p. 7A.

13 "A Scholar Finds His Books," *Charlotte News*, May 19, 1961, p. 14A (reprinted from *Chapel Hill Weekly*).

14 "How Did Attorney Earn Those Fees?," *Charlotte News*, March 18, 1975, p. 1B.

15 "Chambers a Low-Key Crusader," *Charlotte Observer*, July 27, 1965, p. 7A.

16 "Bombings Have Shocked New Bern," *Charlotte Observer*, January 31, 1965, p. 19A.

17 "Biracial Law Firm to Be Formed Here," *Charlotte Observer*, July 4, 1967, p. 10A.

18 Julius Chambers to Kelly Alexander, November 23, 1964, Chambers Papers.

19 "The Legacy of Busing Hearings a Time for Remembering Charlotte's Past," *Charlotte Observer*, January 10, 1988, p. 1C.

20 Interview, Darius Swann, December 6, 1944; Carlton Watkins, unpublished and undated essay on Charlotte's school desegregation experience. Watkins Papers, Charlotte.

21 Interview, Darius Swann, December 6, 1944; "The Legacy of Busing Hearings a Time for Remembering Charlotte's Past," *Charlotte Observer*, January 10, 1988, p. 1C.

22 Interview, Raymond Worsley, October 15, 1992; Interview, Darius Swann, December 6, 1944.

23 "Civil Rights Legacy Swann Suit Grew Out of Something Personal," *Charlotte Observer*, February 5, 1989, p. 1A.

24 Interview, Darius Swann, December 6, 1944; Darius Swann to Charlotte-Mecklenburg Board of Education, September 2, 1964, Chambers Papers.

25 "Negro Mother Challenges Pupil Assignment Plan," *Charlotte Observer*, September 4, 1964, p. 21A; Interview, Reginald Hawkins, October 12, 1992.

26 Interview, Darius Swann, December 6, 1944; "State Has 25 Newly Desegregated School Districts," *Southern School News*, October 1964, p. 5.

27 Interview, Darius Swann, December 6, 1944; Interview, Vera Swann, December 7, 1994.

28 "Minutes of the Board of Directors Meeting of the North Carolina Teachers Association, May 19, 1965," pp. 3, 9–10, Chambers Papers.

29 "Defendant's Proposed Findings of Fact and Conclusions of Law and Order," *Swann v. Charlotte-Mecklenburg Board of Education*, April 1969, p. 13, Horack Papers, Charlotte; "Deposition of William Poe," *Swann v.*

Charlotte-Mecklenburg Board of Education, January 29, 1969, p. 11, Chambers Papers.

30 *Bradley v. School Board of City of Richmond*, 345 F.2d 310, 320 (4th Cir. 1965).

31 Loftus Carson, "Community Approach toward Implementation of the Supreme Court Decision on Public Education in North Carolina," (1954), Box II-A-227, NAACP Papers, Washington, D.C. (noting in some parts of North Carolina strong opposition among black teachers to school desegregation on the grounds that they would lose their jobs).

32 Lamanna, "The Negro Public School Teacher and School Desegregation," p. 21.

33 "Negro Teacher Firings Rise in South," *Charlotte Observer*, July 8, 1965, p. 1A.

34 "Schools Warned on Negroes' Jobs," *New York Times*, June 11, 1965, p. 64.

35 Murray, *History of the North Carolina Teachers Association*, p. 93.

36 "Negro Teacher Firings Rise in South," *Charlotte Observer*, July 8, 1965, p. 1A.

37 Allen, "The Effects of School Desegregation on the Employment Status of Negro Principals in North Carolina," pp. 85–86, 94.

38 "Complaint in Intervention," *Swann v. Charlotte-Mecklenburg Board of Education*, June 1, 1965, Chambers Papers.

39 "Answer," *Swann v. Charlotte-Mecklenburg Board of Education*, February 5, 1965, p. 12, Chambers Papers; "Affidavit of David Harris," *Swann v. Charlotte-Mecklenburg Board of Education*, February 18, 1965, p. 1, Chambers Papers.

40 42 U.S.C. Sec. 2000d (1964).

41 Ibid., p. 2000d-1.

42 Wasby, D'Amato, and Metrailer, *Desegregation from Brown to Alexander*, p. 212.

43 U.S. Office of Education, *General Statement of Policies under Title VI*.

44 White House Conference, *To Fulfill These Rights*, p. 63.

45 "N.C. Ruling Says Schools Required to Desegregate," *Charlotte Observer*, January 27, 1965, p. 1B; "U.S. Law Orders Total, Complete School Integration in N.C.: Moody," *Raleigh News and Observer*, January 27, 1965, p. 1.

46 "N.C. Schools Agree to Comply on Rights," *Charlotte Observer*, February 12, 1965, p. 10A.

47 "New School, Desegregation Ahead for Southwest Area," *Charlotte Observer*, February 12, 1965, p. 16A.

48 "Pupil Assignment Plan to Be by Zones," *Charlotte Observer*, March 12, 1965, p. 1C; "Answer to Motion for Preliminary Injunction," *Swann v. Charlotte-Mecklenburg Board of Education*, May 27, 1965, p. 4, Chambers Papers.

49 Order, *Swann v. Charlotte-Mecklenburg Board of Education*, 4th Cir., August 24, 1965, p. 2, Chambers Papers.

50 March 11, 1965, resolution of Charlotte-Mecklenburg Board of Education, pp. 7–11, Chambers Papers.

51 *Swann v. Charlotte-Mecklenburg Board of Education*, 243 F. Supp. 667, 668 (W.D.N.C. 1965); "School Board Adopts Assignment by Zone," *Charlotte News*, March 11, 1965, p. 1A; "Pupil Assignments to Be by Zone," *Charlotte Observer*, March 12, 1965, p. 1B.

52 "School Faculties to Desegregate," *Charlotte Observer*, April 14, 1965, p. 1D.

53 Testimony of Reginald Hawkins, *Swann v. Charlotte-Mecklenburg Board of Education*, July 12, 1965, p. 31, Chambers Papers.

54 "Brief in Support of Motion for Injunction Pending Appeal," *Swann v. Charlotte-Mecklenburg Board of Education*, August 1965, p. 2, Chambers Papers.

55 "Affidavit of Julius L. Chambers," *Swann v. Charlotte-Mecklenburg Board of Education*, May 1965, pp. 1–2, Chambers Papers.

56 "Charlotte School Board Okays 2,919 Transfers," *Charlotte Observer*, July 6, 1965, p. 15A; Charlotte-Mecklenburg Schools, Pupil Assignment, 1965–66, Chambers Papers.

57 Craven, "Legal and Moral Aspects of the Lunch Counter Protests," *Chapel Hill Weekly*, April 28, 1960, p. 1B.

58 *Swann v. Charlotte-Mecklenburg Board of Education*, 243 F. Supp. 667, 670 (W.D.N.C. 1965).

59 Ibid. (emphasis in the original).

60 "School Race Suit Decision Due Today," *Charlotte Observer*, July 14, 1965, p. 1B.

61 *Swann v. Charlotte-Mecklenburg Board of Education*, 243 F. Supp. 667, 669 (W.D.N.C. 1965).

62 *Wheeler v. Durham City Board of Education*, 346 F.2d 768, 772–73 (4th Cir. 1965); *Nesbit v. Statesville City Board of Education*, 345 F.2d 333, 334–35 n. 3 (4th Cir. 1965).

63 *Swann v. Charlotte-Mecklenburg Board of Education*, 243 F. Supp. 667, 671 (W.D.N.C. 1965) (quoting *Bradley v. School Board of City of Richmond*, 345 F.2d 310, 320–21 [4th Cir. 1965]).

64 Ibid., 668.

65 Order, *Swann v. Charlotte-Mecklenburg Board of Education*, 4th Cir. August 24, 1965, Chambers Papers.

66 *Swann v. Charlotte-Mecklenburg Board of Education*, 369 F.2d 29, 32 (4th Cir. 1966) (en banc).

67 Judges Simon Sobeloff and Spencer Bell of the U.S. Court of Appeals for the Fourth Circuit had suggested as much in their separate opinion in *Bradley v. School Board of City of Richmond*, 345 F.2d 310, 321 (4th Cir. 1965).

68 *Swann v. Charlotte-Mecklenburg Board of Education*, 369 F.2d 29, 32 (4th Cir. 1966) (en banc).

69 Ibid., p. 33.

70 Ibid., pp. 29, 34 (Sobeloff, J., and Bell, J., concurring) (quoting *Bradley v.*

School Board of City of Richmond, 345 F.2d 310, 321 [4th Cir. 1965] [Sobeloff, J. and Bell, J., concurring in part and dissenting in part]) (emphasis in the original).

71 Schwartz, Swann's Way, p. 11.

72 "U.S. Accepts School Desegregation Plan," Charlotte Observer, August 13, 1965, p. 1B; "Negroes File School Desegregation Suit," Charlotte Observer, January 20, 1965, p. 8A.

73 "School Officials Told Substantial Integration Required," Raleigh News and Observer, March 19, 1966, p. 20.

74 U.S. Office of Education, Policies on Elementary and Secondary School Compliance.

75 "Desegregation in the Schools to Be Tripled," Charlotte Observer, July 6, 1965, p. 1B.

76 "School Board Plans Faculty Shift in Fall," Charlotte Observer, August 15, 1965, p. 1C; "School Board Plans Start of Faculty Desegregation," Charlotte Observer, August 18, 1965, p. 1D.

77 "Dan Reveals School Threats, Vows to Preserve Order," Charlotte Observer, August 27, 1965, p. 1A.

78 "County's 1st Day of School Is One of Smoothest Ever," Charlotte Observer, August 28, 1965, p. 1B.

79 "Law Agencies Mass to Probe Bombings," Charlotte Observer, November 23, 1965, p. 1A.

80 "Bomb News Flashed across U.S.," Charlotte Observer, November 23, 1965, p. 1A; "After Bombings, Nation Saw a Different Charlotte," November 24, 1965, p. 10A; "Roy Wilkins to Visit City: No Marches," Charlotte Observer, November 23, 1965, p. 2A; "4 Negro Homes Hit by Bombs in South," New York Times, November 23, 1965, p. 30; "Blasts Rip Charlotte Homes of 4 Civil Rights Leaders," Washington Post, November 23, 1965, p. A3.

81 "4 Negro Homes Hit by Bombs in South," New York Times, November 23, 1965, p. 30.

82 "After Bombings, Nation Saw a Different Charlotte," Charlotte Observer, November 24, 1965, p. 10A.

83 Ibid.

84 "Council Says Indignantly — 'Rebuild,'" Charlotte Observer, November 23, 1965, p. 1A.

85 "Charlotte Bomb Victims Get Material Aid and Sympathy," Charlotte Observer, November 24, 1965, p. 1A; "Anti-Terror Fund Gets Variety of Support," Charlotte Observer, December 3, 1965, p. 1A; "'Operation Rebuild' Plans Payment on 2 Negroes' Bombed Houses," Charlotte Observer, June 2, 1966, p. 1C.

86 "Crowd Packs Auditorium in Concern over Bombings," Charlotte Observer, November 29, 1965, p. 1A; "Voluntary Race Progress Needed," Charlotte Observer, December 11, 1965, p. 2B.

87 "City Should Fill the Hall to Express Bomb Outrage," Charlotte Observer, November 26, 1965, p. 2C.

88 "Good Attendance Sunday Will Repudiate Bombings — Mayor," *Charlotte Observer*, November 27, 1965, p. 1A.

89 "120 Ministers Meet at Site of Bombings," *Charlotte Observer*, December 6, 1965, p. 1C.

90 "Klan Growth Here Worries Stephens," *Charlotte News*, November 5, 1965, p. 1A.

91 "Suit to Halt Shrine Bowl Football Contest Is Filed," *Charlotte Observer*, November 13, 1965, p. 1B.

92 "The Decision Was Mine — Walker," *Charlotte Observer*, November 10, 1965, p. 6C.

93 "Court Won't Block Shrine Bowl Game," *Charlotte Observer*, November 20, 1965, p. 1B.

94 Harry Golden to Ralph McGill, November 29, 1965, Box 35-5, Kelly Alexander Papers, Charlotte.

95 Interview, Adam Stein, December 4, 1992.

96 "Local Negroes Call for End to Bias," *Charlotte Observer*, December 9, 1965, p. 1C; "Negroes' Deadline Passes Quietly," *Charlotte Observer*, December 11, 1965, p. 1B.

97 "Negroes Stress Need for Unity," *Charlotte Observer*, December 13, 1965, p. 1B.

98 "Voluntary Race Progress Needed," *Charlotte Observer*, December 11, 1965, p. 2B.

99 "County Schools Planning Athletic Desegregation," *Charlotte Observer*, December 15, 1965, p. 15A.

100 "Schools Will End Race Assignment," *Charlotte Observer*, April 22, 1966, p. 1B.

101 "Age, Parent Protests Are Major Causes," *Charlotte News*, May 12, 1966, p. 1B.

102 "Negroes Blast School Officials at Protest Rally," *Charlotte Observer*, May 14, 1966, p. 1C; "Angry Negroes Denounce Board," *Charlotte Observer*, May 18, 1966, p. 1B.

103 Interview, Reginald Hawkins, October 12, 1992.

104 "Chairman Explains School Board Reversal," *Charlotte News*, May 7, 1966, p. 1B.

105 *Swann v. Charlotte-Mecklenburg Board of Education*, 300 F. Supp. 1358, 1375–80 (W.D.N.C. 1969).

106 Hanchett, "Sorting Out the New South City," p. 520.

107 Orfield, *Public School Desegregation in the United States*, p. 8.

108 In July 1965, President Johnson replaced HEW Secretary Anthony Celebrezze with John Gardner, who then hired Harold Howe as commissioner of education. Under Gardner and Howe, HEW enforcement efforts increased. Metcalf, *From Little Rock to Boston*, p. 9.

109 U.S. Office of Education, *Revised Statement of Policies for School Desegregation Plans*, section 181.54.

110 Ibid.

111 North Carolina was the last southern state to experience a fund cutoff.

"Law Firm That Aided School Fight Dropped," *Charlotte Observer*, January 31, 1969, p. 1B.

112 "'Guidelines'—A Simple Word Becomes Bombshell," *Raleigh News and Observer*, May 29, 1966, p. 18I; "School Guidelines Come Under Fire," *Raleigh News and Observer*, April 8, 1966, p. 1.

113 HEW press release, January 16, 1969, Chambers Papers; "HEW Lists Southern Gains on School Desegregation," *Charlotte Observer*, January 19, 1969, p. 14A.

114 *Briggs v. Elliott*, 132 F. Supp. 776 (E.D. S.C. 1955).

115 The Fifth Circuit encompassed most of the states of the old Confederacy: Texas, Louisiana, Mississippi, Alabama, Georgia, and Florida.

116 Bass, *Unlikely Heroes*, pp. 41–53.

117 The three opinions were *Singleton v. Jackson Municipal Separate School District* (Singleton I), 348 F.2d 729 (5th Cir. 1965), *Singleton v. Jackson Municipal Separate School District* (Singleton II), 355 F.2d 865 (5th Cir. 1966), and *United States v. Jefferson County Board of Education* (Jefferson I), 372 F.2d 836 (5th Cir. 1966). A fourth significant Fifth Circuit decision during this time period was the circuit's en banc consideration of Jefferson I, *United States v. Jefferson County Board of Education* (Jefferson II), 380 F.2d 385 (5th Cir. 1967), a per curiam opinion.

118 *Singleton v. Jackson Municipal Separate School District* (Singleton I), p. 730 n. 5.

119 Ibid., p. 731.

120 Read, "Judicial Evolution of the Law of School Integration," p. 23.

121 *United States v. Jefferson County Board of Education* (Jefferson I), p. 848.

122 *United States v. Jefferson County Board of Education* (Jefferson II), pp. 385, 387 (emphasis supplied).

123 *Bradley v. School Board of City of Richmond*, 345 F.2d 310 (4th Cir. 1965); *Bowman v. County Board of Education*, 382 F.2d 326 (4th Cir. 1967).

124 *Bradley v. School Board of Richmond*, 382 U.S. 103 (1965); *Rogers v. Paul*, 382 U.S. 198 (1965).

125 Interview, Julius Chambers, August 16, 1993.

126 *Green v. County School Board*, 391 U.S. 430 (1968).

127 Ibid., p. 442.

128 WBTV Editorial, "Freedom of Choice Outlawed," May 31, 1968, Box 37–15, Kelly Alexander Papers.

129 "NAACP to Reopen Integration Suits," *Charlotte Observer*, May 29, 1968, p. 16A.

CHAPTER SIX

1 *Green v. County School Board*, 391 U.S. 430 (1968).

2 Motion for Further Relief, *Swann v. Charlotte-Mecklenburg Board of Education*, September 6, 1968, Chambers Papers, Charlotte.

3 Interview, Julius Chambers, August 16, 1993.

4 "Charlotte Bar Eyes District Judgeship," *Charlotte Observer*, October 22, 1967, p. 4C; "Lawyers Think Ervin Will Okay McMillan," *Charlotte News*, November 2, 1967, p. 1C.

5 "McMillan Elected District Bar Head," *Charlotte Observer*, June 18, 1957, p. 1B; "Mecklenburg Bar Supporting McMillan for Federal Judge," *Charlotte News*, November 9, 1967, p. 5A.

6 "Charlotteans Win Top NC Bar Positions," *Charlotte Observer*, June 21, 1959, p. 1D; "Terry Picks 2 for NC Board," *Charlotte News*, March 31, 1962; "Charlottean Named to Court Job," *Charlotte News*, August 9, 1963, p. 1B; "Local Lawyer Appointed to UA Position," *Charlotte News*, September 2, 1964.

7 "Bathing Pool in Charlotte Integrated," *Greensboro Daily News*, July 28, 1960, p. 1A; Interview, Joseph Grier, July 8, 1992.

8 Interview, William Sturges, October 12, 1992; Interview, James McMillan, October 11, 1989, Southern Oral History Program, University of North Carolina Library, Southern Historical Collection, Chapel Hill.

9 "'Lawyer' McMillan Will Soon Realize Dream of Judgeship," *Charlotte News*, May 13, 1968, p. 16B; Interview, Adam Stein, December 4, 1992.

10 Interview, James McMillan (with Walter H. Bennett), November 1, 1991, pp. 36–37, Southern Oral History Program, University of North Carolina Library, Southern Historical Collection, Chapel Hill.

11 Harry Golden to Robert Kennedy, June 30, 1966, Box 36–9, Kelly Alexander Papers, Charlotte; "McMillan Favored for Warlick Post," *Charlotte Observer*, February 18, 1968, p. 1C.

12 Statement of James B. McMillan, in U.S. Senate Committee on the Judiciary, *Hearings before the Subcommittee on the Separation of Powers*, p. 527; McMillan to Edward Hipp, December 18, 1969, Series 1.1, Folder 14, McMillan Papers, Chapel Hill.

13 Edward LaMotte to James McMillan, February 3, 1970, Series 1, Folder 17A, McMillan Papers.

14 H. Clay Hodges, "The Hard Light of Fact," pp. 9–11.

15 Interview, James McMillan, October 11, 1989, Southern Oral History Program, University of North Carolina Library, Southern Historical Collection, Chapel Hill; "Career of Courage, Compassion," *Charlotte Observer*, November 27, 1994, p. 1A.

16 "McMillan to Try for Senate Seat," May 22, 1961, p. 1B; "James B. McMillan Will Head UA Special Gifts, Professional Group," *Charlotte Observer*, September 3, 1964, p. 15A; "Chamber Unit Refuses to Review Position," *Charlotte Observer*, July 9, 1967, p. 3D; "McMillan Quits N.C. Senate Race," *Charlotte News*, November 25, 1961, p. 1A; "Terry Picks 2 for N.C. Board," *Charlotte News*, March 31, 1962, p. 12B; "Charlottean Named to Court Job," *Charlotte News*, August 9, 1963, p. 1B; "'Lawyer' McMillan Will Soon Realize Dream of Judgeship," *Charlotte News*, May 13, 1968, p. 16B.

17 "Justice's Quiet Spokesman: Judge McMillan's Modesty Belies His Impact since '68," *Charlotte Observer*, March 26, 1989, p. 1A (quoting Charlotte attorney Jonathan Wallas).

18 "McMillan Favored for Warlick Post," *Charlotte Observer*, February 18, 1968, p. 1C; "McMillan Interview 'Friendly,'" *Charlotte Observer*, May 9, 1968, p. 1B.

19 Statement of James B. McMillan, in U.S. Senate Committee on the Judiciary, *Hearings before the Subcommittee on the Separation of Powers*, p. 527.

20 Interview, James McMillan, October 11, 1989, p. 22, Southern Oral History Program, University of North Carolina Library, Southern Historical Collection, Chapel Hill. Judge John Parker had written the lower-court opinion upholding separate but equal in one of the four cases that constituted *Brown v. Board of Education*.

21 Statement of James B. McMillan, in U.S. Senate Committee on the Judiciary, *Hearings before the Subcommittee on the Separation of Powers*, p. 528.

22 McMillan was probably referring to a 1963 decision by the City of Rochester Board of Education to transfer 118 students from an almost all-black school to one that was virtually all white. The Appellate Division in New York eventually found that the board of education had the discretion to make such assignments notwithstanding the fact that one of the purposes for the transfer was "the desire to reduce to some extent the racial imbalance existing in the public schools." *Strippoli v. Bickal*, 250 N.Y.S.2d 969, 972, 21 A.D.2d 365 (1964).

23 "Bar Ass'n Told to Take Leadership in Race Relations," *Charlotte Observer*, June 29, 1961, p. 9A.

24 H. Clay Hodges, "The Hard Light of Fact," p. 2.

25 "Judge James McMillan: Catching the Desegregation Flak," *Raleigh News and Observer*, February 15, 1970. Further evidence of McMillan's willingness to challenge the status quo on civil rights issues came in 1967 in a chamber of commerce vote on whether to seek a constitutional amendment reversing *Baker v. Carr*, 369 U.S. 186 (1962), the Supreme Court decision that had struck down disproportionate legislative districts and that had been widely heralded as one of the high points of Warren Court activism. The chamber supported the amendment reversing *Baker*; McMillan was the lone dissenter and sought unsuccessfully to have the organization reconsider its position. "Chamber Unit Refuses to Review Position," *Charlotte Observer*, July 9, 1967, p. 3D.

26 "Editorial—Judge McMillan," *Charlotte News*, March 2, 1968, p. 12A.

27 "Mecklenburg Bar Supporting McMillan for Federal Judge," *Charlotte News*, November 9, 1967, p. 5A.

28 "'Lawyer' McMillan Will Soon Realize Dream of Judgeship," *Charlotte News*, May 13, 1968, p. 16B.

29 Interview, Adam Stein, December 4, 1992; Interview, Julius Chambers, August 16, 1993.

30 *Wheeler v. Goodman*, 298 F. Supp. 935, 942 (W.D.N.C. 1969).

31 Ibid.

32 Statement of James B. McMillan, in U.S. Senate Committee on the Judiciary, *Hearings before the Subcommittee on the Separation of Powers*, p. 528; Interview, James B. McMillan, August 27, 1981.

33 *Swann v. Charlotte-Mecklenburg Board of Education*, 300 F. Supp. 1358, 1372 (W.D.N.C. 1969).

34 "Charlotte Busing Winds Up Historic Year," *Durham Morning Herald*, May 18, 1972, p. 2D.

35 Statement of James B. McMillan in U.S. Senate Committee on the Judiciary, *Hearings before the Subcommittee on the Separation of Powers*, p. 528.

36 *Swann v. Charlotte-Mecklenburg Board of Education*, 66 F.R.D. 483, 484–85 (W.D.N.C. 1975).

37 Statement of James B. McMillan in U.S. Senate Committee on the Judiciary, *Hearings before the Subcommittee on the Separation of Powers*, p. 528.

38 Interview, Fred Hicks, October 14, 1992.

39 McMillan would later characterize the case as "an application of accepted constitutional principles to a hitherto unlitigated set of facts." *Swann v. Charlotte-Mecklenburg Board of Education*, 66 F.R.D. 483, 485 (W.D.N.C. 1975).

40 "Defendant's Proposed Findings of Fact and Conclusions of Law," *Swann v. Charlotte-Mecklenburg Board of Education*, March 31, 1969, p. 5, Chambers Papers.

41 Interview, William Poe, July 9, 1992.

42 Of the one hundred cities with the largest school systems in 1960, only thirteen were more residentially segregated than Charlotte. Taeuber and Taeuber, *Negroes in Cities*, pp. 32–34, 40–41; "Analysis of Student Enrollment and Professional Instructional Staff of One Hundred Largest School Districts," Chambers Papers.

43 "Statement of James McMillan," *Swann v. Charlotte-Mecklenburg Board of Education*, March 10, 1969, in U.S. Supreme Court Records and Briefs, pp. 36a, 45a, Williamsburg, Va.

44 See, e.g., *Deal v. Cincinnati Board of Education*, 369 F.2d 55, 60 n. 4 (6th Cir. 1966).

45 *Brewer v. School Board of the City of Norfolk*, 397 F.2d 37 (4th Cir. 1968).

46 Other courts had agreed with the Fourth Circuit's *Norfolk* decision. See, e.g., *Henry v. Clarksdale Municipal Separate School District*, 409 F.2d 682, 689 (5th Cir.), *cert. denied*, 396 U.S. 940 (1969): "A school board's zoning policy may appear to be neutral but in fact tend to retard desegregation because it binds pupils to custom-segregated neighborhoods."

47 "HEW Tightens School Guidelines," *Charlotte Observer*, March 18, 1969, p. 1A.

48 "Statement of James McMillan," *Swann v. Charlotte-Mecklenburg Board of Education*, March 16, 1969, in U.S. Supreme Court Records and Briefs, pp. 179a–82a, 218a.

49 *Swann v. Charlotte-Mecklenburg Board of Education*, 300 F. Supp. 1358, 1365–66 (W.D.N.C. 1969).

50 Hanchett, "Sorting Out the New South City," p. 520.

51 Ibid., pp. 499–507; "Birth of a Possible Ghetto—Obscure and Slow," *Charlotte Observer*, December 26, 1966, p. 1B; "The '60s in Charlotte a Decade of Challenge and Change," *Charlotte Observer*, January 15, 1989, p. 1C; Goldfield, *Black, White, and Southern*, p. 182; Testimony of Yale Rabin, *Swann v. Charlotte-Mecklenburg Board of Education*, March 1969, in U.S. Supreme Court Records and Briefs, p. 210a; *Swann v. Charlotte-Mecklenburg Board of Education*, 300 F. Supp. 1358, 1365 (W.D.N.C. 1969).

52 This practice was consistent with an express policy that the Charlotte School Board followed, before the *Brown* decision, of locating schools in the middle of single-race neighborhoods. "Natural Borders Would Stop Extensive City Integration," *Charlotte News*, June 3, 1955, p. 1A (quoting School Superintendent Elmer Garinger).

53 "Plaintiffs' Answers to Interrogatories," *Swann v. Charlotte-Mecklenburg Board of Education*, March 3, 1969, pp. 5–6, and "Plaintiffs Supplementary Proposed Findings of Fact," *Swann v. Charlotte-Mecklenburg Board of Education*, March 1969, pp. 2–7, both in Chambers Papers. To be sure, there were some notable exceptions to this practice of building schools in single-race neighborhoods. In the mid-1960s the school board chose not to place a new high school adjacent to York Road Junior High School, as planned, because of concerns that the school would be all black. Instead, the board found other property and built Olympic High School on the alternative site. The experience was repeated in the placement of Randolph Junior High School. Testimony of William Self, *Swann v. Charlotte-Mecklenburg Board of Education*, March 1969, in U.S. Supreme Court Records and Briefs, pp. 361a–62a. At the time of the March 1969 hearings, both Olympic High School and Randolph Junior High School were fully desegregated. *Swann v. Charlotte-Mecklenburg Board of Education*, 300 F. Supp. 1358, 1379–80 (W.D.N.C. 1969).

54 Transcript of Hearing, *Swann v. Charlotte-Mecklenburg Board of Education*, March 10, 1969, in Record on Appeal to United States Court of Appeals, p. 17, U.S. Courthouse, Charlotte.

55 *Swann v. Charlotte-Mecklenburg Board of Education*, 402 U.S. 1, 20–21 (1971).

56 *Allen v. Board of Public Instruction*, 312 F. Supp. 1127 (S.D. Fla.), rev'd, 432 F.2d 362 (5th Cir. 1970) (Ft. Lauderdale); *Flax v. Potts*, 333 F. Supp. 711 (N.D. Tex. 1970), rev'd, 450 F.2d 1118 (5th Cir. 1971) (Fort Worth); *Goss v. Board of Education*, 320 F. Supp. 549 (E.D. Tenn. 1970) (Knoxville); *Northcross v. Board of Education of Memphis*, 397 U.S. 232 (1970), and *Robinson v. Shelby County Board of Education*, 311 F. Supp. 97 (W.D. Tenn. 1970), rev'd, 442 F.2d 255 (6th Cir. 1971) (Memphis metropolitan area).

57 *Swann v. Charlotte-Mecklenburg Board of Education*, 300 F. Supp. at 1379–80 (W.D.N.C. 1969).

58 Colloquy, *Swann v. Charlotte-Mecklenburg Board of Education*, March 10, 1969, in U.S. Supreme Court Records and Briefs, p. 191a.

59 *Green v. County School Board*, pp. 430, 432.

60 *Swann v. Charlotte-Mecklenburg Board of Education*, 300 F. Supp. 1358, 1360 (W.D.N.C. 1969). In 1969, the Charlotte-Mecklenburg school system was the forty-third largest in the United States. Ibid., p. 1364.

61 "Plaintiffs' Proposed Findings of Fact and Conclusions of Law and Order," *Swann v. Charlotte-Mecklenburg Board of Education*, March 1969, p. 19, Chambers Papers.

62 "Attorney's Goal: Total Integration," *Charlotte News*, May 8, 1969, p. 1A.

63 Oral Argument, *Swann v. Charlotte-Mecklenburg Board of Education*, in Kurland and Casper, *Landmark Briefs and Argument* 70:608–10.

64 *Swann v. Charlotte-Mecklenburg Board of Education*, 300 F. Supp. 1358, 1363 (emphasis in the original), 1372 (W.D.N.C. 1969).

65 Ibid., pp. 1361, 1372 (emphasis in the original), 1368.

66 Ibid., pp. 1371, 1373.

67 Ibid., p. 1369 (emphasis in the original).

68 "Poe Calls Court Rule Revolutionary," *Charlotte Observer*, April 25, 1969; "School Board Splits 5–4 against Appeal," *Charlotte Observer*, April 29, 1969, p. 1C.

69 "Who's Deciding School Issue?," *Charlotte Observer*, May 7, 1969, p. 1C; "Poe Says He Won't Seek Reelection to School Board," *Charlotte News*, April 26, 1971, p. 1A; "Poe Won't Run for Board Again," *Charlotte News*, April 16, 1976, p. 1A.

70 "Dr. Hawkins Will Support Scott, Poe," *Charlotte Observer*, June 25, 1964, p. 11A.

71 Interview, Julia Maulden, December 14, 1994; Interview, Carlton Watkins, July 6, 1992.

72 "Aftershocks," *Charlotte Observer*, May 13, 1979, p. 14A; Interview, William Poe, July 9, 1992.

73 Quoted in "Editorial—Board of Education Wavers from True Academic Goals," *Charlotte Observer*, May 19, 1966, p. 2C.

74 "Poe Says Quarrel with Judge, Not Law," *Charlotte Observer*, May 2, 1969, p. 8A.

75 Interview, Robert Culbertson, October 14, 1992; Interview, Adam Stein, December 4, 1992.

76 "Smith Calls Court Ruling 'Disruptive,'" *Charlotte Observer*, April 25, 1969, p. 1B.

77 "Courts Must Decide Schools' Racial Issue," *Charlotte Observer*, May 25, 1969, p. 1B.

78 "'We'll Learn the Hard Way,'" *Charlotte Observer*, June 18, 1969, p. 1A.

79 "2,000 Turn Out to Protest 'Busing' School Children," *Charlotte Observer*, May 3, 1969, p. 1C.

80 "The Paper War," *Charlotte Focus* 1, no. 6 (1970): 1, in Series 1, Folder 33, McMillan Papers.

81 "Out of the Court and into the Future — with Hope," *Charlotte Observer*, July 12, 1975, p. 1A.

82 See Formisano, *Boston against Busing*.

83 "The Paper War," *Charlotte Focus* 1, no. 6 (1970): 1, in Series 1, Folder 33, McMillan Papers.

84 "Fear of 'Busing' Premature, Say School Officials," *Charlotte Observer*, May 4, 1969, p. 1C.

85 "Chairman Explains School Board Reversal," *Charlotte News*, May 7, 1966, p. 1B.

86 Quoted in Maniloff, "Community Attitudes," p. 90.

87 "Plaintiffs' Proposed Findings of Fact, Conclusions of Law and Order," *Swann v. Charlotte-Mecklenburg Board of Education*, March 2, 1970, p. 6, Chambers Papers.

88 Barrows, "School Busing," p. 18.

89 "Note: New Perspectives on Court Ordered Busing," pp. 329–33.

90 Testimony of Marion Wright Edelman, Washington Research Group, in U.S. Senate Committee on Labor and Public Welfare, *Hearings before the Subcommittee on Education*, p. 625.

91 Tom Wicker, "In the Nation: The Outcry against Busing," *New York Times*, March 8, 1970, p. 11E.

92 *Morrow v. Mecklenburg County Board of Education*, 195 F. Supp. 109 (W.D.N.C. 1961).

93 McMillan to Mrs. C. A. Hartis, December 12, 1969, Series 1.1, Folder 14, McMillan Papers.

94 "Judge: Support School Board," *Charlotte Observer*, May 2, 1969, p. 1A.

95 See, e.g., "Judge Talks to Critics," *Charlotte News*, November 8, 1969, p. 1A; "'Can't Rise above Law,' Judge Says," *Charlotte News*, January 14, 1970, p. 4A; "Double Standard for Judges," *Charlotte Observer*, December 18, 1969; "Old-Style Schools Miss the Boat — McMillan," *Charlotte Observer*, January 18, 1974, p. 1B.

96 "Law Made by Statute and Judicial Decision," *Charlotte Observer*, May 7, 1969.

97 "Judge: Support School Board," *Charlotte Observer*, May 2, 1969, p. 1A.

98 "Old-Style Schools Miss the Boat — McMillan," *Charlotte Observer*, January 18, 1974, p. 1B (emphasis supplied).

99 "Poe Says Quarrel with Judge, Not Law," May 2, 1969, p. 8A; "Judge: Support School Board," *Charlotte Observer*, May 2, 1969, p. 1A.

100 Interview, Julia Maulden, December 14, 1994; Interview, Fred Hicks, October 14, 1992; Interview, Adam Stein, December 4, 1992; Interview, James McMillan, August 27, 1981; McMillan to Lee Abernethy, Jr., December 10, 1969, Series 1.1, Folder 14, McMillan Papers; "Judge, School Board Delegates to Confer," *Charlotte Observer*, June 14, 1973, p. 1A.

101 "Negroes Back Court Order, Rap School Board Action," *Charlotte News*, May 28, 1969.

102 Alabama Council on Human Relations, "It's Not Over in the South: Desegregation in Forty-Three Southern Cities Eighteen Years after Brown,"

(May 1972), p. 28, Charlotte-Mecklenburg Community Relations Committee Papers, Charlotte (CMCRC).

103 See, e.g., "The School Decision In Detail: Here's What the Judge Said," *Charlotte Observer*, May 5, 1969, p. 1A; Claiborne, *The Charlotte Observer*, pp. 287–88.

104 "Editorial—C. A. McKnight," *Charlotte Observer*, May 11, 1969, p. 1C.

105 Claiborne, *The Charlotte Observer*, pp. 274–75.

106 "Editorial—Board, Parents Must Offer 'Conspicuous Public Service,'" *Charlotte Observer*, May 1, 1969.

107 Claiborne, *The Charlotte Observer*, p. 290.

108 Rossell, "Desegregation Plans, Racial Isolation, White Flight, and Community Response," pp. 35–36.

109 Claiborne, *The Charlotte Observer*, p. 288.

110 L. M. Wright, Jr., to C. A. McKnight, memorandum, June 26, 1969, and June 27, 1969, Watkins Papers, Charlotte.

111 Claiborne, *The Charlotte Observer*, p. 291.

112 See, e.g., "Editorial—Some Thoughts and Hopes as the Local Schools Approach a Turning Point," *Charlotte News*, January 31, 1970, p. 14A.

113 "Board to Fight for Neighborhood Schools," *Charlotte Observer*, May 20, 1969, p. 1A.

114 "Judge Hopes for 'Useful' Decision," *Charlotte Observer*, June 19, 1969, p. 1A.

115 "School Board Splits 5–4 against Appeal," *Charlotte Observer*, April 29, 1969, p. 1C; *Swann v. Charlotte-Mecklenburg Board of Education*, 300 F. Supp. 1381, 1382 (W.D.N.C. 1969).

116 "Plaintiffs' Response to Defendants' Plan for Desegregation of Schools and Motion for Civil Contempt," *Swann v. Charlotte-Mecklenburg Board of Education*, June 11, 1969, p. 3, Chambers Papers.

117 James McMillan to William Waggoner and Brock Barkley, May 5, 1969, Chambers Papers; "Judge Offers School Board More Time," *Charlotte Observer*, May 7, 1969, p. 1A.

118 "U.S. Court Asked to Halt Local School Construction," *Charlotte Observer*, May 16, 1969, p. 1B.

119 McMillan memorandum to the file, July 18, 1969, Series 1.1, Folder 35, McMillan Papers.

120 *Swann v. Charlotte-Mecklenburg Board of Education*, 300 F. Supp. 1381, 1383–84 (W.D.N.C. 1969).

121 "Mrs. Kelly Charges Poe Intimidation Try," *Charlotte Observer*, June 18, 1969, p. 1A; "Poe Denies Charges; School Hearing Ends," *Charlotte Observer*, June 22, 1969, p. 1A; Memorandum of telephone conversation between Mrs. Betsey Kelly and Mr. Hicks, June 11, 1969, McMillan Papers. Watkins denied he tried to unseat Poe. Interview, Carlton Watkins, July 6, 1992.

122 *Swann v. Charlotte-Mecklenburg Board of Education*, 300 F. Supp. 1381, 1383 (W.D.N.C. 1969).

123 *Martin v. Charlotte-Mecklenburg Board of Education*, 475 F. Supp. 1318, 1329 (W.D.N.C. 1979); Interview, James B. McMillan, August 27, 1981.

124 "Chambers: Orders Disobeyed," *Charlotte Observer*, June 17, 1969, p. 1A.

125 *Swann v. Charlotte-Mecklenburg Board of Education*, 300 F. Supp. 1381, 1382 (W.D.N.C. 1969).

126 "'We'll Learn the Hard Way,'" *Charlotte Observer*, June 18, 1969, p. 1A.

127 "Mrs. Kelly Charges Poe Intimidation Try," *Charlotte Observer*, June 18, 1969, p. 1A.

128 "'We'll Learn the Hard Way,'" *Charlotte Observer*, June 18, 1969, p. 1A; "Poe Denies Charges; School Hearings End," *Charlotte Observer*, June 19, 1969, p. 1A; Memorandum of telephone conversation between Mrs. Betsey Kelly and Mr. Hicks, June 11, 1969, McMillan Papers.

129 "Chambers Attacks School Plan," *Charlotte Observer*, June 13, 1969, p. 1B.

130 *Swann v. Charlotte-Mecklenburg Board of Education*, 300 F. Supp. 1381, 1386 (W.D.N.C. 1969).

131 "Judge Hopes for 'Useful' Decision," *Charlotte Observer*, June 19, 1969, p. 1A.

132 *Swann v. Charlotte-Mecklenburg Board of Education*, 300 F. Supp. 1381, 1382 (W.D.N.C. 1969).

133 *Swann v. Charlotte-Mecklenburg Board of Education*, 306 F. Supp. 1291, 1295 (W.D.N.C. 1969); "Plaintiffs' Supplemental Complaint," *Swann v. Charlotte-Mecklenburg Board of Education*, July 1969, Chambers Papers; N.C.G.S. Sec. 115–176.1 (Supp. 1969).

134 "Law Firm Plans Test of Antibusing Law," *Charlotte Observer*, July 3, 1969.

135 "Agnew Speaks Soothing Words to South's GOP," *Charlotte Observer*, July 12, 1969, p. 1A.

136 Orfield, *Must We Bus?*, p. 242; "Nixon Hits Guidelines on Schools," *Washington Post*, September 13, 1968, p. 1A; "Nixon Scores U.S. Method of Enforcing Integration," *New York Times*, September 13, 1968, p. 1.

137 "How U.S. Has Softened School Integration Policy," *Charlotte Observer*, May 3, 1970, p. 1B.

138 Interview, James B. McMillan, August 27, 1981.

139 Statement of Ruby B. Martin, Washington Research Project, in U.S. Senate Committee on Labor and Public Welfare, *Hearings before the Subcommittee on Education*, p. 529.

140 *Swann v. Charlotte-Mecklenburg Board of Education*, 306 F. Supp. 1291, 1296 (W.D.N.C. 1969).

141 Charlotte-Mecklenburg Board of Education, "Report in Connection with Amendment to Plan for Further Desegregation," August 4, 1969, Chambers Papers.

142 Even the plaintiffs' proposed plan had recommended closing five of the black schools. Jack Larsen, John Finger, and Robert Passy, "The Charlotte-Mecklenburg School System: Analysis and Recommendations," p. 3, Charlotte-Mecklenburg Community Relations Committee Papers, Char-

lotte (CMCRC); Charlotte-Mecklenburg Board of Education, "Report in Connection with Amendment to Plan for Further Desegregation," August 4, 1969, Chambers Papers.

143 "School Plan Attacked, Defended at Hearing," *Charlotte Observer*, August 6, 1969, p. 1A.

144 "Agreement on Schools Collapses," *Charlotte Observer*, August 13, 1969, p. 1C; *Swann v. Charlotte-Mecklenburg Board of Education*, 306 F. Supp. 1291, 1293 (W.D.N.C. 1969).

145 "Protestors Still Adamant in Rejection," *Charlotte News*, August 16, 1969, p. 1A; "The School Situation Is Worsening, Who Is Responsible," *Star of Zion*, August 14, 1969, p. 4.

146 See, e.g., "Resolution of Simpson-Gillespie United Methodist Church," October 6, 1969, Series 1.1, Folder 14, McMillan Papers.

147 *Swann v. Charlotte-Mecklenburg Board of Education*, 243 F.2d 667, 671 (W.D.N.C. 1965).

148 Defendants' Brief, *Swann v. Charlotte-Mecklenburg Board of Education*, March 1969, p. 12, and "Defendant's Proposed Findings of Fact and Conclusions of Law and Order," *Swann v. Charlotte-Mecklenburg Board of Education*, April 1969, p. 15, both in Chambers Papers.

149 Bell, "Serving Two Masters," pp. 485–87.

150 "Why School Busing Is in Trouble," *U.S. News and World Report*, October 13, 1969, p. 42.

151 Fred Hicks to James McMillan, memorandum, August 7, 1969, Series 1, Box 4, Folder 35, McMillan Papers.

152 Orfield, *Must We Bus?*, p. 415 n. 67.

153 Interview, Julius Chambers, August 16, 1993.

154 Interview, Darius Swann, December 6, 1994.

155 *Swann v. Charlotte-Mecklenburg Board of Education*, 306 F. Supp. 1291, 1293 (W.D.N.C. 1969).

156 "School Plan Attacked, Defended at Hearing," *Charlotte Observer*, August 6, 1969, p. 1A.

157 Transcript of Testimony, *Swann v. Charlotte-Mecklenburg Board of Education*, August 5, 1969, in Record on Appeal to United States Court of Appeals, pp. 53–55, U.S. Courthouse, Charlotte.

158 Testimony of William Self, August 5, 1969, *Swann v. Charlotte-Mecklenburg Board of Education*, in U.S. Supreme Court Records and Briefs, p. 528a.

159 Ibid., pp. 546a, 530a, 533a.

160 *Swann v. Charlotte-Mecklenburg Board of Education*, 306 F. Supp. 1291, 1296, 1298 (W.D.N.C. 1969).

161 Colloquy, *Swann v. Charlotte-Mecklenburg Board of Education*, August 5, 1969, in U.S. Supreme Court Records and Briefs, pp. 569a–570a.

162 *Swann v. Charlotte-Mecklenburg Board of Education*, 306 F. Supp. 1291, 1297 (W.D.N.C. 1969).

163 Ibid., p. 1294 (emphases in the original).

164 Ibid., p. 1293.

165 "Editorial—Public's Reaction Should Be as Sound as Judge's Ruling," *Charlotte Observer*, August 17, 1969, p. 2C.

166 Interview, Adam Stein, December 4, 1992.

167 Testimony of Julia Maulden, in U.S. House Committee on the Judiciary, *Hearings before Subcommittee No. 5*, p. 1304.

168 *Swann v. Charlotte-Mecklenburg Board of Education*, 306 F. Supp. 1291, 1297 (W.D.N.C. 1969).

169 Interview, William Sturges, October 12, 1992.

170 Statement of James B. McMillan, in U.S. Senate Committee on the Judiciary, *Hearings before the Subcommittee on the Separation of Powers*, p. 529.

171 *Swann v. Charlotte-Mecklenburg Board of Education*, 306 F. Supp. 1291, 1297 (W.D.N.C. 1969).

172 McMillan to Mrs. R. Zach Thomas, November 17, 1969, Series 1.1, Folder 14, McMillan Papers.

173 Graglia, *Disaster by Decree*, pp. 105–11.

174 See, e.g., Crain and Mahard, "Desegregation and Black Achievement."

CHAPTER SEVEN

1 "Desegregation below Total Envisioned in Board's Plan," *Charlotte News*, November 11, 1969, p. 1B.

2 *Swann v. Charlotte-Mecklenburg Board of Education*, 306 F. Supp. 1299, 1303–4 (W.D.N.C. 1969).

3 *Alexander v. Holmes County*, 396 U.S. 19 (1969) (per curiam).

4 Orfield, *Must We Bus?*, p. 326 (quoting Greenberg, "Revolt at Justice," p. 24).

5 Orfield, *Must We Bus?*, pp. 326–27.

6 *Alexander v. Holmes County*, p. 20.

7 Cooper v. Aaron, 358 U.S. 1 (1958).

8 "All Public Schools Must Desegregate at Once, Supreme Court Rules," *Charlotte Observer*, October 30, 1969, p. 1A.

9 *Swann v. Charlotte-Mecklenburg Board of Education*, 306 F. Supp. 1299, 1301 (W.D.N.C. 1969).

10 Ibid., p. 1301.

11 Ibid., pp. 1305–6 (quoting the school board's plan) (emphasis in the original).

12 Ibid., p. 1306.

13 Ibid., p. 1307 (quoting the school board's plan) (emphasis in the original).

14 Ibid., p. 1308.

15 "Editorial—School Board Passing Buck to Courts on Desegregation," *Charlotte Observer*, November 18, 1969, p. 2C.

16 "Lawyers Attack School Plan," *Charlotte Observer*, November 22, 1969, p. 1C.

17 *Swann v. Charlotte-Mecklenburg Board of Education*, 306 F. Supp. 1299, 1314 (W.D.N.C. 1969).

18 James McMillan to Jesse Riley, November 18, 1969, Series 1.1, Folder 14, McMillan Papers, Chapel Hill.

19 At least one other judge had done so in Oklahoma City. *Dowell v. School Board of Oklahoma City*, 244 F. Supp. 971 (W.D. Okla. 1965).

20 Rule 53 of the *Federal Rules of Civil Procedure* permits district courts in nonjury cases to name special masters or experts in "any action . . . upon a showing that some exceptional condition requires it." Judge Jack Weinstein later relied in part on McMillan's actions to justify his appointment of a special master in the Coney Island school desegregation case. *Hart v. Community School Board*, 383 F. Supp. 699, 766 (E.D. N.Y. 1974), *aff'd*, 512 F.2d 37 (2d Cir. 1975).

21 "Like Raleigh, Charlotte Races with Time," *Raleigh News and Observer*, February 1, 1970, p. 1I.

22 The Fourth Circuit later mildly chastised McMillan for the selection of Finger but found that the "error, if any, in his selection, was harmless." *Swann v. Charlotte-Mecklenburg Board of Education*, 431 F.2d 138, 148 (4th Cir. 1970).

23 "Interim School Plan May Be Drawn Soon," *Charlotte Observer*, December 5, 1969, p. 1C.

24 *Swann v. Charlotte-Mecklenburg Board of Education*, 306 F. Supp. 1299, 1313 (W.D.N.C. 1969).

25 "Editorial — Board Has Its Last Chance to Help Draw School Plan," *Charlotte Observer*, December 3, 1969, p. 2D.

26 "School Board Puts Off Decision on Ruling," *Charlotte Observer*, December 9, 1969, p. 1C.

27 *Swann v. Charlotte-Mecklenburg Board of Education*, 306 F. Supp. 1299, 1304–5 (W.D.N.C. 1969).

28 "Editorial — Schools: Appeal Needed," *Charlotte News*, November 11, 1969, p. 10A.

29 *Beckett v. School Board of City of Norfolk*, 308 F. Supp. 1274, 1279 (E.D. Va. 1969).

30 "3 Virginia Schools Get Rulings," *Charlotte Observer*, August 13, 1970, p. 2A.

31 "Virginia Judge's Views Differ from McMillan's," *Charlotte News*, January 9, 1970, p. 1A.

32 "New Court Decision Puts Appeal in Doubt," *Charlotte Observer*, December 3, 1969, p. 1D.

33 James McMillan to James Johnson, December 10, 1969, Series 1, Folder 14, McMillan Papers.

34 James McMillan to Jesse Riley, November 18, 1969, Series 1, Folder 14, McMillan Papers.

35 *Swann v. Charlotte-Mecklenburg Board of Education*, 306 F. Supp. 1299, 1305 (W.D.N.C. 1969).

36 *Nesbit v. Statesville City Board of Education*, 418 F.2d 1040 (4th Cir. 1969) (en banc).

37 "New Court Decision Puts Appeal in Doubt," *Charlotte Observer*, December 3, 1969, p. 1D.

38 "Mixing Delay OK If Board Skips Appeal?," *Charlotte News*, December 10, 1969; "Mid-Year Mixing Feared," *Charlotte News*, December 31, 1969, p. 1A; "Appeal Now 'Premature, Unwise'—School Board," *Charlotte Observer*, January 1, 1970, p. 1B.

39 James McMillan to Charles Myers, December 9, 1969, Series 1, Folder 14, McMillan Papers.

40 *Stanley v. Darlington County School District*, 424 F.2d 195, 196–97 (4th Cir. 1970).

41 Frank, *Clement Haynsworth*, p. 30.

42 "Haynsworth 'Unfit' For High Court, Says Negro Leader," *Charlotte Observer*, November 5, 1969, p. 4C.

43 *Carter v. West Feliciana Parish School Board*, 396 U.S. 290 (1970) (per curiam).

44 Ibid., p. 293 (Harlan and White, concurring) and (Black, Douglas, Brennan and Marshall, concurring).

45 "Plaintiffs Petition for Writ of Certiorari," p. 7, *Swann v. Charlotte-Mecklenburg Board of Education*, in Kurland and Casper, *Landmark Briefs and Arguments* 70:18.

46 "Statesville School Plan Approved," *Asheville Citizen*, December 20, 1969, p. 1; "Statesville Told to Pair 4 Schools," *Charlotte Observer*, December 20, 1969, p. 1C.

47 Statement of James B. McMillan, in U.S. Senate Committee on the Judiciary, *Hearings before the Subcommittee on the Separation of Powers*, pp. 529–30.

48 "Motion to Vacate Partial Suspension of, and to Reinstate an Order of the United States District Court for the Western District of North Carolina Ordering Implementation of a School Desegregation Plan," *Swann v. Charlotte-Mecklenburg Board of Education*, March 9, 1970, Chambers Papers, Charlotte.

49 *Swann v. Charlotte-Mecklenburg Board of Education*, 311 F. Supp. 265, 270 (W.D.N.C. 1970); Systems Associates Report, Inc., January 23, 1970, p. 1, Chambers Papers.

50 "Nation Listens as Judges Hear School-Case Debate," *Charlotte Observer*, April 10, 1970, p. 1A.

51 *Charlotte Observer*, February 3, 1970.

52 "175 Get Inside, 500 Stand in Hall," *Charlotte News*, February 3, 1970, p. 8A.

53 "More School Mixing Sure This Year," *Charlotte News*, February 3, 1970, p. 1A. A few days earlier, another Jim McMillan, of Charlotte, had died.

54 Ibid.

55 Testimony of William Self, *Swann v. Charlotte-Mecklenburg Board of Ed-*

ucation, February 3, 1970, in U.S. Supreme Court Records and Briefs, Williamsburg, Va., pp. 773a–74a.

56 "School Hearing Lays Groundwork for Appeal of Local Court Decision," *Charlotte Observer*, February 6, 1970, p. 5A.

57 *Swann v. Charlotte-Mecklenburg Board of Education*, 311 F. Supp. 265, 269 (W.D.N.C. 1970).

58 Ibid.

59 Ibid., p. 270.

60 "Like Raleigh, Charlotte Races with Time," *Raleigh News and Observer*, February 1, 1970, p. 1I.

61 "Moderate Leaders Fall Silent in South," *New York Times*, February 23, 1970, p. 1A.

62 "Nation Listens as Judges Hear School-Case Debate," *Charlotte Observer*, April 10, 1970, p. 1A.

63 "McMillan's Home Picketed," *Charlotte Observer*, February 9, 1970, p. 4C; "Prosecution of Pickets at Judge's Home Vowed," *Charlotte News*, February 10, 1970, p. 7A.

64 "Parents Picket Observer—Rap Anti-Busing Coverage," *Charlotte Observer*, February 14, 1970, p. 5B.

65 Interview, James McMillan, August 27, 1981. The judge answered much of this mail. See, generally, McMillan Papers.

66 Anonymous correspondent to Julius Chambers, March 27, 1970, Chambers Papers.

67 See, e.g., anonymous letter to James McMillan, August 28, 1970, Series 1, Box 5, McMillan Papers.

68 "Judge James McMillan: Catching the Desegregation Flak," *Raleigh News and Observer*, February 15, 1970. See, generally, McMillan Papers.

69 See, e.g., J. F. Gallimore to James McMillan, August 16, 1969, Series 1.1, Folder 14, McMillan Papers. Gallimore included Leon Panetta, a Nixon administration official, and NAACP President Kelly Alexander in this list of "Anti-Christ Jews."

70 "Out of Court and into the Future—with Hope," *Charlotte Observer*, July 12, 1975, p. 1A; "Justice's Quiet Spokesman: Judge McMillan's Modesty Belies His Impact since '68," *Charlotte Observer*, March 26, 1989, p. 1A; James McMillan to J. C. Goodman, March 5, 1970, Series 1, Folder 17, McMillan Papers.

71 Bass, *Unlikely Heroes*; Peltason, *Fifty-Eight Lonely Men*; Bacigal and Bacigal, "A Case Study of the Federal Judiciary's Role in Court-Ordered Busing," p. 693.

72 James McMillan to Frank Porter Graham, February 3, 1970, Series 1, Folder 16, McMillan Papers.

73 Mordecai Johnson to James McMillan, April 2, 1970, Chambers Papers. On Judge Waring, see Yarbrough, *A Passion for Justice*.

74 See, generally, McMillan Papers.

75 Interview, Fred Hicks, October 14, 1992.

76 *Charlotte Observer*, February 15, 1970.

77 Barrows, "School Busing," p. 18.

78 *Charlotte Observer*, February 15, 1970.

79 Mrs. James E. Sullivan to James McMillan, January 29, 1970, Series 1, Folder 15, McMillan Papers.

80 "1700 Protest Desegregation, Busing Order," *Charlotte Observer*, February 9, 1970, p. 1C.

81 "Concerned Parents Propose Boycott," *Charlotte Observer*, February 6, 1970, p. 19A.

82 "The Paper War," *Charlotte Focus* 1, no. 6 (1970), in Series 1, Folder 33, McMillan Papers.

83 Ibid.

84 *Charlotte News*, February 10, 1970.

85 "Editorial—With Its Schools in Crisis, the Community Must Press for Supreme Court Decision," *Charlotte News*, July 11, 1970, p. 4A.

86 "Editorial—More about Schools Appeal," *Charlotte News*, February 5, 1970, p. 18A; "Editorial—Why the School Board Should Appeal and the Courts Should Answer," *Charlotte News*, February 7, 1970, p. 14A (Atlanta, Miami); *Allen v. Board of Public Instruction*, 312 F. Supp. 1127 (S.D. Fla.), *rev'd*, 432 F.2d 362 (5th Cir. 1970) (Fort Lauderdale); *Flax v. Potts*, 333 F. Supp. 711 (N.D. Tex. 1970), *rev'd*, 450 F.2d 1118 (5th Cir. 1971) (Fort Worth); *Goss v. Board of Education*, 320 F. Supp. 549 (E.D. Tenn. 1970) (Knoxville); *Northcross v. Board of Education of Memphis*, 397 U.S. 232 (1970), and *Robinson v. Shelby County Board of Education*, 311 F. Supp. 97 (W.D. Tenn. 1970), *rev'd*, 442 F.2d 255 (6th Cir. 1971) (Memphis metropolitan area); *Beckett v. School Board of City of Norfolk*, 308 F. Supp. 1274 (E.D. Va. 1969) (Norfolk); "'Unitary' Plan Leaves 3 Schools All Black," *Charlotte News*, February 18, 1970, p. 14A (Orlando); *Scott v. Winston-Salem/Forsyth County Board of Education*, 317 F. Supp. 453 (M.D.N.C. 1970); "Judge Denies Mixing Suit," *Charlotte Observer*, February 20, 1970 (Winston-Salem); Statement of William Poe, in U.S. House Committee on the Judiciary, *Hearings before Subcommittee No. 5*, p. 1294 (Mobile and Atlanta).

87 "Editorial—Some Thoughts and Hopes as the Local Schools Approach a Turning Point," *Charlotte News*, January 31, 1970.

88 "1700 Protest Desegregation, Busing Order," *Charlotte Observer*, February 9, 1970, p. 1C.

89 *Congressional Record* 116 (February 10, 1970): 3071 (Senator Ervin).

90 Quoted in Schwartz, *Swann's Way*, p . 3.

91 Statement of James B. McMillan, in U.S. Senate Committee on the Judiciary, *Hearings before the Subcommittee on the Separation of Powers*, p. 521.

92 Scott, "On School Integration," *Addresses and Public Papers of Robert Walter Scott*, p. 549.

93 Craig Phillips to William Self, February 23, 1970, Chambers Papers.

94 Scott, "On School Integration," *Addresses and Public Papers of Robert Walter Scott*, pp. 549–50, 561.

95 "Will HEW Offer 3rd Plan Here?," *Charlotte Observer*, February 21, 1970, p. 1A.

96 Chambers to HEW Secretary Robert Finch, February 24, 1970, Chambers Papers.

97 Panetta and Gall, *Bring Us Together*; Statement of Ruby G. Martin, Washington Research Group, in U.S. Senate Committee on Labor and Public Welfare, *Hearings before the Subcommittee on Education*, pp. 531–32.

98 *Congressional Record* 116 (March 24, 1970): S4351, Daily Edition.

99 "Nixon Plans $1.5 Billion to Improve Segregated Schools," *New York Times*, March 25, 1970, p. 1A.

100 "Congress Pushes Ban on Busing," *Charlotte Observer*, February 20, 1970, p. 1A.

101 "City in Louisiana Told: Don't Bus," *Miami Herald*, February 25, 1970, p. 1A.

102 Congress of Racial Equality, "A True Alternative to Segregation: A Proposal for Community School Districts," February 1970, in "Brief for CORE as Amicus Curiae," *Swann v. Charlotte-Mecklenburg Board of Education*, in Douglas, *The Development of School Busing*, p. 258.

103 Ibid., pp. 259, 263 (emphasis in original).

104 Ibid., p. 265.

105 Testimony of Roy Innis, director, CORE, in U.S. Senate Committee on Labor and Public Welfare, *Hearings before the Subcommittee on Education*, p. 677.

106 "'Respond without Open Defiance,' Poe Urges Parents," *Charlotte Observer*, February 3, 1970, p. 1C.

107 Statement of Lucy W. Benson, president, League of Women Voters of the United States, in U.S. House Committee on the Judiciary, *Hearings before Subcommittee No. 5*, pp. 324, 327–28.

108 "400 'Interested' Parents Back Integration Order," *Charlotte Observer*, February 12, 1970, p. 1B.

109 "Citizens Propose a 'Truth Squad,'" *Charlotte Observer*, February 15, 1970, p. 1C.

110 "Editorial—School Decision Will Test Belief in the System Here," *Charlotte Observer*, February 8, 1970, p. 2B.

111 "The Paper War," *Charlotte Focus* 1, no. 6 (1970), in Series 1, Folder 33, McMillan Papers.

112 "Editorial—'Charlotte Way' Will Serve Us Again in School Crisis," *Charlotte Observer*, January 30, 1970, p. 2C.

113 Interview, Robert Culbertson, October 14, 1992.

114 Ibid.

115 "Where Are You, Charlotte?," *North Carolina Law Record* (April 1970), p. 7.

116 See, e.g., Louis Bledsoe to James McMillan, August 20, 1969, Series 1, Folder 14, McMillan Papers.

117 McMillan to Samuel Williams, February 10, 1970, Series 1, Folder 16, McMillan Papers.

118 Order, *Harris v. Self*, 70-CVS-1097, Mecklenburg County Superior Court, January 30, 1970, Chambers Papers; "Court Order Halts More Pay to Finger," *Charlotte News*, January 30, 1970, p. 1A.

119 Order, *Harris v. Self*, 70-CVS-1097, Mecklenburg County Superior Court, February 12, 1970, Chambers Papers; "Superior Court Judge Clears Way to Pay Finger," *Charlotte Observer*, February 10, 1970, p. 16A.

120 *Swann v. Charlotte-Mecklenburg Board of Education*, 312 F. Supp. 503, 505 (W.D.N.C. 1970).

121 Order, *Harris v. Self*, 70-CVS-1097, February 12, 1970, Chambers Papers.

122 "Order Suspending Superior Court Order," *Swann v. Charlotte-Mecklenburg Board of Education*, March 6, 1970, Chambers Papers.

123 "Court Hears Arguments in Mecklenburg Case," *Southern School News*, March 1961, p. 15.

124 *Morrow v. Mecklenburg County Board of Education*, 195 F. Supp. 109, 114 (W.D.N.C. 1961).

125 "Order Suspending Superior Court Order," *Swann v. Charlotte-Mecklenburg Board of Education*, March 6, 1970, Chambers Papers.

126 *Swann v. Charlotte-Mecklenburg Board of Education*, 312 F. Supp. 503, 505 (W.D.N.C. 1970); Order, *Swann v. Charlotte-Mecklenburg Board of Education*, W.D.N.C. March 6, 1970, Chambers Papers.

127 Order, *Swann v. Charlotte-Mecklenburg Board of Education*, 4th Cir. March 5, 1970, Chambers Papers.

128 *Swann v. Charlotte-Mecklenburg Board of Education*, 397 U.S. 978 (1970).

129 "Motion to Vacate Partial Suspension of, and to Reinstate an Order of the United States District Court for the Western District of North Carolina Ordering Implementation of a School Desegregation Plan," *Swann v. Charlotte-Mecklenburg Board of Education*, March 9, 1970, p. 22, Chambers Papers.

130 *Northcross v. Board of Education*, 397 U.S. 232 (1970) (Burger, C. J., concurring).

131 "Editorial—School Delay Best Course," *Charlotte News*, March 27, 1970, p. 19A.

132 Interview, Adam Stein, December 4, 1992.

133 Ibid.

134 "Supplemental Findings of Fact," *Swann v. Charlotte-Mecklenburg Board of Education*, March 21, 1970, Chambers Papers.

135 "McMillan Disagrees on Figures," *Charlotte News*, March 23, 1970, p. 1A.

136 "Renewal of Application for Stay of Portion of Court Order of February 5, 1970, as Amended by Order of March 3, 1970," *Swann v. Charlotte-Mecklenburg Board of Education*, March 22, 1970, Chambers Papers.

137 "Motion for Further Relief and for Show Cause," *Swann v. Charlotte-Mecklenburg Board of Education*, September 2, 1969, Chambers Papers.

138 Interview, Adam Stein, December 4, 1992.

139 "The Week That Was, Was Only Like the Year," *Charlotte Observer*, March 29, 1970, p. 1D.

140 Order, *Swann v. Charlotte-Mecklenburg Board of Education*, March 25, 1970, Chambers Papers.

141 Ibid.

142 McMillan to C. P. Street, March 6, 1970, Series 1, Folder 17, McMillan Papers.

143 "Poe Hails Stay as 'Necessary,'" *Charlotte Observer*, March 26, 1970, p. 1A.

144 "Reasonableness Set as Integration Test," *Washington Evening Star*, May 27, 1970, p. 1A.

CHAPTER EIGHT

1 Motion, *Swann v. Charlotte-Mecklenburg Board of Education*, March 4, 1970, and "Motion to Recuse and Disqualify," *Swann v. Charlotte-Mecklenburg Board of Education*, March 5, 1970, both in Chambers Papers, Charlotte. Both Chief Judge Haynsworth and Judge McMillan denied the requests on March 6. Order, *Swann v. Charlotte-Mecklenburg Board of Education*, 4th Cir. March 6, 1970, and Order, *Swann v. Charlotte-Mecklenburg Board of Education*, W.D.N.C. March 6, 1970, both in Chambers Papers.

2 *Swann v. Charlotte-Mecklenburg Board of Education*, 312 F. Supp. 503, 504, 510 (W.D.N.C. 1970).

3 Ibid.

4 Ibid., pp. 503, 508 n. 4.

5 Interview, Adam Stein, December 3, 1992.

6 Interview, Julius Chambers, August 16, 1993; NAACP Legal Defense and Educational Fund to Contributors, memorandum, October 1970, and Bob Valder to Julius Chambers, memorandum, June 27, 1968, Chambers Papers.

7 "U.S. Brief Critical of Busing Order in Southern Case," *New York Times*, April 9, 1970, p. 1A; "National Teachers Group Backs McMillan Decision," *Charlotte Observer*, April 8, 1970, p. 1A.

8 James B. McMillan to Davison M. Douglas, September 7, 1982, letter in possession of author.

9 "How U.S. Has Softened School Integration Policy," *Charlotte Observer*, May 3, 1970, p. 1B.

10 "U.S. Brief Critical of Busing Order in Southern Case," *New York Times*, April 9, 1970, p. 1A.

11 "No-Busing Plan Meets Test, School Board Lawyers Say," *Charlotte News*, April 7, 1970, p. 1A.

12 *Swann v. Charlotte-Mecklenburg Board of Education*, 431 F.2d 138, 147 (4th Cir. 1970) (en banc).

13 Ibid., p. 145.

14 Ibid., p. 143.

15 Ibid., pp. 138, 154 (Sobeloff, J., concurring in part and dissenting in part).

16 Rosen, "Judge Sobeloff's Public School Race Decisions," p. 499.

17 James McMillan to John Hunter, June 10, 1970, Series 1, Folder 17C, McMillan Papers, Chapel Hill.

18 Oral Argument, *Swann v. Charlotte-Mecklenburg Board of Education*, in Kurland and Casper, *Landmark Briefs and Argument* 70:622 (quoting Board attorney William Waggoner at July 1970 hearing).

19 "Statement of Minority Board Members Watkins, Kerry, Mauldin, and Kelly," Chambers Papers; "Minority Plan Would Mix All Schools," *Charlotte News*, June 29, 1970, p. 1A; Interview, Carlton Watkins, July 6, 1992.

20 "Self Rips HEW Plan for Charlotte Schools," *Charlotte Observer*, July 16, 1970, p. 1A.

21 "Plaintiffs' Response to the Defendants' Submission to Order of the Court of Appeals for the Fourth Circuit," *Swann v. Charlotte-Mecklenburg Board of Education*, July 7, 1970, p. 4, Chambers Papers; "HEW Official Raps Own Plan," *Charlotte Observer*, July 17, 1970, p. 1A.

22 "Defendants' Submission Pursuant to Order of Court of Appeals for the Fourth Circuit," *Swann v. Charlotte-Mecklenburg Board of Education*, June 29, 1970, p. 5, Chambers Papers.

23 "School Case Again Returns to Court," *Charlotte Observer*, July 15. 1970, p. 1C.

24 "HEW Official Raps Own Plan," *Charlotte Observer*, July 17, 1970, p. 1A.

25 Statement of Ruby G. Martin, Washington Research Group, in U.S. Senate Committee on Labor and Public Welfare, *Hearings before the Subcommittee on Education*, p. 535.

26 *Swann v. Charlotte-Mecklenburg Board of Education*, 318 F. Supp. 786, 790, 803 (W.D.N.C. 1970).

27 Ibid., pp. 794–98; "Catchword Is Ironic in No. 1 Busing State," *Charlotte Observer*, February 20, 1970, p. 3B; NAACP Legal Defense and Educational Fund, *It's Not the Distance*, p. ix.

28 *Swann v. Charlotte-Mecklenburg Board of Education*, 318 F. Supp. 792 (W.D.N.C. 1970).

29 "Self Won't Back Minority School Plan," *Charlotte News*, July 17, 1970, p. 1A.

30 "Finger: Clustering Reasonable," *Charlotte News*, July 18, 1970, p. 1A; "Tests Show Wide Academic Gap," *Charlotte News*, July 24, 1970.

31 "Negro Schools Lowest, White Highest, on Tests," *Charlotte News*, July 24, 1970, p. 12A.

32 "Judge Changes Mind, Won't Rule on Mixing Today," *Charlotte News*, July 20, 1970, p. 1A.

33 "U.S. School Policy Brings Hot Debate," *Charlotte Observer*, June 16, 1971, p. 7A.

34 Testimony of Julius Chambers, in U.S. Senate, Select Committee on Equal Educational Opportunity, *Hearings on the Status of School Desegregation Law*, p. 5433; "U.S. School Policy Brings Hot Debate," *Charlotte Observer*, June 16, 1971, p. 7A.

35 "Integration Beneficial, Lawyer Says," *Charlotte Observer*, March 31, 1972, p. 4C.
36 *Swann v. Charlotte-Mecklenburg Board of Education*, 318 F. Supp. 801 (W.D.N.C. 1970) (emphasis in the original).
37 Ibid., p. 792.
38 Ibid., p. 793.
39 *Swann v. Charlotte-Mecklenburg Board of Education*, 399 U.S. 926 (1970).
40 Read and McGough, *Let Them Be Judged*, p. 524.
41 *Swann v. Charlotte-Mecklenburg Board of Education*, 399 U.S. 926 (1970).
42 See, e.g., Black Papers, Douglas Papers, and Marshall Papers, Washington, D.C.
43 *Swann v. Charlotte-Mecklenburg Board of Education*, 399 U.S. 926 (1970) (Black, J., dissenting).
44 "Will Supreme Court Break Recess for School Case?," *Charlotte Observer*, July 2, 1970, p. 1A.
45 See, e.g., John Harlan to Chief Justice Burger, memorandum, August 27, 1970, Black Papers.
46 "3 Groups Urge School Decision," *Charlotte News*, July 11, 1970, p. 1B.
47 "Here's the Text of Resolution," *Charlotte News*, July 14, 1970, p. 3B.
48 "High Court School Ruling Asked," *Charlotte News*, July 14, 1970, p. 3B.
49 "Charlotte School Officials Request Justice Dept. Help," *Charlotte Observer*, August 7, 1970.
50 "Justice Department Rejects Charlotte Plea," *Charlotte Observer*, August 14, 1970, p. 3A; "Mitchell Fears Dixie Problems If Court Tightens School Rules," *Los Angeles Times*, August 20, 1970, p. 1; "Administration Is Hoping for Delay in Bus Ruling," *Fayetteville Observer*, August 20, 1970, p. 1A.
51 "CPA Petitioning for Mixing Delay," *Charlotte News*, August 13, 1970, p. 1A.
52 "Haynsworth Asked to Stay Mix Order," *Charlotte News*, p. 2A, August 13, 1970.
53 "Judge Haynsworth: No Authority to Postpone Desegregation Order," *Charlotte Observer*, August 18, 1970, p. 1A.
54 "Legislators Ask Stay of Order," August 20, 1970, p. 1C; "School Need Desegregation Guide—Scott," *Charlotte Observer*, August 25, 1970, p. 6A.
55 "Four Cities Lose 11th Hour Appeal," *Charlotte Observer*, August 26, 1970, p. 1A.
56 Schwartz, *Swann's Way*, p. 93.
57 "Schools Face Huge Busing Problem," *Fayetteville Observer*, August 26, 1970, p. 1A.
58 "Stay Would Strengthen Appeal to Supreme Court, Board Chairman Says," *Charlotte News*, August 5, 1970 p. 5C; Interview, William Poe, July 9, 1992.
59 "Charlotte Schools Prepare to Implement Busing Plan," *Fayetteville Observer*, September 8, 1970, p. 9A.

60 "School Board Majority Blasted by Watkins," *Charlotte News*, August 5, 1970, p. 1A.

61 "Stay Would Strengthen Appeal to Supreme Court, Board Chairman Says," *Charlotte News*, August 5, 1970, p. 5C.

62 Memorandum, *Swann v. Charlotte-Mecklenburg Board of Education*, August 7, 1970, Chambers Papers; "Board Decides to Appeal, Ask Stay of Order," *Charlotte Observer*, August 7, 1970, p. 1A.

63 "Board Decides to Appeal, Ask Stay of Order," *Charlotte Observer*, August 7, 1970, p. 1A; "Options Rejected by Board," *Charlotte News*, August 7, 1970, p. 1A.

64 "CPA Asks Telegrams of Protest," *Charlotte Observer*, July 22, 1970, p. 1B; Fancher, *Voices from the South*, p. 30.

65 Lord, *Spatial Perspectives on School Desegregation and Busing*, pp. 26–27.

66 Abstract of Votes for County Board of Education, May 2, 1970, May 30, 1970, Mecklenburg County Board of Elections, Charlotte; Moye, "Charlotte-Mecklenburg Consolidation," pp. 157–58; Lord, *Spatial Perspectives on School Desegregation and Busing*, pp. 26–27.

67 Lord, *Spatial Perspectives on School Desegregation and Busing*, p. 26.

68 Interview, Jane Scott, October 15, 1992.

69 Lord, *Spatial Perspectives on School Desegregation and Busing*, p. 26.

70 Charles Lowe to William Self, July 8, 1970, Chambers Papers.

71 "Schools Planning Massive Busing," *Fayetteville Observer*, August 26, 1970, p. 1A.

72 "Challenge Fails to Stop Bus Shipping to Charlotte," *Fayetteville Observer*, September 5, 1970.

73 "Defendants' Interim Report of Desegregation, 1970–1971," *Swann v. Charlotte-Mecklenburg Board of Education*, September 18, 1970, p. 1, Chambers Papers; "40,000 Pupils Bused Daily to Charlotte, N.C. Schools," *Boston Globe*, November 22, 1970, p. 4A.

74 "2,000 Student Drop Could Mean Teacher Slash," *Charlotte News*, November 6, 1970, p. 1A.

75 "40,000 Pupils Bused Daily to Charlotte, N.C. Schools," *Boston Globe*, November 22, 1970, p. 4A; "Decision on Schools Next Week," *Charlotte News*, July 25, 1970, p. 1A.

76 Rossell, *The Carrot or the Stick*, p. 161.

77 Quoted in Maniloff, "Community Attitudes," pp. 88–89.

78 "Mixed Charlotte School Rolls Off," *Fayetteville Observer*, September 9, 1970, p. 1A.

79 Quoted in Maniloff, "Community Attitudes," p. 93.

80 "2,000 Student Drop Could Mean Teacher Slash," *Charlotte News*, November 6, 1970, p. 1A.

81 "Should Small Whites Be Bused to Inner City," *Charlotte News*, February 15, 1974, p. 18A.

82 Lord and Catau, "School Desegregation."

83 Dale, "City-County Educational Consolidation in Charlotte and Mecklenburg," p. 111.

84 Rossell and Hawley, "Understanding White Flight," p. 169.
85 "40,000 Pupils Bused Daily to Charlotte, N.C. Schools," *Boston Globe*, November 22, 1970, p. 4A.
86 "Tar Heels Balk at Busing Plan," *Fayetteville Observer*, August 25, 1970, p. 1A.
87 Interview, Julian Mason, December 6, 1994.
88 "The Legacy of Busing Hearings a Time for Remembering Charlotte's Past," *Charlotte Observer*, January 10, 1988, p. 1C.
89 To be sure, at least one social scientist has suggested that public pronouncements by business, civic, and political leaders in support of school desegregation did not reduce the level of community protest during the 1970s, but she concedes that the evidence is not conclusive. Rossell, "Desegregation Plans, Racial Isolation, White Flight, and Community Response," in pp. 19–20.
90 "C of C Urges Quiet School Opening," *Charlotte News*, August 31, 1970, p. 1A.
91 "40,000 Pupils Bused Daily to Charlotte, N.C. Schools," *Boston Globe*, November 22, 1970, p. 4A.
92 Statement of Lucy W. Benson, president, League of Women Voters of the United States, in U.S. House Committee on the Judiciary, *Hearings before Subcommittee No. 5*, pp. 324, 327–28.
93 "Damage to House Extensive," *Charlotte News*, February 4, 1971, p. 1A.
94 "35 Pitch In to Reopen Law Firm," February 8, 1971, p. 1C; "Law Profs Help Ex-Pupil Chambers," *Charlotte Observer*, February 17, 1971, p. 5A.
95 "Editorial—Arsonists' Work Threatens Basis for Justice, Liberty," *Charlotte Observer*, February 6, 1971, p. 18A.
96 Oral Argument, *Swann v. Charlotte-Mecklenburg Board of Education*, in Kurland and Casper, *Landmark Briefs and Argument* 70:618.
97 Ibid., pp. 608–10.
98 Oral Argument, *Swann v. Charlotte-Mecklenburg Board of Education*, in *United States Law Week* 39 (October 1970): 3159.
99 Oral Argument, *Swann v. Charlotte-Mecklenburg Board of Education*, in Kurland and Casper, *Landmark Briefs and Argument* 70:635.
100 Interview, William Poe, July 9, 1992.
101 Schwartz, *Swann's Way*, 101–5.
102 Ibid., pp. 113–18.
103 Ibid., pp. 118–29.
104 Ibid., pp. 130–42.
105 Ibid., pp. 143–71.
106 Quoted in ibid., p. 179.
107 Ibid., pp. 179–84.
108 *Swann v. Charlotte-Mecklenburg Board of Education*, 402 U.S. 1, 5 (1971).
109 Ibid., p. 25.
110 Ibid., p. 26.
111 Ibid., pp. 30–31.
112 "Court Backs McMillan," *Charlotte News*, April 20, 1971, p. 1A.

113 *Swann v. Charlotte-Mecklenburg Board of Education*, 401 U.S. 1, 31–32 (1971).

114 See generally Diver, "The Judge as Political Powerbroker"; Combs, "The Federal Judiciary and Northern School Desegregation"; Starr, "Accommodation and Accountability."

115 William Brennan to Warren Burger, March 8, 1971, Box 436, Black Papers.

116 Orfield, *Must We Bus?*, p. 25.

117 Statement of Ruby G. Martin, Washington Research Group, in U.S. Senate Committee on Labor and Public Welfare, *Hearings before the Subcommittee on Education*, pp. 539–40.

118 Statement of Elliott L. Richardson, Secretary of Health, Education and Welfare, U.S. Senate Committee on Labor and Public Welfare, *Hearings before the Subcommittee on Education*, p. 263.

119 Erwin Griswold to James McMillan, Series 1, Folder 18-C, McMillan Papers.

120 McMillan to Stanley Kaplan, April 29, 1971, Series 1, Folder 18-C, McMillan Papers.

121 *Swann v. Charlotte-Mecklenburg Board of Education*, 401 U.S. 424 (1971).

122 "Let's Rise to Challenge, Civic Leaders Urge Parents," *Charlotte Observer*, April 21, 1971, p. 1C.

123 "Racial Strife Disrupts Schools in Charlotte," *Washington Evening-Star*, February 1971, p. 1A, in Chambers Papers.

124 Quoted in "Charlotte's Day in Court 20 Years Ago This Week," *Charlotte Observer*, April 14, 1991, p. 1C.

125 "Poe: School Plan Could be Changed," *Charlotte News*, April 21, 1971, p. 1A.

126 "Editorial—The High Court's Decision," *Charlotte News*, April 21, 1971, p. 20A.

127 "Board to Ask High Court to Rehear Mixing Case," *Charlotte News*, May 7, 1971, p. 1A.

128 "School Board Would Ban Assignment on Race Basis," *Charlotte News*, April 28, 1971, p. 2A.

CHAPTER NINE

1 "2,000 Student Drop Could Mean Teacher Slash," *Charlotte News*, November 6, 1970, p. 1A.

2 Pratt, *The Color of Their Skin*; "Atlanta Sidesteps Massive Crosstown School Busing," *Charlotte Observer*, August 1, 1971, p. 10A.

3 *Swann v. Charlotte-Mecklenburg Board of Education*, 328 F. Supp. 1346, 1347 (W.D.N.C. 1971).

4 Ibid., pp. 1350–51.

5 "Redrawn Lines Included," *Charlotte News*, April 29, 1969, p. 1B.

6 *Swann v. Charlotte-Mecklenburg Board of Education*, 328 F. Supp. 1350–51 (W.D.N.C. 1971). By the school board's estimates, the operational costs

of the Finger Plan were about $600,000. *Swann v. Charlotte-Mecklenburg Board of Education*, 431 F.2d 138, 143 (4th Cir. 1970).

7 *Swann v. Charlotte-Mecklenburg Board of Education*, 334 F. Supp. 623, 626 (W.D.N.C. 1971).

8 "McMillan Questions School Board Plan," *Charlotte Observer*, June 18, 1971, p. 1A.

9 WBTV Editorial, "The School Assignment Plan, 1971," June 17, 1971, Chambers Papers, Charlotte.

10 "Atlanta Sidesteps Massive Crosstown School Busing," *Charlotte Observer*, August 1, 1971, p. 10A.

11 Rossell and Hawley, "Understanding White Flight," pp. 165–66; Rossell, "Desegregation Plans, Racial Isolation, White Flight, and Community Response," pp. 33–34.

12 Lord, "School Busing and White Abandonment," p. 88.

13 *Swann v. Charlotte-Mecklenburg Board of Education*, 328 F. Supp. 1346, 1350, 1352 (W.D.N.C. 1971).

14 Ibid., p. 1348 ; *Monroe v. Board of Commissioners*, 391 U.S. 450, 459 (1968).

15 Rossell and Hawley, "Understanding White Flight," p. 170.

16 "Finger Plan Reordering Predicted," *Charlotte News*, June 25, 1971, p. 1A.

17 Interview, Julia Maulden, December 14, 1994; Interview, Carlton Watkins, July 6, 1992.

18 Interview, Robert Culbertson, October 14, 1992.

19 "Last Meeting," *Charlotte News*, October 13, 1976, p. 1B.

20 Interview, Carlton Watkins, July 6, 1992.

21 Charlotte-Mecklenburg Board of Education, "Pupil Assignment Plan, 1971–1972," June 25, 1971, Chambers Papers; *Swann v. Charlotte-Mecklenburg Board of Education*, 328 F. Supp. 1346, 1348–49 (W.D.N.C. 1971).

22 Charlotte-Mecklenburg Board of Education, "Pupil Assignment Plan, 1971–1972," June 25, 1971, Chambers Papers; "Keeps Students Together," *Charlotte Observer*, June 22, 1971, p. 1A.

23 *Swann v. Charlotte-Mecklenburg Board of Education*, 328 F. Supp. 1346, 1349 (W.D.N.C. 1971).

24 Ibid., pp. 1347–50.

25 *Swann v. Charlotte-Mecklenburg Board of Education*, 334 F. Supp. 623, 627, 629 (W.D.N.C. 1971).

26 *Swann v. Charlotte-Mecklenburg Board of Education*, 328 F. Supp. 1346, 1349 (W.D.N.C. 1971).

27 "Current Plan Called 'Unfair,'" *Charlotte Observer*, August 26, 1971; Testimony of Julia Maulden, in U.S. House Committee on the Judiciary, *Hearings before Subcommittee No. 5*, p. 1304.

28 "School Feeder Plan Complaint Hearing Set," *Charlotte Observer*, September 2, 1971, p. 1C; *Swann v. Charlotte-Mecklenburg Board of Education*, 334 F. Supp. 623 (W.D.N.C. 1971).

29 *Swann v. Charlotte-Mecklenburg Board of Education*, 334 F. Supp. 625, 626 (W.D.N.C. 1971).

30 "Report with Respect to West Charlotte High School," *Swann v. Charlotte-Mecklenburg Board of Education*, January 21, 1972, Chambers Papers.

31 "Schools File Imbalance Proposals," *Charlotte Observer*, September 24, 1970, p. 1B; *Swann v. Charlotte-Mecklenburg Board of Education*, 334 F. Supp. 623, 628 (W.D.N.C. 1971).

32 "Editorial—Let's Settle School Issue before Fall Arrives Again," *Charlotte Observer*, July 1, 1971; "New School Mix Appeal Is Ready," *Charlotte News*, July 19, 1971, p. 1B.

33 "Board's Attorney Criticizes School Rulings of McMillan," *Charlotte Observer*, October 14, 1971, p. 20C; Pettigrew and Green, "School Desegregation in Large Cities," p. 35.

34 Orfield, *Must We Bus?*, pp. 25–16; *Calhoun v. Cook*, 332 F. Supp. 804 (N.D. Ga. 1971).

35 *Swann v. Charlotte-Mecklenburg Board of Education*, 453 F.2d 1377 (4th Cir. 1972) (en banc).

36 Statement of Ruby G. Martin, Washington Research Group, in U.S. Senate Committee on Labor and Public Welfare, *Hearings before the Subcommittee on Education*, pp. 542–43.

37 Orfield, "Congress, the President, and Anti-Busing Legislation," p. 108.

38 "Text of Legislative Message," *Congressional Quarterly*, March 25, 1972, pp. 642–48.

39 "School Board Members to Appeal to Congress," *Charlotte News*, February 18, 1972, p. 1A.

40 Jefferson Standard Broadcasting Co., "Editorial: The Constitution and Busing," (February 7, 1972), in U.S. House Committee on the Judiciary, *Hearings before Subcommittee No. 5*, p. 146.

41 Interview, Julia Maulden, December 14, 1994; Statement of Sam McNinch Accompanied by Mrs. Jane B. Scott, Statement of William Poe, Statement of Julia Maulden, in U.S. House Committee on the Judiciary, *Hearings before Subcommittee No. 5*, pp. 276, 1292, 1301.

42 Statement of William Poe, in U.S. House Committee on the Judiciary, *Hearings before Subcommittee No. 5*, pp. 1292, 1300 (quotation).

43 Quoted in Myerson, *Nothing Could Be Finer*, p. 52.

44 Luebke, *Tar Heel Politics*, pp. 162–64.

45 Lord, *Spatial Perspectives on School Desegregation and Busing*, p. 26.

46 "Busing Expected Key Issue on May 6," *Charlotte News*, April 29, 1972, p. 2C.

47 Barrows, "School Busing," p. 18.

48 Quoted in Maniloff, "Community Attitudes," p. 75.

49 Maniloff, "Busing in Charlotte," pp. 1–8.

50 "Charlotte 'Survives' Busing," *Washington Post*, November 19, 1972, p. 1A.

51 Coleman Kerry, the first African American member of the Charlotte-Mecklenburg Board of Education, had been appointed to the board to fill a vacancy in the late 1960s.

52 "A Quiet Voice for Schools," *Charlotte Observer*, November 5, 1976, p. 1A.

53 "Jones, Poe Agree: Robinson's Good," *Charlotte News*, April 19, 1977, p. 1B.

54 "Charlotte Busing Winds Up Historic Year," *Durham Morning Herald*, May 28, 1972, p. 2D.

55 Bob Valder to Hayes Mizell, memorandum, February 22, 1972, p. 6, Chambers Papers.

56 Roland M. Smith to Jane Scott, March 2, 1972, in U.S. House Committee on the Judiciary, *Hearings before Subcommittee No. 5*, p. 287.

57 Daniels, "In Defense of Busing," p. 36; "Aftershocks," *Charlotte Observer*, May 13, 1979, p. 14A.

58 Executive Staff of Charlotte-Mecklenburg Schools, "Position Paper on School Disruptions," December 10, 1971, p. 1, Charlotte-Mecklenburg Community Relations Committee Papers, Charlotte (CMCRC).

59 "Report Says School Board Must Lead," *Charlotte Observer*, March 15, 1972, p. 1A.

60 "3 Members Sue Education Board," *Charlotte News*, May 10, 1973, p. 1B; "School Board 'Talks' May Spark Suit," *Charlotte Observer*, May 3, 1973, p. 1C.

61 "Discipline Is Biased, Study Says," *Charlotte Observer*, November 30, 1973, p. 1B.

62 Bob Valder to Hayes Mizell, memorandum, February 22, 1972, p. 6, Chambers Papers.

63 *Givens v. Poe*, 346 F. Supp. 202, 210 (W.D.N.C. 1972).

64 Ibid., pp. 205, 209–10.

65 Unpublished Order, *Givens v. Poe* (No. 2615, W.D.N.C. November 1, 1972), Chambers Papers.

66 *Lynch v. Snepp*, 350 F. Supp. 1134, 1140 (W.D.N.C. 1972).

67 U.S. Commission on Civil Rights, *School Desegregation in Ten Communities*, p. 95.

68 Reginald Smith to Bob Valder, memorandum, March 20, 1973, Chambers Papers.

69 U.S. Commission on Civil Rights, *School Desegregation in Ten Communities*, p. 93.

70 Complaint, *Cuthbertson v. Charlotte-Mecklenburg Board of Education*, March 29, 1973, Chambers Papers; "New Suit Challenges City School Mixing," *Charlotte News*, March 29, 1973, p. 1A.

71 *Cuthbertson v. Charlotte-Mecklenburg Board of Education*, 535 F.2d 1249 (4th Cir.), *cert. denied*, 429 U.S. 831 (1976).

72 *Swann v. Charlotte-Mecklenburg Board of Education*, 362 F. Supp. 1223, 1230 (W.D.N.C. 1973).

73 "Motion for Further Relief," *Swann v. Charlotte-Mecklenburg Board of Education*, November 8, 1972, Chambers Papers.

74 "Pupil Assignment Study," pp. 13–14, quoted in *Swann v. Charlotte-*

Mecklenburg Board of Education, 362 F. Supp. 1223, 1232 (W.D.N.C. 1973) (emphasis supplied).

75 Lord and Catau, "School Desegregation Policy and Intra-School District Migration," pp. 787–88; "Out of the Court and into the Future—with Hope," *Charlotte Observer*, July 12, 1975, p. 1A.

76 National Education Association, *Three Cities That Are Making Desegregation Work*, p. 32.

77 "Board to Advise Integration Plans," *Charlotte Observer*, May 1, 1973, p. 1B.

78 "Board Votes Not to Ask Busing Relief for Pupils," *Charlotte News*, April 25, 1973, p. 1A.

79 *Swann v. Charlotte-Mecklenburg Board of Education*, 362 F. Supp. 1223, 1230–31 (W.D.N.C. 1973).

80 Ibid.

81 Interview, Julian Mason, December 6, 1994.

82 Quoted in Gaillard, *Dream Long Deferred*, p. 116.

83 Julian Mason to Charlotte-Mecklenburg Board of Education, May 30, 1973, Chambers Papers.

84 Interview, Julian Mason, December 6, 1994.

85 "Out of the Court and into the Future—with Hope," *Charlotte Observer*, July 12, 1975, p. 1A.

86 "School Case Near End, Judge Says," *Charlotte Observer*, May 10, 1973, p. 1A.

87 "Judge, School Board Delegates to Confer," *Charlotte Observer*, June 14, 1973, p. 1A.

88 "Board Will Seek Advice on School Mix Guideline," *Charlotte News*, June 13, 1973, p. 1A.

89 Ibid.; "Judge, School Board Delegates to Confer," *Charlotte Observer*, June 14, 1973, p. 1A; Julian Mason to Members of the Board of Education, June 15, 1973, Chambers Papers.

90 "School Staff Awaits Word from Board on Changes," *Charlotte News*, June 15, 1973, p. 1B.

91 "School Plan Gets Work," *Charlotte News*, June 21, 1973, p. 1A.

92 "Editorial—Meeting in Judge's Office Brought End to 'Theater,'" *Charlotte Observer*, June 16, 1973, p. 12A.

93 *Swann v. Charlotte-Mecklenburg Board of Education*, 362 F. Supp. 1223, 1233, 1237 (W.D.N.C. 1973).

94 Ibid., p. 1238; Charlotte-Mecklenburg Board of Education, "Summary of Staff Presentations and Board Actions Relative to Court Order of June 19, 1973," Chambers Papers.

95 *Swann v. Charlotte-Mecklenburg Board of Education*, 362 F. Supp. 1223, 1237 (W.D.N.C. 1973).

96 Ibid., p. 1238 (emphasis in original).

97 Charlotte-Mecklenburg Board of Education, "Summary of Staff Presentations and Board Actions Relative to Court Order of June 19, 1973," Chambers Papers.

98 *Swann v. Charlotte-Mecklenburg Board of Education*, 362 F. Supp. 1223, 1240, 1242 (W.D.N.C. 1973).

99 "Report Pursuant to the Order of the Court Issued on August 16, 1973," *Swann v. Charlotte-Mecklenburg Board of Education*, September 5, 1973, Chambers Papers; "71% of Lottery Students Enrolled at W. Charlotte," *Charlotte News*, September 19, 1973, p. 1B.

100 "The Schools: Bad Timing Crushes Fragile Alliance," *Charlotte Observer*, July 7, 1973, p. 11A.

101 Quoted in Gaillard, *Dream Long Deferred*, p. 132.

102 "School Plan Gets Work," *Charlotte News*, June 21, 1973, p. 1A.

103 Lord, *Spatial Perspectives on School Desegregation and Busing*, p. 30.

104 In the meantime, in June 1973, Chambers took additional action against the board, challenging the board's placement of kindergartens. The school board planned to operate kindergartens in twenty schools; every one of the schools was in a white neighborhood, thereby placing a greater burden on black children seeking to attend these schools and notwithstanding the fact that many of the black elementary schools were already underutilized. "Motion for Further Relief," *Swann v. Charlotte-Mecklenburg Board of Education*, June 28, 1973, Chambers Papers; "Chambers to Challenge Local Kindergarten Plan," *Charlotte News*, June 22, 1973, p. 7C. McMillan, already consumed by the West Charlotte issue, deferred action on the kindergarten issue. *Swann v. Charlotte-Mecklenburg Board of Education*, 362 F. Supp. 1223, 1242 (W.D.N.C. 1973).

105 "Editorial — Schools: A Point of Decision," *Charlotte News*, June 26, 1973, p. 16A.

106 "Out of the Court and into the Future — with Hope," *Charlotte Observer*, July 12, 1975, p. 1A; "Integration: Can Boston Follow Charlotte's Lead?," *Charlotte Observer*, February 8, 1975, p. 15A.

107 "150 Parents, Teens Protest School Plan," *Charlotte Observer*, August 16, 1973, p. 1C.

108 "Most City Leaders Favor Equal Busing," *Charlotte Observer*, June 24, 1973, p. 6D.

109 Interview, William Waggoner, October 14, 1992.

110 Interview, William Sturges, October 12, 1992.

111 "School Board Votes 5–4 for Appeal," *Charlotte Observer*, July 3, 1973, p. 1A.

112 "Editorial — Old Illusions: The Board Clings to Them," *Charlotte Observer*, July 6, 1973, p. 16A.

113 "The Schools: Bad Timing Crushes Fragile Alliance," *Charlotte Observer*, July 7, 1973, p. 11A.

114 "Timetable Approved by Board," *Charlotte News*, August 15, 1973, p. 1B.

115 "McNinch Wants 'Split' Board to Quit," *Charlotte Observer*, September 28, 1973, p. 1A.

116 *Swann v. Charlotte-Mecklenburg Board of Education*, 489 F.2d 966 (4th Cir. 1974) (per curiam) (en banc).

117 Interview, Margaret Ray, October 15, 1992.

118 "School Truce Took Painstaking Efforts," *Charlotte Observer*, July 17, 1974, p. 1A; "CAG Now Has Some Clout," *Charlotte Observer*, April 5, 1974, p. 1A.

119 "At Center of a Bag of Porcupines—Maggie Ray," *Charlotte Observer*, May 31, 1974, p. 1B.

120 "Citizens Advisory Group Report," *Swann v. Charlotte-Mecklenburg Board of Education*, April 22, 1974, and "Transcript of Testimony of Margaret Ray," *Swann v. Charlotte-Mecklenburg Board of Education*, April 1974, p. 651, both in Chambers Papers.

121 "Editorial—Good Signs for Charlotte Schools," *Charlotte News*, December 2, 1973.

122 "Parents Poll: Don't Bus Children for All 12 Years," *Charlotte Observer*, January 9, 1974, p. 1A; "Citizens Advisory Group Report to the Court," *Swann v. Charlotte-Mecklenburg Board of Education*, April 22, 1974, Chambers Papers.

123 Interview, Margaret Ray, October 15, 1992; Gaillard, *Dream Long Deferred*, pp. 139–40.

124 "Minutes, Special Meeting of the Charlotte-Mecklenburg Board of Education," February 11, 1974, Chambers Papers.

125 John Finger to Julius Chambers, April 12, 1973, and Julius Chambers to John Finger, April 20, 1973, Chambers Papers.

126 "W. Charlotte Plan Draws Fire," *Charlotte Observer*, February 21, 1974, p. 1A.

127 "Feeder Plan Going to McMillan Tomorrow," *Charlotte News*, February 28, 1974, p. 1A.

128 "Minutes, Special Meeting of the Charlotte-Mecklenburg Board of Education," February 27, 1974, Chambers Papers.

129 "Booe Critical of Appeal," *Charlotte News*, January 18, 1974, p. 1B.

130 "Board Refuses McMillan's Request," *Charlotte Observer*, March 29, 1974, p. 1A.

131 *Northcross v. Board of Education*, 489 F.2d 15 (6th Cir. 1973), *cert. denied*, 416 U.S. 962 (1974); *Goss v. Board of Education*, 482 F.2d 1044 (6th Cir. 1973), *cert. denied*, 414 U.S. 1171 (1974).

132 *Charlotte Observer*, May 6, 1974, p. 1C.

133 Unpublished order, *Swann v. Charlotte-Mecklenburg Board of Education*, April 3, 1974, p. 4, Chambers Papers.

134 Quoted in "Citizens Panel to Help Devise School Plan," *Charlotte Observer*, April 4, 1974, p. 1A.

135 "As School Hearings Reopen, Board Is Pulled by Legal and Community Concerns," *Charlotte News*, April 13, 1974, p. 6A.

136 "Editorial—Help for the Court?," *Charlotte News*, April 8, 1974, p. 14A.

137 "Booe Wants School Board to Get Stay," *Charlotte News*, April 8, 1974, p. 1B; "Board to Obey Court Order to Aid CAG on Assignment," *Charlotte Observer*, April 11, 1974, p. 1B.

138 "CAG Pupil Plan Takes 'Near-Home' Approach," *Charlotte Observer*,

April 24, 1974, p. 1A; "Board Needs School Mix Reply Soon—Poe," *Charlotte News*, April 26, 1974, p. 1A.

139 "Board's Cautious on Busing," *Charlotte Observer*, May 23, 1974, p. 1B.

140 "Citizens Plan May Mean White Flight Poe Says," *Charlotte News*, May 21, 1974, p. 1B.

141 "Stability Draws Some White Support," *Charlotte Observer*, May 22, 1974, p. 1C.

142 "Harris Sees Support for 'Fair' Pupil Plan," *Charlotte Observer*, May 23, 1974, p. 1B; "School Truce Took Painstaking Efforts," *Charlotte Observer*, July 17, 1974, p. 1A.

143 Gaillard, *Dream Long Deferred*, p. 150.

144 "School Truce Took Painstaking Efforts," *Charlotte Observer*, July 17, 1974, p. 1A.

145 *Charlotte Observer*, June 7, 1974, p. 1A.

146 "Candidates Give Goals for Schools," *Charlotte Observer*, April 19, 1974, p. 1B.

147 "Anti-Busing Group Backs 3 Candidates," *Charlotte News*, May 6, 1974, p. 1B.

148 "School Tension Subsides," *Charlotte Observer*, September 6, 1957, p. 1A.

149 "Poe: Busing Drove Off 20% of Whites," *Charlotte News*, September 25, 1974, p. 1B.

150 "Plan Would Bus Southeast Whites to West Charlotte," *Charlotte Observer*, July 10, 1974, p. 1A.

151 *Swann v. Charlotte-Mecklenburg Board of Education*, 379 F. Supp. 1102, 1105 (W.D.N.C. 1974).

152 "Plaintiffs' Response to Final Report of the Citizens' Advisory Group," *Swann v. Charlotte-Mecklenburg Board of Education*, June 7, 1974, Chambers Papers; Interview, Julius Chambers, August 16, 1993.

153 "Judge McMillan Gives Approval to Joint Pupil Assignment Plan," *Charlotte News*, July 10, 1974, p. 1A.

154 *Swann v. Charlotte-Mecklenburg Board of Education*, 379 F. Supp. 1102, 1103 (W.D.N.C. 1974); "New Pupil Assignment Plan Is Approved," *Charlotte Observer*, July 10, 1974, p. 1A.

155 *Swann v. Charlotte-Mecklenburg Board of Education*, 379 F. Supp. 1102, 1103, 1105 (W.D.N.C. 1974).

156 *Swann v. Charlotte-Mecklenburg Board of Education*, 67 F.R.D. 648 (W.D.N.C. 1975).

157 Quoted in National Education Association, *Three Cities That Are Making Desegregation Work*, p. 34.

158 Hochschild, *The New American Dilemma*, pp. 93–107.

159 "Out of the Court and into the Future—with Hope," *Charlotte Observer*, July 12, 1975, p. 1A.

160 Interview, Robert Culbertson, October 14, 1992.

161 Hanchett, "Sorting Out the New South City," pp. 510–12.

162 Edds, *Free at Last*, p. 199.

163 Quoted in Egerton, *School Desegregation*, p. 19.

1 *Swann v. Charlotte-Mecklenburg Board of Education*, 67 F.R.D. 648 (W.D.N.C. 1975).

2 "Local Schools May Undergo More Changes," *Charlotte Observer*, June 5, 1977, p. 1A; "The Busing Plans," *Charlotte News*, May 25, 1977; Nadler, "Charlotte-Mecklenburg," p. 311.

3 Nadler, "Charlotte-Mecklenburg," p. 311. The U.S. Supreme Court ruling the previous year was *Pasadena Board of Education v. Spangler*, 427 U.S. 424 (1976).

4 *Martin v. Charlotte-Mecklenburg Board of Education*, 475 F. Supp. 1318 (W.D.N.C. 1979); Nadler, "Charlotte-Mecklenburg," pp. 315–16.

5 "Divided We Stand: The Resegregation of Our Public Schools," *Atlanta Constitution*, October 1987.

6 See, e.g., Kalodner and Fishman, *Limits of Justice*; Dimond, *Beyond Busing*; Wilkinson, *From Brown to Bakke*; Monti, *A Semblance of Justice*; Formisano, *Boston against Busing*; Graglia, *Disaster by Decree*; Wolters, *The Burden of Brown*; Wolf, *Trial and Error*; Kirp, *Just Schools*; Metcalf, *From Little Rock to Boston*; Pratt, *The Color of Their Skin*; Pride and Woodard, *The Burden of Busing*.

7 See, e.g., Graglia, *Disaster by Decree*; Wolters, *The Burden of Brown*; Wolf, *Trial and Error*.

8 U.S. Commission on Civil Rights, *New Evidence on School Desegregation*, pp. 37–41.

9 The one exception was Hidden Valley Elementary, which both the court and the school board allowed to remain majority black.

10 Lord, *Spatial Perspectives on School Desegregation and Busing*, p. 31.

11 Daniels, "In Defense of Busing," p. 37.

12 Rossell, *The Carrot or the Stick*, p. 153.

13 Ibid., p. 67; Pettigrew and Green, "School Desegregation in Large Cities."

14 Social scientists who have examined urban school desegregation have concluded that the greater the minority enrollment, the greater the white flight. Rossell and Hawley, "Understanding White Flight," p. 169.

15 Rossell, "Desegregation Plans, Racial Isolation, White Flight, and Community Response," p. 32; Hochschild, *Thirty Years after Brown*, p. 10; Orfield, *Must We Bus?*, p. 63.

16 *Milliken v. Bradley*, 418 U.S. 717 (1974).

17 Hochschild, *Thirty Years after Brown*, p. 7.

18 Charlotte had a metropolitan area of 571,000, whereas Richmond had 553,000 residents. Orfield, *Must We Bus?*, p. 63; U.S. Bureau of the Census, *Statistical Abstract of the United States: 1973*, pp. 850, 890.

19 Orfield, *Must We Bus?*, p. 63.

20 Egerton, *School Desegregation*, p. 17.

21 Alabama Council on Human Relations, "It's Not Over in the South: Desegregation in Forty-Three Southern Cities Eighteen Years after Brown," p.

13, Charlotte-Mecklenburg Community Relations Committee Papers, Charlotte (CMCRC).

22 Statement of James B. McMillan, in U.S. Senate Committee on the Judiciary, *Hearings before the Subcommittee on the Separation of Powers*, pp. 555–61.

23 By 1980, the city was considerably more desegregated by residence than it had been in 1970. Pearce, *Breaking Down Barriers*; Spence, "Has Busing Hit the Skids?," p. 59.

24 Orfield, *Toward a New Strategy for Urban Integration*, pp. 23–24, 67.

25 Quoted in Egerton, *School Desegregation*, p. 19.

26 A 1981 study of Charlotte real estate found that in the determination of housing values, perceived school quality was a much more important factor than was the racial composition of schools. Jud and Watts, "Real Estate Values, School Quality, and the Pattern of Urban Development in Charlotte, North Carolina," p. 88. This study stood in contrast to earlier studies that had found that the racial composition of public schools had a significant impact on housing values. Clotfelter, "The Effect of School Desegregation on Housing Prices," p. 446.

27 Statement of James B. McMillan, in U.S. Senate Committee on the Judiciary, *Hearings before the Subcommittee on the Separation of Powers*, pp. 555–61; Egerton, *School Desegregation*, p. 16; "First in Busing," *Charlotte News*, September 12, 1975, p. 1A; "Test Scores Up but Black-White Gap Widens," *Charlotte News*, July 15, 1981, p. 4D; "In a District That Made It Work, Questions about Busing's Future," *Philadelphia Inquirer*, April 23, 1989; "Charlotte's Blacks View Nine Years of Busing as a 'Necessary Evil,'" *Wall Street Journal*, November 6, 1979, p. 1; "Rulings on School Integration Key Target for Conservatives," *New York Times*, May 17, 1982, p. 1. These results in Charlotte are consistent with various studies that have found educational gains for minority students in the wake of school desegregation, particularly in the elementary grades and particularly when the minority population is relatively small. Mahard and Crain, "Research on Minority Achievement in Desegregated Schools."

28 Statement of James B. McMillan, in U.S. Senate Committee on the Judiciary, *Hearings before the Subcommittee on the Separation of Powers*, pp. 555–61.

29 Quoted in Gaillard, *Dream Long Deferred*, p. 168.

30 California Achievement Test Results for Ethnic Groups, 1978–92, Charlotte-Mecklenburg Public Schools, Charlotte.

31 "Editorial," *Charlotte Observer*, October 9, 1984, quoted in "That Busing Success Story," *Wall Street Journal*, January 21, 1985, p. 22.

32 "Justice's Quiet Spokesman: Judge McMillan's Modesty Belies His Impact since '68," *Charlotte Observer*, March 26, 1989, p. 1A.

33 Kratt, *Charlotte: Spirit of the New South*, p. 148.

34 Quoted in Egerton, *School Desegregation*, p. 18.

35 Tom Wicker, "In the Nation—Busing after a Decade," *New York Times*,

in U.S. Senate Committee on the Judiciary, *Hearings before the Subcommittee on the Separation of Powers*, p. 352.

36 "In a District That Made It Work, Questions about Busing's Future," *Philadelphia Inquirer*, April 23, 1989.

37 "First in Busing," *Charlotte News*, September 12, 1975, p. 1A.

38 "West Charlotte and Its Boston Guests," *Jefferson Standard Editorial*, October 22, 1974, Series 1, Box 5, McMillan Papers, Chapel Hill; "20 Queen City Pupils to Make Boston Visit," *Durham Morning Herlad*, November 11, 1974, p. 13A.

39 Gaillard, *Dream Long Deferred*, p. 155.

40 Edds, *Free at Last*, p. 192.

41 Charles S. Bullock, "The Election of Blacks in the South."

42 Quoted in National Education Association, *Three Cities That Are Making Desegregation Work*, p. 36.

43 "Tournament Invigorates Charlotte," *New York Times*, April 2, 1994, p. 7A; Edds, *Free at Last*, p. 196.

44 "Divided We Stand: The Resegregation of Our Public Schools," *Atlanta Constitution*, October 1987.

45 In 1985, Charlotte attorney Ralph McMillan challenged—in a *Wall Street Journal* editorial—the claim that busing had "succeeded" in Charlotte. *Wall Street Journal*, "That Busing Success Story," January 21, 1985, p. 22.

46 "Tate Buoyed by Black Vote," *Charlotte Observer*, June 6, 1990, p. 1A.

47 "Charlotte's Black Community Divided over Magnet Schools," *Charlotte Observer*, March 1, 1992, p. 1A. A 1994 survey of opinion in Charlotte found that 68 percent of the black respondents believed that busing was necessary to ensure equal educational opportunities, whereas only 35 percent of the white respondents agreed. "Survey Spotlights the Black-White Social Distance," *Charlotte Observer*, May 3, 1994, p. 1C.

48 "For the Record: Dr. John Murphy," *Charlotte Observer*, May 3, 1994, p. 8A.

49 "Charlotte's Black Community Divided over Magnet Schools," *Charlotte Observer*, March 1, 1992, p. 1A.

50 Rosenberg, *The Hollow Hope*; Klarman, "*Brown*, Racial Change, and the Civil Rights Movement."

51 Bell, "*Brown v. Board of Education* and the Interest-Convergence Dilemma."

52 Niebuhr, *Moral Man and Immoral Society*, pp. 252–53.

Bibliography

Manuscript Collections

Atlanta, Georgia
Paul Ervin, Jr.
  Paul Ervin Papers

Boston, Massachusetts
Massachusetts Institute of Technology Library
  Anti-Defamation League, "The High Cost of Conflict: A Roundup of
    Opinion from the Southern Business Community on the Economic
    Consequences of School Closing and Violence," 1983

Chapel Hill, North Carolina
University of North Carolina Library, North Carolina Collection
  American Friends Service Committee, *Newsletter*, October 1959
  Stanford Brookshire, "Brookshire Lives," 1979
  Department of Public Instruction, Raleigh, "Report of Governor's
    Commission for the Study of Problems in the Education of Negroes in
    North Carolina," 1935
  James Farmer, "Mass Action Makes N.C. Live Up to Liberal Reputation,"
    CORE-lator, July 1963
  Office of State Superintendent of Public Instruction, Raleigh, "Biennial
    Report of the Superintendent of Public Instruction of North Carolina,"
    1879, 1880, 1908–9, 1909–10
  James E. Shepard, "Racial Relationships in North Carolina," 1947
University of North Carolina Library, Southern Historical Collection
  James McMillan Papers
  Southern Oral History Program

Charlotte, North Carolina
Charlotte-Mecklenburg Community Relations Committee
  Charlotte-Mecklenburg Community Relations Committee Papers (CMCRC)
Charlotte-Mecklenburg Public Schools
  California Achievement Test Results for Ethnic Groups, 1978–92
Mecklenburg County Board of Elections
  Abstract of Votes for County Board of Education, May 2, 1970, May 30,
    1970
Public Library of Charlotte and Mecklenburg County
  Charlotte-Mecklenburg Council on Human Relations, "The New Negro and
    Carver College," August 1961
United States Courthouse
  Record on Appeal to the United States Court of Appeals, *Swann v.
    Charlotte-Mecklenburg Board of Education*

University of North Carolina at Charlotte, Atkins Library
    Frederick Douglass Alexander Papers
    Kelly Miller Alexander, Sr., Papers
    Stanford Brookshire Papers
    Julius L. Chambers Papers
    Charlotte-Mecklenburg Community Relations Committee Papers (UNCC)
    Harry Golden Papers
    Joseph Grier Papers
    Reginald Hawkins Papers
    Benjamin Horack Papers
Carlton Watkins
    Carlton Watkins Papers

Raleigh, North Carolina
North Carolina State Archives
    Luther Hartwell Hodges Papers

Washington, D.C.
Library of Congress
    Hugo Black Papers
    William O. Douglas Papers
    Thurgood Marshall Papers
    NAACP Papers

Microfilm Collections

Williamsburg, Virginia
College of William and Mary, Marshall-Wythe Law Library
    U.S. Supreme Court Records and Briefs

Wilmington, Delaware
Microfilm Collection of Scholarly Resources
    FBI File on the Black Panther Party of North Carolina
    FBI File on the National Association for the Advancement of Colored People
    (NAACP)

Newspapers and Periodicals

Asheville Citizen
Atlanta Constitution
Boston Globe
Carolina Times
Chapel Hill Weekly
Charlotte News
Charlotte Observer

Charlotte Post
Congressional Record
Durham Morning Herald
Fayetteville Observer
Greensboro Daily News
New York Times
Race Relations Law Reporter

Raleigh News and Observer
Southern School News
Star of Zion

Washington Post
Winston-Salem Journal

Interviews

All interviews are by the author.
Betsy Blackwell, May 20, 1992, Williamsburg, Virginia
Jack Bullard, December 14, 1994, Charlotte, North Carolina
Julius Chambers, August 16, 1993, Durham, North Carolina
Daniel Clodfelter, July 30, 1981, Charlotte, North Carolina
Robert Culbertson, October 14, 1992, Charlotte, North Carolina
Paul Ervin, Jr., January 23, 1992, Atlanta, Georgia
Sidney Freeman, December 15, 1994, Charlotte, North Carolina
Cloyd Goodrum, December 14, 1994, Charlotte, North Carolina
Joseph Grier, July 8, 1992, Charlotte, North Carolina
Reginald Hawkins, October 12, 1992, Charlotte, North Carolina
Fred Hicks, October 14, 1992, Charlotte, North Carolina
Calvin Hood, October 15, 1992, Charlotte, North Carolina
Benjamin Horack, October 13, 1992, Charlotte, North Carolina
Charles Jones, December 16, 1994, Charlotte, North Carolina
Clifford Jones, October 13, 1992, Charlotte, North Carolina
James McMillan, August 27, 1981, Charlotte, North Carolina
Julian Mason, December 6, 1994, Charlotte, North Carolina
Julia Maulden, December 14, 1994, Concord, Tennessee
James Paul, February 24, 1993, Newark, New Jersey
William Poe, July 9, 1992, Charlotte, North Carolina
Elizabeth Randolph, October 15, 1992, Charlotte, North Carolina
Margaret Ray, October 15, 1992, Charlotte, North Carolina
Thomas Ray, October 15, 1992, Charlotte, North Carolina
Ed Sanders, October 12, 1992, Charlotte, North Carolina
Jane Scott, October 15, 199,. Charlotte, North Carolina
Adam Stein, December 3, 4, 1992, Chapel Hill, North Carolina
William Sturges, October 12, 1992, Charlotte, North Carolina
Darius Swann, December 6, 1994, Atlanta, Georgia
Vera Swann, December 7, 1994, Atlanta, Georgia
William Waggoner, October 14, 1992, Charlotte, North Carolina
Jonathan Wallas, October 14, 1992, Charlotte, North Carolina
Carlton Watkins, July 6, 1992, Charlotte, North Carolina
Raymond Worsley, October 15, 1992, Charlotte, North Carolina

Books, Articles, and Dissertations

Alexander, Roberta Sue. "Hostility and Hope: Black Education in North Carolina during Presidential Reconstruction, 1865–1867." *North Carolina Historical Review* 53 (April 1976): 113–32.

————. *North Carolina Faces the Freedmen: Race Relations during Presidential Reconstruction, 1865–1867*. Durham: Duke University Press, 1985.

Allen, Jesse. "The Effects of School Desegregation on the Employment Status of Negro Principals in North Carolina." Ed.D. dissertation, Duke University, 1969.

Anderson, Eric. *Race and Politics in North Carolina, 1872–1901: The Black Second*. Baton Rouge: Louisiana State University Press, 1980.

Armor, David. "The Evidence on Busing." *Public Interest* 28 (Summer 1972): 90–126.

Ashmore, Harry S. *An Epitaph for Dixie*. New York: W. W. Norton and Co., 1958.

————. *The Negro and the Schools*. Chapel Hill: University of North Carolina Press, 1954.

Bacigal, Ronald J., and Margaret F. Bacigal. "A Case Study of the Federal Judiciary's Role in Court Ordered Busing: The Professional and Personal Experiences of U.S. District Court Judge Robert R. Merhige." *Journal of Law and Politics* 3 (Spring 1987): 693–725.

Bailey, Kenneth. *Southern White Protestantism in the Twentieth Century*. New York: Harper and Row, 1964.

Barksdale, Marcellus C. "The Indigenous Civil Rights Movement and Cultural Change in North Carolina: Weldon, Chapel Hill, and Monroe, 1946–1965." Ph.D. dissertation, Duke University, 1977.

Barrows, Frank. "School Busing: Charlotte, N.C." *Atlantic Monthly* 230 (November 1972): 17–22.

Bartley, Numan V. *The Rise of Massive Resistance: Race and Politics in the South during the 1950's*. Baton Rouge: Louisiana State University Press, 1969.

Bass, Jack. *Unlikely Heroes: The Dramatic Story of the Southern Judges of the Fifth Circuit Who Translated the Supreme Court's Brown Decision into a Revolution for Equality*. New York: Simon and Schuster, 1981.

Bass, Jack, and Walter DeVries. *The Transformation of Southern Politics: Social Change and Political Consequence since 1945*. New York: Basic Books, 1976.

Batchelor, John. "Rule of Law: North Carolina School Desegregation from *Brown* to *Swann*, 1954–1974." Ed.D. dissertation, North Carolina State University, 1992.

————. "Save Our Schools: Dallas Herring and the Governor's Special Advisory Committee on Education." M.A. thesis, University of North Carolina at Greensboro, 1983.

Bell, Derrick A., Jr. "*Brown v. Board of Education* and the Interest-Convergence Dilemma." *Harvard Law Review* 93 (1980): 518–33.

————. "Serving Two Masters: Integration Ideals and Client Interests in School Desegregation Litigation." *Yale Law Journal* 85 (1976): 470–516.

Beyle, Thad L. "The Paradox of North Carolina." In *Politics and Policy in*

North Carolina, edited by Thad L. Beyle and Merle Black. New York: MSS Information Corp., 1975.

Bickel, Alexander. "The Decade of School Desegregation: Progress and Prospects." *Columbia Law Review* 64 (1964): 193–229.

Black, Earl. *Southern Governors and Civil Rights: Racial Segregation as a Campaign Issue in the Second Reconstruction*. Cambridge: Harvard University Press, 1976.

Blythe, LeGette, and Charles Brockmann. *Hornets' Nest: The Story of Charlotte and Mecklenburg County*. Charlotte: Published for the Public Library of Charlotte and Mecklenburg County by McNally, 1961.

Bond, Horace Mann. *The Education of the Negro in the American Social Order*. New York: Prentice-Hall, 1934.

Bracey, John, August Meier, and Elliott Rudwick, eds. *Conflict and Competition: Studies in the Recent Black Protest Movement*. Belmont, Calif.: Wadsworth Publishing Co., 1971.

Branch, Taylor. *Parting the Waters: America in the King Years, 1954–1963*. New York: Simon and Schuster, 1988.

Brauer, Carl. *John F. Kennedy and the Second Reconstruction*. New York: Columbia University Press, 1977.

Brooks, Thomas R. *Walls Come Tumbling Down: A History of the Civil Rights Movement, 1940–1970*. Englewood Cliffs, N.J.: Prentice-Hall, 1974.

Bullock, Charles. "The Election of Blacks in the South: Preconditions and Consequences." *American Journal of Political Science* 19 (November 1975): 727–39.

Bullock, Henry. *A History of Negro Education in the South: From 1619 to the Present*. Cambridge: Harvard University Press, 1967.

Burk, Robert F. *The Eisenhower Administration and Black Civil Rights*. Knoxville: University of Tennessee Press, 1984.

Burns, Augustus. "North Carolina and the Negro Dilemma, 1930–1950." Ph.D. dissertation, University of North Carolina, 1968.

Burstein, Paul. *Discrimination, Jobs, and Politics: The Struggle for Equal Employment Opportunity in the United States since the New Deal*. Chicago: University of Chicago Press, 1985.

Carson, Clayborne. *In Struggle: SNCC and the Black Awakening of the 1960s*. Cambridge: Harvard University Press, 1981.

Cash, W. J. "Close View of a Calvinist Lhasa." *American Mercury* 28 (April 1933): 443–51.

Cecelski, David S. *Along Freedom Road: Hyde County, North Carolina, and the Fate of Black Schools in the South*. Chapel Hill: University of North Carolina Press, 1994.

Center for Urban Affairs, ed. *Paths Toward Freedom: A Biographical History of Blacks and Indians in North Carolina by Blacks and Indians*. Raleigh: Center for Urban Affairs, 1976.

Chafe, William. *Civilities and Civil Rights: Greensboro, North Carolina, and the Black Struggle for Freedom*. New York: Oxford University Press, 1980.

Charlotte-Mecklenburg Council on Human Relations. "The School Board

Must Move toward Full Compliance." *New South* 14 (December 1959): 11–12.

Claiborne, Jack. *The Charlotte Observer: Its Time and Place, 1869–1986.* Chapel Hill: University of North Carolina Press, 1986.

Clay, James W., ed. "Atlas of Charlotte-Mecklenburg." UNCC Monograph Series in Geography, No. 3. Charlotte: University of North Carolina at Charlotte, 1981.

Clayton, Bruce. *W. J. Cash: A Life.* Baton Rouge: Louisiana State University Press, 1991.

Clotfelter, Charles. "The Effect of School Desegregation on Housing Prices." *Review of Economics and Statistics* 57 (November 1975): 446–51.

Cobb, James C. *Industrialization and Southern Society, 1877–1984.* Lexington: University Press of Kentucky, 1984.

———. *The Selling of the South: The Southern Crusade for Industrial Development, 1936–1980.* Baton Rouge: Louisiana State University Press, 1982.

Cochran, A. B. "Desegregating Public Education in North Carolina." In *Politics and Policy in North Carolina*, edited by Thad L. Beyle and Merle Black. New York: MSS Information Corp., 1975.

Colburn, David. *Racial Change and Community Crisis: St. Augustine, Florida, 1877–1980.* New York: Columbia University Press, 1985.

Combs, Michael W. "The Federal Judiciary and Northern School Desegregation: Judicial Management in Perspective." *Journal of Law and Education* 13 (July 1984): 345–99.

Conner, Robert D. W., and Clarence Poe. *The Life and Speeches of Charles Brantley Aycock.* Garden City, N.Y.: Doubleday, Page and Co., 1912.

Coogan, William H. "School Board Decisions on Desegregation in North Carolina." Ph.D. dissertation, University of North Carolina at Chapel Hill, 1971.

Coon, Charles. "The Beginnings of the North Carolina City Schools, 1867–1887." *South Atlantic Quarterly* 12 (July 1913): 235–47.

———. *Public Taxation and Negro Schools.* Cheyney, Penn.: Committee of Twelve for the Advancement of the Interests of the Negro Race, 1909.

———. "School Support and Our North Carolina Courts, 1868–1926." *North Carolina Historical Review* 3 (July 1926): 399–438.

Crain, Robert, and Rita Mahard. "Desegregation and Black Achievement: A Review of the Research." *Law and Contemporary Problems* 42 (Summer 1978): 17–56.

Cramer, M. Richard. "School Desegregation and New Industry: The Southern Community Leaders' Viewpoint." *Social Forces* 41 (May 1963): 384–89.

Crow, Jeffrey. "Cracking the Solid South: Populism and the Fusionist Interlude." In *The North Carolina Experience: An Interpretive and Documentary History*, edited by Lindley S. Butler and Alan D. Watson. Chapel Hill: University of North Carolina Press, 1984.

Crow, Jeffrey, Paul Escott, and Charles Flynn, eds. *Race, Class, and Politics in*

Southern History: Essays in Honor of Robert F. Durden. Baton Rouge: Louisiana State University Press, 1989.

Crow, Jeffrey, Paul Escott, and Flora Hatley. *A History of African Americans in North Carolina.* Raleigh: North Carolina Division of Archives and History, 1992.

Crow, Jeffrey, and Robert Winters, eds. *The Black Presence in North Carolina.* Raleigh: North Carolina Museum of History, 1978.

Dale, Charlene Thomas. "City-County Educational Consolidation in Charlotte and Mecklenburg: An Historical Appraisal of Change." Ph.D. dissertation, University of North Carolina, 1968.

Daniels, Lee A. "In Defense of Busing." *New York Times Magazine,* April 17, 1983, 34–98.

Davis, Gregory. "A Multi-Disciplinary Critique of the Protest-Accommodationist Analysis of the Black Church and Black Leadership Styles, with an Analysis of the Leadership Style of Dr. Reginald Armistice Hawkins." Ph.D. dissertation, Union Graduate School, 1985.

Days, Drew, III. "The Other Desegregation Story: Eradicating the Dual System in Hillsborough County, Florida." *Fordham Law Review* 61 (October 1992): 33–37.

———. "School Desegregation Law in the 1980's: Why Isn't Anybody Laughing?" *Yale Law Journal* 95 (July 1986): 1737–68.

Dimond, Paul. *Beyond Busing: Inside the Challenge to Urban Segregation.* Ann Arbor: University of Michigan Press, 1985.

Dittmer, John. *Local People: The Struggle for Civil Rights in Mississippi.* Urbana: University of Illinois Press, 1994.

Diver, Colin. "The Judge as Political Powerbroker: Superintending Structural Change in Public Institutions." *Virginia Law Review* 65 (February 1979): 43–106.

Douglas, Davison M. "The Rhetoric of Moderation: Desegregating the South during the Decade after *Brown.*" *Northwestern University Law Review* 89 (Fall 1994): 92–139.

———, ed. *The Development of School Busing as a Desegregation Remedy.* New York: Garland Publishing, 1994.

Du Bois, W. E. B. *The Negro Common School.* Atlanta: University Press, 1901.

Du Bois, W. E. B., and A. Dill. *The Common School and the Negro American.* Atlanta: Atlanta University Press, 1911.

Dudziak, Mary. "Desegregation as a Cold War Imperative." *Stanford Law Review* 41 (November 1988): 61–120.

Dunn, Charles. "An Exercise of Choice: North Carolina's Approach to the Segregation-Integration Crisis in Public Education." M.A. thesis, University of North Carolina, 1959.

Dunn, James. "Title VI, the Guidelines, and School Desegregation in the South." *Virginia Law Review* 53 (January 1967): 42–88.

Eagles, Charles W., ed. *The Civil Rights Movement in America.* Jackson: University Press of Mississippi, 1986.

Earnhardt, Elizabeth. "Critical Years: The North Carolina Commission on Interracial Cooperation, 1942–1949." M.A. thesis, University of North Carolina, 1971.

Edds, Margaret. *Free at Last: Black Political Power in the South, 1965–1985.* Bethesda, Md.: Adler and Adler, 1987.

Edmonds, Helen. *The Negro and Fusion Politics in North Carolina, 1894–1901.* Chapel Hill: University of North Carolina Press, 1951.

Edsall, Preston, and Oliver Williams. "North Carolina: Bipartisan Paradox." In *The Changing Politics of the South*, edited by William C. Havard. Baton Rouge: Louisiana State University Press, 1972.

Egerton, John. *School Desegregation: A Report Card from the South.* Atlanta: Southern Regional Council, 1976.

———. "When Desegregation Comes, the Negro Principals Go." *Southern Education Report* 3 (December 1967): 8–12.

Emory, Frank. "Some Aspects of the Black Experience in Politics." In *Paths toward Freedom: A Biographical History of Blacks and Indians in North Carolina by Blacks and Indians*, edited by Center for Urban Affairs. Raleigh: Center for Urban Affairs, 1976.

Erskine, Hazel. "The Polls: Race Relations." *Public Opinion Quarterly* 26 (Spring 1962): 137–48.

Escott, Paul. *Many Excellent People: Power and Privilege in North Carolina, 1850–1900.* Chapel Hill: University of North Carolina Press, 1985.

Fairclough, Adam. *To Redeem the Soul of America: The Southern Christian Leadership Conference and Martin Luther King, Jr.* Athens: University of Georgia Press, 1987.

Fancher, Betsy. *Voices from the South: Blacks Students Talk about Their Experiences in Desegregated Schools.* Atlanta: Southern Regional Council, 1970.

Federal Housing Administration. *FHA Underwriting Manual.* Washington, D.C.: GPO, 1938.

Finch, Minnie. *The NAACP: Its Fight for Justice.* Metuchen, N.J.: Scarecrow Press, 1981.

Formisano, Ronald P. *Boston against Busing: Race, Class, and Ethnicity in the 1960s and 1970s.* Chapel Hill: University of North Carolina Press, 1991.

Foy, Marjorie Anne Elvin. "Durham in Black and White: School Desegregation in Durham, North Carolina, 1954–1963." M.A. thesis, University of North Carolina at Greensboro, 1991.

Frank, John. *Clement Haynsworth, the Senate, and the Supreme Court.* Charlottesville: University Press of Virginia, 1991.

Franklin, John Hope. *The Free Negro in North Carolina, 1790–1860.* Chapel Hill: University of North Carolina Press, 1943.

———. *From Slavery to Freedom: A History of American Negroes.* New York: Knopf, 1956.

Freyer, Tony. *The Little Rock Crisis: A Constitutional Interpretation.* Westport, Conn.: Greenwood Press, 1984.

Gaillard, Frye. *The Dream Long Deferred*. Chapel Hill: University of North Carolina Press, 1988.

Gaillard, Frye, and Polly Paddock. "Charlotte's Busing Breakthrough." *The Progressive* 39 (October 1975): 36–37.

Garrow, David. *Bearing the Cross: Martin Luther King, Jr., and the Southern Christian Leadership Conference*. New York: W. Morrow, 1986.

————. *Protest at Selma: Martin Luther King, Jr., and the Voting Rights Act of 1965*. New Haven: Yale University Press, 1978.

Gavins, Raymond. "The NAACP in North Carolina during the Age of Segregation." In *New Directions in Civil Rights Studies*, edited by Armstead L. Robinson and Patricia Sullivan. Charlottesville: University Press of Virginia, 1991.

Goldfield, David R. *Black, White, and Southern: Race Relations and Southern Culture 1940 to the Present*. Baton Rouge: Louisiana State University Press, 1990.

————. *Cotton Fields and Skyscrapers: Southern City and Region, 1607–1980*. Baton Rouge: Louisiana State University Press, 1982.

Graglia, Lino. *Disaster by Decree: The Supreme Court Decisions on Race and the Schools*. Ithaca, N.Y.: Cornell University Press, 1976.

Graham, Hugh. *The Civil Rights Era: Origins and Development of National Policy, 1960–1972*. New York: Oxford University Press, 1990.

Greenberg, Jack. *Crusaders in the Courts: How a Dedicated Band of Lawyers Fought for the Civil Rights Revolution*. New York: Basic Books, 1994.

————. "The Supreme Court, Civil Rights, and Civil Dissonance." *Yale Law Journal* 77 (July 1968): 1520–44.

Greenwood, Janette Thomas. "Bittersweet Legacy: The Black and White 'Better Classes' in Charlotte, North Carolina, 1850–1910." Ph.D. dissertation, University of Virginia, 1991.

————. *Bittersweet Legacy: The Black and White "Better Classes" in Charlotte, 1850–1910*. Chapel Hill: University of North Carolina Press, 1994.

Halperin, Edward C. "Special Report: Desegregation of Hospitals and Medical Societies in North Carolina." *New England Journal of Medicine* 318 (January 7, 1988): 58–63.

Hanchett, Thomas W. "The Rosenwald Schools and Black Education in North Carolina." *North Carolina Historical Review* 65 (October 1988): 387–444.

————. "Sorting Out the New South City: Charlotte and Its Neighborhoods." Ph.D. dissertation. University of North Carolina at Chapel Hill, 1993.

Harlan, Louis. *Separate and Unequal: Public School Campaigns and Racism in the Southern Seaboard States, 1901–1915*. Chapel Hill: University of North Carolina Press, 1958.

Hawley, Willis, ed. *Effective School Desegregation: Equity, Quality, and Feasibility*. Beverly Hills, Calif.: Sage Publications, 1981.

Hochschild, Jennifer. *The New American Dilemma: Liberal Democracy and School Desegregation*. New Haven, Conn.: Yale University Press, 1984.

—. *Thirty Years after Brown*. Washington, D.C.: Joint Center for Political Studies, 1985.

Hodges, H. Clay. "The Hard Light of Fact: Judge James Bryan McMillan and the *Swann* Case." Honors Essay, Department of History, University of North Carolina at Chapel Hill, 1990.

Hodges, Luther. *Businessman in the Statehouse: Six Years as Governor of North Carolina*. Chapel Hill: University of North Carolina Press, 1962.

—. *Messages, Addresses, and Public Papers of Luther Hartwell Hodges, Governor of North Carolina, 1954–1961*, vol. 1. Edited by James W. Patton. Raleigh: Council of State, State of North Carolina, 1960.

Hoey, Clyde. *Addresses, Letters, and Papers of Clyde Roark Hoey, Governor of North Carolina, 1937–1941*. Edited by David Corbett. Raleigh: Council of State, State of North Carolina, 1944.

Horowitz, David. "White Southerners' Alienation and Civil Rights: The Response to Corporate Liberalism, 1956–1965." *Journal of Southern History* 54 (May 1988): 173–200.

Jacoway, Elizabeth. "An Introduction: Civil Rights and the Changing South." In *Southern Businessmen and Desegregation*, edited by Elizabeth Jacoway and David Colburn. Baton Rouge: Louisiana State University Press, 1982.

Jacoway, Elizabeth, and David Colburn, eds. *Southern Businessmen and Desegregation*. Baton Rouge: Louisiana State University Press, 1982.

Johnson, Charles S. *Backgrounds to Patterns of Negro Segregation*. New York: Crowell, 1943.

—. *Into the Main Stream: A Survey of Best Practices in Race Relations in the South*. Chapel Hill: University of North Carolina Press, 1947.

Johnson, Elmer D. "James Yadkin Joyner, Educational Statesman." *North Carolina Historical Review* 33 (July 1956): 359–83.

Jud, G. Donald, and James M. Watts. "Real Estate Values, School Quality, and the Pattern of Urban Development in Charlotte, North Carolina." *Economics of Education Review* 1 (Winter 1981): 87–97.

Kalodner, Howard, and James Fishman, eds. *Limits of Justice: The Courts' Role in School Desegregation*. Cambridge, Mass.: Ballinger Publishing Co., 1978.

Kaufman, Irving. "Masters in Federal Courts: Rule 53." *Columbia Law Review* 58 (1978): 452–69.

Kellogg, Charles. *NAACP: A History of the National Association for the Advancement of Colored People*. Baltimore: Johns Hopkins Press, 1967.

Key, Valdimer O. *Southern Politics in State and Nation*. New York: A. A. Knopf, 1949.

King, William. "The Era of Progressive Reform in Southern Education: The Growth of Public Schools in North Carolina, 1885–1910." Ph.D. dissertation, Duke University, 1970.

Kirp, David. *Just Schools: The Idea of Racial Equality in American Education*. Berkeley: University of California Press, 1982.

Klarman, Michael J. "*Brown*, Racial Change, and the Civil Rights Movement." *Virginia Law Review* 80 (1994): 7–150.

Kluger, Richard. *Simple Justice: The History of Brown v. Board of Education and Black America's Struggle for Equality*. New York: Knopf, 1975.

Knight, Edgar. *Public School Education in North Carolina*. Boston: Houghton Mifflin Co., 1916.

Kousser, J. Morgan. *Dead End: The Development of Nineteenth-Century Litigation on Race Discrimination in the Schools*. Oxford: Clarendon Press, 1986.

Kratt, Mary. *Charlotte: Spirit of the New South*. Tulsa: Continental Heritage Press, 1980.

Kurland, Philip B., and Gerhard Casper, eds. *Landmark Briefs and Arguments of the Supreme Court of the United States*, vols. 49a, 70. Arlington, Va.: University Publications of America, 1975.

Kushner, James A. *Apartheid in America: An Historical and Legal Analysis of Contemporary Racial Segregation in the United States*. Gaithersburg, Md.: Associated Faculty Press, 1980.

Lamanna, Richard. "The Negro Public School Teacher and School Desegregation: A Survey of Negro Teachers in North Carolina." Ph.D. dissertation, University of North Carolina at Chapel Hill, 1966.

Lawson, Steven F. *Black Ballots: Voting Rights in the South, 1944–1969*. New York: Columbia University Press, 1976.

———. *In Pursuit of Power: Southern Blacks and Electoral Politics, 1965–1982*. New York: Columbia University Press, 1985.

Leach, Damaria. "Progress under Pressure: Changes in Charlotte Race Relations, 1955–1965." M.A. thesis, University of North Carolina, 1976.

Lefler, Hugh, and Albert Newsome. *North Carolina, the History of a Southern State*. Chapel Hill: University of North Carolina Press, 1963.

LeLoudis, James. "'A More Certain Means of Grace': Pedagogy, Self, and Society in North Carolina, 1880–1920." Ph.D. dissertation, University of North Carolina, 1989.

Lewis, Kenneth. "The History of Black Lawyers in North Carolina." *Bar Notes* (December 1987/January 1988), 9.

Logan, Frenise. *The Negro in North Carolina, 1876–1894*. Chapel Hill: University of North Carolina Press, 1964.

Lord, J. Dennis. "School Busing and White Abandonment of Public Schools." *Southeastern Geographer* 15 (November 1975): 81–92.

———. *Spatial Perspectives on School Desegregation and Busing*. Washington, D.C.: Association of American Geographers, 1977.

Lord, J. Dennis, and John C. Catau. "School Desegregation Policy and Intra-school District Migration." *Social Science Quarterly* 57 (1977): 784–96.

Luebke, Paul. "Corporate Conservatism and Government Moderation in North Carolina." In *Perspectives on the American South: An Annual Review of Society, Politics, and Culture*, edited by Merle Black and John Shelton Reed. New York: Gordon and Breach Science Publishers, 1981.

———. *Tar Heel Politics: Myths and Realities*. Chapel Hill: University of North Carolina Press, 1990.

Lukas, J. Anthony. *Common Ground: A Turbulent Decade in the Lives of Three American Families*. New York: Knopf, 1985.

McAdam, Doug. *Political Process and the Development of Black Insurgency, 1930–1970*. Chicago: University of Chicago Press, 1982.

McDaniel, Clyde O. "Housing and Segregation of Blacks in the South." In *Urban Housing Segregation of Minorities in Western Europe and the United States*, edited by Elizabeth Huttman. Durham: Duke University Press, 1991.

McMillen, Neil. *The Citizens' Council: Organized Resistance to the Second Reconstruction, 1954–64*. Urbana: University of Illinois Press, 1971.

McNeil, Genna Rae. "Charles Hamilton Houston." *Black Law Journal* 3 (Fall 1973): 123–31.

Mahard, Rita, and Robert Crain. "Research on Minority Achievement in Desegregated Schools." In *The Consequences of School Desegregation*, edited by Christine Rossell and Willis Hawley. Philadelphia: Temple University Press, 1983.

Maniloff, Howard. "Busing in Charlotte." *South Today* 1 (January–February 1973): 1–8.

———. "Community Attitudes toward a Desegregated School System: A Study of Charlotte, North Carolina." Ed.D. dissertation, Columbia University, 1979.

Marable, Manning. *Race, Reform, and Rebellion: The Second Reconstruction in Black America, 1945–1990*. Jackson: University Press of Mississippi, 1991.

Marney, Carlyle. *Structures of Prejudice*. New York: Abingdon Press, 1961.

Marshall, Thurgood. "An Evaluation of Recent Efforts to Achieve Racial Integration in Education through Resort to the Courts." *Journal of Negro Education* 21 (Summer 1952): 316–27.

Martin, Arthur. "Segregation of Residences of Negroes." *Michigan Law Review* 32 (April 1934): 721–42.

Martin, John B. *The Deep South Says "Never."* New York: Ballantine Books, 1957.

Matthews, Donald, and James Prothro. *Negroes and the New Southern Politics*. New York: Harcourt, Brace and World, 1966.

Matney, Brian. "Two Decades after *Swann*: A Qualitative Study of School Desegregation Efforts in Charlotte and Mecklenburg County, North Carolina." Ph.D. dissertation, University of North Carolina, 1992.

Meador, Daniel. "The Constitution and the Assignment of Pupils to Public School." *Virginia Law Review* 45 (May 1959): 517–71.

Meier, August, and Elliott Rudwick. *CORE: A Study in the Civil Rights Movement, 1942–1968*. New York: Oxford University Press, 1973.

Metcalf, George. *From Little Rock to Boston: The History of School Desegregation*. Westport, Conn.: Greenwood Press, 1983.

Monti, Daniel. *A Semblance of Justice: St. Louis School Desegregation and Order in Urban America*. Columbia: University of Missouri Press, 1985.

Morris, Aldon. *The Origins of the Civil Rights Movement: Black Communities Organizing for Change*. New York: Free Press, 1984.

Moye, William T. "Charlotte-Mecklenburg Consolidation: Metrolina in Motion." Ph.D. dissertation, University of North Carolina, 1975.

Murphy, Walter. "The South Counterattacks: The Anti-NAACP Laws." *Western Political Quarterly* 12 (June 1959): 371–90.

Murray, Percy. *History of the North Carolina Teachers Association.* Washington, D.C.: National Education Association, 1984.

Muse, Benjamin. *Ten Years of Prelude: The Story of Integration since the Supreme Court's 1954 Decision.* New York: Viking Press, 1964.

Myerson, Michael. *Nothing Could Be Finer.* New York: International Publishers, 1978.

Myrdal, Gunnar. *An American Dilemma: The Negro Problem and Modern Democracy.* New York: Harper, 1944.

Nadler, Mark. "Charlotte-Mecklenburg." In *Busing U.S.A.*, edited by Nicholaus Mills. New York: Teachers College Press, 1979.

National Association for the Advancement of Colored People (NAACP). *In Freedom's Vanguard: NAACP Report for 1963.* New York: NAACP, 1964.

———. "The Negro Common School in North Carolina." *Crisis* 34 (May 1927): 79–80, 96–97; 34 (June 1927): 117–18, 133–35.

———. *Progress and Portents: NAACP Annual Report for 1958.* New York: NAACP, 1958.

National Association for the Advancement of Colored People (NAACP) Legal Defense and Educational Fund. *It's Not the Distance, "It's the Niggers."* New York: NAACP Legal Defense and Educational Fund, 1972.

National Education Association. *Three Cities That Are Making Desegregation Work.* Washington, D.C.: National Education Association, Human and Civil Rights, 1984.

Newbold, N. C. "Some Achievements in the Equalization of Educational Opportunities in North Carolina." *Educational Forum* 9 (May 1945): 451–66.

Niebuhr, Reinhold. *Moral Man and Immoral Society: A Study in Ethics and Politics.* New York: C. Scribner's, 1932.

Noble, Marcus C. S. *A History of Public Schools of North Carolina.* Chapel Hill: University of North Carolina Press, 1930.

Norrell, Robert J. *Reaping the Whirlwind: The Civil Rights Movement in Tuskegee.* New York: Alfred A. Knopf, 1985.

North Carolina Advisory Committee to the United States Commission on Civil Rights. *Equal Protection of the Laws in North Carolina.* Washington, D.C.: GPO, 1962.

"Note: New Perspectives on Court Ordered Busing." *Columbia Journal of Law and Social Problems* 8 (1972): 321–37.

Oppenheimer, Martin. *The Sit-In Movement of 1960.* Brooklyn: Carlson Publishing, 1989.

Orfield, Gary. "Congress, the President, and Anti-Busing Legislation, 1966–1974." *Journal of Law and Education* 4 (January 1975): 81–139.

———. *Must We Bus? Segregated Schools and National Policy.* Washington, D.C.: Brookings Institution, 1978.

———. *Public School Desegregation in the United States, 1968–1980.* Washington, D.C.: Joint Center for Political Studies, 1983.

———. *The Reconstruction of Southern Education: The Schools and the 1964 Civil Rights Act.* New York: Wiley-Interscience, 1969.

———. "Research Politics and the Antibusing Debate." *Law and Contemporary Problems* 42 (Autumn 1978): 141–73.

———. *Toward a New Strategy for Urban Integration.* New York: Ford Foundation, 1981.

Orr, Oliver. *Charles Brantley Aycock.* Chapel Hill: University of North Carolina Press, 1961.

Panetta, Leon, and Peter Gall. *Bring Us Together: The Nixon Team and the Civil Rights Retreat.* Philadelphia: J. B. Lippincott Co., 1971.

Paul, James, and Albert Coates. *The School Segregation Decision.* Chapel Hill: University of North Carolina Press, 1954.

Pearce, D. *Breaking Down Barriers: New Evidence on the Impact of Metropolitan School Desegregation on Housing Patterns.* Washington, D.C.: National Institute of Education, 1980.

Peebles, Wilma C. "School Desegregation in Raleigh, North Carolina, 1954–1964." Ph.D. dissertation, University of North Carolina, 1984.

Peltason, J. W. *Fifty-Eight Lonely Men: Southern Federal Judges and School Desegregation.* New York: Harcourt, Brace and World, 1961.

Penniger, Randy. "The Emergence of Black Political Power in Charlotte, North Carolina: The City Council Tenure of Frederick Douglass Alexander, 1965–1974." M.A. thesis, University of North Carolina at Charlotte, 1989.

Pettigrew, Thomas F., and Robert L. Green. "School Desegregation in Large Cities: A Critique of the Coleman 'White Flight' Thesis." *Harvard Educational Review* 46 (February 1976): 1–53.

Pleasants, Julian M., and Augustus M. Burns. *Frank Porter Graham and the 1950 Senate Race in North Carolina.* Chapel Hill: University of North Carolina Press, 1990.

Powell, William. *North Carolina through Four Centuries.* Chapel Hill: University of North Carolina Press, 1989.

Pratt, Robert A. *The Color of Their Skin: Education and Race in Richmond, Virginia, 1954–89.* Charlottesville: University Press of Virginia, 1992.

Pride, Richard, and J. David Woodard. *The Burden of Busing: The Politics of Desegregation in Nashville, Tennessee.* Knoxville: University of Tennessee Press, 1985.

Rabinowitz, Howard. *Race Relations in the Urban South, 1865–1890.* New York: Oxford University Press, 1978.

Randolph, Elizabeth, ed. *The Black Experience in Charlotte and Mecklenburg County.* Charlotte, N.C.: Public Library of Charlotte and Mecklenburg County, 1992.

Read, Frank. "Judicial Evolution of the Law of School Integration since Brown v. Board of Education." *Law and Contemporary Problems* 39 (Winter 1975): 7–49.

Read, Frank, and Lucy McGough. *Let Them Be Judged: The Judicial Integration of the Deep South.* Metuchen, N.J.: Scarecrow Press, 1978.

Roland, Charles. *The Improbable Era: The South since World War II.* Lexington: University Press of Kentucky, 1975.

Rosen, Sanford Jay. "Judge Soboloff's Public School Race Decisions." *Maryland Law Review* 34 (1974): 498–531.

Rosenberg, Gerald N. "*Brown* Is Dead! Long Live *Brown*!: The Endless Attempt to Canonize a Case." *Virginia Law Review* 80 (1994): 161–71.

————. *The Hollow Hope: Can Courts Bring About Social Change?* Chicago: University of Chicago Press, 1991.

Rossell, Christine. *The Carrot or the Stick for School Desegregation Policy: Magnet Schools or Forced Busing.* Philadelphia: Temple University Press, 1990.

————. "Desegregation Plans, Racial Isolation, White Flight, and Community Response." In *The Consequences of School Desegregation*, edited by Christine Rossell and Willis Hawley. Philadelphia: Temple University Press, 1983.

Rossell, Christine, and Willis Hawley. "Understanding White Flight and Doing Something about It." In *Effective School Desegregation: Equity, Quality, and Feasibility*, edited by Willis Hawley. Beverly Hills, Calif.: Sage Publications, 1981.

————, eds. *The Consequences of School Desegregation.* Philadelphia: Temple University Press, 1983.

Sarratt, Reed. *The Ordeal of Desegregation: The First Decade.* New York: Harper and Row, 1966.

Schwartz, Bernard. *Swann's Way: The School Busing Case and the Supreme Court.* New York: Oxford University Press, 1986.

Scott, Robert. *Addresses and Public Papers of Robert Walter Scott, Governor of North Carolina, 1969–1973.* Edited by M. F. Mitchell. Raleigh: Division of Archives and History, Department of Cultural Resources, 1974.

Seawell, Malcolm. "North Carolina at a Crossroad." *New South* 14 (January 1959): 3–5.

Smith, J. Clay, Jr. *Emancipation: The Making of the Black Lawyer.* Philadelphia: University of Pennsylvania Press, 1993.

Sosna, Morton. *In Search of the Silent South: Southern Liberals and the Race Issue.* New York: Columbia University Press, 1977.

Southern Education Reporting Service. *Statistical Summary of School Segregation-Desegregation in the Southern and Border States.* Nashville: Southern Educational Reporting Service, 1965.

Spence, Susan. "Has Busing Hit the Skids?" *Tarheel Magazine* 59 (October 1981): 52–62.

Starr, Michael G. "Accommodation and Accountability: A Strategy for Judicial Enforcement of Institutional Reform Decrees." *Alabama Law Review* 32 (Winter 1981): 399–440.

Swanson, Ernst W., and John A. Griffin, eds. *Public Education in the South*

Today and Tomorrow: A Statistical Survey. Chapel Hill: University of North
Carolina Press, 1955.
Taeuber, Karl, and Alma Taeuber. *Negroes in Cities: Residential Segregation
and Neighborhood Change.* Chicago: Adline Publishing, 1965.
Thompson, Ernest Trice. *Presbyterians in the South,* vol. 3. Richmond: John
Knox Press, 1973.
Towe, William. *Barriers to Black Political Participation in North Carolina.*
Atlanta: Voter Education Project, 1972.
Trillin, Calvin. "Remembrance of Moderates Past." *New Yorker* 53 (March 21,
1977): 85–97.
Tumin, Melvin. *Segregation and Desegregation: A Digest of Recent Research.*
Westport, Conn.: Greenwood Press, 1957.
Tushnet, Mark. *Making Civil Rights Law: Thurgood Marshall and the
Supreme Court, 1936–1961.* New York: Oxford University Press, 1994.
———. *The NAACP's Legal Strategy against Segregated Education, 1925–
1950.* Chapel Hill: University of North Carolina Press, 1987.
Umstead, William. *Public Addresses, Letters, and Papers of William Bradley
Umstead, Governor of North Carolina, 1953–1954.* Edited by David
Corbitt. Raleigh: Council of State, State of North Carolina, 1957.
U.S. Bureau of the Census. *Census of Population, 1950: Characteristics of
Population, North Carolina.* Washington, D.C.: GPO, 1952.
———. *Census of Population and Housing, 1960: Charlotte, N.C.*
Washington, D.C.: GPO, 1963.
———. *1970 Census of Population and Housing: Charlotte, N.C.* Washington,
D.C.: GPO, 1972.
———. *1980 Census of Population and Housing: Charlotte-Gastonia, N.C.*
Washington, D.C.: GPO, 1982.
———. *1990 Census of Population and Housing: Survey Population and
Housing Characteristics, North Carolina.* Washington, D.C.: GPO, 1993.
———. *Report on Population of the United States at the Eleventh Census:
1890.* Washington, D.C.: GPO, 1897.
———. *Statistical Abstract of the United States: 1973.* Washington, D.C.:
GPO, 1973.
———. *Thirteenth Census of the United States Taken in the Year 1910:
Population, Occupation Statistics.* Washington, D.C.: GPO, 1914.
———. *Twelfth Census of the United States: Special Reports, Occupations.*
Washington, D.C.: GPO, 1904.
U.S. Commission on Civil Rights. *Civil Rights U.S.A.: Public Schools,
Southern States, 1962.* Washington, D.C.: GPO, 1962.
———. *New Evidence on School Desegregation.* Washington, D.C.: GPO,
1987.
———. *School Desegregation in Ten Communities.* Washington, D.C.: GPO,
1973.
———. *Survey of School Desegregation in the Southern and Border States,
1965–66.* Washington, D.C.: GPO, 1966.
U.S. Commission on Civil Rights and Richard Day. *Civil Rights U.S.A.: Public*

Schools, Southern States, 1963, North Carolina. Washington, D.C.: GPO, 1964.

U.S. House. Committee on the Judiciary. *Hearings before Subcommittee No. 5 of the Committee on the Judiciary.* 92d Cong., 2d sess., 1972.

U.S. Office of Education, Department of Health, Education and Welfare. *General Statement of Policies under Title VI of the Civil Rights Act of 1964 Respecting Desegregation of Elementary and Secondary Schools.* Washington, D.C.: GPO, 1965.

———. *Policies on Elementary and Secondary School Compliance with Title VI of the Civil Rights Act of 1964.* Washington, D.C.: GPO, 1968.

———. *Revised Statement of Policies for School Desegregation Plans under Title VI of the Civil Rights Act of 1964.* Washington, D.C.: GPO, 1966.

U.S. Senate. Committee on Labor and Public Welfare. *Hearings before the Subcommittee on Education.* 92d Cong., 2d sess., 1972.

———. Committee on the Judiciary. *Hearings before the Subcommittee on the Separation of Powers.* 97th Cong., 1st sess., 1981.

———. Select Committee on Equal Educational Opportunity. *Hearings on the Status of School Desegregation Law.* 92d Cong., 1st sess., 1971.

Vaughn, William. *Schools for All: The Blacks and Public Education in the South, 1865–1877.* Lexington: University Press of Kentucky, 1974.

Villard, Oswald Garrison. "The Crumbling Color Line." *Harpers Magazine* 66 (July 1929): 156–67.

Ware, Gilbert. "*Hocutt*: Genesis of Brown." *Journal of Negro Education* 52 (Summer 1983): 227–33.

Wasby, Stephen, Anthony D'Amato, and Rosemary Metrailer. *Desegregation from Brown to Alexander: An Exploration of Supreme Court Strategies.* Carbondale: Southern Illinois University Press, 1977.

Watters, Pat. *Charlotte.* Atlanta: Southern Regional Council, 1964.

Waynick, Capus, John Brooks, and Elsie Pitts, eds. *North Carolina and the Negro.* Raleigh: North Carolina Mayors' Cooperating Committee, 1964.

Weare, Walter B. *Black Business in the New South: A Social History of the North Carolina Mutual Life Insurance Company.* Urbana: University of Illinois Press, 1973.

Weaver, Robert. *The Negro Ghetto.* New York: Harcourt, Brace, 1948.

Weinberg, Meyer. *A Chance to Learn: The History of Race and Education in the United States.* New York: Cambridge University Press, 1977.

———. *Race and Place: A Legal History of the Neighborhood School.* Washington, D.C.: GPO, 1967.

Wettach, Robert. "North Carolina School Legislation—1956." *North Carolina Law Review* 35 (1956): 1–16.

Wey, Herbert, and John Carey. *Action Patterns in School Desegregation: A Guidebook.* Bloomington, Ind.: Phi Delta Kappa, 1959.

White House Conference. *To Fulfill These Rights.* Washington, D.C.: GPO, 1966.

Whitener, Daniel. "Public Education in North Carolina during Reconstruction, 1865–1876." In *The James Sprunt Studies in History and Political Science,* vol. 31, edited by Fletcher Green. Chapel Hill: University of North Carolina Press, 1949.

Wilkinson, J. Harvie. *From Brown to Bakke: The Supreme Court and School Integration: 1954–1978.* New York: Oxford University Press, 1979.

Williams, Juan. *Eyes on the Prize: America's Civil Rights Years, 1954–1965.* New York: Viking Press, 1987.

Williamson, Joel. *The Crucible of Race: Black/White Relations in the American South since Emancipation.* New York: Oxford University Press, 1984.

Wolf, Eleanor. *Trial and Error.* Detroit: Wayne State University Press, 1981.

Wolters, Raymond. *The Burden of Brown: Thirty Years of School Desegregation.* Knoxville: University of Tennessee Press, 1984.

Woodward, C. Vann. *Origins of the New South, 1877–1913.* Baton Rouge: Louisiana State University Press, 1951.

Wright, Marion A. "Integration and Public Morals." *New South* 12 (November 1957): 7–14.

Yarbrough, Tinsley. *Judge Frank Johnson and Human Rights in Alabama.* University: University of Alabama Press, 1981.

———. *A Passion for Justice: J. Waties Waring and Civil Rights.* New York: Oxford University Press, 1987.

Index

Newbold, Nathan, 14, 18
New Hanover County, N.C., 21
New Kent County, Va., 127–28, 139
Newman, Don, 74
Newsweek, 251
New York City, N.Y., 252
New York Herald Tribune, 102
New York Times, 72, 120, 251
Niebuhr, Reinhold, 6, 254
Nixon, Richard, 159; criticizes judges, 153; sets forth busing policy, 180–81, 188, 192, 193; petitioned by CPA, 200; asks for antibusing legislation, 222–23, 224
Nixon administration: and school desegregation in Charlotte, 153, 178, 180–81; and *Swann* litigation, 192–93, 200, 207, 212; opposes antibusing constitutional amendments, 222
Norfolk, Va., 20, 130, 137, 168, 170, 179, 245
North Carolina: and education financing, 7–9, 12–15, 21–22; and segregated schools, 7–11, 17–18, 19–20, 23–24, 43–44; and political power, 12, 42–43; and teacher salaries, 20–21; and business growth, 39, 42; and school integration, 45, 46
North Carolina Agricultural and Technical College, 20
North Carolina Association of Rabbis, 67
North Carolina Attorney General, 113–14
North Carolina Bar Association, 132, 133
North Carolina Board of Dental Examiners, 105
North Carolina Central University, 109
North Carolina College for Negroes, 18, 19, 20, 23, 108
North Carolina Commission on Interracial Cooperation, 23

North Carolina Constitution: requires segregated schools, 7; prohibits racial discrimination in the schools, 8, 14; and disfranchisement amendment, 12, 16; and separate taxation amendment, 13; and amendment allowing school closures and tuition grants, 33, 34
North Carolina Constitutional Convention of 1868, 7
North Carolina Dental Society, 93, 105, 286 (n. 130)
North Carolina Department of Administration, 180
North Carolina General Assembly: establishes public school system, 7; requires school segregation, 7; and school finance, 7; permits separation taxation for schools, 8–9; and appointment of school board members, 9; permits school board discretion in financial matters, 9; and segregation laws, 12; and suffrage amendment, 12; permits separate white school districts, 13; establishes graduate programs at black colleges, 19, 20; and teacher salaries, 20, 21; and school appropriations, 21–22; improves black education, 22; seeks to avoid judicial action, 22; vests local school boards with assignment authority, 31, 44–45; establishes education commission, 32; rejects legislation abolishing public schools, 32; ratifies Pearsall Plan, 33; responds to *Brown* decision, 33; and efforts to restrict NAACP, 40, 185; imposes speaker ban, 133–34; prohibits state funds for busing, 153, 180, 191
North Carolina Institute of Government, 27–28
North Carolina Law Record, 183
North Carolina Law Review, 109

176, 186, 188; and Clement Haynsworth nomination, 171–72; and *Carter* case, 172, 186, 188; allows stay of desegregation, 185–86; and Memphis case, 186, 191, 238; and *Griggs* case, 213; and *Monroe* case, 218; and Knoxville case, 238

Vandiver, Ernest, 37
Veterans Administration, 54
Vienna Youth Festival, 85
Villa Heights Elementary School, 195
Villa Heights neighborhood, 52, 138
Vinson, Fred, 26, 28
Virginia, 26, 35, 38, 43, 49, 70, 171, 261 (n. 2), 267 (n. 105)
Voice of America, 74, 101
Voting Rights Act of 1965, 4

Waggoner, William, 150, 174–75, 207
Wagner-Steagall Act of 1937, 54
Wake Forest College, 142
Wall Street Journal, 98
Wallace, George, 202, 222
Waller, Harcourt, 66
Waring, Waties, 177
Warlick, John, 72
Warlick, Mrs. John, 72
Warlick, Wilson, 77–78, 82, 131
Warren, Earl, 26
Washington County, N.C., 21
Washington Heights neighborhood, 52–53
Washington Post, 120, 251
Watkins, Carlton, 150, 151, 170, 201, 231
Wayne County, N.C., 45

WBT radio station, 63
WBT television station, 128, 218
Wesley Heights neighborhood, 52
West Charlotte High School: building of, 54; integration of, 216, 229–30, 231–32, 233, 234–35, 239, 240–41; black population of, 221, 228; as open school, 237; proposed closure of, 237; and Boston students, 251
West Mecklenburg High School, 224–25
Westside Parents Council, 89
Wheeler, Raymond, 58
White, Byron, 172
White, George, 13
White, Hugh, 26
White, Walter, 21
White Citizens' Council, 71, 100
White flight, 215–19, 233–34, 240, 246–47, 322 (n. 14)
White House, 35, 113, 178
White supremacy, 12
Whitfield, Paul, 156–57
Whitsett, Kenneth, 40, 70, 71
Wilkins, Roy, 121–22
Wilmington, N.C., 12, 50, 101
Wilson, N.C., 11, 21
Winston-Salem, N.C., 44, 68, 179
Wisdom, John Minor, 126–27
Woolworth's, 86
Wright, L. M., 148

Yancey County School Board, 82
Yarborough, Edward, 45
YMCA, 104–5
Yoder, Ed, 98

Zeb Vance Elementary School, 92